BLOOD RUNS GREEN

Chicago and sites relating to the Cronin murder case, 1889.

BLOOD RUNS GREEN
THE MURDER THAT TRANSFIXED GILDED AGE CHICAGO

Gillian O'Brien

THE UNIVERSITY OF CHICAGO PRESS

CHICAGO AND LONDON

Gillian O'Brien is senior lecturer in history at Liverpool John Moores
University. She is coeditor of *Georgian Dublin* and *Portraits of the City:
Dublin and the Wider World*.

The University of Chicago Press, Chicago 60637
The University of Chicago Press, Ltd., London
© 2015 by The University of Chicago
All rights reserved. Published 2015.
Printed in the United States of America

24 23 22 21 20 19 18 17 16 15   1 2 3 4 5

ISBN-13: 978-0-226-24895-0 (cloth)
ISBN-13: 978-0-226-24900-1 (e-book)
DOI: 10.7208/chicago/9780226249001.001.0001

LIBRARY OF CONGRESS CATALOGING-IN-PUBLICATION DATA

O'Brien, Gillian, author.
  Blood runs green : the murder that transfixed gilded age
Chicago / Gillian O'Brien.
      pages   cm — (Historical studies of urban America)
    Includes bibliographical references and index.
    ISBN 978-0-226-24895-0 (hardcover : alkaline paper) —
ISBN 978-0-226-24900-1 (e-book)   1. Cronin, Patrick Henry,
1846–1889.   2. Murder—Illinois—Chicago—Case studies.
3. Irish—Illinois—Chicago—History—19th century.
4. Republicanism—Ireland—History—19th century.
5. Secret societies—Ireland—History—19th century.
I. Title.   II. Series: Historical studies of urban America.
    HV6534.C4O27 2015
    364.152'3092—dc23
                                                      2014025348

♾ This paper meets the requirements of ANSI/NISO Z39.48–1992
(Permanence of Paper).

For Alistair Daniel
and in memory of
Mai Crowe
Garret FitzGerald
&
Denis O'Brien

CONTENTS

CAST OF CHARACTERS

M. E. Ames	Lawyer for the defense in the murder trial
John F. Beggs	Lawyer; Senior Guardian of Camp 20
Martin Burke	Unskilled laborer; member of Camp 20
Theodore and Cordelia Conklin	Friends of Dr. Cronin; Cronin lived with the Conklins
Daniel Coughlin	Detective; member of Camp 20
Patrick H. Cronin	Physician; member of Clan na Gael; murder victim
Michael Davitt	Founder of the "New Departure" and the Irish National Land League; friend of Alexander and Margaret Sullivan
John Devoy	Senior figure in Clan na Gael and strong supporter of Cronin
Luke Dillon	Member of Clan na Gael; involved in the "Dynamite War"; supporter of Cronin
Dan Donohoe	Lawyer for the defense in the murder trial
Maurice Dorney	Catholic pastor of St. Gabriel's Parish, Canaryville; member of Clan na Gael; close friend of Alexander Sullivan
Frederick Ebersold	Police inspector at the time of Cronin's murder; key member of the Cronin murder investigation
Patrick Egan	Treasurer of the Irish National Land League who gave Alexander Sullivan $100,000 of league funds; later president of Irish National League of America; ally of Sullivan
Patrick A. Feehan	First Catholic archbishop of Chicago; friend of Alexander Sullivan
John Finerty	Owner and editor of the *Citizen*; onetime congressman; member of Clan na Gael; supporter of Alexander Sullivan
William S. Forrest	Chief lawyer for the defense in the murder trial
William Foster	Lawyer for the defense in the murder trial
Andy Foy	Bricklayer; member of Camp 20; hostile to Cronin; friend of Daniel Coughlin

Lizzie Foy   Wife of Andy Foy; accused him of involvement in the Cronin murder

Francis Hanford   School principal; shot by Alexander Sullivan in 1876

George W. Hubbard   Police chief in Chicago at the time of the Cronin murder

William J. Hynes   Lawyer; member of Clan na Gael; onetime supporter of Alexander Sullivan, but a lawyer for the prosecution in the Cronin murder trial

George C. Ingham   Lawyer for the prosecution in the murder trial

William B. Kennedy   Lawyer for the defense in the murder trial

John Kunze   Petty crook with links to Daniel Coughlin

Henri Le Caron   Member of Clan na Gael; knew both Alexander Sullivan and Patrick Cronin; testified at the Parnell Commission

Mackey Lomasney   Member of Clan na Gael; involved in the "Dynamite War"; killed trying to set a bomb on London Bridge in December 1884

Joel Longnecker   State's Attorney for Illinois; chief prosecutor in the Cronin murder trial

Luther Laflin Mills   Lawyer for the prosecution in the murder trial

Patrick O'Sullivan   Iceman; member of Camp 20

Charles Stewart Parnell   Leader of the Irish Parliamentary Party; Member of the British Parliament; key figure in the Home Rule movement

Colonel W. P. Rend   Wealthy Irish American businessman; constitutional nationalist; supporter of Cronin

Scanlan family   Key figures in Irish Chicago; friends of Cronin

Kickham Scanlan   Lawyer for the prosecution in the murder trial

Michael Schaack   Captain in the police force; based at the East Chicago Avenue Police Station; led the investigation into Cronin's disappearance

Herman Schuettler   Police officer who replaced Schaack as senior figure in the Cronin investigation

Alexander Sullivan   Controversial and influential Irish American; lawyer; leader of Clan na Gael in the 1880s; leader of the Irish National Land League in the mid-1880s; member of Camp 20; enemy of Cronin

Margaret Buchanan Sullivan   Journalist; wife of Alexander Sullivan

R. W. Wing   Lawyer for the defense in the murder trial

CHRONOLOGY

1845   Great Potato Famine begins

1846   Patrick Henry Cronin born in County Cork, Ireland

1848   Alexander Sullivan born in Amherstberg, Ontario

1847   Cronin family emigrates from Ireland to North America

1858   Founding of the Fenians and the Irish Republican Brotherhood

1861   April: American Civil War begins

1863   Cronin returns to the United States from St. Catharine's, Ontario, where his family had settled

1865   May: American Civil War ends

1866   First Fenian raids on Canada

1867   Fenian uprisings in Britain; John Devoy sentenced to fifteen years' hard labor
       ●JUNE: *Founding of Clan na Gael in New York*

1868   Sullivan's shoe store in Detroit destroyed by fire

1869   First Clan na Gael camp established in Chicago; Sullivan becomes Collector of Internal Revenue in territory of New Mexico

1870   Second attempted Fenian invasion of Canada; Sullivan buys *Santa Fe Gazette*, renames it *Santa Fe Post*

1871   Third attempted Fenian invasion of Canada; Sullivan flees Santa Fe after shoot-out with General H. H. Heath
       ●JANUARY: *Partial amnesty for Fenian prisoners; Devoy arrives in New York*
       ●OCTOBER: *Great Chicago Fire devastates city*

1873   Sullivan arrives in Chicago

1874   Sullivan appointed secretary of Board of Public Works; marries journalist Margaret F. Buchanan

1875   Establishment of the "Skirmishing Fund"

1876
       ●APRIL: Catalpa *rescues Fenian prisoners in Australia*
       ●AUGUST: *Sullivan shoots and kills school principal Francis Hanford*

●**AUGUST**: Catalpa *arrives triumphantly in New York*
●**OCTOBER**: *First Hanford murder trial begins*
●**FALL**: *Sullivan's Clan na Gael membership application rejected; Cronin joins Clan na Gael*

1877　Revolutionary Directory established with members from Clan na Gael and the Irish Revolutionary Brotherhood; Sullivan becomes a member of Clan na Gael; Devoy takes control of the "Skirmishing Fund" from Jeremiah O'Donovan Rossa and renames it the "National Fund"

●**MARCH**: *Second Hanford murder trial—Sullivan acquitted*

1878　Sullivan admitted to the Illinois bar; "New Departure" begins

1879–81　Land War in Ireland

1880

●**JANUARY–MARCH**: *Charles Stewart Parnell goes on fund-raising tour of North America*
●**FEBRUARY**: *Parnell visits Chicago*
●**NOVEMBER**: *Patrick A. Feehan becomes archbishop of Chicago; Maurice Dorney establishes St. Gabriel's Parish in Canaryville*

1881　Irish American republicans organize series of bombings in Britain; Coercion Acts pass in Ireland; Patrick Egan flees to Paris with Land League funds

●**AUGUST**: *Clan national convention held in Chicago; Sullivan becomes chair of the Executive Committee*
●**OCTOBER**: *Parnell arrested and imprisoned in Kilmainham Jail, Dublin*

1882　Cronin moves from St. Louis to Chicago; Sullivan visits Patrick Egan in Paris to obtain $100,000 in Land League funds

●**JANUARY**: *John Finerty launches first edition of the* Citizen
●**APRIL**: *Sullivan moves $100,000 in Land League money into his personal bank account*
●**MAY**: *Phoenix Park Murders—Chief Secretary Lord Frederick Cavendish and Undersecretary Thomas Burke murdered in Dublin by a secret Irish republican society, the Invincibles*

1883　Founding of the Irish National League of America; Irish American republicans bomb Glasgow and London locations

●**APRIL**: *Sullivan elected president of the new Irish National League of America*

1884　Irish Americans bomb London locations

●**AUGUST**: *National convention of Clan na Gael held in Boston*
●**DECEMBER**: *London Bridge explosion—Mackey Lomasney killed*

1885

●**JANUARY**: *Clan bombs London locations; Devoy's Clan camp suspended from Clan na Gael*
●**MAY**: *Cronin expelled from Clan na Gael*

1886

●**MAY 1**: *Strikes begin in Chicago to demand an eight-hour workday*
●**MAY 3**: *Four strikers killed by police near McCormick Reaper Works*
●**MAY 4**: *Haymarket bombing and police response kills or injures more than fifty people*
●**AUGUST**: *Susan Lomasney requests financial assistance from Alexander Sullivan*

1887   Cronin acts as expert witness in two medical negligence cases and for the "Wilson Estate"; Luke Dillon begins financial support of the Lomasney family

1888
- **JUNE**: *Clan national convention agrees to examine charges against the Triangle*
- **AUGUST**: *Triangle trial begins*
- **SEPTEMBER**: *Parnell Commission begins*

1889
- **JANUARY**: *Triangle trial verdict reached; Sullivan found not guilty, but Michael Boland censured*
- **FEBRUARY 5**: *Henri Le Caron begins testimony at the Parnell Commission*
- **FEBRUARY 8**: *Camp 20 meeting condemns Cronin's actions*
- **FEBRUARY 15**: *Trial committee of Camp 20 meets to try Cronin on treason charges*
- **FEBRUARY 17**: *"J. B. Simonds" rents flat at 117 Clark Street*
- **MARCH**: *Cronin receives two suspicious emergency calls*
- **MARCH 20**: *"Frank Williams" rents Carlson cottage in Lake View*
- **APRIL**: *Patrick O'Sullivan, iceman in Lake View, retains Cronin as his company's physician*
- **MAY 4**: *Cronin summoned to attend injured O'Sullivan worker*
- **MAY 5**: *Cronin's friend Theo Conklin reports Cronin missing; bloody trunk found in Lake View*
- **MAY 9**: *Frank Woodruff arrested for horse stealing*
- **MAY 10**: *Cronin sightings in Toronto reported*
- **MAY 22**: *Cronin's body found*
- **MAY 23**: *Police discover crime scene at the Carlson cottage*
- **MAY 24**: *Bloody trunk identified as that bought by "Simonds"; Daniel Coughlin, detective working on the Cronin case, suspected of involvement in his murder*
- **MAY 25**: *Cronin's coffin on view in First Cavalry Armory; Coughlin arrested*
- **MAY 26**: *Cronin's funeral and burial services held*
- **MAY 27**: *O'Sullivan arrested*
- **JUNE 5–11**: *Coroner's inquest held*
- **JUNE 11**: *Sullivan arrested in Chicago; John J. Maroney and Charles McDonald arrested in New York*
- **JUNE 14**: *Sullivan released on $20,000 bail*
- **JUNE 16**: *Martin Burke arrested in Winnipeg*
- **JUNE 29**: *Coughlin, O'Sullivan, Burke, John F. Beggs, and John Kunze charged with Cronin's murder*
- **AUGUST 26**: *Trial opens*
- **AUGUST 30**: *Jury selection begins*
- **OCTOBER 11**: *Jury fixing plot discovered*
- **OCTOBER 22**: *Jury secured*
- **OCTOBER 23**: *Prosecution begins*
- **NOVEMBER 16**: *Defense begins its case*
- **DECEMBER 12**: *Jury deliberations begin*
- **DECEMBER 16**: *Trial verdict reached*

REQUIEM

Reporter: It strikes me, doctor, that your funeral would be very largely attended.

Dr. C——: Yes, and the cause of death extensively inquired into.

Chicago hadn't seen its like since Abraham Lincoln's body had lain in state at the Cook County Courthouse in 1865. When the doors to the First Cavalry Armory on Michigan Avenue opened on the afternoon of Saturday, May 25, 1889, almost twelve thousand people flooded into the building and filed past the coffin. The crowd represented all classes and all ages, "from the child scarcely able to toddle to the aged man, walking with faltering, uncertain steps. Parents took their children and children their grandparents. The day laborer walked beside the well-dressed professional man."

The body was too decomposed, its wounds too gruesome, to permit a public viewing. Instead, it was enveloped in a French walnut casket decorated with gold and silver and placed high on a catafalque. Every last detail associated with the public viewing and funeral had been carefully choreographed. The huge, militaristic interior of the armory was transformed into something resembling a botanic garden. The platform upon which the casket had been placed was draped with flags, its edges softened by displays of potted plants; armed sentries from the Hibernian Rifles stood at attention in one corner. The coffin was covered with ferns, white hyacinths, and ropes of smilax. An enormous crucifix of pink roses and daisies lay at its head while at its foot stood an enormous floral harp. A large portrait of the dead man, draped in black, was displayed beside the coffin, and a candelabrum with seven tapers cast its flickering light across the scene.

The following day, Chicago was brought to a standstill as the funeral cortege made slow, mournful progress through the streets. At

Cronin's funeral procession. In Henry M. Hunt, *The Crime of the Century; or, The Assassination of Dr. Patrick Henry Cronin* (Chicago: H. L. and D. H. Kockersperger, 1889), 233. Collection of the author.

10:45 a.m. the casket was carried from the armory and placed in a hearse drawn by four black horses. Several carriages filled with friends and family traveled behind. They were followed by a procession of seven thousand mourners led by Reed's Drum Corps and members of the Hibernian Rifles, who marched with weapons reversed, the traditional military mark of respect. The funeral route was crowded with upwards of forty thousand onlookers; according to the *Chicago Tribune*, it took an hour for the entire procession to pass a given point, and all that could be seen from its perspective was one "solid line of humanity" occupying the sidewalks, "lampposts, stairways in blocks [and] the tops of the blocks themselves."

Inside Holy Name Cathedral, a congregation of four thousand squeezed into every seat and crammed the aisles while crowds overflowed onto the streets. Amid a hushed silence the coffin was placed below the altar, which had been draped in black velvet. The *Chicago Evening News* reported that "the dirges of the bands and the roll of the drums that came in through the window . . . threw a shadow . . . over the funeral vestments of the priests and into the solemn intoning of the requiem service and the . . . responses of the organ."

Several priests concelebrated the Requiem Mass, and Father Peter J. Muldoon, a friend of the dead man, gave an emotional eulogy, praising the deceased's devotion to others: "He was told that a fellow-man was sick, and instantly, without hesitation, with his heart full of charity, and in his hands the very instruments to bring relief and mercy to a fellow being, he goes forth with good will to his fellow-man and meets what? An atrocious death!"

At the conclusion of the funeral mass, the procession once again assembled and began its slow march south toward Union Depot. Over 20,000 people gathered outside the station, with a further 5,000 inside. Three trains had been specially hired to take 2,500 mourners from Chicago to Calvary Cemetery in Evanston to witness the interment. Hundreds more took carriages out to the burial site, and a crowd in excess of 3,000 stood in the rain while the casket was placed in a public vault amid a murmuring of prayers.

It wasn't just Chicago that mourned this loss. The violent death of this man had made global headlines, and the investigation and trial were regularly reported in the *New York Times*, the *Los Angeles Herald*, the *Times* of London, the *Belfast Newsletter*, the *Glasgow Herald*, *Baner ac Amserau Cymru* in Wales, the *Timaru Herald* in New Zealand, and the *Sydney Morning News*, among many others. His murder sparked an extensive police investigation through the United States and Canada, culminating in what was at the time the longest-running trial in US history. The aftermath of the murder was far-reaching and long-lived. It was, as one newspaper editor put it, "one of the ghastliest and most curious crimes in civilized history. . . . To the horrors of the French criminal history, to the exploits of 'Jack the Ripper' in London, or to the darkest and bloodiest mysteries of secret crime in New York resort must be had to find a parallel for this case"—and yet today the story of the murder and its consequences remains, like the victim, buried and largely forgotten. At the edge of Calvary Cemetery, near the junction of two paths, surrounded by large, ornate mausoleums, there lies, half buried in the grass, a small, flat piece of granite measuring two by one and a half feet. It bears a simple inscription: "Dr. P. H. Cronin, 1846–1889. Rest in Peace."

CHAPTER ONE

"CITY OF BIG SHOULDERS"

The Convergence of the Clan

That astonishing Chicago—a city where they are always rubbing the
lamp and fetching up the genii, and contriving and achieving new
possibilities.

Mark Twain

I n the spring of 1873, a short, dapper man with "piercing and magnetic eyes"
stepped off the train into the charred, scarred streets of Chicago.
Dressed in his trademark black suit, complete with cowboy boots
and pearl-handled pistol, Alexander Sullivan was trying to rebuild
himself and his reputation, much like the city itself. Huge swaths
of Chicago had been destroyed by the Great Fire of 1871 that began
at the back of DeKoven Street on the West Side, leapt the Chicago
River, and traveled north as far as Fullerton Avenue in Lincoln Park.
For a day and a half the fire had raged, and when it was over, little
remained of the city center apart from the limestone Water Tower
on Michigan Avenue (then Pine Street) and Mahlon D. Ogden's residence on West Walton Street. An estimated three hundred people
had died, eighteen thousand buildings had been reduced to glowing
embers, and almost a third of the city's population had lost their
homes.

Faced with disaster, the citizens of Chicago rallied, and as soon
as land was cleared of the smoking debris, new, bigger, better, taller
buildings rose to replace the old. Despite the depression that gripped
much of the United States in the early 1870s, by June 1873 the city was
sufficiently resurgent to host a jubilee week to celebrate the rebuild-
ing. Chicago began to rival and then to overtake the expansion of
New York, Boston, and Philadelphia; within twenty years of the Great
Fire, the city boasted the first skyscrapers and the fastest-growing
population in the country.

For Sullivan, as for others arriving in Chicago in the aftermath of the Great Fire, the city was a place of opportunity, of hope, and of expectation. Every week thousands of young men and women clambered out of trains to seek their fortune in the bustling metropolis. As the trains slowed on the approach to the station the iconic sights and sounds that would define the city for several generations became clear. Emerging from the bustle and smoke and clamor of engines and bells in Union Depot, new Chicagoans caught their first glimpses of the "dingy houses, smoky mills, [and] tall elevators" that surrounded the station. Aside from Alexander Sullivan, 1873 also saw the arrival in Chicago of Albert Parsons and Louis Sullivan. Parsons's involvement with anarchists would culminate in a pivotal moment for the city and for labor history during the Haymarket Riot of 1886, while Louis Sullivan's buildings would come to define the Chicago of the late nineteenth century.

Alexander Sullivan was determined to make his mark too, and his appearance frequently attracted attention. Always clean-shaven and impeccably dressed in a black suit, he was a slim man with gray eyes and arresting facial features. One admiring contemporary observed that "his features have the delicacy of sculpture and indicate a refined, proud and sensitive nature" while in the "the frank and penetrating glance of his eyes is easily discerned a character of extraordinary mental capacity which is combined with courage, tact and persistence." Not everyone was so impressed. William O'Brien, a member of the Irish Parliamentary Party, thought him "a liverish man, strong-browed and strong-jawed, about whose bloodless lips and sharp white teeth there played a certain pitilessness which all his softness of voice and studious airs of deference could not change to anything better than cold self-control." Wherever Sullivan went, opinion tended to be sharply divided, and he had become, of necessity, something of a master of reinvention. Between 1865 and 1895, he was variously a respectable businessman, the owner of a shoe store, a tax collector, a newspaper owner, a journalist, a city official, a postmaster, the leader of a secret revolutionary society, a lawyer, an abolitionist, a Republican, a Democrat, the president of the Irish National League of America, a gambler, and a murderer. America was the land of opportunity, and Alexander Sullivan was a great opportunist.

ALEXANDER SULLIVAN.   [143]

Alexander Sullivan. In John T. McEnnis, *The Clan-na-Gael and the Murder of Dr. Cronin* (Chicago: F. J. Schulte and J. W. Iliff, 1890), 143. Collection of the author.

Born in 1848 in Amherstberg, Ontario, Sullivan was the son of Irish immigrants—his father was a British army officer. As a young man he moved to Detroit, where he invested in a shoe store, but in 1868 it was destroyed by a fire. Accused of arson, Sullivan was put on trial. Several witnesses claimed that he had purchased cans of oil, that they had seen him leaving the shop at about the time that the fire started, and that traces of oil had been discovered in the destroyed shop. However, two additional witnesses, one of whom—Margaret Buchanan—was his future wife, swore that he had been attending church with them at the time of the fire. The case was dismissed amid much talk of corruption, and Sullivan, unable to find work in Detroit, left for New Mexico, where he became postmaster in Santa Fe. In 1869, as a reward for his support of the Republican General Ulysses S. Grant in the presidential election, he was appointed Collector of Internal Revenue for the territory of New Mexico. The following year he bought the *Santa Fe Gazette*, which he renamed the *Santa Fe Post* and ran as a Republican newspaper. This was a short-lived investment, as in 1871 Sullivan was forced to flee the city following a dramatic shooting match in which he and General H. H. Heath (then Secretary for the Territory) took potshots at each other, and the discovery that $10,000 was missing from Internal Revenue accounts.

Sullivan's departure from New Mexico also severed his ties (albeit temporarily) with the Republican Party, and in the 1872 presidential election he supported the failed bid of newspaper editor Horace Greeley, the nominee of the short-lived Liberal Republican Party. After a brief stint in New York, he wended his way to Chicago. Drawing on his newspaper experience, Sullivan's first job in the city was as a journalist with the *Chicago Evening Post*, and he went on to work for both the *Chicago Inter Ocean* and the *Chicago Times*.

Within eighteenth months, Sullivan had settled in Chicago and appeared to have put his somewhat shady past behind him. His career in the press was brief, however: in 1874, with the support of City Treasurer Daniel O'Hara, he was appointed secretary of the Board of Public Works, a position carrying considerable influence and power, particularly as the city began to rebuild after the Great Fire. O'Hara's patronage convinced Sullivan that the fleetingly popular People's Party, and later the Democratic Party, was worthy of his support. Through the 1870s and 1880s, Sullivan's political loyalty flipped between the Republican and Democratic Parties and largely depended on which one promised him the greater rewards for his support.

Having secured a good job, Sullivan married Margaret Buchanan, a journalist and former teacher, in November 1874. Like Sullivan, Buchanan was of Irish stock. Born in Ireland, she moved to the United States in the aftermath of the Great Potato Famine, and the couple met in Detroit in the late 1860s. Following Sullivan's hasty departure from Detroit, she established herself in Chicago as one of the finest journalists not only in the Midwest but in the nation. She secured her first job at the *Chicago Evening Post* after she submitted articles via a third party. The editor, C. H. Ray, was so impressed that he made a job offer without meeting the author, and was surprised to find his new journalist was a woman. Margaret Sullivan was regarded by John R. Walsh, the owner of the *Chicago Herald*, as "the best living writer of English," and William O'Brien, who had little time for her husband, described her as "a lady journalist of remarkable gifts." She was on the editorial staff of the *Chicago Herald*, the *Chicago Evening Post*, and the *Chicago Times* during the late 1870s and early 1880s, but by 1888 she wrote primarily for the *Chicago Tribune*, where she was both an editorial writer and an art critic.

Margaret Sullivan played a key part in Alexander Sullivan's impressive reinvention of himself as a respectable, responsible member of society. However, it wasn't long before he ran into trouble again. In August 1876 he shot and killed a school principal, Francis Hanford. In an anonymous letter to the City Council of Chicago, Hanford had implied that Mrs. Sullivan had had an improper relationship with the mayor, Harvey Colvin. He claimed that she had used her influence not only to secure her husband the position of secretary of the Board of Public Works but also to cripple the public school system on behalf of the Catholic Church, which was desperate for church—rather than state-led—schools. Incensed, Sullivan and confronted Hanford at his home. When Hanford refused to retract his allegations, Sullivan shot and killed him. After trials in October 1876 and March 1877, both before the same judge, W. K. McAllister, Sullivan was acquitted despite evidence that he had gone to Hanford's house with a pistol and shot dead an unarmed man. There were allegations of corruption on the bench and in the jury—the judge had repeatedly taken the side of the defense and allowed Sullivan's supporters to applaud and cheer the defendant throughout the case. According to a contemporary commentator, "The acquittal of the defendant upon the second trial has helped to create a wide-spread belief . . . that in the conduct of these trials justice was outraged." At the second trial, Sullivan was prosecuted by State's Attorney Luther Laflin Mills, and his key defense lawyer was William J. Hynes. In 1889 all three would meet again.

Despite the scandal associated with the killing of Hanford, Sullivan retained his job with the Board of Public Works. The board had responsibility for a wide range of services, including public buildings, parks, water, streets, and building permits, and as its secretary there was little going on in Chicago that Sullivan did not know about, and many favors he could and did arrange. But this wasn't enough for him. He set his sights on a legal career, enrolling at the Union College of Law. He was registered there at the time of the Hanford shooting but, following his arrest, was expelled. However, by 1878 the Illinois Supreme Court had admitted him to the Illinois bar upon the recommendation of a Chicago judge (an occurrence that also had about it the whiff of corruption—a familiar odor in all the dealings of Alexander Sullivan). Soon after his admission to the bar, he established a legal practice in partnership with Thomas G. Windes, who later became chief justice of the Circuit Court. Once again, Sullivan proved adept at reinventing himself. In the fall of 1876, he declared himself an ardent devotee of the cause of Ireland, and sought membership in a rapidly growing and influential secret society, Clan na Gael. His membership in the Clan would define the course of his life and bring him into close contact with the man whose funeral would bring Chicago to a standstill in 1889: Dr. P. H. Cronin.

><+>•O•<+><

Clan na Gael was a secret Irish republican society founded in New York in 1867. Like its predecessor, the Fenians, the Clan was dedicated to winning Irish independence from Britain through the use of force. The official name of Clan na Gael was the United Brotherhood, though few ever called it that.

At the outset the Clan's main stronghold was on the East Coast of the United States, where the majority of the Irish in America lived. Senior figures, including Jerome Collins, John Devoy, John J. Breslin, and William Carroll, were all based in either New York or Philadelphia. The East Coast was also where the Fenians had been strongest, and it was where the most important Irish American newspapers, such as Patrick Ford's *Irish World* and John Boyle O'Reilly's *Pilot*, were published. However, by the early 1880s the Clan's center of influence had moved seven hundred miles west to Chicago. A young, vibrant, and growing Irish population, a charismatic leader in Alexander Sullivan, and the tacit support of the Catholic hierarchy combined to make that city the new center of Clan activity.

The first Clan "camp" in Chicago was established in 1869 in the strongly Irish neighborhood of Bridgeport, and camps soon spread throughout the city. Membership was open to all men who were Irish-born or of Irish descent, and in Chicago thousands fell into that category. In 1870 there were almost 40,000 Irish-born residents of Chicago; by 1890 there were 70,000. If residents with at least one Irish-born parent are taken into account, the total "Irish" population in 1890 jumps to almost 180,000, or 17 percent of the city's population.

The first wave of Irish immigrants consisted primarily of laborers who had worked on the Erie Canal in New York State in the 1820s. When the Illinois and Michigan Canal was commissioned, they moved west to Chicago, and when it was completed in 1848 they stayed, the vast majority of them settling on the city's South Side, around Bridgeport. These men worked in nearby slaughterhouses, steel mills, brickyards, and brewing companies, and from 1865 onward at the sprawling Union Stock Yard. After the fire of 1871, so many Irish were working in construction that it led to "the boast that it was the Irish who had rebuilt the city." Yet many of them lived in little more than hovels. By the early 1880s, the *Chicago Tribune* declared that "Bridgeport has, in Chicago, become a generic term for smells, for riots, bad whiskey and poor cigars." Though there were considerable numbers of Germans, Poles, and Lithuanians living in that neighborhood, it remained overwhelmingly Irish in character, with the Irish accounting for 48 percent of its population. Just beyond Bridgeport's limits, in the streets that surrounded the stockyards, that figure rose to 70 percent.

Like other immigrant communities, the Irish in Chicago faced many challenges. Although a steady stream of Irish had landed in the United States during the first half of the nineteenth century, their numbers soared after the Great Potato Famine that devastated Ireland in the 1840s. Those who left Ireland for the United States were primarily Catholic, and for the Irish in America the church proved to be a very strong bond. Further, many Irish shared an antipathy toward Britain, or more specifically England. Young Irelanders such as John Mitchel encouraged that feeling—that the Irish in America were exiles forced from their land by the brutality of foreign landlords and the British government. Fraternal, charitable, political, sporting, and secret revolutionary societies sprang up to cater to the Irish immigrant, and these organizations formed a local network that provided friendship, a social life, and, in many cases, jobs. By the end of the 1870s, Clan members held a number of influential positions throughout the city, frequently helping Irishmen to secure jobs, obtain liquor licenses, and purchase homes. Membership in Clan na Gael also enabled the politically minded to participate in the struggle to free Ireland.

In an era of considerable anti-Irish and anti-immigrant sentiment, there was comfort in numbers. In Chicago, as elsewhere, Irishmen had many options when it came to seeking out the company and support of their countrymen. By the 1880s the three most significant Irish organizations in Chicago were the Ancient Order of Hibernians, an Irish Catholic fraternal organization established in New York in 1836; the Land League of America, founded in 1880 as an open, visible organization pledged to support the Irish Land League and later the Irish Parliamentary Party; and Clan na Gael. Like many others, Alexander Sullivan was a member of all three. His initial attempt to join the Clan was rejected when he was blackballed by one Chicago camp because he was out on bail awaiting the second trial for the murder of Hanford, but following his acquittal in 1877 he found favor in another. Sullivan rose quickly through the Clan system, and by 1879 he was the head of the Illinois, Indiana, and Ohio District, a position that gave him direct access to Clan leadership. He was articulate and charismatic, and he inspired both great devotion and great antipathy among those who knew him.

The leadership of the Clan generally consisted of well-educated men, many of whom, like Sullivan, chose to live in salubrious areas on the North Side rather than the poorer Irish neighborhoods on the South Side. They included professional men such as John Finerty, one-term congressman and newspaper owner and editor; John P. Hopkins, Chicago's first Catholic mayor; mine owner Colonel W. P. Rend; businessman Frank T. Scanlan; lawyer William J. Hynes; and Patrick Cronin, physician (and later, murder victim). Many Irish and

Irish American policemen were members of the Clan, and despite considerable opposition from the Catholic Church, several priests belonged, including Father Maurice Dorney, the "Stockyards Priest," who became an influential figure. But the Clan was far from an organization simply for professionals; the rank and file of the secret society consisted of men who worked in the packing plants and the stockyards of Chicago.

Within a decade of his arrival in Chicago, using his connections within Irish republicanism and in the fields of journalism, politics, business, and law, Sullivan had become the most influential Irishman in the city. As one contemporary journalist observed, "Nobody ever came into anything like close relations with Alexander Sullivan without liking or hating him thoroughly. . . . He is . . . a powerful man and one who out of the very nature of things was born to be a leader." Yet this was far from the limits of his ambition. It was not enough to lead the Irish in Chicago; Sullivan was determined to spread his influence nationwide and beyond. If New York's Tammany Hall boasted "Honest" John Kelly and Richard Croker, then Chicago had Alexander Sullivan. Through the 1880s, Sullivan's influence was felt all the way from dingy saloons in Bridgeport to the Oval Office in Washington, DC, and the Palace of Westminster in London.

Sullivan was meticulous about cultivating relationships with political and church leaders in Ireland and Chicago as well as across the United States. In 1880 he acted as chaperone for Charles Stewart Parnell on the Midwest portion of his American tour. Parnell was a member of the British Parliament, president of the Land League, soon to be leader of the Irish Parliamentary Party, and a man many believed could restore an independent Irish Parliament (a cause better known as Home Rule). In many ways Parnell was an unlikely hero for Irish nationalists. He came from a family of wealthy Protestant landlords, and his great-grandfather, John Parnell, had been Chancellor of the Exchequer in Ireland at the time of the 1798 Rebellion. Yet despite this unpromising background (from a nationalist perspective), Parnell endeared himself to radicals in his maiden speech in Parliament when he asked, "Why should Ireland be treated as a geographical fragment of England? . . . Ireland is not a geographical fragment, but a nation." His association with Michael Davitt and John Devoy, two senior Fenians who were greatly respected in Ireland and in Irish America, also served to enhance his credibility.

Parnell's trip was a risky one. As one member of the Irish Parliamentary Party observed the day before Parnell's departure,

> If he can hold his ground with the Clan na Gael, and afterwards hold it in the House of Commons, he will win Home Rule. The Clan na Gael are the open and avowed enemies of England. . . . What is Parnell going to say to them? If he speaks with an eye to the House of Commons his speeches won't go down with the Clan. If he speaks with an eye to the Clan his speeches will be used against him in the House.

The key issue on which Parnell had to walk a delicate tightrope was violence—if he condemned the use of force in the campaign to free Ireland, he risked losing huge swaths of Irish America; if he condoned the use of force, he risked the immediate termination of his parliamentary career and any prospect Ireland had of achieving Home Rule. Parnell was also hopeful of converting the American public and government to the cause of Home Rule—by highlighting Britain's injustices toward Ireland. In some ways Parnell's appeal transcended ethnic boundaries. He appealed to Americans who had no connection with Ireland by stressing his close ties to America: his grandfather, Rear Admiral Charles Stewart, had served with distinction in the United States Navy in the early part of the century; his mother, Delia, was American, and she and his sisters Fanny and Anna lived in Bordentown, New Jersey, in the early 1880s.

Parnell's tour was initially intended to raise money for the Land League, which had been established in 1879 with two key aims: to ensure fair rents and to assist tenants in purchasing the land they farmed. However, these aims were rapidly overtaken by a humanitarian effort to avert famine in Ireland, which after forty years was once again feared to be imminent. Parnell's trip was a whirlwind tour of forty cities in fifteen states, and a brief hop across the Canadian border to speak in Toronto and Montreal. His excursion included an address to the House of Representatives in Washington, DC, and speeches in Boston, Philadelphia, New York, Cincinnati, and Chicago, but Parnell was not an inspired public speaker. "I hate public assemblies," he claimed, "I am always nervous"—but however poorly he spoke, the content of the speeches was well received, and his rhetoric appealed to both the moderate and the radical. His speeches were carefully tailored to his audience and often implied acceptance of violence, or at least an understanding that some might find that route palatable. Such ambiguity toward the use of force incensed the British authorities but thrilled many Irish Americans. In Cleveland, talking about the armed Irish American regiments that frequently greeted him on his tour, he remarked, "I thought that each one of them must have wished . . . 'Oh, that I could carry these arms for Ireland!' Well it may come to that some day or other."

It was in Chicago that Parnell met with the most support. Whereas 7,000 came out to greet him in New York, a crowd of between 15,000 and 20,000 assembled in the Interstate Exposition Building in Chicago on the night of February 23, 1880. A huge procession of religious, fraternal, military, and semimilitary Irish societies, accompanied by marching bands, escorted Parnell from his hotel to the Exposition Building, where a civic reception was held in his honor and Mayor Carter Harrison presented him with the Key to the City. Parnell's arrival at the hall was delayed by over an hour by large crowds lining the street. As Michael Davitt later recalled,

> The hall was full of a vast audience, restive and impatient, full of eagerness to hear the envoys. But if the organizers of receptions in the United States are loyal to any American institution more than another, it is to that of ceremony. . . . Among the items on the program which preceded the . . . speakers was the recitation of a long poem of welcome . . . and this task was performed by a dramatic artiste, a young lady . . . who with other striking attractions, stood over six feet high. . . . The handsome young giantess poured into them and over them for nearly half an hour an elocutionary torrent of praise and worship.

The poem, written by Margaret Sullivan, Alexander's wife, was followed by the enthusiastic singing of "The Battle Hymn of the Republic," with words adapted for the occasion:

Says every true American, Parnell thy cause is ours
We pray for Heaven's blessing to strew your course with flowers
The land-sharks dare not harm thee with our united powers
To set Ireland free
Welcome, welcome, onward, onward
Welcome, welcome, onward, onward . . .

Finally, Parnell rose to speak. He entreated his Chicago supporters to continue sending money to Ireland, claiming that "if you help us to keep our people alive during this winter . . . we will kill the Irish land system. And when we have killed the Irish land system we shall have plucked out and ground to powder the corner stone of British misrule in Ireland." Later, back at his hotel, Parnell raged about "tall women, public reciters and versified welcomes," but he must have been mollified by the knowledge that over $10,000 (approximately $250,000 in today's currency) had been raised.

Alexander Sullivan accompanied Parnell around the Midwest and was enormously impressed by the Irish parliamentarian, though he criticized his stage presence, complaining of his "defective articulation, his feeble monotone and excessive shyness." However, he concluded that he "never heard any human being, whether uncouth or cultivated, doubt his sincerity, or hesitate, after seeing and hearing, to trust and follow him." But Parnell and Sullivan's relationship over the next decade was often difficult. Overtly, Sullivan was an enthusiastic supporter of the leader of the Irish Parliamentary Party, while covertly many of his actions undermined Parnell's politics.

>—!—◆>—○—<◆—!—<

Parnell was not the only notable Irishman to arrive in Chicago in 1880. Irish Catholics received a significant boost when, in the autumn, Patrick A. Feehan from County Tipperary was appointed the first Catholic archbishop of Chicago. Feehan's presence influenced the development of a robust Irish nationalism in the city. Unlike Archbishop John Williams in Boston and Archbishop Michael Corrigan in New York, Feehan did not take a hard line when it came to extreme elements of Irish American republicanism.

Although the Clan (unlike the Fenians) was never formally condemned by the Catholic Church, most church leaders were vehemently opposed to the organization for a number of reasons. First, the church hierarchy in Ireland and the United States condemned the existence of secret societies; second, the nondenominational republic that the Fenians and the Clan proposed to establish did not conform to the church's idea of an Irish Catholic state. However, Archbishop Feehan did not criticize the Clan and instead chose to ignore, or tacitly approve, its activities. Indeed, by his choice of friendships and his refusal to issue proclamations condemning secret societies, he in effect encouraged the spread of violent republicanism.

Feehan was a subtle patriot. He sympathized with the aspirations of the radical members of Clan na Gael and "never hesitated on proper occasions to lift up his voice against the crimes and intrigues of her oppressors." In an 1882 address he noted,

> England, being stronger than Ireland was, destroyed her temples and her monuments . . . robbed her of her jewels, and then placed upon her shoulders a robe of mockery, and attempted to point her out to the derision of the nations and said "See how poor she is now and how ignorant her people are"—when she had made them so.

Perhaps this awareness of oppression made Feehan sensitive to the needs of a number of communities within the Catholic Church in Chicago, and as archbishop he actively promoted the establishment of "national" parishes for non-English-speaking Catholics. Following Feehan's death in July 1902, the United Irish Societies of Chicago observed that

> his heart and purse were always at the service of the land that cradled him. While he was known and respected generally as a distinguished churchman and conspicuous for his learning and piety, those engaged in active work for the cause of Ireland had a close acquaintance with him, and always knew him as a man whose devotion to the old land had never faltered.

Throughout his time in Chicago, Feehan tolerated, befriended, and financially supported the Irish cause. One of his closest associates was Alexander Sullivan.

Feehan may have been the most influential, but he was far from the only ally Sullivan had in the Catholic Church. One of the highest-profile Chicago clerics was Father Maurice Dorney, "the Stockyards Priest." Dorney was born in 1851 in Springfield, Massachusetts, but spent most of his life in Chicago, where his father, a Limerickman, was a lumber buyer for the Illinois Central Railroad. Following his ordination in 1874, he served in several parishes in Chicago, but it was his involvement in the establishment in 1880 of St. Gabriel's Parish in the Canaryville neighborhood, close to the Union Stock Yard, that brought him to a position of prominence within the Irish community. Dorney was a popular, enthusiastic, charismatic, and strongly republican priest. Within a decade he had transformed St. Gabriel's into a vibrant parish complete with its own school, and a church designed by the notable architects Daniel Burnham and John Root. The Sisters of Mercy educated the young in the parish's grammar and high schools, and Father Dorney made the parish hall available for meetings of Irish social, political, and revolutionary societies. Dorney, himself a member of Clan na Gael, held an annual celebration of the birth of the Irish republican martyr Robert Emmet, regularly spoke at the Irish republican events, and was a very close friend of Alexander Sullivan.

>—¦◆>·O·◆¦—<

By 1881 it was clear to those involved that the center of Irish republicanism in America was in Chicago. Alexander Sullivan nominally shared the leadership of the Clan with Denis Feely and Michael Boland, but all the key decisions were his, and he was intolerant of dissent. Anyone hoping to progress to a position of leadership in the Clan would have to position himself close to Sullivan, both geographically and politically. One man intent on doing this was Dr. Patrick Henry Cronin.

Cronin was "a fine-looking, muscular man, with a clear, bold eye, a resolute jaw, and refined features of the best Irish type." According to the journalist and writer Eugen Seeger, he was "a typical Irishman, brave, loyal and warm-hearted; impulsive, vindictive and relentless." Cronin was born in Buttevant, County Cork, at the height of the Great Potato Famine, and as an infant he and his family moved

Dr. Patrick Henry Cronin (detail). Photographer: V. Georg & Company.
Chicago History Museum, ICHi-QF38KC88.

to America. The family initially settled in New York and later moved
to Baltimore before finally settling in St. Catharines, Ontario, which
had a considerable Irish population. In 1863 Cronin returned to the
United States and found work in the oil fields of Pennsylvania. However, he did not linger there and soon moved west to St. Louis, where
he got a job as a warehouse porter.

Cronin had a fine tenor voice, and frequently sang at Irish events
and at both his local Catholic Church and, rather unusually, the Second Baptist Church in St. Louis. His talent brought him to the attention of some influential businessmen in the city, and one of them,

R. P. Tansey, elevated him to the position of city ticket agent for the St. Louis and Southeastern Railway. Keen to pursue a long-held dream of being a physician, Cronin persuaded a local timber and railroad firm, the Bagnal Timber Company, to sponsor his studies. He enrolled at the Missouri Medical College, where he graduated in the late 1870s; later he received both a master's degree and a PhD from St. Louis University. Cronin was an ambitious and capable physician who with a number of colleagues helped revive the St. Louis College of Physicians and Surgeons, and by the early 1880s he was its professor of eye and ear diseases. He was sufficiently embedded in St. Louis society to attend the 1878 World's Fair in Paris (the Exposition Universelle) as one of Missouri's state commissioners.

Cronin's commitment to his profession was rivaled by his dedication to the Irish cause. He was a member of a number of societies, including the Ancient Order of Hibernians and, from late 1876, Clan na Gael. By 1882 he had recognized that proximity to Alexander Sullivan was key to progressing in the Clan, so he decided to move to Chicago. The two men had become acquainted through Clan channels earlier, and Sullivan paved the way for Cronin's arrival in Chicago by securing him a position at Cook County Hospital.

However, Cronin soon established his own private medical practice, opening two offices: one in the Chicago Opera House Block in the downtown business district, the other at the residence he shared with his friends, Theo and Cordelia Conklin, in the Windsor Theatre Building on North Clark Street. The vast majority of his patients were Irish, and he quickly integrated himself into the Irish community. He was a prominent member of a number of charitable and fraternal societies, and was often spotted walking his Skye Terrier, Dixie, in the streets around his home. And as in St. Louis, Cronin's musical talents did not go to waste. He regularly sang at Holy Name Cathedral on State Street, and at concerts organized by other Irish Americans, where he was renowned for his rendition of the unofficial Irish national anthem, "God Save Ireland." Most important, he threw himself enthusiastically into Clan activity, and quickly became the most senior member of his local Clan camp.

CHAPTER TWO

THE UNITED BROTHERHOOD

lan na Gael was far from being the first Irish secret revolutionary so-
ciety. It built on a tradition that reached back to the foundation
of the Society of United Irishmen in Belfast in 1791, and followed
in the footsteps of groups such as the Young Irelanders and, more
directly, the Fenians. In 1858 the Fenians were founded as an organization intent on launching an insurrection against Britain. The Fenians in the United States would provide the money while their Irish
counterparts, the Irish Republican Brotherhood, would provide the
manpower. However, a combination of hesitant leadership and the
outbreak of the American Civil War curtailed any notions of funding
an Irish rebellion, at least while the war raged. By the time the insurrection was organized, the movement had been infiltrated by spies
and informers, and most of the leadership had been detained by British and Irish authorities.

Then, in 1867, uprisings began with an aborted raid on the arse-
nal at Chester Castle near Liverpool, England. The failure to secure a
substantial arms cache meant that a large-scale rebellion was impossible, but through the spring and summer of 1867 a series of Fenian
attacks took place in both Britain and Ireland. In early September
several Fenians were arrested in Manchester, and a plot was hatched
to spring them from the prison van transporting them from court to
jail. In the course of the rescue a police officer, Sergeant Charles Brett,
was shot dead, and two Fenian prisoners, Thomas J. Kelly and Timothy Deasy, escaped and fled to America. Within weeks six men had
been captured, convicted of murder, and sentenced to death. Three—
William Allen, Michael Larkin, and Michael O'Brien, the "Manchester Martyrs"—were publicly hanged outside Salford Prison in Manchester on November 23, 1867. While many condemned the killing of

Brett, it was widely regarded in both Ireland and Britain as unintentional, and the executions were seen as an excessive reaction.

Out of disaster came triumph of a sort—the creation of a new generation of republican martyrs alongside men such as Theobald Wolfe Tone and Robert Emmet to inspire further attacks on British domination of Ireland. The fact that the Fenian movement could operate (albeit largely unsuccessfully) in Ireland, Britain, and the United States was a propaganda victory for the rebels, and had a profound effect on both republicans and the British authorities—on the one hand it offered hope of future success, and on the other it spread fear. William Gladstone, soon to be prime minister, privately conceded that Fenian activity did prompt a reconsideration of Irish claims, and ultimately brought about the disestablishment of the Church of Ireland in 1871. John Devoy, a leading Irish republican, later recalled that Gladstone's concessions "proved a stronger argument in favor of physical force and even of terrorism on the part of Ireland to secure justice and freedom than any Irishman ever made."

These victories were still some way off in December 1867, when an attempt was made to free Fenian military leader Ricard O'Sullivan Burke from the Clerkenwell Jail in London. The plan was straightforward—a cask filled with gunpowder would be placed by the prison yard wall. A small white Indian rubber ball would be thrown over the wall while the prisoners were in the exercise yard as the signal for Burke to fall out of line, wait for the explosion, and then, in the midst of the confusion, escape through the hole in the wall. However, at the first attempt the fuse failed to light, and at the second the gunpowder exploded and the prison wall collapsed, as did several laborers' cottages across the road, killing twelve people and injuring at least 120. O'Sullivan Burke did not escape, as the prison authorities had been alerted to the plan and confined all prisoners to their cells. Five men and one woman were accused of murder, though only one, Michael Barrett, was found guilty. After this disaster, a significant amount of the support that the Fenians had previously enjoyed among the British working class evaporated.

On the other side of the Atlantic, the Fenians were also failing to cover themselves in glory. In 1866 they launched an attack on the small island of Campobello (at the time British territory), just off the coast of Maine, in the somewhat ludicrous hope of offering it in exchange for Irish independence. Though they were easily repulsed by a combination of American, Canadian, and British forces, the Fenians made several further attempts to invade Canada between 1866 and 1871, all of which were rebuffed. The excursions were widely regarded as fiascoes; the movement, never entirely united, splintered as disillusioned members left. From the various factions, Clan na Gael emerged as the bearer of the Irish republican flame. Its ideological aims were no different from those of the Fenians, and many regarded the Clan simply as a better-organized, better-led version. Colloquially, both at the time and in later generations, many reporters, commentators, members, and historians referred to the Fenians when they really meant Clan na Gael.

>─┤◆>─○─<◆┤─<

In June 1867 Jerome Collins, a Fenian and a journalist on the *New York Herald*, founded the Napper Tandy Club, named for an Irish republican of the late eighteenth century. This club, and others that stemmed from it, attracted many disillusioned Fenian men, and in 1870 these associated clubs became known collectively as Clan na Gael.

The Clan, like many secret societies, was a mix of the theatrical, the secretive, and the absurd. It modeled some of its rituals and ceremonies on those used by groups such as the Ancient Order of Hibernians (which had many Clan members), the Freemasons, and other fraternal societies. Within the Clan there was an acute awareness of the need to keep its revolutionary plans secret. In an attempt to thwart spies, the organization decided to encode some of its communications. But Clan leaders settled on a ridiculously simplistic system in which each letter was replaced by the one that came after it alphabetically. "Ireland" became "Jsfmboe," "England" was "Fohmboe," and "Revolutionary" became "Sfwpmoujposbsz." Later additions to the secret communications system included symbols and code words used to indicate senior members of the Clan. James J. O'Kelly, senior Clan man and brother of the painter Aloysius O'Kelly, advised John Devoy to write in ink made from a "weak solution of yellow prussaite of potash," using a "quill pen" on "rough unglazed paper." The secret message would then be developed using "a solution of copperas." Gestures were also used to convey messages—signals such as twice rubbing the inner corner of the right eye with a handkerchief on the index finger of the right hand, or placing the little finger of the left hand in the left ear.

The organization of the Clan was relatively straightforward. At the top of its pyramidal structure was the Executive Committee (sometimes called the Executive Directory), which consisted of eighteen men based in the United States. From 1877 onward there was also a seven-man Revolutionary Directory, three members of which were nominated by the Executive Committee, three nominated by the Irish Republican Brotherhood, and the seventh member elected by the other six. The Revolutionary Directory was a key component of the Clan, since it coordinated republican activity on both sides of the Atlantic. It was intended to

> take charge of the immediate preparation for a struggle with Fohmboe [England]; [it had] power to declare xbs [war]; to negotiate with foreign powers hostile to Fohmboe, and to assume all powers, functions and authority of a provisional government in Jsfmboe [Ireland] when xbs has been declared.

The Clan in America would supply money, arms, and ammunition while their sister organization the IRB would provide strategy and manpower.

At a state level the Clan was divided into districts, and each district was subdivided into camps. New York (where the Clan was founded) was District A, and Chicago was part of District K, which included all of Illinois and Michigan. Every camp had both a name and a number. The number was secret, known only to members; the name, such as the Wolfe Tone Club or the Columbus Club, was the Clan's face in public, where it masqueraded as a simple fraternal society. Each camp elected its own officers, the most important of whom were the Senior Guardian and the Junior Guardian. Officers of individual camps would know the corresponding officers in their district, but were not supposed to meet with the rank and file of other camps to ensure that secrecy was maintained. Every two years district conventions elected delegates to the national convention, and they in turn elected the members of the Executive Committee.

Membership in Clan na Gael was restricted to Irishmen and men of Irish ancestry. At first Greenhorns (members born in Ireland) were deemed naturally more devoted to the cause than Narrowbacks (members born outside Ireland of Irish parentage), who were subjected to additional inquiries about their "history, character and sentiments." But by the 1880s this approach was outdated, because the Clan's ranks were swollen by North American–born members like Sullivan.

Prospective members could not simply attend a Clan meeting; they had to be nominated and seconded by two members, and character references had to be produced. Camps voted anonymously, and three black balls cast during the voting process were enough to reject a candidate. Twice a year every camp was required to submit a list of rejected and expelled members to the Executive Committee, which then circulated the complete list to all camps to prevent spies and informers. However, these lists were often incomplete. Men (including Alexander Sullivan) who were blackballed by one camp were often accepted by another.

Secrecy within the Clan proved impossible. The Irish community in America was a close-knit yet fluid one, and information was transmitted through families, friends, and associates and between towns and cities. America in the late nineteenth century was a place of high mobility for young working-class men—the group that made up the majority of Clan na Gael. These men were likely to become members of several Clan camps, and such fluidity made the Clan very porous. Moreover, hundreds of Clan men met at district conventions, and on occasion one thousand delegates were dispatched to the national convention, where they discussed politics, rebellion, and Ireland over several alcohol-fueled days. Maintaining a low profile and secrecy amid such conditions was futile.

The need for financial support also forced the Clan into the open, or at the very least made it visible for those who wanted to see it. Securing Irish independence by the use of force was a costly enterprise, and so while time was spent plotting and planning, writing manifestos, stockpiling dynamite, and penning newspaper columns, fund-raising also was a key priority. Picnics, balls, and fairs were the chief fund-raising activities. St. Patrick's Day was one of the days promoted by the United Irish Societies of Chicago, an umbrella group representing many Irish and Irish American organizations but run by the Clan. However, their primary focus was on three other annual events—Robert Emmet's birthday (March 4), the Feast of the Assumption (August 15), and the anniversary of the execution of the Manchester Martyrs in 1867 (November 23).

In Chicago, St. Patrick's Day was observed with enthusiasm by the Irish; thousands attended functions in halls across the city. The halls were decked out with green ribbon, and concerts of Irish traditional music and rebel songs were held. Republican songs such as "The Wind That Shakes the Barley" and "The Rising of the Moon" were particular favorites. Most popular of all was T. D. Sullivan's "God Save Ireland," written in 1867 and inspired by the last words of the Manchester Martyrs as they were led from the dock after being sentenced to death. It was set to the tune of the American Civil War song "Tramp, Tramp, Tramp!" and by the early 1870s it was regularly referred to as the Irish national anthem. T. P. O'Connor, a journalist and Home Rule Member of the British Parliament, noted in 1886 that "whenever in any part of the globe there is now an assembly of Irishmen, social or political—a concert in Dublin, a Convention in Chicago, or a Parliamentary dinner in London—the proceedings regularly close with a singing of 'God save Ireland.'" At the St. Patrick's Day celebration in 1888, Patrick Cronin led the crowd in a rendition of the song that was so loud "that the rafters shook and the [building] seemed in serious danger of collapsing . . . and the street-car horses on Madison Street shied as they passed a block away."

Celebrations on the Feast of the Assumption took the form of a picnic. From 1876 onward this was held at Ogden's Grove, near the junction of North Avenue and Halsted Street. If eating, drinking, dancing, and speeches full of fire and brimstone could defeat Britain, then Irish chances of success were high. As "Mr. Dooley," the comic creation of journalist Finley Peter Dunne, wryly observed, "There's wan thing about th' Irish iv this town . . . they give picnics that does bate all. Be hivins if Ireland cud be freed be a picnic, it'd not on'y be free to-day, but an impre." Thousands attended the picnics, designed largely as a social gathering for families. Entertainment was laid on for adults and children. There was Irish dancing alongside the "usual paraphernalia" of merry-go-rounds, fat men's races, thin men's races, three-legged races, girls' sack races, long jumps and high jumps, the wheel of fortune, shot putting and hammer throwing, lung testers, and "try your weights." Booths sold food and drink, and in the evening, following the inevitable political speech making, bands played a range of Irish and American dance tunes, with a fireworks display often providing the finale for the day.

The speaker's rostrum and the dance area at the picnic were usually festooned with both American and Irish flags. Further evidence of Irish Americans' desire to straddle both cultures was visible at the St. Patrick's Day celebrations in Chicago in 1888, when, after the traditional Irish music and speeches, the chairs were cleared away and "a regular American ball" then took place: the waltz and quadrille took center stage, and the "Irish boys and girls needed no coaching in the dancing of them."

Picnics and balls were the public face of the Clan—a family day out, a day to reminisce about the "old country" for those who had left Ireland, a day to imagine it for those born in the United States. It was a day for family and friends, a day when the laborer, the stockyards worker, the lawyer, and the doctor stood side by side as Irishmen. The vast majority of picnickers were Irish nationalists, republicans even, but few ever thought in concrete terms about where the money they spent at these gatherings ended up. It was enough to know that they were buying into Irish freedom, buying into a clear identity, buying into a close community in a land that often rejected them.

>⚬➤⚬◅

The public face of the Clan masked a secret interior, complete with rituals designed to reinforce the aims of the organization. An elaborate ceremony surrounded the initiation of members, and its early incarnations involved blindfolding the candidates and tying their hands behind their backs. It was essential that the Senior Guardian give a stirring performance at these proceedings; the "Ritual of the United Brotherhood" noted that it was an indispensable qualification for the position of S. G. [Senior Guardian] [or] J. G. [Junior Guardian] that members . . . should be good readers, capable of delivering their part in an impressive, animated, but not hurried manner.

The purpose of the ritual was "as much to impress the old members, refreshing their minds with their obligations and principles of the Order, as to instruct candidates." Camps often personalized the ceremony with "appropriate vocal and instrumental music." Rousing patriotic tunes or ballads extolling the heroics of Ireland's martyrs or listing the great ills done to Ireland by Britain were popular. On the day of initiation, the camp's meeting room was specially decorated. Green, white, and yellow pendants were displayed throughout the room, and an Irish republican tricolor was draped across the main table.

Candidates for Clan membership were sequestered in an antechamber, where the "conductor" asked each man a series of questions. When answered correctly, the "conductor" presented the candidate to the rest of the camp:

> The Conductor . . . will knock distinctly three times on the door. The S[entry] . . . will partly open the door and demand: "Halt! Who comes there?" Conductor—"Friends who desire to unite with us in the cause of Irish Freedom." S[enior] G[uardian]—"Advance Friends!". . . . Conductor—"Forward! March!"

The Senior Guardian then made a rousing speech to the candidate in which the purpose of the Clan was outlined:

> We are Irishmen banded together for the purpose of aiding the people of Ireland in securing their independence, and to elevate the position of the Irish Race. The lamp of the bitter past plainly points out our path, and we believe that the first step on the road to freedom is secrecy . . . once a member of this Order, you must stand by its watchwords of secrecy, obedience and love.

The new member then swore an oath of obligation on the Bible:

> I __ do solemnly swear in the presence of Almighty God, and members
> here assembled, that I will labor while life is left me to aid the people
> of Ireland in establishing a republican form of government in Ireland.
> That I will never reveal the secrets of this organization to any per-
> son. . . . That I will foster a spirit of Unity, Nationality and Brotherly
> Love among the people of Ireland.

Membership did not come without financial cost. Every member
was required to pay a fee, which varied from camp to camp: those in
well-off districts paid more than those in working-class areas. In 1881
the initiation fee was at least one dollar, and the weekly dues not
less than ten cents, with every camp obliged to meet at least twice a
month. Any member in arrears could be suspended or expelled from
his camp, unless he could prove that his indebtedness was the result
of a "want of employment." Central control of finances was important, so each camp was warned that their money must

> not be invested in any project that would make it unavailable in case
> of the F.C. [Executive Directory] requiring it for immediate use, and no
> monies of the V.C. [Revolutionary Directory] shall be loaned on mort-
> gages or otherwise, except that they may be invested in U.S. bonds.

All camps had their own code or "special words," which were used
to gain access to meetings. At these gatherings members discussed
fund-raising activities, debated the policies pursued by the Clan,
reminisced about Ireland, and, most important for many, organized
jobs for Clan members. Every camp meeting closed in the same manner, with a reminder of the express purpose of the organization:

> Brothers! Our work for this night is performed. We part as we met
> in a spirit of unity and brotherly love—principles that should actu-
> ate us continually as Irish revolutionists. We again separate to mingle
> with the outside world. Let us bear with us a vivid recollection of our
> mission—to heal the wounds of the past, and open the prospects of
> a glorious future by counseling and practicing unity and fraternity
> among the exiled children of our land. Until we meet again secrecy, as
> silent as that of the tomb, must guard the knowledge we possess; and

amidst the vicisitudes [sic] and toils of life, never forget that Ireland has entrusted her safety to us, and expects a faithful fulfillment of our pledges.

At the close of the meeting, camp members adjourned to a favorite spot in the outside world—usually a nearby saloon, where drinking and singing commenced.

>—!—‹›—•—O—•—‹›—!—‹

Clan membership was greatly enhanced as a result of the partial amnesty granted to Fenian prisoners in 1871. Many of the released men came to America, keen to continue to fight for Irish freedom. Newly arrived immigrants such as John Devoy, William Mackey Lomasney—the "Little Captain"—and Jeremiah O'Donovan Rossa gave new life to the republican movement.

Devoy was an astute, articulate, and acerbic commentator and came to have a dominant role in the Clan. He was a talented journalist and a skilled organizer, and he inspired great loyalty. However, he was also quick to anger and slow to forgive—traits that John Dillon, Member of the British Parliament for East Mayo, saw as common among the Irish. Writing of Devoy, he noted that "it is a miserable characteristic of our people that they seem to be utterly unable to differ on a political question without immediately becoming ferocious personal enemies."

Devoy arrived in America with impeccable republican credentials—he had become a member of the Irish Republican Brotherhood in 1861, and by 1865 he was in charge of IRB recruitment in the British army. That same year he helped IRB leader James Stephens escape from Richmond Prison in Dublin. Devoy was arrested in 1866, and the following year was sentenced to fifteen years' hard labor.

Fenian prisoners were not treated as political prisoners, and most served their time in British prisons—particularly Millbank, Portland, and Pentonville. They were harshly treated, and stories of abuse proliferated. To secure better treatment and also the early release of the Fenian prisoners, the Amnesty Association was established in 1869. It highlighted the dire conditions and appalling treatment of those imprisoned, drawing attention to one notorious incident in which O'Donovan Rossa had his hands cuffed behind his back for thirty-five days. The association succeeded in generating considerable public sympathy for the prisoners, and in 1871 Gladstone agreed to a partial amnesty under which many of the men, including Devoy, were released on the condition that they went into exile.

Upon his arrival, the *New York Herald* described Devoy as being "in good health and spirits, five foot six in height with the square broad shoulders of a young Hercules, close-cropped hair surmounting a square massive forehead, small deep-set eyes, giving an assurance of shrewdness to a face massed into firmness by a compressed mouth and strong chin." Alongside men such as Jerome Collins and William Hynes of Chicago, Devoy quickly established himself as a key figure in the Clan; his endorsement of the organization encouraged many others to join.

Devoy was determined that the Clan would not stagnate as the Fenians had done. A dramatic show of strength was required, and he decided that an audacious rescue mission was just the way to do it. Since many of Devoy's comrades in the IRB had been convicted and transported to Freemantle Prison in Western Australia, he was determined to free them and bring them to the United States. Such an attempt was fraught with danger, but it was not without precedent—in 1869 an American whaling boat, the *Gazelle*, had helped the Irish Fenian, journalist, and poet John Boyle O'Reilly to escape from Western Australia. If Devoy's rescue was successful, the propaganda victory would be immense.

>─!─◆>─○─<◆─!─<

In 1874, under Devoy's direction, James Reynolds—a Fenian based in New Haven, Connecticut—bought a whaling bark, the *Catalpa*, with the express purpose of dispatching it to Australia to aid in the escape of six Fenian prisoners. While Reynolds and others prepared the ship for its long voyage another Fenian, John J. Breslin, traveled to Australia to organize the prison break. The *Catalpa*, captained by George S. Anthony, left New Bedford, Maine, in April 1875, but on several occasions the rescue mission was nearly scuppered: at a stop in the Azores, many of the crew deserted and a new crew had to be hired; bad weather and faulty navigation devices delayed the *Catalpa's* arrival in Australia; and the presence of many Royal Navy ships in the vicinity caused further delay.

Finally, on April 17, 1876, a full year after the *Catalpa* had set sail, the rescue plan was put into action. Six Fenian prisoners who were working outside the Freemantle Prison walls absconded and, using carriages organized by Breslin, traveled forty miles to the coast, where they boarded a rowboat to take them to the waiting ship. However, the steamship *SS Georgette* and a police cutter appeared and gave chase. As the fugitives reached the *Catalpa* and were hauled aboard, Captain Anthony raised the American flag and dared the *Georgette* to open fire. The captain of the *Georgette* balked at causing an international incident, and as the ship sailed into the Indian Ocean the *Georgette* and the police cutter gave up the pursuit.

The outrageous and daring rescue made headlines around the world. In Dublin and Cork, torchlight processions welcomed the news of the men's escape, and in New York the former prisoners received heroes' welcomes. The success of the mission prompted a huge surge in the membership of the Clan (it was around this time that both Alexander Sullivan and Patrick Cronin joined) and ensured that Clan na Gael, not the Fenian Brotherhood, would dominate Irish republicanism in the United States through the 1870s and 1880s. As John Boyle O'Reilly, now editor of the *Boston Pilot*, put it, "It is a most memorable and honorable affair, and will do more good for Ireland than a whole unsuccessful attempt at revolution. It will put vim and confidence into men, and make them feel that they can trust each other."

At the welcome reception for the escaped prisoners held in Manhattan in August 1876, the masterminds of the *Catalpa* rescue were introduced to John P. Holland, a teacher and inventor from County Clare in Ireland. Although sympathetic to the Irish cause, Holland was not an activist, nor was he a member of any secret republican society. Yet over the course of an eight-year collaboration, he became a key figure in the campaign to secure Irish freedom from Britain.

At the time of this rescue, Holland was working on a submarine design. He had immigrated to America in 1873, and within two years had refined his design sufficiently to approach the United States Navy for funding. But the navy dismissed his plans, deeming them impractical. Therefore, the timing of his meeting with leading men in Clan na Gael and the Fenians was fortuitous. Buoyed by the success of the *Catalpa* rescue and in possession of a growing war chest of funds, the Irish republicans agreed to fund Holland's submarine experiments. In return they were entitled to a 50 percent interest in all patents and the use of his finished submarine. The work was to be carried out in secret, and Holland's submarine would be fitted with a "dynamite gun" intended to attack British ships, both military and merchant.

The money to invest in Holland's enterprise came from the "Skirmishing Fund" established in 1875 by Irish republicans, most notably Jeremiah O'Donovan Rossa and Patrick Ford (editor of *The Irish World*). Ford justified this fund by arguing that "the Irish cause requires skirmishers. It requires a little band of heroes who will initiate and keep up without intermission a guerrilla war." The money raised would be spent on training young men to use dynamite and financing bombing raids in Britain. One of the more outlandish proposals put forward was to use aerial bombs transported in hot air balloons, or "Jove's thunderbolts," as Ford put it, which would rain down "showers of explosives upon an army." Though this plan was never put into practice, the submarine was a more serious project.

Few knew the precise details of the development of the "torpedo boats," but their existence was an open secret. The "salt water enterprise," as it was known in Clan circles, attracted much attention from both the US press and the British Foreign Office. Blakely Hall, a reporter for the *New York Sun*, christened Holland's invention "the Fenian Ram," while the Foreign Office received a number of reports about the "Fenian Navy," which included the "torpedo boats" *Exterminator* and *Devastator*. Most of the construction work was carried out at J. C. Todds and Company in Paterson, New Jersey, and the Delameter Iron Works on West Thirteenth Street, New York, with the completed vessels being tested and docked at Bayonne, New Jersey.

Much of the Skirmishing Fund was spent either on propaganda, such as the Fenian Ram, or on the repatriation of the body of the Fenian movement's founder, John O'Mahony, whose funeral in 1877 was used as a republican demonstration; seventy thousand mourners lined the streets of Dublin as the coffin was carried to Glasnevin Cemetery. But as time passed, there was little evidence of success-

ful skirmishing, and contributors to the fund grew anxious. A further problem with the fund was O'Donovan Rossa, who was more
ridiculed than respected. Stories of his drunkenness and bizarre behavior were rife, and so in 1877 Devoy wrested control of the fund
and renamed it the "National Fund." This fund was controlled by
a seven-member Board of Trustees who represented both the Clan
and the Fenians. Gradually, plans for skirmishing were replaced
by a new strategy for Irish (and Irish American) nationalists and
republicans—the "New Departure." This was concocted by Devoy,
Parnell, and a recently released IRB prisoner, Michael Davitt. Transatlantic in its reach, it linked Irish land reformers, constitutional
nationalists, and determined republicans together in a campaign
to improve tenants' rights in Ireland, restore an Irish Parliament to
Dublin, and finally achieve the ultimate goal of an Irish republic. All
this was to be done through constitutional agitation, not skirmishing, which had reaped few rewards. It was time to shelve the use of
violence and pursue, at least for a while, a more peaceful solution to
"Ireland's difficulty."

With the change in the Clan's focus, the continued funding of
the Fenian Ram proved controversial, and mutual suspicion grew
between Holland and his backers. Though Holland had worked on a
number of prototype submarines with considerable success between
1876 and 1883, no vessel was ready for active service. He was afraid
that the Clan would walk away before the project was complete,
while Clan leaders feared that Holland might take his invention elsewhere. To ensure that this would not happen, the Clan hatched a
plan to steal the prototypes. One night in July 1883, a number of Clan
men, led by John J. Breslin, navigated a tugboat up the East River and
Long Island Sound to New Haven, Connecticut, pulling behind them
the Fenian Ram and a smaller model submarine that they had just
removed from Holland's dock. In an inauspicious development, the
model submarine sank as they towed it, but the larger Fenian Ram
was successfully smuggled and hidden inside a brass foundry owned
by James Reynolds. There she was abandoned until 1916, when she
was exhibited at Madison Square Garden, New York, to help raise
money for those injured during the Easter Rising. Holland, initially
furious about the theft, made only limited (and unsuccessful) at-

tempts to negotiate the return of his submarine, but he did have the last laugh: in 1900 he sold his prototype submarine to the US Navy after all.

>—I—◄►—O—◄►—I—◄

Despite the success of the *Catalpa* mission, the Clan had failed to capitalize on its increased membership and support. There had been no thunderbolts from the skies, nor, despite the investment of over $60,000 ($1.4 million in today's dollars), torpedoes from the sea. There was a growing fear within elements of the Clan that both the New Departure movement and Parnell's tour of the United States had turned the focus away from revolutionary activity and toward the Land League and constitutional politics. From his base in Chicago, Sullivan began to articulate the views of the discontented, those who feared that the Clan would become nothing more than a talking shop, a forum for disgruntled Irishmen to air their grievances. A growing number of Clan members favored using the "terrible agencies of dynamite," but believed they were being held back by a lack of will from the sister organization, the IRB, in Ireland. Without support from the IRB, the Clan was largely impotent. In a letter to Devoy in September 1880, Sullivan suggested breaking with that organization:

> I am quite convinced that the IRB is not in good hands. . . . I fear our work and money are wasted, while the IRB is under control of men who lack activity and brains. . . . I must confess for myself that I am sorely disappointed at affairs in Ireland, especially when I am forced to believe that there never was better material there to form a revolutionary organization. Unless a change is made, my judgment is that the home connection [the IRB] ought to be dropped. We could do something if *alone*. We can do nothing unless the home management is changed.

The Clan's national convention was scheduled to take place on Sullivan's home turf, Chicago, in August 1881. For this ambitious Clansman, the assembly provided the ideal opportunity to orchestrate a coup against the leadership, including Devoy. Despite their overt cordiality, Sullivan blamed Devoy for the lack of progress since the *Catalpa* rescue and held him responsible for the New Departure, which, as far as Sullivan was concerned, had brought with it few benefits. Wresting control of the Clan from the incumbents had been made easier for Sullivan by the May 1880 resignation of the chairman of the Executive Committee, Dr. William Carroll. Carroll felt he had been personally snubbed by Parnell on his American tour, and he believed Parnell's promotion of the League was intended to undermine the Clan. Carroll's absence created a vacancy that Sullivan was determined to fill. A consummate organizer, he set about ensuring that men favoring the immediate use of force against the British would dominate the convention. And of course these men would be loyal to Sullivan.

On August 3, 1881, two thousand delegates, all registered under assumed names that would "not give any indication of [their] . . . nationality," met in the opulent Palmer House Hotel, at the corner of State and Monroe Streets. Sullivan's groundwork paid off: the delegates elected him and several of his most ardent supporters to senior positions. They also voted for significant changes in the structure of the Clan organization—the Executive Committee was reduced from eighteen members to five, and the makeup of the Revolutionary Directory, which coordinated both Clan and IRB policy, was altered as well. Sullivan was elected to the Executive Committee along with Michael Boland, Denis Feely, James Treacy, and James Reynolds. He and his sidekicks Boland and Feely became the Clan's representatives on the Revolutionary Directory. With these alterations, Sullivan's position as leader of the Clan was secured. Then the convention promptly voted to pursue "an active policy" that ended the polite negotiations that Sullivan and his supporters associated with the New Departure. Instead, arms, ammunition and explosives would be procured, men trained, targets selected, and a new, dynamic, successful version of skirmishing begun. This policy would be known as the Dynamite War.

There was an element of Greenhorns versus Narrowbacks in this changing of the guard in Clan na Gael. In many respects this was not surprising, because by 1880, over half of all Irish Americans had been born in the United States. Greenhorns often regarded Narrowbacks with a degree of contempt, claiming that their Irishness wasn't quite the equivalent of men who had been born and bred on Irish soil. But by the 1881 national convention of the Clan, it was the Narrowbacks who were in the ascendancy within the organization. Devoy, Carroll, and Hynes were all Greenhorns, but the Narrowbacks (Sullivan, Boland, and Feely) now controlled both the Executive Committee and the Revolutionary Directory. By 1884 the Clan leadership was known as the Triangle, and in memoranda and circulars the symbol was used to denote them. But Feely and Boland were of little significance, beyond being necessary to ensure that Sullivan kept a hold on power. As William O'Brien, an Irish Parliamentary Party M.P., observed, Alexander Sullivan was the "one man who confuted a proposition of old Euclid by proving that there was a triangle of which one side was greater than the second and third put together." Throughout the 1880s Sullivan would dictate Clan policy, commandeer Clan funds, and implement the "active policy." The transfer of power was complete, and the first real fissures of the split that was to come began to appear.

Until the Chicago convention of August 1881, Sullivan, Devoy, and Hynes had maintained a civil relationship, though Devoy and others had some reservations about Sullivan's dedication to the cause. However, all were impressed by his ability as an organizer, and many found him to be excellent company. In 1876, when Sullivan was charged with the Hanford murder, Hynes was one of his attorneys. Moreover, as late as October 1880, Sullivan agreed to take over some legal cases for Hynes while Hynes campaigned to be elected State's Attorney for Illinois. Sullivan observed that "the belief here is that ordinarily when a man goes into politics, he is not of much use to us; but that Hynes is an exception, and, if made master of his own time and independent, he could serve the *cause* and the Irish people of Chicago to great advantage." Clearly, Sullivan was anxious to get Clan men into positions of influence and power within the US judicial system, where they could promote both Irish republicanism and Sullivan himself. But Hynes lost the election to Joel Longnecker, a man Sullivan would later regard as an enemy. And despite their apparent closeness, Sullivan regarded Hynes as part of the old guard of the Clan. Shortly after he became chairman of the Executive Committee, he suspended Hynes's clan camp and reconstituted it without Hynes as a member.

>─┼─◆>─•─O─•─<◆─┼─◁

Not content with shoring up power within the Clan, Sullivan was also determined to control the coffers of the Land League of America, the sister organization of the Land League in Ireland. Land League funds were not intended to fund bombing campaigns, but Sullivan wanted an additional injection of cash to add to the Clan's reserves, and decided to place pressure on the Land League, although—officially at least—the two organizations were completely separate. Despite their differences, Sullivan met with Devoy in early 1882 to outline his forthcoming trip to Paris to see Patrick Egan, treasurer of the Land League. Egan had been based in Paris since 1881, when the Protection of Persons and Property (Ireland) Act, one of the Coercion Acts, was introduced. This act gave the authorities in Ireland powers of arrest and detention without trial, and allowed for the suppression of the Land League. Before it became law, however, Egan fled to France with the League's account books.

The British consul in New York, Sir Edward Archibald, was convinced that "a considerable portion . . . if not the greater part of the monies remitted [by the Land League of America] to Paris are to be . . . used to promote rebellion in Ireland." Though he lacked evidence to back up his claim, his speculation was quite close to the truth. The purpose of Sullivan's Parisian visit in the spring of 1882 was to obtain $100,000 ($2.65 million in today's dollars) from Egan, a sum amounting to half the Land League's funds, and he wanted to extract a guarantee that half of all future donations to the Land League would find their way into Clan-controlled accounts. Devoy was horrified by such a proposal, fearful of tainting the Land League (and by association Parnell) with links to a terror campaign. Yet despite Devoy's objections, Sullivan made his demands to Egan. Egan resented Sullivan's hectoring style and was reluctant to concede, but when Sullivan threatened to break off relations between the American and Irish sides of the Land League, he finally agreed to hand over the money.

Despite Devoy's growing antipathy toward Sullivan, the men remained in regular, if somewhat touchy, contact over various Clan and personal financial matters. Devoy was a prickly character, so Sullivan warned him against taking criticism too seriously: "You were not abused half as much as I have been in Chicago. If I noticed assaults they would last forever. By treating them with contempt . . . you make more friends and preserve your dignity." Events would later show that neither man heeded Sullivan's advice.

Reflecting on the early 1880s, Devoy recalled that Sullivan spent 1882 and the beginning of 1883 focusing on securing his power base: "Old leaders had to be got rid of and discredited and obedient tools put back in their places, and a certain amount of 'work' done to keep the steam up." In April 1883, Sullivan consolidated his grip on power when he was elected president of the Irish National League of America at a special convention held at Philadelphia's Horticultural Hall. The National League replaced the defunct Land League of America, and its stated objective was to achieve self-government for Ireland through support for Parnell, though many within its ranks hankered for a republic won through force. The convention was attended by twelve hundred delegates representing a wide range of organizations, including Clan na Gael, the Ancient Order of Hibernians, and the Catholic Total Abstinence Union. At its proceedings, loyal members followed Clan policy, which demanded that when any movement was organized "in which members of the [Clan] can conscientiously participate, no pains should be spared to secure the control of these movements . . . by the [Clan]. A few of our good men can always manage to secure this control." The National League Convention was heavily packed with many delegates having dual loyalties—officially representing one organization, but in reality representing the Clan. Many attended in response to a letter issued by Clan leaders that reminded members of the "necessity of securing as full an attendance as possible at the convention in Philadelphia [as] it presents the first opportunity to secure the union of all the elements of our race on this continent." Father Maurice Dorney acted as temporary chairman, and Sullivan's election as president of the League was something of a formality.

From April 1883, as National League president and as chairman of the Executive Directory of Clan na Gael, Sullivan controlled both the overt and the covert means of making money for the Irish "cause." It's no surprise that he was keen to secure control of the National League, for it (and the Land League before it) attracted a much broader (and often wealthier) membership than the Clan. Sullivan's involvement with both the Clan and the League was a clever sleight of hand, for "Irishmen who would not join a secret society and abhorred the use of dynamite applauded him as one who implicitly accepted the leadership of Parnell, while the clansmen rejoiced in the knowledge that at the head of the Irish league was a dynamiter who had taken the oath of the brotherhood and as one of its directing minds was projecting mysterious expeditions against England." This assessment by the *Chicago Times* was astute: Sullivan was a chameleon who blended seamlessly with whatever company he kept.

As president of the National League, Sullivan claimed that the Irish nationalist movements in the United States were resolved to follow the lead of those based in Ireland: "It is for them [those in Ireland] to choose the road which leads to liberty, it is for us to march with them upon it." Public statements were one thing, but privately Sullivan was frustrated by what he regarded as the timidity of the IRB leadership, and he was determined to take decisive action. A new and explosive chapter in the story of Irish republicanism was about to begin.

CHAPTER THREE

THE DYNAMITE WAR

T hroughout the early 1880s, Clan na Gael trained and dispatched young men from the United States to Britain to plant bombs in English and Scottish cities. There were a few explosions in Britain in 1881 and 1882 led by O'Donovan Rossa's men, but the most sustained attacks orchestrated by Sullivan's Clan took place between October 1883 and February 1885, when "infernal machines" (as many of the rudimentary bombs were called) were detonated or discovered in a host of locations.

The first significant bombings took place in January 1883: bombs exploded in Glasgow's gasworks and the Caledonia Railway's freight house; in March the offices of the London *Times* were targeted, and in October explosions rocked the London Underground. In February 1884 a small explosion in the cloakroom of Victoria Station in London injured seven people; on one day in May bombs were thrown into two clubs in that city, and there was a failed attack on Scotland Yard. In December there was an attempt to blow up London Bridge, and on January 24, 1885, the bombers carried out their most audacious attack, detonating explosives at the center of British power—the Parliament at Westminster and the iconic Tower of London. Though no one was killed, the bombs injured a number of people and caused considerable damage to some of the most famous landmarks in Britain. The *Irish World* celebrated this attack on the heart of the British establishment, claiming it as "a victory that all patriotic Irishmen and justice loving Americans will appreciate." Under Sullivan the Clan had changed tack, and in spectacular fashion.

>⋅I⋅‹›⋅O⋅‹›⋅I⋅<

The "dynamite policy" pursued by the Triangle of Sullivan, Feely, and Boland was controversial within the Clan. Many felt that planting bombs in public spaces in Britain seriously undermined Parnell's political campaign, a campaign that the majority of Irish America supported. By commandeering the Land League funds and taking the war to Britain, the Clan was casting doubt on Parnell's claim to have no links to any group prepared to use violent means to achieve its aims; his dedication to a purely political solution was coming under increasing scrutiny at a time when numerous rumors linked him to the brutal Phoenix Park murders of Chief Secretary Lord Frederick Cavendish and his undersecretary, Thomas Burke, in Dublin in 1882.

The debate was not just a political one. Many Irish republicans believed that although British military and political targets were legitimate, British civilians were not, and they feared a repeat of the Clerkenwell Jail explosion of 1867 which resulted in the deaths of twelve civilians. For their part, both Devoy and Cronin opposed the "Dynamite War." Cronin told a close friend, Tom F. O'Connor, who was considering taking part in a bombing mission, that he was against it in principle, that he thought the "war" would be a disaster, and that "there were enough good, honest Irishmen behind English bars" already. But perhaps it was the death of William Mackey Lomasney, "the Little Captain," that prompted the decisive break between Devoy and Sullivan.

A slight, retiring man who spoke with a lisp, Lomasney was in many ways the archetypal Irish republican hero. He was born into an Irish republican family in Cincinnati, Ohio, in 1841. His grandfather had reputedly been a United Irishman who was killed during the failed Rebellion of 1798. Lomasney joined the Fenians as a young man, later becoming a member of the Clan. After serving in the Union army, he went to Ireland, where he was promptly arrested, imprisoned, and banished from that country and Britain. After a brief spell back in the United States, he returned in 1867 to Ireland, where he quickly gained notoriety for a series of dramatic and successful raids on coast guard stations and police barracks. Lomasney was captured in Cork in February 1868, tried, and sentenced to twelve years' penal servitude. He spent much of his incarceration in Millbank Prison, London, where he became close friends with John Devoy and was released alongside him under the terms of the amnesty of 1871. Devoy had great respect for Lomasney, commenting that while "modest and retiring in manner, one who did not know him well would never take him for a desperate man, but no one in the Fenian movement ever did more desperate things."

Lomasney and his new wife—a Cork woman, Susan Mahon—settled in Detroit, where he established himself as a stationer, bookseller, and aspiring playwright. Yet it was not long before he found himself once again involved in Irish republican activity. He joined the Clan and served with Devoy on the Executive Committee until Sullivan took over in August 1881. Lomasney was strongly in favor of Parnell, believing he was "eminently deserving of our support, and that he means to go as far as we do in pushing the business"—but he was unwilling to entirely forgo the prospect of using force against the British if it might bring success.

Despite somewhat diverging political views, Lomasney and Devoy remained close even when—in late 1880—Lomasney began to experiment with dynamite. As he told Devoy, however, "I scarcely think there will be need for what I am preparing for, but it is best to be ready, and none will be better pleased than myself if there never happens to be use for what I am preparing." In February 1881 there were explosions in Manchester, and a boy of seven was killed. In response, an irate Lomasney wrote to Devoy:

> Those foolish affairs in England are believed to be the work of O'Donovan Rossa's men. The amount of folly and bungling in connection with these attempts is simply disgraceful. . . . If allowed to go on confusion and anarchy would be the result.

Yet despite his reservations, when Sullivan embarked on the Dynamite War, Lomasney chose to follow. He claimed that his aim was to "strike terror into the British ruling class" without "hurting a hair on an ordinary Englishman's head."

In August 1884 Lomasney, his brother-in-law Peter Mahon, and John Fleming sailed to England. On the evening of December 13, close to six o'clock, the three men boarded a small boat, rowed out to London Bridge, attached a bomb to iron gratings, and lit the fuse. As the men prepared to row away, the bomb exploded prematurely, blowing the men "to atoms," destroying the boat, and shattering

THE DYNAMITE WAR || 43

windows, but leaving London Bridge largely undamaged. According to Devoy, Lomasney had never intended to destroy the bridge; rather, the explosion was designed to spread fear. It is possible that Lomasney had agreed to participate in the dynamite campaign so that he could direct attacks away from areas where civilians might be injured or killed and toward iconic buildings and landmarks. Certainly, this is what Devoy chose to believe.

The Dynamite War, like the skirmishing campaign, was a disaster, both militarily and politically. Sullivan believed that "the mystery of an unknown power striking in the dark, always able to evade detection, is far more terrible than the damage inflicted." In many respects he was correct, but his bombers failed to evade detection; the Clan were not an unknown power; and although injuries were inflicted, some property was damaged, and fear was spread, the cost (financial and otherwise) to the Clan was high. Between 1881 and 1885, thousands of dollars were spent, three men were killed, and eighteen were arrested and imprisoned. In the vast majority of cases, the would-be bombers were arrested before they could detonate their "infernal machines," indicating that, as in so many Irish republican organizations before theirs, a spy had infiltrated Clan na Gael.

The British authorities placed the blame for the bombings firmly at the feet of Irish America, because in almost every case the would-be bombers were US citizens or resident in the United States; almost all the dynamite used came from the United States; and all the explosive devices were constructed using American material. The British government believed that many Irish republicans became US citizens for the sole purpose of enlisting the support of the US government if arrested while on "active service" in Britain or Ireland. Edward O'Meagher Condon, for example, was sentenced to death for his role in the murder of Sergeant Brett in 1867, but his death sentence was commuted partly as a result of intervention from President Ulysses S. Grant.

Back in June 1881, Edward Thornton, the British minister in Washington, DC, met with James G. Blaine, the US secretary of state, to discuss "the very violent and hostile language which was being made use of by certain newspapers published at New York which supported . . . the Fenians." The British government wanted the United

States to take action regarding "this incendiary language." Blaine refused, arguing that the Fenians had little influence except among the Irish, and were "treated with the greatest contempt by the vast majority of the Americans" until the arrival of "telegrams from England had given [them] a certain importance." He conceded that if his government discovered that "armed expeditions were being prepared in his country with hostile intentions against Her Majesty's Government, or . . . for the destruction of life or property in Great Britain by means of explosives manufactured here, it would take the most energetic measures to prevent such expeditions." Blaine said he had written to J. R. Lowell, the US ambassador to Britain, and "strongly recommended him not to take up too warmly the cause of American citizens . . . who went to England or Ireland with the express object of agitating and of then appealing to their Government for protection." He agreed to "recommend the President [James A. Garfield] not to grant protection to Irishmen who had come to the United States for the sole purpose of being naturalized." But Garfield was shot and fatally wounded a week after Thornton's meeting with Blaine, and so nothing came of it.

The real sea change in American political opinion came following the Clan's audacious attacks on the House of Commons, Westminster Crypt, and the Tower of London on "Dynamite Saturday," January 24, 1885. The attacks at the very heart of British government rattled the US politicians, so much so that there was an attempt to pass a bill in the Senate to prevent "the organization of conspiracies in this country for using dynamite or other explosive for the purposes of assassination at home or abroad." The bill was defeated, but there was growing disquiet among senior politicians. Then, in a State of the Union address in December 1885, President Grover Cleveland announced that US citizenship "should be withheld from those who . . . may acquire the rights of American citizenship for no other [reason] than a hostile purpose towards their original governments." Cleveland's speech was well received in Britain, though tensions remained between the governments with regard to the tolerance shown by American authorities toward declared Irish republicans. The debate about Irish republicans seeking US citizenship to protect themselves should they be arrested in Britain or Ireland was revived during 1889 as newspapers devoted thousands of words to discussing whether an Irishman's loyalty to America was pragmatic rather than passionate.

For the Clan, the cost of the dynamite campaign in terms of men and money was significant, but the real damage was internal. It split over the dynamite policy, and the campaign further strained its already difficult relations with both constitutional nationalists and the Irish Republican Brotherhood. Like many of the other dead or imprisoned Clansmen, Lomasney left behind a wife and children. The Clan recognized the sacrifices of these men and pledged to support their families, but manifestly failed to do so. In August 1886, Lomasney's widow approached Devoy for assistance, claiming that she and her five children had been left destitute, and that Sullivan had promised but failed to provide for them. Devoy, Cronin, and others opposed to the Triangle were quick to bring the tragic story of Susan Lomasney to the fore. Sullivan's offhand treatment of the widow of an Irish martyr was simply one more reason for Devoy and Cronin to begin a campaign against the leader of the Clan. It was a campaign that would divide and almost destroy the Clan itself.

><+>+O+<+><

Fractures in Irish republican organizations were not unusual. Frequently, members shared little more than antipathy toward England and a desire to secure Ireland's freedom. How and when that freedom would be achieved was a matter for much discussion. In the United States, many of those drawn to the Fenians and Clan na Gael were inspired by John Mitchel's *The Last Conquest of Ireland (Perhaps)*; published in 1860, it had become the classic narrative of oppression. Mitchel, himself an exile from Ireland after having been sentenced to fourteen years' transportation under the Treason Felony Act of 1848, assuaged the survivor's guilt of many Irish immigrants to the United States by casting them as unwilling exiles: "There began an eager desire in England to get rid of the Celts by emigration; for though they were perishing fast of hunger and typhus, they were not perishing fast enough." The cruelties of the English would be avenged, the wrongs of centuries of British misrule set right by the thousands of Irish Americans who accepted Mitchel's version of Irish history without question.

Taking on the British Empire was an immense challenge, but as all Irish republican societies had discovered, their more immediate problems were often internal. Spies, informers, and personal quarrels frequently destroyed any possibility of launching a sustained or substantial attack on Britain. From the Society of United Irishmen in the 1790s onward, every Irish republican organization was weakened by splits. Inspired by the French Revolutionary slogan of "Liberty, Equality, Fraternity," the United Irishmen attempted to ignore the sectarian divisions within Ireland and unite under the "common name of Irishman" to "break the connection with England." But before the rebellion even began, the organization had been so thoroughly penetrated by spies and informers that most of the leadership had been arrested, imprisoned, and sent into exile. Nonetheless, the uprising still took place, and by August 1798, thirty thousand combatants and civilians were dead; within two years the Act of Union was passed, the Irish Parliament closed, and a new United Parliament based in Westminster established in its place. Despite their failure, the United Irishmen proved inspirational to all future Irish republican organizations, including Clan na Gael. The societies, divided by almost seventy years from the United Irishmen, were secret, oath-bound, and committed to using force to obtain Irish freedom. The Clan consciously linked itself with previous versions of Irish republicanism, and the names of its clubs often recalled heroes of earlier eras, such as Theobald Wolfe Tone, James Napper Tandy, and Robert Emmet.

Yet the nineteenth-century societies also adopted many of the United Irishmen's weaknesses. Despite secrecy being crucial to their survival, Irish republican organizations were very porous—perhaps because they often met in bars and saloons. By 1880 there was an acute awareness of the flaws that had damaged previous republican movements, and Alexander Sullivan reflected sadly on the fact that—time and again—the Irish were divided: "It is the same sad, sad, old story. Divisions, ill-wills, lack of common courtesy to one another, and a failure, therefore, to present a front of unity to the world." Somewhat ironically, Sullivan's correspondent was John Devoy; within three years the men presided over a split that was to tear the Clan apart.

And yet despite its divisions the Clan thrived. In the late 1870s it had a membership of around 10,000, a figure that rose to 13,000 in 1882, when the British consul in New York noted that the Clan was "a thoroughly organized and efficient . . . organization with increasing membership revenue." As a result of that organization and efficiency, membership increased to over 20,000 by 1884 and to 40,000 by 1889. Despite the failure of skirmishing, the Fenian Ram, the New Departure, and the Dynamite War, the Clan continued to grow, perhaps because the local advantages of being a Clan member in terms of access to jobs, accommodation, and community had become more significant than the achievement of Irish independence, which, however desirable, still seemed a distant prospect at best.

>—⦙—‹›—◦—‹›—⦙—≺

In Chicago everything was possible, at least in the imagination. The city was, in Louis Sullivan's words,

> magnificent and wild: a crude extravagance: an intoxicating rawness: a sense of big things to be done. For "Big" was the word. "Biggest" was preferred, and the "biggest in the world" was the braggart phrase on every tongue. Chicago had the biggest conflagration "in the world." It was the biggest grain and lumber market "in the world." It slaughtered more hogs than any city "in the world." It was the greatest railroad center, the greatest this, and the greatest that. . . . What they said was true: and had they said, in the din, we are the crudest, rawest, most savagely ambitious dreamers and would-be doers in the world, that might also be true."

Some of those "savagely ambitious dreamers and would-be doers" were members of Clan na Gael, and thousands of young Irish men and women arrived in Chicago determined to play their part in making that city the biggest and the most magnificent. To do that, they needed jobs.

The Clan was key to getting jobs for the Irish, though it wasn't the only organization to perform this function. The Irish were well placed to become players in the political system, particularly at the local level, for a number of reasons: first, there was a history of underground societies in Ireland, from agrarian societies such as the Whiteboys and Rightboys to the more overtly political United Irishmen. Throughout the eighteenth century, the penal laws had reduced Irish Catholics to second-class citizens and forced the Catholic population to become self-reliant, with some assistance from the church. Daniel O'Connell and the Catholic emancipation movement of the 1820s had politicized a new generation of the working class, who now had a voice in politics, or at least the potential for a voice. The new immigrants to the United States, radicalized by their experience of the Great Potato Famine, spoke English for the most part and were determined to make their voice heard. Second, the Clan found it relatively easy to get members elected to city and town councils, because the Irish voted in far greater numbers than most immigrant groups; further, Irish candidates benefited from their Catholicism, as other Catholic immigrants often voted for them. In the 1880s every senior Clan member was heavily involved in machine politics. By 1883 the Irish dominated overt and covert domestic affairs in Chicago.

Alexander Sullivan was a consummate political operator. Even his critics conceded that he was "incontestably the ablest Irish American of his day . . . a lawyer and politician of vast, if devious talents" who "had the gift of attracting the fast friendship of more than one man." Walter Wellman, the journalist and explorer, thought he had a "striking gift for diplomacy and intrigue" and was "always calm and well poised . . . never known to lose the cool and almost cruel equanimity which is his predominant outward trait."

Sullivan recognized the importance of looking after the immediate needs of Clan members, aware that loyalty could be bought by securing employment. Much of his success stemmed from the influx of new Irish residents to the city. John Devoy recalled that "most of the organized Irish were his loyal supporters, though in Clan na Gael the majority of the old timers disliked and distrusted him. But for years the flood of new members attracted by the hope of obtaining political jobs swamped them." Sullivan gathered a motley crew of "'toughs,' ward 'heelers,' gamblers, liquor dealers and thugs, all of whom would leave him to-morrow if he was 'thrun down' as a politician." Devoy complained that under Sullivan's control, the Clan had become an American political machine "not for the purpose of . . . promoting the cause of Ireland but for securing jobs for individuals." It is a charge that has some substance, though securing jobs for the Irish was an important and necessary function if money was to be raised for the Irish cause. Membership dues were vital to the organization. Whatever the motivations of those who joined, what really mattered was that the Clan had a steady stream of cash coming in.

Sullivan carefully cultivated the support of all shades of political opinion. On the Democratic side, he was an active supporter of Harvey Colvin in the mayoral election of 1873 and also of Carter Harrison, who served four terms as mayor between 1879 and 1887. He was friendly with other leading Democrats in Chicago, including Dan Corkery, a wealthy, Bridgeport-based mine owner and coal merchant and a Clan man, and Mike McDonald, owner of the Store at the northwest corner of Clark and Monroe. The Store was a saloon, a gambling den, and a flophouse for many young Irish immigrants. It was a hub of activity, frequented by "politicians, gamblers, pugilists and celebrities of all shades." The success of the Store, alongside his huge real estate portfolio and his stone quarries in Lemont, Illinois, meant that by 1887 McDonald's fortune was estimated at over $1 million. But he was not content with wealth alone—political influence was also important, and he was "acknowledged to have made the political fortunes of more people than any other individual in the west," including that of Carter Harrison. It was no wonder Sullivan sought him out.

Sullivan was also well regarded in Republican circles, where one of his closest friends was John M. Smyth, a senior Republican, a successful furniture dealer, and a member of the Clan. Treading a careful line between local, national, and international politics, Sullivan secured support from both political parties and from within the Board of Public Works, where his two years as secretary had provided him with valuable contacts. These he used to secure Irishmen positions across the city in a wide range of jobs, including within the police force, the hospitals, and the stockyards. Although some Irish found jobs in skilled professions, the rest were overrepresented in a number of unskilled jobs, including laborers, freight handlers, hod carriers, and lumber vessel unloaders, and they frequently earned less than their British and Scandinavian counterparts. Few were as privileged as Sullivan or Cronin.

Clan membership in Chicago was highest in poor areas of the city such as Bridgeport, home to the first Clan camp. In the packinghouse and stockyard districts, Sullivan relied on the support of a number of labor leaders and "fixers," such as Michael McInerney, a wealthy funeral director in Canaryville and the leading Democrat in the stockyards, and Father Maurice Dorney. Dorney, along with other nationalist priests such as Father Thomas Hodnett and Father J. M. Hagan, frequently found jobs for newly arrived Irish immigrants in the factories that surrounded Bridgeport. One of the camps of that neighborhood, Camp 41, was particularly influential. Its leader was Dan Corkery, and powerful members included James Strain, clerk in the Court Commissioner's Office, and City Council Aldermen John Powers and Edward P. Burke.

Although the Irish often favored the nod-and-a-wink approach to obtaining and keeping jobs, some Clan men were active in the burgeoning union movement, particularly in areas near the stockyards. Hundreds of Irish butchers and meat cutters took part in the Great Railroad Strike of 1877. By the time the strike spread from Maryland and West Virginia to Chicago, many workers who were not directly part of the railroad industry had become involved. At the "Battle of the Viaduct" near Halsted and Sixteenth Streets, several hundred Irish took part, marching under Irish republican banners. At least thirty protesters were killed and hundreds injured; most of the names on the list of the dead or injured were Irish. The Irish were also heavily involved with the Knights of Labor, whose founder, Terence Powderly, was the Senior Guardian of the Clan camp in Scranton, Pennsylvania. In the early 1880s, 35 percent of the Knights officers were Irish, but following a failed telegraphers' strike in the summer of 1883 the union's influence fell away. But for most Irish workers in Chicago, unions were of little benefit—they were unskilled and easily replaced if they became embroiled in labor issues.

Alexander Sullivan was happy to make it known that he had secured jobs, found housing, and fixed problems. On occasion he even involved himself in labor disputes. In May 1882, twenty-four mostly

Irish iron ore workers at the Joliet Iron and Steel Company were fired because they had joined a union organized by local saloonkeepers. The local community was outraged, particularly when it was discovered that the men had been replaced by lower-paid, largely unskilled workers. The police force turned a blind eye to the Irishmen's attacks on the new employees until the level of violence escalated to such an extent that it could no longer be ignored. Seven men were indicted for attacks on Italian and black workers, and at their trial they were defended by Sullivan.

>—!—◆>—◌—<◆—!—◅

Sullivan's ambitions went beyond both the city of Chicago and the call of Ireland. He had dabbled in American politics as early as 1868, when he actively supported Ulysses S. Grant in the presidential election and was rewarded with the position of Collector of Internal Revenue in the territory of New Mexico. In advance of the 1884 presidential election, he began—at least in public—to distance himself from exclusively Irish organizations. He stood down as president of the National League and was replaced by Patrick Egan (whom O'Donovan Rossa scathingly referred to as "a man who had been groomed to become a pliant tool"). Unbeknownst to members of the League, Sullivan had resigned to pursue his political ambitions in the United States. He had been in negotiations with Grover Cleveland's supporters, with a view to gathering Irish American support for the Democratic candidate in the upcoming presidential election. In return, Sullivan would secure the nomination as the vice-presidential candidate. When those negotiations broke down, he approached James G. Blaine, the Republican candidate; after receiving assurances that if Blaine was victorious Sullivan would be rewarded with the position of secretary of the interior, he campaigned vigorously on Blaine's behalf. Sullivan promised the Irish American vote, and in many ways he delivered it—Irish Americans were much more likely to vote than other immigrant communities, and he was in a position to influence many of those votes.

Devoy later claimed that he thought Sullivan's American ambition was "grotesque in its absurdity, but nobody liked to say so in Sullivan's presence." He argued that "it would do more to create prejudice against us than anything that has yet occurred in America. . . . It would enable our enemies to say that we put men in positions of forcing them on the political parties for nomination for public office." At the time, however, Devoy's newspaper, the *Irish Nation*, steadfastly supported Blaine's presidential campaign.

It was somewhat ironic that Blaine's campaign foundered the week before the election, when a Republican, Reverend Samuel D. Burchard, described the Democrats as the party of "Rum, Romanism, and Rebellion." Irish American voters were outraged, and Blaine's refusal to distance himself from the comment contributed to his defeat and the end of Alexander Sullivan's domestic political ambitions. Sullivan's engagement with American local and national politics was enthusiastic but ultimately doomed, and he was sufficiently pragmatic to realize that his real power base lay within Clan na Gael and the broader Irish American community. His foray into American politics proved to Devoy that he was not to be trusted.

Until 1883 the Clan had held a national convention every two years to elect men to the Executive and the Revolutionary Directories. However, Sullivan postponed the 1883 convention, claiming that English detectives were watching the Clan, and that to hold a convention would attract undesirable attention—though its postponement may also have been to allow him time to focus on his American political ambition. Critics of Sullivan believed the postponement was simply a dodge so he would not have to account for the $100,000 of Land League funds he had obtained from Patrick Egan in Paris in 1882. The convention that took place in Boston in August 1884 was far less representative than previous ones, and no envoys from the Irish Republican Brotherhood were invited to attend. The national convention of 1881 had almost two thousand delegates; the Boston convention of 1884 had twenty-seven, and these had been chosen by specially convened district conventions largely controlled by pro-Sullivan camps. Sullivan had successfully consolidated his control of the Clan.

This so-called Triangle Convention of 1884 made sweeping changes to the structure of the Clan. The Executive Directory was reduced to three—Sullivan and his henchmen Feely and Boland—

and allowed for a break with the IRB. The constitution was altered so that the Clan oath now bound members to decisions taken by the Executive Directory, whether "known or unknown." At the convention, the Triangle submitted a financial report that was accepted by the delegates, despite the fact that thousands of dollars remained unaccounted for. Rumors of fraud and theft that had been mere whispers became louder and more insistent, encouraged by members who were suspicious of the Triangle. Questions were raised that remained unanswered. Poor Clan accounting may have been responsible, but if it was neither fraud nor theft, it was certainly incompetence, and it left the way open to charges of embezzlement.

Many members of the Clan, including Devoy and Cronin, were furious that they had been excluded from the Triangle Convention. Devoy's frustration was part personal, part professional. Focused entirely on securing Irish freedom, he was disturbed by Sullivan's foray into American domestic politics. Writing of the Land League in the early 1880s, he made it clear that "we are fighting for the Irish people and for the Irish people alone," and he condemned those who wanted to use the League "in America for American purposes." Sullivan, on the other hand, regarded the Land League (and later the National League) as "a positive Americanizing influence." Devoy attacked the Triangle for adopting dictatorial powers, for downgrading the relationship with the IRB, and for being less than transparent with regard to the Clan accounts. His criticisms may have been grounded in personal animosity, as he resented Sullivan's refusal to provide Clan funding to his struggling newspaper, the *Irish Nation*, and he was angered by the fact that the Boston convention confirmed he was no longer near the center of power in the Clan.

At the urging of Devoy, John J. Breslin, and others, the Clan's District A (the New York District) passed a resolution protesting the decisions taken at Boston. The Triangle took immediate action, declaring the "so-called convention of District A an illegal body," and suspending Devoy's Napper Tandy Club for its "insulting, untruthful and insurrectionary actions." This suspension was followed by others in New York, Brooklyn, and Boston. Most of the suspended camps were in the original Clan stronghold on the East Coast, but opposition to the Triangle also came from Chicago, with William Hynes, Sullivan's attorney at the Hanford murder trial, and Patrick Cronin leading the charge. Hynes had been ejected from the Clan because his camp had held a public meeting in Chicago without the permission of the Triangle. The offense was not a significant one, but Sullivan's close friend and member of the Clan's finance committee, Timothy Crean, believed in coming down on "Kickers" (as those who opposed the Triangle became known) "like a triphammer."

The suspended camps decided not to establish a rival organization (as had happened many times before in Irish republican circles) but instead to set up a temporary committee dedicated to rekindling a close relationship with the IRB and attempting to forge a reunion with the other camps, but without the Triangle. Sullivan's portion of the Clan remained the larger and the stronger, but the anti-Triangle side was not insignificant. Devoy recalled that so many were opposed to Sullivan that a conference in New York of suspended clubs had as many delegates as earlier national conventions. William Hoare, the British consul in New York, estimated that the Sullivan branch of the Clan accounted for two-thirds of the Clan membership, but the Devoy faction was financially much better off. For the British, the split was good news: as Hoare reminded the prime minster, Robert Gascoyne-Cecil, 3rd Marquess of Salisbury, "The division . . . cannot . . . but lessen its power for mischief [and] . . . the prospect of a reunion of the factions is very remote."

The Triangle issued a robust circular in April 1885 that attacked the reputations of the men who had charged the Clan leadership with improper conduct. The circular implied that they must be spies or dupes of Scotland Yard to concoct such allegations, and aimed a particular barb at Breslin (and, to a lesser extent, Devoy) for involvement in the Fenian Ram scheme:

> Very few today can be found who can show that their experiments cost the enemy a cent of damage. Yet men who have spent tens of thousands in experimenting are very willing to criticize others and even to make insinuations against other men's purity of acts and motives. This is referred to for the purpose of reminding men how much easier it is to criticize than to do.

Yet despite the growing hostility between the Sullivan and the Devoy wings of the Clan, many of the rank-and-file members on both sides remained friendly. Indeed, John Boyle O'Reilly, a senior figure in Irish American circles, articulated the frustration of most ordinary members when he wrote in despair to Devoy: "I am sick to death of the deadly bitterness of these fights and I think . . . the interests of the Irish people are best served by ignoring them. . . . I dislike Sullivan's intense planning and manipulating; but it is his natural way, and his whole career so far as I have seen it, has been highly beneficial for Ireland." As for those involved in the split, he thought they were "crochety but good men. . . . They have each written pages of hatred against the others . . . but both charge and counter-charge *cannot* be true—so I concluded that neither is quite correct—and that both had better be forgotten." But because neither side listened to O'Reilly, the split became a gaping chasm. Attempting to bridge the chasm was to prove fatal.

CHAPTER FOUR

"SECRET HATREDS"

A Tale of Two Trials

P atrick Cronin soon became Alexander Sullivan's most tenacious and vocal opponent. Though they were members of different camps of
Clan na Gael, the two men both had offices in the Chicago Opera House Block, lived close to each other, moved in the same social circles, and met at Clan and National League events. Cronin had
moved from St. Louis to Chicago to become more involved in the
Clan and the National League, and had quickly established himself
in the broader Irish American community. He was Senior Guardian of Camp 96 of the Clan, and also president of the 18th Ward of
the National League of America. In addition, he was a member of a
number of fraternal and benevolent societies, including Royal Arcanum, Catholic Foresters, Independent Order of Foresters, the Royal
League, the Ancient Order of Hibernians, the Knights of St. Patrick,
and others. His circle of friends and acquaintances was expanded
both by his membership in the choir at Holy Name Cathedral, and by
the fact that he sang at almost every Irish event held in the city. By
1884 his prominence was such that he presided over the annual com-
memoration of the Manchester Martyrs at the North Side Turner
Hall on Clark Street near Chicago Avenue. As always, the evening
concluded with a rousing rendition of "God Save Ireland," which he
led. Cronin may have lacked Sullivan's political connections and ability to secure employment for new arrivals to Chicago, but he became
known for providing medical care to the Irish regardless of their ability to pay, and by the mid-1880s he certainly regarded himself as a
realistic alternative to Sullivan as leader of the Clan in the city.

Cronin was convinced that Sullivan was more interested in promoting himself than securing Irish freedom. He also suspected him
of embezzling $100,000 of Clan funds, and he objected to his oppo-

sition to continuing Irish immigration. Sullivan had embraced the Immigration Act (1882), which, in addition to levying a fifty-cent tax on all immigrants landing in US ports, declared that "any convict, lunatic, idiot or any person unable to take care of himself . . . shall not be permitted to land." In June 1883, Sullivan, as president of the Irish National League of America, met with Chester A. Arthur, president of the United States, and encouraged the rigorous enforcement of legislation concerning Irish immigration. He was anxious that the US government take action to end the stream of destitute immigrants from Ireland—a category that in the 1840s would have included Cronin's family. These new arrivals, Sullivan (and many others) alleged, were preventing the Irish already in America from getting jobs, and were contributing to the bad reputation the Irish had for fecklessness, idleness, and drunkenness. He produced the standard Narrowback argument, which claimed that continued emigration and the remittances sent back home to Ireland merely perpetuated British misrule in Ireland, as Britain could continue to shirk her responsibilities toward Ireland by exporting the problem.

Cronin knew well enough to be cautious about publicizing his opposition to Sullivan. In 1882, as a new resident in the city, he had watched with interest as Clan member P. W. Dunne accused Sullivan of misappropriating Clan funds. Incensed, Sullivan claimed to "have no idea why the scoundrel persists in seeking to misrepresent me. I have never done him anything but an act of kindness." Sullivan offered to have an "independent" assessor examine his personal accounts, and nominated his close friend Father Maurice Dorney, confident that no one would question a priest's integrity, whatever the finding. Unsurprisingly, Dorney reported that Sullivan's accounts were all in order. Dunne was tried by an internal Clan court and expelled from the organization. His fate persuaded Cronin to proceed with a degree of caution. As his dislike and suspicion of Sullivan grew he carefully avoided direct confrontation until after the Triangle Convention of August 1884.

>—⊷⟩⟶O⟵⟨⊷—⟨

By the end of 1884, Cronin had quietly allied himself with the Devoy wing of the Clan, and the following year he embarked on a dogged campaign against Sullivan. A contemporary observer noted that Cronin was "a friend for life and a foe till death," as Sullivan was to discover. Armed with "evidence" of Sullivan's corruption, Cronin gave talks to local Clan camps and circulated letters to members further afield in which he (and others, including John Devoy and former dynamiter Luke Dillon) set out a series of charges against the Triangle. In a letter to the rank and file of the Sullivan wing, the Devoy faction criticized Sullivan's leadership and accused him of centering all power and control in his own hands, which boded "no good to the [Clan] or the object which it was formed to promote." Documents circulated by Cronin and his allies directly attacked the dynamite policy of Sullivan's Clan on several grounds: it had been unsuccessful; it had wasted money; it had turned the British public against the Irish living in Britain; and, almost as an afterthought, it had caused injury to innocent people:

> We find that $128,000 [$3.4 million in today's dollars] has been paid to the executive, which . . . "favors action." What are we to understand by favoring "action"? Is it the policy of explosion? Of spending large sums of money on failures? Is it the scattering of mortar, stone and brick, the breaking of windows and the maiming of innocent men, women and children, among whom are your own race, travelling on railway trains or standing at railway stations? Are these the lofty heights to which the organization aspires? . . . We know as a result of this policy that the Irish residents in England are looked upon with hate and suspicion and threatened with dismissal from their occupations.

The letters and documents were intended to open up a broad debate about the leadership of the Triangle and the future direction of the movement. Yet it seemed that beyond the senior figures in the Clan, few paid much attention. At least at first.

><del>+<>+O+<>+<

In fact Cronin's actions backfired, bringing not unity between his camp and Sullivan's but a charge of treason from Dan Brown, a member of his own camp. The Clan constitution listed eleven offenses that were "deemed cause for expulsion, suspension, reprimand, or degradation from office":

> Treason; Violation of Constitution, Malfeasance in office; Slander or libel of a member of the V. C. [United Brotherhood]; Habitual drunkness [sic]; Embezzlement; Conviction of felony; Wilful neglect to pay dues when able; Disobedience of orders; Desertion; Conduct prejudicial to the good of the order.

Cronin was charged with three of these: treason, violation of constitution, and slander or libel (of Sullivan). A seven-man trial committee (or jury) was appointed, including members of both Cronin's camp (Camp 96) and Sullivan's (Camp 20). Sullivan acted as the prosecutor, while Cronin defended himself. It is no surprise that Cronin was found guilty and expelled.

Cronin refused to accept his dismissal from the Clan meekly, and as member Henri Le Caron recalled, "On his expulsion [he] joined the ranks of seceders, which by this time included such well-known men as Devoy, Luke Dillon, Peter McCahey and others . . . on the executive of the new body." His expulsion may have disappointed him, but it made little practical difference: he soon established his own rival camp, allied himself still closer with Devoy and Dillon, and continued his campaign against Sullivan and his supporters. In September 1885 he was one of the authors of a letter to members of the Sullivan wing that urged these "honest men [who] have been led to sustain wrong" to break with Sullivan, as the division

> is serious enough to menace the existence of a once powerful organization. . . . The strength and vitality of the national movement has been shattered. The oldest and strongest Ds [camps] are being driven out one by one, and a system of repression of free speech and sham trials . . . is brought into requisition for the purpose of crushing all independence of thought. . . . We charge that the three members . . . of the Triangle, are solely responsible for the evils of the present situation, and that deceit and trickery have characterized their action at every step.

The letter went on to denounce the Triangle for weakening the Revolutionary Directory, which had "provided the means of [making] one united Irish revolutionary policy throughout the world." In addition, it called the Triangle's dismissal of the IRB "a direct blow at the integrity of the national movement." The letter concluded with a plea for a general convention that would

> pronounce a final judgment, and calmly and impartially set aside all men who stand in the way of union. . . . The only possible means of securing it . . . is by your shaking off the lethargy that has overtaken you and joining hands with us. . . . The cause of truth, justice and patriotism will triumph, the confidence now broken will be restored, the gloom hovering over the organization dispelled and with brightening hopes we will march on to the accomplishment of our object—the restoration of national independence under a republican form of government to our native land.

Cronin's actions were not without consequences. His campaign made Chicago the focus of the dispute, raising a fury in Clan circles. As the dispute raged on this fury only grew, and by Feburary 1886 rumors began to circulate that Cronin was "doomed."

⊱━◈━○━◈━⊰

In the spring of 1887, several incidents took place that aroused Cronin's suspicions that a plot was being hatched against him. First, he was asked to be an expert witness in two legal cases, one in Chicago, the other in New York. William Starkey, a lawyer and Clan man, requested him to testify concerning another physician's alleged medical negligence. When he took the witness stand under oath, however, he was subjected to a barrage of personal questions, as the opposing counsel, David Callaghan, seemed determined to unmask a secret past. Later, Callaghan asked Cronin to be his expert witness in a case about a doctor's fee. Despite his unpleasant experience at Callaghan's hands, Cronin agreed. On this occasion he was cross-examined by C. M. Hardy, who pursued a line of aggressive questioning about when he was born and when he came to live in America. Around the same time, two men appeared at Cronin's sister's house in St. Catharine's, Ontario, seeking information about Cronin's date of birth. They claimed to be private detectives looking for Cronin in connection with the proceeds of a will from the "Wilson Estate" in Winnipeg.

Suspecting some link between the court cases and the so-called estate, Cronin went to Callaghan's office to confront him, only to find both Starkey and Hardy there also. He later discovered that all three were friendly with Sullivan. Convinced that the court cases and the "private detectives" in Ontario were all part of Sullivan's "deep-laid plan to ruin him," Cronin consulted a lawyer, R. S. Iles, who advised him that the evidence of a conspiracy was inconclusive, so a case could not be made. Cronin was disappointed, as he had hoped to force "Aleck out of his hole as a persistent persecutor of myself . . . through his malicious story-telling." He was convinced that Sullivan would ratchet up his harassment, so he warned Iles that "Alexander Sullivan is as black as hell. He has tried to ruin my reputation and, failing in that, he will seek my life." The following year, his old school friend Thomas P. Tuite, the Detroit city treasurer, visited Cronin; he later recalled that "the doctor talked much of his coming death at the hands of assassins."

Cronin was undoubtedly paranoid, but there is substantial evidence to suggest that Sullivan had been behind both the "Wilson Estate" and the "expert witness" cases. He was determined to prove that Cronin had perjured himself when he became a citizen of the United States, and hoped that the doctor would incriminate himself under oath. In a letter to Clan members, Sullivan alleged that Cronin had lied about the length of time he had lived in the United States and had not met the minimum residency requirement for obtaining his citizenship papers, and had therefore secured his papers illegally. But the cross-examinations failed to prove that Cronin was a perjurer, and in any case this was a weak argument within the Irish American community—many thousands had secured their citizenship through economies with the truth, and few would have judged Cronin harshly had Sullivan's suspicions been borne out. Additionally, encouraging investigation into Cronin's background was a risky strategy, as it invited a new and unwelcome focus on Sullivan's own antecedents, which also had potential for scandal. It was rumored (admittedly by those who opposed him) that Sullivan's mother had had an affair with a "Captain Fortescue," and that he was Sullivan's father. As Devoy rather crudely put it, "The Chief of the Triangle is the cross-born offspring of an English cad, born in a British camp, nursed in a British barrack, with the Union Jack flying over it, fed on British rations and educated in British schools. There is nothing Irish about him except his name, which does not properly belong to him." Stories also circulated which suggested that, in addition to his brother Florence, a journalist with the *Chicago Herald*, he had two half-brothers living in Chicago: one a policeman, the other a female impersonator on the stage. When it came to muckraking, the Cronin and Devoy faction gave as good as it got.

>─┤─◆〉─◆─○─◆─〈◆─┤─<

Despite continual attacks by opposing members of the Clan, behind the scenes a number of attempts were made to reconcile the divided organization. At a convention in Chicago in June 1888, delegates agreed to air the grievances that had split the Clan, and to establish a committee to examine the charges brought by Devoy against Sullivan, Boland, and Feely. Devoy listed four specific charges:

> Charge First: Violation of their Oaths of Membership and Office.
> Charge Second: Misappropriation of the Funds of the United
>   Brotherhood.
> Charge Third: Betrayal of Trust and of the Interests of the United
>   Brotherhood.
> Charge Fourth: Malfeasance in office.

In total the Triangle faced eleven charges. The three most significant accused Sullivan, Boland, and Feely of of stealing, spending, or losing between $100,000 and $128,000 "without any direct benefit to the order"; falsifying accounts between 1881 and 1884; and "scandalously and shamefully" neglecting the wives and families of the dynamiters. A six-man jury was established, with three men representing each side of the dispute—Cronin was appointed to the prosecution side. When the jury members were announced, Sullivan objected to Cronin's presence, claiming that he did not have the "decency of a dog," that the word "perjurer was burned into his scoundrel brow," and that he was prejudiced against all members of the Triangle. Sullivan laid out several grounds for omitting Cronin from the panel:

1st He is a personal enemy
2nd He has expressed opinions in this case
3rd He is a perjurer and a scoundrel unfit to be placed on any jury

Sullivan's objections were rejected by the jury, and in the spirit of compromise Cronin agreed to cast his vote with the majority.

Quite by accident, the Clan trial coincided with a sensational judicial inquiry known as the Parnell Commission that was taking place in London. Charles Stewart Parnell had been the subject of Parnellism and Crime, a series of controversial articles published by the London *Times* in 1887. These articles implicated Parnell in the Phoenix Park murders committed in Dublin in 1882, and accused him of having close links with the Fenians and Clan na Gael. Parnell denied all charges, and a Parliamentary Commission was established to investigate the newspaper's claims. The proceedings ran between September 1888 and November 1889 and attracted considerable attention. Onlookers in the public gallery might find themselves sitting alongside Henry James or Oscar Wilde. James apparently found the case fascinating, for he wrote about the "thrilling, throbbing Parnell trial," where "if one had been once and tasted blood, one was quite hungry to go again, and wanted to give everything up and live there." Much of the commission focused on establishing whether or not Parnell had connections with extreme republicanism, and elements of both the British and the American press were desperate to find direct links between Parnell and the Dynamite War. Where better to look than within the ranks of a divided Clan?

The first sessions of the Clan trial took place in Buffalo, New York, in August 1888, but to avoid press intrusion the trial later decamped to the Hotel Westminster in New York City; when journalists arrived there, it moved to Mike Ledwith's saloon on Third Avenue. The real bite to this story was Devoy's (and Dillon's and Cronin's) allegation that Sullivan had embezzled up to $128,000, most of which he had obtained from Patrick Egan in Paris. This was Land League money, intended for use as part of the dynamite campaign. From a British perspective, the fact that Devoy and others alleged that the money had been stolen for personal use would not deflect from the fact that it had been earmarked for training dynamiters and purchasing explosives—in other words, donations given by Parnell supporters had been used to make bombs. This, if proved, would destroy Parnell's political career and any prospect of Home Rule for Ireland. But the men who almost ruined Parnell's career with their financial shenanigans also saved it. In October 1888, Egan and Sullivan dispatched Father Dorney to London; the priest was armed with documents proving that a down-on-his-luck, disillusioned Irish nationalist journalist named Richard Pigott had forged the "Parnell letters" that implicated Parnell in terrorist activity. With Pigott exposed, the accusations against Parnell appeared weak and circumstantial.

The atmosphere during the Clan trial was fraught. All the bitterness of the last few years came to the fore, and many (including Devoy) attended the proceedings armed, fearing that Sullivan would "make a morgue" of the room if the judgment went against him. Devoy was heavily criticized for not taking the stand himself, which those on the side of the Triangle saw as "evidence of moral cowardice." He was dismissed by them as being "not free from prejudice and selfishness," and criticized for being petty enough to embark on a vendetta against Sullivan because he had failed to subsidize Devoy's newspaper. Devoy's refusal to testify certainly gave credence to the view that he was a coward who would not face those he was criticizing from afar.

In contrast, Luke Dillon was regarded as a man "who honestly believed his charges were true," and was prepared to publicly defend his belief. Although he had raised serious allegations against the Triangle, Dillon managed to straddle both camps in the early days of the split within the Clan. He was Devoy's friend, yet he was opposed to the New Departure movement and in favor of Sullivan's Dynamite War, and took part in two bombing expeditions himself. In May 1884 he and others bombed the Junior Carlton Club in London. He was one of the few participants who avoided arrest, and in January 1885 embarked on a second mission in which he detonated a bomb in the House of Commons. But Dillon returned to the United States disillusioned with Sullivan's leadership, arguing that the bombers had been poorly treated, and the families of those arrested or killed ignored. By 1887 he was firmly on the side of Cronin and Devoy, but there remained considerable respect for him across Clan ranks.

A number of witnesses came forward to testify that the dynamiters' families had been left destitute. The most compelling of these was Susan Lomasney, widow of Mackey Lomasney. In the summer of 1886, she had asked Sullivan for assistance and he had refused, instructing her to go to Father Dorney; he too failed to provide any aid. Eventually, Sullivan offered her a loan of one hundred dollars, which she and many others felt was inadequate. Luke Dillon, the former dynamiter, was outraged by Sullivan's indifference, and in 1887 he began to send funds to support the Lomasney family. Of all the charges leveled at the Triangle, this was the one that had the greatest chance of success.

On January 16, 1889, the trial verdict was returned. It was a compromise that pleased neither side and ensured that any façade of unity within the Clan remained just that. Jury members C. F. Byrnes and J. D. McMahon reported that "by a vote of four to two of the said committee, Alexander Sullivan is acquitted of all charges presented against him . . . the testimony adduced fully convinced the undersigned of the manhood, honor, integrity and patriotism of Alexander Sullivan." However, it was not complete exoneration for the members of the Triangle, for Michael Boland was particularly censured for financial irregularities. Additionally, it was found "unanimously that the family of Captain Lomasney was sorely neglected and left destitute, and that . . . said neglect was culpable and deserving of severe condemnation." Further, the jury found that "large sums of money were expended which brought no fruit, and might, therefore, be termed injudicious outlay; yet there was no evidence of the conversion of said funds by any one of the gentlemen against whom charges were preferred."

Before the trial began, Cronin had made a commitment to cast his vote with any four members of the jury in the hope of obtaining a unanimous verdict and unity within the Clan. However, he reneged on this, and in the aftermath of the judgment he and his ally Peter McCahey justified their refusal to agree to a unanimous verdict: the jury was "unable to elicit all the facts connected with the charges because of the refusal of several witnesses to answer many of the questions asked them." They outlined twelve areas where they felt that the Clan's leadership had been in the wrong, including misappropriating at least $87,000 and "scandalously and shamefully" neglecting the family of Mackay Lomasney and other dynamiters.

Jury members were supposed to hand over or destroy any notes they had made during the trial. Cronin refused to do so, instead visiting as many Clan camps as would have him, armed with sheaves of his trial observations as he continued his campaign against Sullivan. His notes also formed the basis of a bizarre fictional account of his own murder entitled *Is It a Conspiracy?*, an imagined conversation between Cronin and a journalist. The pamphlet, which Cronin circulated among his associates, was later described as a "jumble of incoherency," but it contained sections where Cronin seemed to fear for his life and believe that Alexander Sullivan would be the instigator of his death. In the conversation, Cronin sets out his arguments against Sullivan and the Triangle, and foresees his own violent death. In a bizarre (if prophetic) conclusion, the fictional journalist says to the fictional Cronin, "It strikes me that your funeral would be a largely attended one." The doctor agrees with him, and adds that "the cause of death [would be] extensively inquired into."

Sullivan may have been cleared by the Clan, but Cronin was determined to show that the trial was a sham in which the odds were always stacked in Sullivan's favor. He told his friend Stephen Conley that he would not desist: "I will do my duty. . . . I am alone, a single man, have no wife or children to feed and consequently do not fear to die. No one will be injured by my death. I will do my duty fearlessly, come what may."

Cronin's behavior was not well received in some areas. John F. Beggs, the Senior Guardian of Camp 20 (Sullivan's camp), wrote what would become a very significant letter to Edward Spelman, the Clan's district officer, imploring him to take some action to silence Cronin. Beggs despaired of Cronin's behavior and asked,

> Why, in God's name, if men are sincere, will they insist upon opening old sores? The majority of our men believes the parties charged [the

Triangle] to be innocent . . . and to have the charges made continually that they are guilty, creates a bitterness and ill-feeling. . . . If we are true men . . . we will rather conciliate than keep up a war. . . . The rank and file are sincere. They want peace and . . . they will have it even if it has to come to war . . . a day of punishment will come. I am very much discouraged at the present outlook, but hope no trouble will result.

In his reply Spelman said he regretted Cronin's behavior, but insisted there was little he could do to stop Cronin from making his allegations public. The ructions were no longer contained within the Clan, and by early February 1889 the *Chicago Tribune* carried reports on the split. Cronin's dogged campaign had succeeded only in making the operations of a supposedly secret society far from secret. For some members of the Clan, this was entirely unacceptable.

>—I ◀▶▪○▪◀▶ I—<

Though the trial of Sullivan and the Triangle had concluded, one member of the Clan was still preparing for his day in court. He was Henri Le Caron, a wiry, cigar-smoking Frenchman who was turning his attention from Clan business in America to activities of the Parnell Commission in London. Le Caron was memorably described by Devoy as "short and slightish in build; erect like a soldier— imperturbably cool; he has a lofty forehead, and smallish alert eyes . . . [and] one of the boniest faces . . . like a death's head with a tight skin of yellow parchment." On the morning of Tuesday, February 5, he took the stand in Probate Court One at the Royal Courts of Justice. Le Caron's sensational testimony, if genuine, clearly tied Parnell to revolutionary activity.

Le Caron began his testimony with a startling announcement: he was not a Frenchman dedicated to the cause of Irish freedom but an Englishman named Thomas Beach from Colchester, Essex, and he had been a spy for the British government for twenty-five years. As a young man he had lived in Paris, where he worked for Arthur & Co., an estate agency, bank, and wine merchant who dealt with American and British residents of the French capital. When the American Civil War began, a number of Arthur & Co.'s clients returned to the United States; seeking adventure, Le Caron decided to go with them. On

Henri Le Caron (*Thomas Miller Beach [Henri Le Caron],* by
Sydney Prior Hall). © National Portrait Gallery, London, NPG 2238.

his way to fight in that war, Le Caron changed his name, because
he didn't want his parents to discover he had abandoned Paris for
the dangers of the American battlefields. In August 1861 he enlisted
in the Union army and fought alongside many Irishmen, including
General John O'Neill. As a result of his friendship with O'Neill, Le
Caron joined the Fenians (claiming that his mother was Irish) and
served on its Council of War. He became a spy in the late 1860s, when
his father brought a letter he had written about Fenian activities to
the attention of J. G. Rebow, Member of Parliament for Colchester.
Rebow put Le Caron in direct touch with Scotland Yard, where he
worked very closely with Robert Anderson, one of the first spymas-
ters (and an inspiration for Inspector Heat in Joseph Conrad's novel
The Secret Agent).

Le Caron was a largely idle spy during the 1870s, so he spent the decade pursuing a career as both a chemist and a physician. He settled in Illinois, where he was resident medical officer at Joliet Prison. Later, he completed his medical training in Detroit. Back in Illinois, he established his own pharmacy and medical practice in Braidwood, a town about sixty miles southwest of Chicago.

Le Caron was, in many ways, larger than life and stranger than fiction. For a time he supplemented his income by becoming involved in the murky, but lucrative, world of grave robbing and body snatching. The number of bodies donated to medical schools fell short of the demand, and it was estimated that most of the five thousand cadavers dissected annually were obtained illegally from pauper's graves, African American burial grounds, hospitals, prisons, mental institutions, and morgues. In 1885, when Illinois passed an anatomy act, Le Caron's supplementary income began to dry up as it became legal to donate unclaimed bodies to medical schools.

During his time on the stand at the Parnell Commission, Le Caron denied that he was either an informer or a traitor; rather, he saw himself as "a military spy, serving among the enemies of my country," whose testimony would do "a great public good." He stated he had met Parnell a number of times, both in the United States and in London, and was adamant that Parnell knew of Clan na Gael's plan to use violence to achieve Irish freedom. Le Caron's information had formed the basis of a number of the articles in the London *Times*, and his reports had been partly responsible for the capture of many of the men sent to blow up key targets in London during the Dynamite War.

Within the Clan few, with the exception of Cronin, had suspected Le Caron. He was close to many senior Clan men and "out-Heroded Herod in his zeal for the cause of Irish liberation." Dr. George Cunningham, who knew Le Caron from the mid-1860s, recalled that he was so active "that Irish Americans called him the 'Lafayette of the Irish cause.'" Although Cronin had long been an enemy of Le Caron, who had been part of the committee that secured his expulsion from the Clan, he must have greeted some of his testimony with a knowing nod, though he would undoubtedly have hated the manner in which this information was made public. Le Caron maintained that the vast majority of Irishmen are perfectly sincere and perfectly honorable, but there can be no question that the professional Irish patriot is about as unscrupulous, insincere and thoroughly contemptible a person as it is possible to find. The amount of money wasted, misappropriated and stolen outright from the treasuries of these patriotic organizations is almost beyond belief.

Le Caron's testimony damaged both Parnell and Sullivan. Although Le Caron and Cronin had very different agendas, it was possible that Le Caron might topple Sullivan from his pedestal, achieving Cronin's chief aim.

Le Caron was never "outed" by the Clan; he chose to unveil his affiliation at the Parnell Commission, and by so doing put his life at risk. Possibly fearful of being discovered as the Clan began to implode, he may have decided that his chances of survival were higher if he was under the protection of the British police, something that his appearance at the Commission guaranteed. Whatever his motives, it was a risky strategy.

The ripples sent across the Atlantic by Le Caron's testimony caused immense damage to Irish America. Cronin, Devoy, and Dillon were quick to make much of the link between him and Sullivan. Cronin addressed Le Caron's appearance at the Parnell Commission in an editorial he wrote for the *Celto-American*, the newspaper he and his supporters had established in 1889 to promote their side of the Clan argument:

> The fact is Irish affairs are in a deplorable condition in America. The le Caron episode shows how easy it is to be a "Dr. Jekyll and Mr. Hyde" in Irish national affairs. . . . Oh, for a pure, clean, patriotic man like Parnell, free from the "back stairs" love of intrigue and wanton vilification of those who do not agree with him. . . . How in heaven's name can union be looked for when the machine methods of ward primaries are brought into play on every important occasion of our assembling or combining? . . . Let us have the truth, the whole truth, and nothing but the truth, and forever silence the slanderer, no matter who he may be.

The editorial alluded to the rumors circulating in Chicago and, for those in the know, was a clear attack on Sullivan, though he remained unnamed. Unification of Clan na Gael was a more distant prospect than ever before.

For their part, Sullivan, Egan, and Finerty repeated stories allegedly emanating from London which claimed that Le Caron had named four other Clan men who were British spies. This list was allegedly seen by Sir John Russell, counsel for Parnell, and Michael Davitt, who had taken Sullivan's side in the Clan dispute, but there is no evidence that such a list ever existed. However, rumors rapidly circulated, claiming that Cronin was among those named. Fact or fiction, this was a disaster for Cronin—few informers, spies, or suspected spies survived long in Irish republican circles. James Carey famously turned informer on his Invincible colleagues following the Phoenix Park murders of Cavendish and Burke in order to save himself from the hangman's noose, but he could not save himself from assassination as he fled to South Africa.

The whispers, mutterings, and murmurings that had long floated around any mention of Cronin in certain circles became firm statements of fact. Cronin was a spy, Le Caron had said so, and Davitt had seen the list. What further proof was needed? Back in 1883 Sullivan had issued a chilling warning that "the informer is fore-doomed . . . no man can betray and live. No hole too dark, no corner of the earth too obscure or too far to hide the spy and the informer from the avenging arm of Jsjti [Irish] nationality." Many Clan members in America were quick to believe that Le Caron was not acting alone; after all, as one argued, "The English Government would not have taken Le Caron from America if there were not people to take his place here." Whether Cronin was a spy was irrelevant; the belief that he was a spy was. Isolated in Chicago, far from his ablest defenders, Dillon and Devoy, his days were numbered.

CHAPTER FIVE

"BOYS, I GIVE UP"

O**n the evening of Friday, April 19, 1889, Cronin was visited at his office in** the Chicago Opera House Block by two Clan members from Lake View: his friend John A. Mahoney, a recently elected justice of the peace, and Patrick O'Sullivan, an ice dealer. O'Sullivan, "a small and very ordinary-looking Irishman, with beetling black eyebrows which run together across his low forehead," had come with a proposition: Cronin would act as on-call physician to his firm, and would treat any of his employees who became ill or were injured at work. In return O'Sullivan would pay Cronin a retainer of fifty dollars for the summer months, when his ice business flourished. This was a peculiar contract. Why would O'Sullivan leave Lake View, which in April 1889 was still a city in its own right, to seek a medical practitioner in Chicago?

Lake View began in the 1840s as a small, largely German farming settlement, and by 1865 it had grown to be a town. In the aftermath of the Great Fire it expanded rapidly, because after 1871 every new building in Chicago had to have a fireproof exterior. This was unaffordable for the working-class citizens, so many moved from the city to neighboring Lake View. By the time Lake View was granted a city charter in 1887, its population had grown from about 2,000 in 1870 to 45,000. There were seventy-five physicians and surgeons based there, while Cronin's downtown Chicago office was more than five miles from O'Sullivan's icehouse; his home, nearly four miles distant.

The business of an ice dealer was not a hazardous one, and it was much more expensive to retain the services of a physician than to simply summon one if an accident occurred. O'Sullivan employed only four men in his business, and according to his own account, none had ever been injured on the job. Indeed, his doctor's bills for the previous three years amounted to less than ten dollars.

Perhaps O'Sullivan chose to retain Cronin's services because business was booming and he could now afford to do so. He had established his ice dealership in 1885, and it was expanding along with the city. Just before he approached Cronin, he had several thousand new business cards printed. His optimism was well founded, as the summer of 1889 proved a bumper one for ice dealers: demand for ice was such that there was not enough for "the preparation of mint juleps . . . and sweltering manhood may as well resign himself . . . to lukewarm beverages with the down-town lunch." Such scarcity meant that by June 1, 1889, the cost of ice had increased by 20 percent. O'Sullivan sourced his ice from Silver Lake, Wisconsin, about sixty-five miles northwest of Chicago, and sold it from the back of a covered wagon. His employees traveled door to door, cutting small blocks of ice from a much bigger block mounted on the wagon. Customers used some of their purchase to make cold desserts such as ice cream or to chill drinks, but they placed most of it in designated iceboxes, which stored fresh food, particularly fish, meat, and dairy products.

Under Cronin and O'Sullivan's agreement, Cronin would tend any injured O'Sullivan employee, but would not answer a medical summons unless the caller presented him with one of O'Sullivan's business cards, printed with his contact details and illustrated with two horses pulling a covered wagon with ICE in big, bold letters on the stretched canvas. A man stood at the rear of the wagon carrying a large block of ice.

Increasingly anxious about his safety, Cronin feared bogus medical calls. He firmly believed that his life was in danger, and since his expulsion from the Clan in 1885, had almost always traveled armed with his Smith and Wesson revolver. He had told friends of several occasions since his expulsion when he had been called out on "medical emergencies," only to discover that there was no patient but a gang of "five or six suspicious looking men" awaiting him. On each occasion he was able to flee. In April 1888 Cronin was visited in his rooms by a "tough," who confessed that he had been approached by a North Side policeman who offered fifty dollars if he would give Cronin "a good beating and put him out of the way." He refused, because Cronin had been good to his elderly mother. More recently, a month

Patrick O'Sullivan's business card. In Hunt,
Crime of the Century, 20. Collection of the author.

before O'Sullivan's proposition, there had been another disturbing incident in which Cronin was summoned to an address that turned out to be a vacant lot. He was wary and arrived by buggy, accompanied by a friend. Upon finding the site derelict, the pair immediately sped away. Cronin was certain that he had been lured to the spot by a gang who anticipated that he would arrive by streetcar and wander the deserted street alone, looking for the fictitious house. He was convinced that all these incidents were attempts to injure or kill him, and that Alexander Sullivan was behind each one.

Why, then, did Cronin accept O'Sullivan's proposal? He was not a wealthy man, so the promise of fifty dollars a month was undoubtedly a factor. Perhaps he was also reassured by the presence of his friend Mahoney. Whatever his motives, O'Sullivan left Cronin's office after having paid the physician his first installment. Cronin propped the iceman's business card on the mantelpiece, where it remained undisturbed for several weeks.

Close to seven thirty in the evening on Saturday, May 4, there was a frantic knock at the door of Cronin's office in the Windsor Theatre

Building on the northeast corner of Clark and Division. Mrs. Cordelia Conklin, Cronin's landlady, friend, and sometime receptionist,
opened it to a flushed, mustachioed man in his thirties who wore
a soft, low-crowned hat pulled tight on his forehead. The man appeared agitated and demanded to see the doctor immediately, but
was informed that Cronin was with a patient, young Agnes McNearney. For several minutes the man restlessly paced the waiting room,
looking so severe and distressed that Sarah McNearney, who was
waiting for her sister, was afraid to do more than glance at him.
When Cronin finally emerged, the man thrust a business card at
him and urged him to hurry to Patrick O'Sullivan's icehouse, where a
worker had been seriously injured. Swiftly, Cronin packed his medical satchel with plenty of cotton batting and threw on his jacket and
slouch hat. A buggy pulled by an eye-catching white horse awaited
the men outside. As Cronin scrambled into the buggy he spotted his
friend Frank T. Scanlan, who was on his way to meet the shareholders
of the Irish nationalist paper the *Celto-American*. Cronin was also due
to attend this meeting, as in addition to being a shareholder, he was
the paper's political editor. The meeting was to be held in Cronin's
downtown office in the Chicago Opera House Block. Leaning from
the buggy, Cronin threw his office keys to Scanlan, shouted his apolo-
gies, and expressed the hope that he would return in time for at least
the meeting's conclusion.

He was never seen alive again.

>─┤─◆⟩─◆─○─◆─⟨◆─┤─◄

Because Cronin was a man of habit, when he had not returned home
by Sunday morning the Conklins immediately jumped to the conclusion that he had been murdered. This was, perhaps, an overrreaction,
but Cronin had been good friends with the couple for almost twenty
years; for half that time they had shared a home, first in St. Louis and
then, from 1882 onward, in Chicago. The Conklins knew that Cronin
lived in fear of assault or death, though they claimed not to know the
source of the threat, beyond the fact that it was an "Irish American
organization." Theo Conklin feared the worst, particularly since he
knew that Cronin had left his office without taking his revolver.
Conklin headed north to O'Sullivan's home, but the iceman, roused

Dr. Cronin leaves his home in the Windsor Theatre Building on the evening of May 4, 1889. In Anon., *The Great Cronin Mystery; or, The Irish Patriot's Fate: By One of America's Most Famous Detectives* (Chicago: Laird and Lee, 1889), 22. Collection of the author.

from his bed, insisted that none of his employees had been injured the previous day, and that Cronin had not been sent for. Immediately upon returning home, Conklin summoned several of Cronin's close friends, including John Scanlan, Scanlan's nephew Frank, and P. W. Dunne, the man who had first accused Sullivan of misappropriating funds (and lived to tell the tale).

All were convinced that Cronin had been kidnapped and probably murdered. The Scanlans and Dunne decided that the police, the Pinkerton Detective Agency, and the press should be informed. In addition, Dunne and Peter McCahey, Cronin's ally at the trial of the

Triangle, volunteered to set up a fund to aid the search. This fund paid for the Pinkerton detectives and offered a reward of $2,000 (approximately $52,000 in today's dollars) for information proving Cronin was alive, and $5,000 (approximately $131,000) for information leading to the arrest and conviction of his murderers if he was dead.

The Pinkerton Agency had been established in Chicago by Allan Pinkerton in 1850, and by 1889 was the largest provider of investigative services in the United States. In some respects the employment of the Pinkertons in the search for Cronin was a surprise, because many Irish Americans had little respect for them. In 1873 the agency had hired James McParlan to infiltrate the Molly Maguires, an oath-bound and legendarily violent Irish secret society that flourished in the coal fields of Pennsylvania in the 1860s and 1870s. McParlan's testimony contributed to the conviction and execution of twenty men who had been found guilty of murder. Moreover, the agency had provided strikebreakers in Chicago in 1885 and 1886. And Allan Pinkerton was certainly no friend to Irish republicans: in 1882 he had written to the British prime minister, William Gladstone, offering unsolicited advice about the use of spies and informers. This attempt to extend Pinkerton business across the Atlantic was rejected, but from the mid-1880s onward the London Metropolitan Police Special Branch regularly employed Pinkerton's men in the United States. Nonetheless, despite the hostility felt by many Irish toward the Pinkertons, there was also an acceptance that they were a successful agency, and the one most likely to locate the Cronin murder suspects. Cronin's friends had nothing more concrete than suspicion and rumor to guide them, yet within twenty-four hours of his disappearance a substantial search party consisting of friends, journalists, Pinkerton detectives, and several police officers had begun to look for the missing doctor.

News of Cronin's disappearance spread rapidly. On May 8 his old school friend, Thomas Tuite, wrote to Devoy from Detroit, asking, "What horrible thing is this about Cronin? . . . Can't be possible that he has been injured 'in the house of his friends.' It is too horrible to think of." Already writing of Cronin in the past tense, he recalled his friend as "a noble soul, manly and generous, a credit to our people and so devoted to them, but then those very qualities would beget

him enemies . . . and if a blow has been struck whether from the outside or the inside, we must see that justice is done, yes, even to avenging the crime." John Scanlan refused to speculate publicly on what
had happened to Cronin, maintaining that "if Cronin is murdered . . .
then I will speak and speak through the law." However, in private he
confided to Devoy that he and Cronin's friends had to live

> with the terrible fact staring us in the face that Dr. Cronin was decoyed
> away, and [we are] convinced he is dead. We are met on the street cor-
> ners by the gang with their faces wreathed in leers, not smiles, offering
> to bet "he will turn up all right; he is off on a spree, it's a love affair; he
> was a companion of Le Caron; he's gone to England to testify against
> Parnell," . . . lies, lies, lies.

>—⋅◆⟩—◯—⟨◆⋅—◃

The police were slow to react to the Conklins' suspicions. On the
one hand, this is unsurprising; it was not particularly unusual for
an unmarried man in his midforties to fail to return home after a
night out, and no evidence of foul play had been provided. On the
other, many Irishmen on the police force would have been aware of
the strained relationship between Cronin and other elements within
Clan na Gael, and that should have been sufficient for the police to
take the worries of the Conklins seriously. A further factor that made
the police reluctant to investigate the disappearance was the fact
that no reports of suspicious activity had been filed on the night of
Cronin's disappearance.

And yet there *had* been suspicious activity in Lake View that
night—but the two police officers who witnessed it didn't report it
until the following evening. At around two o'clock in the morning,
at the corner of Clark and Diversey, Patrolmen John Smith and Fred
Hayden had seen a bay horse drawing a carpenter's wagon containing a large trunk and traveling north at great speed. The men on the
wagon ignored the officers' order to stop, and about ninety minutes
later at the same junction, the officers saw the wagon again, this time
heading south and without the trunk. Despite the late hour and the
suspicious demeanor of the men, both officers put the activity down

to the fact that it was early May, brushed off their suspicions, and decided not to report it.

The tradition of moving on May 1 was said to have been brought to Chicago by English and Dutch immigrants, as it was the date associated with hiring fairs where servants would change employers. By the late 1800s, up to a third of Chicago residents moved every May 1. Bizarre sights were commonplace in the days surrounding "moving day," such as the lady seen on the Randolph streetcar line "encumbered with the marble top of a wash-stand, three chromos, a caged canary bird and an oil lamp, while another . . . struggled manfully in the attempt to retain possession of a sprinkling can, three potted geraniums, a poodle dog, four umbrellas and a dozen oranges." A trunk transported late at night did not incur great suspicion.

But by 7:30 on Sunday morning, twelve hours after Cronin had last been seen, the wagon and trunk had taken on new significance. Out for an early morning carriage ride, Alderman William P. Chapman spotted several men standing on both sides of a ditch near Montrose Avenue (then Sulzer Street) and Broadway (then Evanston Avenue) in Lake View. He paused to see what had caught their interest, and saw that a large trunk had been discarded there. Its lid had been forced open, and the interior was covered in blood and partially filled with gore-soaked cotton. Chapman reported all this to Captain Francisco Villiers at Lake View Police Station, who sent officers to retrieve the trunk. Villiers examined the trunk at the station and discovered it contained a lock of short brown hair. He concluded that the trunk had once held the body of a murdered adult. Later that evening, the two officers who had seen the speeding wagon identified the trunk as the one that was on the wagon.

The Lake View police were alerted to Cronin's disappearance only late Sunday evening, some ten hours after the trunk had been discovered, and Captain Villiers hastened to O'Sullivan's home at the corner of Bosworth Avenue and Roscoe Street. As he had done when confronted by Theo Conklin, O'Sullivan denied having summoned Cronin. Villiers then visited Cronin's home, where he showed the doctor's friends the lock of hair from the trunk. Mrs. Conklin was certain that the lock matched Cronin's long, soft, and remarkably silky hair, but the following day H. F. Wisch, Cronin's barber, disagreed. Cronin was a regular client, attending up to four times a week to be shaved and occasionally have his hair cut. Wisch and his employees were certain the hair was not Cronin's—his, by their reckoning, was exceptionally coarse, while the lock in Villier's possession was fine. Further, Cronin had had his hair cut less than a week earlier, and the barber was certain that his hair was much shorter than the sample shown. Confused, Villiers returned to Lake View and set about finding a body to fit the trunk.

The bloodied contents and interior of the trunk indicated that foul play had occurred, but there was little to link the evidence to Cronin. However, the discovery caught the interest of the Chicago police force, as it, not the Lake View force, had been approached by Cronin's friends. Captain Michael Schaack of the East Chicago Avenue Police Station and a handful of colleagues were dispatched to work alongside the Lake View force. Together, and with much mutual suspicion, they set about searching for a body, Cronin's or otherwise. Little of note was discovered apart from wagon tracks on a sandy road that led to Lake Michigan. The tracks reached the lakeshore, then turned south and headed back toward Chicago. A local night watchman, John Way, told officers that at one o'clock on Sunday morning he had spoken at the lakeshore with a group of men who were huddled around a wagon containing a box. They claimed to be lost and in search of Lake Shore Drive, which was two miles south. Way directed the men toward the Drive and watched them and their cargo leave.

A missing man, a bloody trunk, and a group of suspicious-looking men behaving strangely at the lakeshore all combined to give the police an easy narrative—Cronin had been killed and then bundled into the trunk, and the attempt to dump his corpse in Lake Michigan had been foiled. But with no body, no wagon, and no suspects, the police were forced to go in search of evidence to sustain their theory. They were joined by many of Cronin's friends as well as crowds of amateur and professional detectives, many of whom knew of Cronin and his dispute with Alexander Sullivan and were intrigued by his disappearance. Others joined the hunt, lured by the substantial reward on offer. By Monday a small army of friends, police, and interested parties of all kinds were looking high and low for the doctor.

The search met with little success. Police visits to stables in Lake View seeking a white horse yielded nothing. The pond in Wunder's Cemetery (the German Lutheran cemetery near where the trunk was found) was searched, as were six hundred feet of the Chicago River close to Fullerton Avenue Bridge, where the wagon had crossed. But nothing of significance was found, and the initial mood of expectation among the police was replaced by despair. Captain Villiers's enthusiasm quickly turned to apathy. Perhaps he had hoped that a bloodied body would turn up as easily as the bloody trunk, and he could mark his final days as police chief in Lake View by solving a spectacular murder case. But with the case stalled, Villiers and other officers lost interest in the missing man, and soon many journalists, and some friends of Cronin, were criticizing the lackluster police effort. The *Chicago Daily News* complained,

> [most of the] hordes of detectives and special officers detailed on the case . . . are attempting to make it appear they are working very hard but they can be seen by the dozens along the north branch of the river, lolling idly under the shade-trees, and inhaling the beautiful aroma from the pellucid stream as it laps and splashes lazily at their feet.

>––+·+>·+O·+‹+·+·‹

The police may have had limited enthusiasm for the search for Cronin, but the press latched on to the story. Mrs. Conklin later recalled that "the reporters came to see me thick and fast . . . [following] the Doctor's disappearance." Many of these journalists were familiar with the dispute between Cronin and Sullivan; they, like Cronin's friends, were quick to jump to conclusions about his fate.

Alexander Sullivan was visited by a number of journalists, and he admitted to them that although he and Cronin had offices in the same building and sometimes met in the elevator, they were "not on speaking terms." He claimed that he held Cronin in contempt, and had told him so to his face. For the last three years, he had "nothing whatever to do with Dr. Cronin," took no interest in him, and knew nothing of his comings and goings. As far as he was concerned,

Cronin's disappearance was simply the unfortunate result of intoxication.

Not all papers thought he had been murdered, and many column inches were filled with wild speculation: Cronin was an alcoholic; he was suffering from amnesia; he was mad; he had performed an illegal abortion that had gone wrong and had fled the city; he had been having an affair and got caught; he had been murdered by Neapolitan brigands; he was a spy and had fled to London to testify at the Parnell Commission.

These stories and more filled column after column of the papers in Chicago and far beyond. The *Chicago Herald* reported that Cronin was "eccentric; so much so that at times his vagaries have caused people to think that he was not of sound mind." The *Chicago Tribune* quoted an unnamed Irish nationalist who claimed that Cronin had left for London so he could testify at the Parnell Commission. The source maintained that Cronin was going to testify that very little of the money raised in America for Irish republicanism ever reached its intended destination; these statements would benefit Parnell by showing that his "connection with certain extreme movements among the Irish factions in America has not been as close as was supposed. If, as a matter of fact, he has received no financial help from these factions, he cannot be responsible for their statements of his advocacy of their actions." The *St. Louis Post-Dispatch* hinted that Cronin may have been involved with Mrs. Conklin or, if he had done nothing to enrage Conklin, then he may have "incurred the mortal hatred of some offended father, brother or husband . . . that he was liable to err in this regard is a fact known to those who were intimately acquainted with him during his residence in this city."

For those who actually were "intimately acquainted" with Cronin, the *Post-Dispatch*'s speculation was implausible, but it was trumped by the bizarre tale put forward by Frank Collier, an Englishman who claimed to have killed Cronin because his friend Queen Victoria had wished it. According to Collier, the queen hated Cronin for his "offensive partisanship on the Irish question," and she would "never rest until the head of Dr. Cronin [was] brought to [her] on a charger." Keen to do his duty, Collier allegedly disguised himself as an Italian brigand and got four Neapolitans, "armed with bowie knives, six shooters, an old fashioned cutlass . . . and a pouch of dynamite cartridges," to carry out the murder. Collier's claim was wisely dismissed by the police as attention seeking: in December 1889 he was declared insane.

The journalists had to expend little effort in coming up with these stories. As Finley Peter Dunne, then city editor of the *Chicago Times*, commented,

> Day after day men, not all of them Irishmen either, whom I knew and respected, dropped in at my office to chat about nothing in particular but always ending with something more than a hint that they knew Cronin was a British spy . . . that he had been killed by his landlord, who had discovered him lying with his landlord's wife, that he had fled to escape the wrath of the brother of a patient he had seduced. But the most concrete evidence was that he had furtively escaped to Canada.

So many rumors abounded that Theo Conklin issued a statement to the press decrying the "wide-spread reports . . . saying that Cronin was off on a spree, it was a love affair, he had gone crazy or turned informer." He furiously defended his friend:

> Dr. Cronin was one of the most moral men I ever knew. He was not a society man and had no lady friends. He never associated with any women of ill-repute. . . . I know that there is no woman in the case and I know that any insinuations to the effect that the doctor is "on a spree" must come from those who do not know him as well as I do. You can rest assured the man was murdered.

Conklin's statement did little to dampen speculation, and Cronin remained the subject of gossip and rumor at every level of Chicago society.

>─┤◆─○─◇┤─<

Information pertaining to Cronin's movements on May 4 began to trickle in. The police were told that he had been seen on the evening of his disappearance in Martin McNulta's saloon on North Wells Street. Annie Murphy, a young woman familiar in Irish circles as a singer and elocutionist, came forward to say that she too had seen Cronin on the night of the fourth. She knew him well from their regular appearances together onstage at concerts, and she told police that she had seen him on streetcar 405, en route to Union Station. Her story was corroborated by the car's conductor, Mr. Dwyer.

Several miles from Lake View, Pat Dinan, a "weather-beaten man about forty-five years old," followed the news of Cronin's disappearance with more than a passing interest. The papers had reported that the buggy taking Cronin from his home had been pulled by a white horse. Dinan, the owner of a livery stable at 260 Clark Street (now 827 North Clark Street), owned such a horse, and it and a buggy had been hired by Dan Coughlin, one of the local detectives, on the evening of Cronin's disappearance. This was not unusual, as detectives regularly hired horses and buggies from Dinan's stable—the East Chicago Avenue station house was about half a block away.

Late on the evening of May 6, Dinan went to the station to report Coughlin's buggy hire to Captain Schaack. Schaack had a reputation for solving high-profile cases and for keeping himself in the public eye. Within weeks of his promotion to captain in 1885, he broke the case that made his name—the Kledzic murder investigation—and the following year he led the search for the men involved in the Haymarket bombing. But as Dinan entered the station he bumped into Dan Coughlin, who begged him not to speak to Schaack because it was well known that Coughlin and Cronin were enemies (he had been on the committee that had expelled Cronin from the Clan), and he feared that Dinan's statement might get him into trouble. Dinan duly left the station, but later that evening he visited Schaack at his home and informed him that on May 4 Coughlin had told Dinan that "if anybody should call for a horse he should give it to him, and that he would be responsible." At seven o'clock in the evening on May 4, an unshaven man with a thick black moustache had called to collect the horse and buggy. He initially refused to take the buggy, because the windows had no curtains and the horse was white. But Dinan had no other horse or buggy available, so eventually the man accepted the rig and drove north.

Armed with this suspicious development, Schaack confronted

Coughlin, who admitted that he had sent a man to get a horse and rig from Dinan, but denied knowing the man, claiming that he was "Thomas Smith," a friend of a friend from Michigan who was in the city for a few days but had left for New Mexico and was uncontactable. Schaack, a friend and mentor of Coughlin, chose not to inform his senior officers of this development. Instead, he went to Dinan's stables and took the rig and white horse to the Conklins' home to see if Mrs. Conklin could identify it. When Dinan's horse and buggy pulled up outside, Mrs. Conklin said it was not the one that had taken Cronin away. However, within days she claimed that she was misled by Schaack, and that on the evening he brought Dinan's horse by her home the horse had been out working all day and thus did not resemble the lively animal she had seen several days earlier. When the same horse was brought again to her on May 25, she immediately identified it as the one whose buggy she had seen Cronin enter. Cordelia Conklin's poor recollection of events would later become a significant issue.

Schaack's relationship with the Conklins was strained. He had little interest in the Cronin case and was "rip-roaring mad at the Conklins," because he believed they were making allegations without a shred of evidence. He told Conklin that if Cronin's friends did not trust him, "they ought to . . . ask the Superintendent of Police to put some other Captain . . . on the case." Although Schaack admitted that he was completely "at sea" with regard to the case, he steadfastly refused to believe that Patrick O'Sullivan might be a suspect, as he knew him and found him "a pretty decent kind of a man."

Newspaper reporters were unaware of Dinan's visit to the police, but after days of largely idle speculation, a dramatic development caught their attention. On May 9 the police arrested Frank Woodruff as he tried to sell a stolen horse and buggy. Woodruff, dressed in cheap clothes and with a bad complexion and a squint in one eye, seemed particularly uneasy when taken into custody. En route to the police station, he announced that he had information about what had happened to Cronin, and he provided a detailed statement in which he said that he had met a stranger at a gambling house and had been persuaded to help him to "do a job." This "job" involved driving a wagon out of the city toward Lincoln Park. There he met three men with a trunk, one of whom was referred to as "Doc." The trunk was loaded onto the wagon and two men climbed aboard, though "Doc" remained behind. When Woodruff reached the north pond in Lincoln Park, he was told to halt. The dismembered body of a woman, referred to by the men as "Allie," was taken from the trunk and dumped in the pond; the trunk was abandoned in the ditch where it was later discovered.

Many aspects of Woodruff's story seemed unlikely, but the press avidly reported his account as fact and Schaack, at least initially, believed it. Combined, Woodruff's and Annie Murphy's stories seemed credible—Cronin had gone on the run to avoid prosecution relating to the death of "Allie." The police thought the body may have been that of Alice Villavose, a young girl who had disappeared from Chicago six weeks earlier. Not all were convinced by Woodruff's story, though, with Cronin's friends and some police officers openly skeptical. Nevertheless, the police began dragging the ponds in Lincoln Park for the remains of Villavose. No body was found.

By May 14 the police had suspended their investigation. As the Chicago Police Chief, George W. Hubbard, explained it, "What do we want of Dr. Cronin? He hasn't done anything for which the police want him." Detective Dan Coughlin, who despite having arranged the buggy that had taken Cronin away was now actively working on the search for the missing man, called the reporters in and announced,

> Boys, I give up. Unless Cronin is a British spy who is now hiding in London, I can't even guess what has happened to him. I've searched high and low until I'm exhausted and I can get nowhere. But this you may be sure of, there isn't a shred of evidence that Cronin was murdered.

Woodruff was increasingly regarded as a fantasist by police and press, but he remained in custody; the police were certain that if not involved in Cronin's disappearance, he was at least involved in selling stolen goods. He already had a criminal record for such activity, and had previously served time in several penitentiaries for petty offences. He told a reporter from the *Tribune* that he regretted making a confession, as he later discovered his arrest had been caused by the suspicion that he was a horse thief, not because he was suspected of involvement with the discovery of a bloodstained trunk.

Following swiftly on from Woodruff, the Chicago press was soon gifted with another story. Early on the morning of May 10, several newspaper editors in the city received a telegram from C. T. Long, formerly a Chicago journalist but now working in Toronto. Long reported that he had bumped into Cronin (whom he had known in Chicago) on the street and persuaded him to give an interview. Long's telegram described Cronin as being "out of his mind." The following day, Long dispatched a second lengthy telegram containing an account of his interview with Cronin, which was published in the Chicago *Herald* and several other newspapers. In the interview Cronin claimed to have left Chicago because of the feud with Sullivan, that he had told the Conklins he was leaving, and that by creating such a fuss afterward they had "made fools of themselves. . . . According to the instructions I left with them, they should not have opened their mouths until I was safely out of the country. But it is the same old story. Tell a woman anything and you are sure to get the worst of it." Upon learning of Cronin's appearance in Canada, the *New York Times* described him as "a scamp who has run away to escape the consequences of a fatal criminal operation." If Long's tale was to be believed, then all the commotion surrounding Cronin's disappearance was mere sensationalism.

The Conklins were incredulous. They, along with Cronin's other friends, insisted that Long's interview was fabricated. Theo Conklin issued a statement in which he claimed that Long was in cahoots with William Starkey, who was one of the lawyers that had summoned Cronin as an expert witness in 1887, only to quiz him about his claim to American citizenship. Long was also a friend of Alexander Sullivan. Yet despite fervent rejections of Long's story, both Cronin's friends and the Chicago police dispatched men to Toronto to investigate his claims. Arriving in the city, Cronin's friend Patrick McGarry went straight to the Rossin House Hotel, where Long claimed Cronin had been staying. No record of his stay, or of anyone answering the same description, was found. He concluded that there was "not an atom of foundation" to the claim that Cronin had fled to Canada.

>─┤─◆>──○──<◆─┤─<

All speculation as to the whereabouts of Dr. Cronin was finally quashed on the afternoon of May 22, when three employees of the Board of Public Works were sent to investigate a putrid smell emitting from the storm sewer at the corner of Foster (then Fifty-Ninth Street) and Broadway (then Evanston Avenue) in Lake View. Peering through the iron bars of the grate, they noticed something large blocking the sewer entrance. At first they thought it was a dog, but it soon became clear that it was not. One of the men, Henry Roesch, went immediately to Lake View Police Station and returned in the patrol wagon with Captain E. H. Wing and several officers. With great difficulty the officers and the public works employees hauled the beaten and naked body of a man out of the sewer. As the corpse lay in front of the group of horrified and repulsed men they realized they had just solved the mystery of what had happened to Dr. Cronin.

CHAPTER SIX

"THE DARKEST AND BLOODIEST MYSTERIES OF SECRET CRIME"

C*ronin was afforded little dignity in death. The sight of the dead man* was grotesque. He had been badly beaten about the head and had spent a considerable amount of time underwater, so his body was swollen and greatly disfigured. A piece of cloth was tied tightly around his throat, and an *Agnus Dei*, a Catholic safeguard against harm, hung from his neck. Clearly, this medallion had been of no benefit to its wearer. So disfigured was Cronin that, apart from Francisco Villiers, none of those who first saw the body recognized it. Yet all assumed it was the missing doctor, because the catch basin was in an isolated area about three hundred yards from the Argyle Park Station on the Chicago and Evanston branch of the Chicago, Milwaukee and St. Paul railroad—less than a mile from where the bloodstained trunk had been discovered at the corner of Montrose (then Sulzer Street) and Broadway (then Evanston Avenue).

When Captain Villiers saw the corpse, he immediately declared that it was Cronin. He summoned Cronin's friends to identify the body, which had been laid out on a zinc table in the temporary morgue in the cellar of the Lake View Police Station. Even before formal identification of Cronin's body took place, the newspapers had published special editions announcing the discovery of the dead doctor.

As reports that a body had been found spread through Lake View, roads around the police station were blocked by throngs hoping to get a glimpse of the corpse. Police armed with batons tried in vain to keep the crowds away. In the midst of their grief, Cronin's loved ones had to contend with a steady stream of the curious and the prurient traipsing in and out of the morgue before, on the morning of

May 23, a long-overdue decision was made to restrict visitors to those involved in the investigation and Cronin's friends and family.

Despite its very advanced decomposition, the corpse was immediately identified as Cronin by his friends. His "baseball finger" and the unusual hairiness of his arms were both identifying features. More precise information came from Cronin's dentist, who recognized his own work in the gold fillings and a lower jaw plate he had made for the deceased. Formal identification came a little after eight o'clock that evening, when a tearful Theo Conklin made a positive identification of the body.

As hordes gathered outside the police station and took turns crouching to peer through the small narrow window and down into the morgue, hundreds of others trampled the bushes around the storm sewer where Cronin had been discovered. The curious who failed to see the body themselves read graphic descriptions in the newspapers. A reporter from the *Chicago Tribune* who saw the corpse reported that its deterioration was extensive:

> [The] action of the dripping water in the sewer . . . had loosened the hair of the scalp, face, chest and shins. The moustache had fallen off and lay in a tangled mess on the right cheek. The lips, swollen and bloated, were stretched wide and at the corners of the mouth showed traces of agony. The two front teeth, a prominent feature of the doctor . . . showed ghastly beneath the half parted lips. The slight goatee remained. . . . The slight baldness at the front of the head was doubly visible beneath the tangled mass of wet hair. . . . At the corner of the left eye was a gash two inches long; over the top of the skull two lengthy wounds . . . on the right temple another deep cut.

Following the its formal identification, Dr. John Brandt of Cook County Hospital conducted a preliminary examination of Cronin's body. Brandt concluded that the head injuries had been inflicted during a sustained attack with both sharp and blunt objects, one of which was probably an ice pick. At least three of the wounds would have proved fatal. He believed that Cronin was "surprised and stunned at the first blow" and rendered unconscious, which accounted for the lack of defense wounds on his hands. A sample of Cronin's hair was compared with the lock taken from the bloody trunk, and Brandt proclaimed himself certain that they were identical. His conclusions added weight to the public's assumption that the bloody trunk and O'Sullivan's icehouse were connected to the murder.

After the initial medical examination, Cronin's body lay overnight in the police station. Water was sprinkled on the corpse throughout the night to stave off further decomposition. The autopsy took place on May 23, immediately after Cronin's brother John, who had just arrived from Arkansas, viewed the body. Seven doctors, led by Dr. James F. Todd, the county-appointed physician, conducted the examination, which took almost five hours to complete. Considerable bruising was found on Cronin's lower limbs and cuts and bruises to his head, but there was no sign of suffocation. His lungs were full of blood, which was attributed to the body being dumped facedown into the catch basin. Despite the blows that had clearly rained down upon Cronin's head, none of the skull bones had been fractured. Like Dr. Brandt, Dr. Todd and his assistants concluded that more than one instrument had been used in the attack, and that the angle of the wounds indicated that Cronin had been hit from behind.

With the autopsy completed, Cronin's body was removed to Birren and Carroll's undertakers on East Chicago Avenue, where it was embalmed. Nicholas Birren was shocked by the condition of the body, but assured journalists that he and the staff were "applying all the skill known to embalmers . . . in our effort to reduce the body to its normal size." Once embalmed, Cronin's body was dressed in a suit of broadcloth and placed in a sealed coffin, as it was too decomposed for a public viewing. A silver plate inscribed with "Philip Patrick Henry Cronin, Born: August 7th, 1846. Died: May 4th, 1889" was placed in the center of the casket. From the undertakers the body was taken to the Armory of the First Cavalry on Michigan Avenue, where it would remain until the funeral.

As the casket was being placed on a catafalque in the middle of the Armory a middle-aged, gray-bearded man came forward and asked for it to be opened. He identified himself as Mr. Carroll, Cronin's brother-in-law. With his wife Ellen, Cronin's sister, he had traveled from St. Catharines, Ontario, to grieve. After a discussion with Cronin's friends, the coffin lid was raised and the doctor's face exposed (albeit covered by glass). Weeping, Ellen Carroll bent over the glass and repeatedly kissed it, muttering, "Goodbye, goodbye asthore." The coffin was resealed, and Mrs. Carroll led away. Later that afternoon, the doors of the armory were opened to allow thousands to pay their respects to the dead man.

>—:—◆>——O——<◆—:—<

Much of the speculation that had circulated while Cronin was missing dissolved like early morning mist as soon as his body was found. As the *Daily News* observed, "In one night the Cronin mystery . . . has assumed an awful importance and solemnity. It is no longer time to bandy quips." Whispers of a conspiracy, an Irish republican conspiracy, rapidly became shouts on the street, in newspaper columns, in saloons, and along the corridors of police stations and legal practices across Chicago. In the public's mind, pieces of the murder puzzle were falling into place. Journalists reported that the residents of Lake View talked of nothing but the murder. The *Inter Ocean* observed,

> [The] male population either gathered in front of the station or in little knots at the street corners and discussed the ghastly find. . . . In all the shops and stores the one topic discussed . . . was the finding of Dr. Cronin's body, and it was not till near midnight that the inhabitants of that erstwhile peaceful little town had securely bolted their doors and windows and retired to their firesides or couches, there to either talk or dream of the horrible find.

For some, the discovery of the body inspired them to become part of the investigation. As the *Evening News* reported, Cronin's murder generated

> an army of amateur detectives. One can see them prowling about. . . . They look wise, kneel down on sidewalks and gaze at little indentations in the planking, find old hats and shoes and declare they belonged to the murdered doctor. Some profess even to this late day to have tracked the wagon which sped away with its ghastly burden after the murder. Others rake under the sidewalks and in the ditches for the clothes of the victim.

The crowd milling around the Lake View Police Station discussed the "incalculable injury" the murder would inflict on the "Irish cause; that it would throw back the movement which it might have been intended to advance." Many said that they had sympathized with the Irish national movement, but if Clan na Gael had resorted to murdering dissenting members, they believed there would be a revulsion of sentiment against Irish republicanism among even its most ardent supporters. Speaking on behalf of Cronin's friends, Theo Conklin declared that Cronin, the "victim of the foulest of murders," had been killed by members of the Clan, and he pointed out that the killers must have been Catholics:

> [The] fact that the *Agnus Dei* was untouched is most significant. It shows that Catholics—and most Irishmen are Catholics—committed the deed. Anyone else would have removed the charm, but a Catholic, even in the commission of a murder, would not dare to do so.

That Cronin had been found naked was a cause of much comment in the newspapers. There was fevered speculation that his clothes and identifying documents had been taken in order to be sent to London, where they would be placed on a decomposing body which would then be dumped in the River Thames. When "Cronin's" body was fished out of the river in London, his enemies in Chicago would claim this as proof that he was a spy who was planning to testify at the Parnell Commission, but had been captured and assassinated before he could do so. In New York, John Devoy was quick to comment on the "savage murder," and he clearly implicated Sullivan when he declared that "Cronin's death is the result of a conspiracy by certain men who were accused of embezzling large sums of money from the Parnell fund." The state's attorney, Joel Longnecker, and Inspector Ebersold of the Chicago police were also quick to conclude that Cronin's murder was the result of a conspiracy carried out by "some Irish secret society faction."

><!--divider--><

In this and many other respects, Cronin's murder was unusual. Most homicides in Chicago in the late nineteenth century were the result of drunken brawls often prompted by gambling debts or rows about women. However, rather than depicting Cronin's murder as the tragic outcome of a liquor-fueled fight, evidence in the case rapidly began to point to an extensive conspiracy. As the investigation continued there were a number of surprising twists that implicated influential figures in Chicago. For the city's police force in particular, the investigation shone an unwanted spotlight into a divided and unruly organization.

By 1889 the Chicago Police Department had an unenviable reputation. Many thought it both incompetent and corrupt despite the reforms that had been brought about during Carter Harrison's time as mayor (1879–87), and they were keen to find flaws in its murder investigation. But, in contrast to popular perception, by 1889 the police force was in some respects quite a sophisticated one. It was salaried and full-time from 1856 onward, uniformed since 1858, and equipped with a detective unit since 1860. In 1880 Harrison introduced a patrol signal service in which telephones were installed in secure boxes around the city. Inside each box was an alarm dial with a pointer and eleven different categories, such as "riot," "forgery," and "thievery." "Respectable" citizens were provided with a key to the boxes; a police wagon was immediately dispatched to the box location where an alarm had been sounded. In addition, patrolmen were obliged to check in via signal box every hour, which reduced the amount of time they could spend in saloons. In 1881 the city began using patrol wagons for transporting arrestees to the local police station and occasionally serving as ambulances. In 1888 the city implemented the Bertillon system of prisoner classification, which combined "mug shots" of suspects with detailed measurements of their head, middle finger, left foot, and the arm from elbow to fingertip.

Throughout the 1880s the police force expanded rapidly. In 1880 it had 473 officers; by the end of 1889 it had 1,624. (In the same period, Chicago's population doubled, from 503,185 to 1,099,850.) In 1880 there had been one police officer for every 1,064 residents; by the end of the decade, that ratio was 1 to 677.

But while the police force was relatively modernized, the behavior of some of its members was not always progressive. Chicago was a restless city in the 1880s. The Great Railroad Strike of 1877, the Streetcar Strike of 1885, and the Haymarket bombing in 1886 had secured it a reputation for labor disputes and violence. Business leaders expected the police to be their protectors, while employees wanted the police to support them. Bars, brothels, and gambling dens were also the focus of much debate: temperance and gambling laws were largely flouted in the late nineteenth century. Saloon owners, who were frequently local leaders of their community and often politically connected, resented police intrusion. Many of the police were close friends with saloon keepers and (in many cases) some of their best customers, and so they were reluctant to enforce any restrictions. The temperance leaders, often wealthy and well connected, threatened to reduce funding for the police if drinking laws were not enforced.

Political influence was often brought to bear on the police officers themselves. Many had obtained their jobs through a network of contacts rather than any formal application procedure. Within the Irish community, Alexander Sullivan was well known as the man to go to for police or public works jobs. At the senior level too, talent was often not enough to secure a promotion. The police chief was usually chosen on the basis of his loyalty to whichever party had recently won the mayoral election, while captains and inspectors generally worked closely with locally powerful ward leaders. In 1897 the Illinois governor, John R. Tanner, complained that "Chicago presents the only instance of a police force used as an instrument for the sole benefit of the political party which happens to be in power after each election."

In the early 1880s Harrison succeeded in improving the image of the police, at least in the eyes of many of the working class, when he instructed the force not to assist in strikebreaking. Consequently, in 1885 the police refused to become involved in a strike at the McCormick Reaper Works. In this instance the striking workers were victorious, and Cyrus McCormick Jr. blamed this on Harrison's non-interventionist policy. There seemed to be no way to keep all sides happy. By the middle of 1885, the delicate balancing act performed by the police looked impossible to maintain. Harrison was reelected for a fourth term that year, but by only 375 votes; his weakened position made his control of the police force tenuous. When a strike at the Chicago West Division Railway Company escalated, Captain John Bonfield decided to order his men to attack the strikers. The intervention broke the strike and won Bonfield the gratitude of the city's employers. Police policy now was to intervene, often using force. In the spring of 1886, an old Irish reporter at the *Daily News* observed to Art Young, a rookie illustrator at the paper, "There's a limit to how far the police can go in the name of law and order. They'll go too far with the clubbing one of these days and the workers will strike back."

A defining moment for the police came on the evening of May 4, 1886, when festering resentment between the anarchists and the law enforcement authorities reached crisis point. Strikes demanding an eight-hour workday had begun on May 1. On May 3 four strikers were killed during violent clashes with police near the McCormick Reaper Works. The following evening, at a meeting called to protest the deaths, a crowd numbering close to two thousand assembled at the Haymarket Square, where they listened to speeches by August Spies and Albert Parsons among others. By ten o'clock, most of the throng had dispersed; only about six hundred remained to listen to Samuel Fielden, "the anarchists' most effective evangelist." At 10:20 p.m., Fielden was asked by Captain William Ward to end his speech. As he wrapped up, the police began to move in, and a bomb was thrown by someone in the crowd. It exploded, killing one policeman at the scene and injuring others.

What followed was heavily disputed, but both sides agreed that after the bomb exploded, the police began firing upon the gathering. At least five of the crowd were killed and an additional forty-five wounded. Seven police officers died: one at the scene, the others in the days that followed. A high-profile police investigation followed, and by the time a grand jury indicted ten men for conspiracy to incite murder, the police had arrested two hundred people and conducted raids on houses, saloons, and newspaper offices associated with the labor or anarchy movements. The trial of the anarchists led to the conviction of eight men, of whom four were executed and one committed suicide before all were pardoned by the governor of Illinois in 1893.

>·‹•›·•·O·•·‹•›·‹

Several members of the Chicago police force who became key figures in the Cronin investigation were prominent at the time of the Haymarket bombing. Frederick Ebersold was police chief, while Michael Schaack was the most important investigator. Schaack was regarded as a maverick. Journalists found him fascinating and a source of stories. One remarked, "Captain Schaack has a lot of gall to talk about 'trouble-makers.' You can bet your life if there was no trouble Schaack would make some. He's a glory hunter—a bastard of the first order." Whatever his methods, Schaack got results: within five years (1869–74) he was credited with 865 arrests, but rumor had it that he often strayed outside the confines of the law to secure convictions. Ebersold's relationship with Schaack was frequently strained, and tensions between the two men flared again during the Cronin case. On the third anniversary of the Haymarket bombing, the day that Cronin disappeared, Schaack's book *Anarchy and Anarchists* was published. In it he criticized his superior officers' handling of the Haymarket investigation, maintaining that

> it would be a false delicacy . . . to pass over the complete incompetency which prevailed at Police Headquarters. . . . It cannot be denied that, had the case been left in the hands of the men of the Central Office, the prosecution would have come to naught . . . the men at headquarters neither appreciated the gravity of the situation, nor were they able to cope with the conspirators. . . . There was neither order, discipline nor brains at headquarters.

Ebersold responded to Schaack's criticism in an interview published in the *Daily News* on May 10:

> It was my policy to quiet matters down. . . . Captain Schaack wanted to keep things stirring. He wanted bombs to be found . . . everywhere. I thought people would lie down and sleep better if they were not afraid that their homes would be blown to pieces any minute. But this man, Schaack, this little boy who must have his glory or his heart would be broken, wanted none of that policy.

Schaack's determination to do things his own way would ultimately bring a premature end to his career.

For a brief period in the aftermath of the Haymarket bombing, the public perception of the police was a positive one. Chicago's citizens had considerable sympathy for the "dead heroes" among the officers, and individuals and businesses gave substantial donations to the force—more than $70,000 was raised by the middle of August. Meanwhile, newspapers carried positive stories, many of them about Schaack, who reveled in his celebrity.

Yet the police force as a whole was often targeted by the press. The increasing independence of many of the city's newspapers made them ideal places for exposing corruption. Under the management of James J. West, the *Chicago Times* conducted a series of civic campaigns, many aimed at exposing incompetence and corruption within the police force, beginning in the late 1880s. In early 1889 the paper ran several articles alleging that Schaack and Bonfield were in the pockets of those running gambling and prostitution operations on the North and West Sides. Schaack and Bonfield reacted by ordering the arrest of James Dunlop, the city editor, and West on charges of criminal libel. The men were swiftly released, and the *Chicago Times* exposé forced Police Chief Hubbard and Mayor John A. Roche to suspend Schaack and Bonfield, though this decision was not implemented until after Schaack's deliberate mishandling of Pat Dinan's allegations had hampered the Cronin murder investigation. For the *Times*, the timing of the Cronin case could not have been better: the paper used the murder investigation to further emphasize the many failings of the Chicago police as it saw them, including "inefficiency in command, jealousy and the spirit of insubordination throughout the force, neglect and sloth everywhere."

The paper was not alone in attacking the police force; other newspapers commented on the inefficiency of the police and implied that certain officers may have colluded with the murderers. As the murder investigation inched forward the *Daily News* insinuated that

> the police are admirable so long as they are asked only to stand at street corners and pilot good looking ladies through a maze of vehicles. . . . But when it comes to a case like the Cronin murder, the supineness, the slowness and the stupidity of the police authorities is marvelous to behold. They sit like so many stone images at first until

the guilty creatures have time to get away. . . . They [the police] walk all around the manhole where the festering corpse was found, and, though it smells to high heaven they cannot find it. . . . Is it mere stupidity? Is it mere laziness?

In an editorial of May 27, the *Inter Ocean* noted that "the developments in the Cronin business show very plainly that the Chicago police force needs a very thorough over-hauling. There seems to be in it very little discipline, and entire absence of esprit de corps, and an alarming amount of dishonesty." The police force was even mocked outside Chicago. The *Omaha Republican* joked, "It is believed that a Chicago policeman cannot find his way to the police station . . . unless someone gives him a clew [*sic*]."

There was no doubt that the Chicago Police Department was riven by division and mutual suspicion, which hampered the murder investigation. A further difficulty for the case was that two police forces were involved—Lake View's and Chicago's. Cronin had been taken from his home in Chicago but found in Lake View, and at least in the early stages of the investigation, there seemed to be no clear chain of command; both forces wanted the glory of a solved crime, and neither wanted the shame of a failed investigation. The tensions between the two forces were partially exacerbated by the upcoming referendum on the annexation of Lake View. The *Chicago Times* used the murder to argue in favor of annexation by Chicago:

> The Cronin case illustrates . . . the need of a municipal union between Chicago and its suburbs. . . . In the inquiry that must follow . . . the police authorities, absolutely independent in law, will clash, and through their jealousies and failures to co-operate because of misunderstandings . . . the vital inquiry will be . . . embarrassed. . . . Here we are, one community in substance, many communities in law. . . . In union there is strength.

After much debate, on June 29, 1889, the population of Lake View (and those of Hyde Park, Lake, Cicero, and Jefferson) voted in favor of annexation by a slim margin. As a result, the 266 officers of the Lake View Police Department became part of Chicago's law enforcement organization when the annexation became effective on July 15. The Cronin investigation was now concentrated in one force.

>—⊢◆>—○—<◆⊢—<

In the late 1880s, the Irish and Irish Americans in Chicago represented less than 17 percent of the population, yet they comprised almost 50 percent of the police force, and many of the officers and detectives owed their positions to Alexander Sullivan. Chicago wasn't unique in this: in 1880 50 percent of the police force in Vicksburg, Mississippi, and Memphis, Tennessee, was Irish-born, while in 1900 in St. Louis, the Irish accounted for a third of the city's police force but only about 3 percent of the population.

In an editorial, the *Inter Ocean* claimed "no prejudice against Irishmen," but could not hide its

> astonishment over the fact that so large a proportion of the police force was born in the Green Isle. At times like these a great many people would be glad to see the police force a little more Americanized. At any rate they would like to know that the men who carry clubs have not taken any oaths to aid in the "removal" of their fellow men when so ordered by a midnight conclave of their clan.

Slason Thompson, editor of the anti-immigration periodical *America: A Journal for Americans*, thought that "it was a wise decision which removed Irish policemen from work on the Cronin case, not that all Irish policemen are murderers or their accomplices, but it is hard to discriminate and cull the true from the traitors." Cronin's friends believed that there was reluctance in the police force to locate his killers; one of them commented that the Chicago police were

> loud in their denunciations of the London police for not bringing to justice a madman . . . but when it comes nearer home they sing a different tune. "If Jack the Ripper was in Chicago, or if London had a few of Chicago's police, the Whitechapel butcher would soon come to grief" they would say. Let them look at their own record and examine it carefully before they complain that the friends of Dr. Cronin lack confidence in their ability.

John Devoy agreed with this assessment. He maintained that "a portion of the Chicago police are in sympathy with the murderers and endeavoring to screen them."

At the time, De Witt Cregier had just taken office as mayor, and in his inaugural address on April 15 he stated that the police department "should be substantially free from the mutations and influence of politics. Personal merit . . . should be the main passport . . . and promotion should be the reward of duties efficiently preformed." However, some journalists and Cronin's friends felt that Cregier was too weak to combat the power of secret societies. They called on him to carry out "the necessary purification of the police force," but believed that he was "bound so tightly by officialism and political influences that he dares not stir."

Police Chief Hubbard didn't believe that having Irish investigators on the case was an issue, and he singled out Detective John Collins, an Irish American, for praise. Yet he was swift to react to accusations of bias, and on May 23 issued an order of "No Irishmen Need Apply" to detectives working on the Cronin case. Although a few Irish detectives and officers remained with the investigation to circulate among the community, almost all Irish detectives and officers were redeployed. According to the police, this was not because any Irishman was under suspicion but because "the Irishman's prejudices are very strong and if any one of them sympathized with any of the warring factions he could not do efficient work on the case."

>−+−◆◆−−O−−◆◆−+−<

The enormous attention paid to the case by the newspapers encouraged both Mayor Cregier and Mayor Boldenweek of Lake View to throw considerable resources behind the investigation. Hubbard hoped to harness public interest; consequently, he issued a statement to all stations under his command:

> In view of the fact that the mutilated body of Dr. Cronin has been found in a catch-basin . . . and that much public comment will be aroused, you will instruct your officers to note the nature of any such comment they may overhear, and follow up all clues. . . . The order is sent out . . . because some person having some criminal knowledge of

how Dr. Cronin met his death may be indiscreet enough to make some
statement when excited that would lead to the solving of the mystery.

Inspector Ebersold also believed that the discovery of the body would
ensure that "tongues will wag" and arrests would be made.

If the police had their ears open, so too did the reporters. Despite
their mutual distrust, both parties had a close relationship. Reporters were desperate for further developments in the Cronin case, and
if the police failed to deliver, then the newspapers would furnish the
stories themselves. The day after Cronin's body was found, Captain
Wing addressed the reporters gathered outside the Lake View station. "I like you boys," he said, "but there's no use asking me any questions because I won't answer them." Wing may have remained tight-
lipped, but the police were porous, so there was little the journalists
didn't know about the progress of the investigation. According to Inspector Ebersold, officers eager to tell their story to the press consti-
tuted a serious problem: "The papers are printing entirely too much.
They hurt the case. There are too many blabbers now without my
telling anything. If officers would learn to keep their mouths shut we
could work better." The inspector's concern about press interference
in the case proved to be well founded, but his attitude inevitably
made him a figure of jest for some journalists. The *Chicago Evening
News* mocked him

> [for wearing] his full police regimentals—star, bright buttoned coat
> and a hat the curve in the brim of which would set a dime-novel read-
> ing boy crazy with delight. This attire was doubtless worn to awe the
> murderers into submission should the Inspector run across them.

However, the journalists were not content to simply rely on leaks;
they were determined to solve the murder themselves. As soon as
Cronin's body was found, several reporters rushed to get Patrick
O'Sullivan's reaction. The *Chicago Tribune* reported that the iceman
"gasped" and began to tremble "like a leaf" when told, though he continued to maintain that he knew nothing about Cronin's disappearance, and he refused to accompany the journalists to the morgue to
see the body. Reporters also visited Alexander Sullivan at his home

on Oak Street, where he deplored Cronin's murder. In addition, Sullivan categorically denied that he had been killed by fellow Irishmen, claiming that

> the Irish American party in this country has its factions and its quarrels as any other political organization has. . . . But there could have been no malicious hostility toward him which would go to the extreme of vengeance against his person in any shape, much less to the extent of murder.

Sullivan also dismissed Cronin as "not particularly prominent as an Irish Nationalist," and he was "inclined to think that he may have been murdered by private enemies for private reasons." But Sullivan occasionally failed to maintain such poise. A week later, when he was surprised on the doorstep of his office by a journalist from the *Evening News*, with his eyes flashing "fire red," he ordered the journalist to "get out of here, I say, or I will assist you very forcibly. . . .—— the reporters and their impertinent questions." With that the door slammed shut.

After the discovery of the body, Patrick O'Sullivan was summoned to meet with Lieutenant Schuettler of the Chicago police and Captain Wing of the Lake View force. O'Sullivan vehemently denied any involvement with Cronin's murder, but conceded that he had noticed suspicious activity in the vicinity of his home. The area around O'Sullivan's house, at the corner of Bosworth and Roscoe, was quite isolated, dotted with houses, sheds, and fields of celery and cabbages. Behind his home was a large barn and a shed used for the ice business. The remainder of the block was vacant, with the exception of two cottages and a few outhouses. The cottages were owned by a Swedish couple, the Carlsons, who lived in one and rented out the other. According to O'Sullivan, the rental cottage had recently been occupied, and he suggested that the policemen pay a visit to the Carlsons. The *Daily News* reported that after speaking with O'Sullivan, "the least suspicion that the police may have had that the ice dealer knew more about Cronin's murder than he cared to tell melted away like an April frost before a hot sun."

Acting on O'Sullivan's tip, Schuettler and Wing headed to the

Carlson cottages. Both properties were on the same plot at 1872 Ash-land Avenue (now the 3400 block of North Roscoe Street), with the Carlsons living in the one set back from the road and behind the rental property. As they approached the cottages the men noticed bloodstains on the sidewalk and two dried streams of blood on the wooden steps that led to the door of the rented cottage. Without pausing to seek permission, Schuettler, an imposing figure standing six feet six inches tall, "quick as a cat, with the physical strength of an elephant," shouldered that door and crossed the threshold. The scene that greeted the officers was shocking: splashes of blood covered the walls and the floor despite apparent efforts to paint over the stains. A broken rocking chair stood forlornly in the center of the room, and damaged and stained furniture was scattered around. Droplets of congealed blood had clung to the lock on a dresser, and the men removed samples of these as evidence. Captain Wing described the scene as "blood, blood, everywhere."

The hasty attempt to conceal the bloodstains had left footprints and fingerprints of paint inside the cottage, leading Schuettler and Wing to conclude that the paint had been applied by a man with small feet. Other than these prints, there were few clues as to the former inhabitants of the cottage. There were no personal belong-ings, though Schuettler and Wing found a bill for curtains, and the markings on the furniture indicated that they had been purchased at Alexander H. Revell & Co., a well-known Chicago furniture shop. The men also found a key, which they later matched to the lock of the trunk found in the ditch on May 5. There was no doubt that a violent assault had occurred in the cottage, but at this stage of their investi-gation the police had nothing to explicitly link it to Cronin.

Horrified and somewhat shaken, Schuettler and Wing stationed a detective at the door to prevent curious visitors from damaging any potential evidence. Their precaution was ineffective: in the heat of the day, the guard decided to go to the back steps and sun himself. Seeing their opportunity, three reporters who had been tailing the policemen burst open the front door. They made a hasty examina-tion of the interior and collected slivers of the bloodstained floor before being ordered out by a "big-whiskered detective with a .44 cal-iber revolver held wickedly in the fingers of his right hand."

The scene of a crime: The Carlsons' cottages (*left*) and O'Sullivan's icehouse and residence (*right*), Lake View, 1889 (detail). Photographer: Reynolds Photograph Company. Chicago History Museum, ICHi-QF38KC88.

Meanwhile, Schuettler and Wing went next door to question Johanna and Jonas Carlson. The couple confessed that they knew about the bloodstained interior, but claimed they had not informed the police because they feared that if it became known that a murder had occurred, it would be impossible to rent out the cottage again. Yet despite their reluctance to involve the police, they were also afraid to destroy the evidence or tamper with what was clearly a crime scene. In fact the Carlsons seemed almost relieved that the police had discovered the bloody cottage, and Johanna Carlson was eager to tell them her version of what happened: on March 20 "Frank Williams," a tall, thin, pale-faced young man, had called to inquire about the rental cottage, which he wanted for himself and his siblings, two brothers and a sister who would be keeping house for them. The family was in Baltimore but intended to join him shortly. After viewing the cottage, he agreed to a monthly rent of twelve dollars. That afternoon some furniture was delivered, but over the following days the Carlsons noticed that the cottage was infrequently occupied, though they had occasional sightings of Williams, who appeared to keep odd hours.

On April 20, when Williams arrived to pay his rent, he explained that his sister was ill, but he hoped his family would move in within a week or two. Three weeks later, on May 13, the Carlsons were visited by a man who claimed to have been sent by Williams. The man explained that Williams's sister was now in a hospital, and he had left Chicago to be with her and his family, who had decided to remain in Baltimore. Williams planned on returning to Chicago, however, and had asked his friend to continue to pay the rent for him. The Carlsons refused to accept this arrangement, because neighbors, including Mr. Dieckman, a milkman who lived nearby, reportedly found Williams and his friends "scary." Five days later, the couple received a letter from Frank Williams; it was postmarked Hammond, Indiana. He wrote,

> My sister is low at present and my business calls me out of town. If you will please put the furniture in your cellar for a few days I will pay you for your trouble. . . . My sister told me to paint the floor for her so that it would not be so hard to keep clean.

In a significant development, the Carlsons told Schuettler and Wing that Williams knew Patrick O'Sullivan, and when Williams's letter arrived they had sought his advice. O'Sullivan advised them to keep Williams's furniture, and if he failed to return for his property O'Sullivan would pay an additional month's rent on his behalf. (If the Carlsons were telling the truth, it seemed peculiar to the officers that O'Sullivan, who was anxious to deflect attention from himself, would lead the police to a crime scene and to people who could link him to it. Perhaps he had counted on the Carlsons' poor grasp of English, or perhaps he had nothing to hide.) The Carlsons then told Schuettler and Wing that having spoken with O'Sullivan and anxious to re-let the cottage, they asked their son Charles to go to the property and remove the furniture. He entered the cottage, saw the bloodstains and broken furniture, and immediately retreated. The family assured the police that the cottage had been untouched since then.

Convinced that they had found the site of Cronin's murder, Schuettler and Wing summoned Dr. Brandt to examine the blood-stains. He concluded not only that it was human blood, but also that it was the same blood that had been found in the trunk. Following the lead suggested by the furniture bill, several detectives visited A. H. Revell & Co. Store records showed that on February 17, "J. B. Simonds" had spent $32.71 on a number of items, including carpet, a bed, a lamp, a rocking chair, and a trunk. The furniture had not been delivered to Lake View; rather, it was sent to rooms 12 and 15, 117 South Clark Street (on the southeast corner of Clark and West Washington Streets, in the downtown business district). The rooms had been rented for forty-two dollars a month from Edward C. Throckmorton of Knight and Marshall Real Estate for Simonds's brother, who was moving to Chicago. The lease had been signed and the first month's rent paid. A month later, on March 20, the rent collector, Herman Goldman, called and found no one home, though peering through the keyhole he saw that the flat had been furnished. When he returned the following day, all the furnishings had been removed, and J. B. Simonds was never seen again. When police officers investigated the rooms, they noticed that room 12 overlooked the main entrance of the Opera House Block, where Cronin had one of his medical offices.

The conspiracy that Cronin's friends talked of was beginning to look plausible. Within days of Cronin's body being dragged from the sewer, the police had found what they believed was the murder scene. The discovery of the Clark Street flat gave credence to the argument that a plot had been hatched to kill Cronin just after Henri Le Caron gave his testimony at the Parnell Commission in early February. It seemed that the plan had been to murder Cronin at the Clark Street flat, but something occurred between February 17 and March 20 which forced the conspirators to switch location from Clark Street to Lake View. But if a narrative was becoming clear, the police still lacked proof. Names were bandied about in the press and between Cronin's friends, but without evidence it was impossible to make arrests. Indeed, the police had no idea who Williams or Simonds were. They had a long way to go.

CHAPTER SEVEN

"THE WHISPER OF SILENCE"

A violent assault had taken place at the Carlson cottage, that much was certain—but the police could not link the cottage to Cronin, nor had they any real suspects, despite the rumors swirling around. Slowly, however, pieces of the puzzle began to fit together. Several people reported seeing suspicious activity at the Carlson cottage on the night of May 4. William Mertes, a milk dealer in Lake View, told police that at about eight thirty he had seen a buggy containing two men pull up outside. One of the men leapt down and ran up the stairs to the door, which opened before he knocked. From where he stood outside, Mertes heard loud, angry voices as the buggy and driver sped away. Police also traced the expressman who had brought the furniture from Clark Street to Lake View. Hakon Mortensen, a young Swede, told them that near the end of March, he was paid $1.50 by a man who matched the description of "Frank Williams" to transport the furniture to the Carlson cottage.

Despite police assurances to journalists that no officers were suspected of involvement in Cronin's death, Detective Dan Coughlin's name was being whispered among Cronin's friends. Born in Michigan of Irish parents, Coughlin had moved to Chicago in 1881, and through his friendship with Timothy Crean and Florence Sullivan, Alexander's brother, had become a member of both Clan na Gael and the police force. Coughlin's antipathy toward Cronin was common knowledge in Clan circles. He had been on the committee that expelled Cronin from the Clan in 1885 and was a member of the same camp as Alexander Sullivan.

Moreover, Coughlin, known as the "Slugger of Market Street," had a reputation for using force to obtain information and confessions from suspects. However, nothing but hearsay connected him to Cronin's disappearance until journalists from the *Chicago Times* got a scoop. Finley Peter Dunne later recalled his newspaper's break-through in the case:

> We had on the paper one of those creatures of the underworld who somehow manage to maintain a position in journalism. . . . One night when our progress on the case had halted . . . Joe Dunlop came in and told our proprietor that he had found . . . the man who hired the horse and buggy . . . Dan Coughlin. . . . It was the biggest "scoop" I ever took part in in my whole newspaper experience.

Three days after Cronin's body was discovered, the *Chicago Times* publicly linked Coughlin to the murder. The article, "He Must Explain It," was published on page one and included interviews with both Police Chief Hubbard and Pat Dinan the liveryman. Hubbard declared that Coughlin needed to make "a satisfactory explanation, or see the inside of a cell." The following day's editorial pulled no punches:

> In the Cronin case look to this man Coughlin, a detective of the East Chicago avenue station. What are his antecedents? How came he by his appointment? Who recommended him? What rational explanation is there of his extraordinary conduct in the . . . investigation. . . . Admittedly an enemy of Cronin he is set to work on the Cronin case. . . . Let us know whether the city of Chicago itself, through police agents, is an accessory both before and after the fact to a horrible murder.

On the morning of the *Chicago Times*'s scoop, Dinan told his story again to the police. This time he met a receptive audience. Coughlin was placed under surveillance, and Hubbard called a meeting of those involved in the investigation. The assembly of Police Chief Hubbard, Mayor Cregier, wealthy Irish American businessman and constitutional Irish nationalist W. P. Rend, and Cronin's friend and lawyer William Hynes showed just how intertwined law enforcement, politics, and Irish America were. Coughlin was summoned to the meeting and quizzed for over two hours. It was a bizarre audience for such an interrogation, as the men (particularly Rend and Hynes) were unlikely to give him an unbiased hearing. The detective's responses to their probing were deemed evasive and vague, and at six thirty on the evening of May 25 he was "locked up on suspicion of being an accomplice to the abduction and murder of Dr. Cronin." Unsurprisingly, the *Chicago Times* took full credit for Coughlin's arrest.

With Coughlin in custody, the police renewed their interest in Patrick O'Sullivan, the iceman. The circumstantial evidence against O'Sullivan was considerable: the arrangement made in mid-April for Cronin to tend to any of his injured men, his connection with Williams, and the call for aid on the night of May 4 all suggested that O'Sullivan knew more than he would admit. The police had no difficulty linking Coughlin and O'Sullivan, as both were members of the same Clan camp. O'Sullivan was arrested on the morning of May 27, and later that day both he and Coughlin were refused bail and moved to the Cook County Jail, where they were placed on "Murderers' Row."

>⋅!⋅◀▸⋅•⊙•⋅◀▸!⋅◀

Meanwhile, the legal wheels were turning. In the immediate aftermath of the discovery of Cronin's body, a six-man coroner's jury was assembled. The *Daily News* thought the jurors were "all intelligent-looking men, evidently well-to-do and far above the average 'flunk' coroner's jury." The panel would be responsible for declaring how, when, and where Cronin died. Unlike a trial jury, the coroner's jury was not governed by "strict rules of evidence"; it could "receive even hearsay evidence if it will tend to put [the jury] on the track of the real evidence which may be obtained in the case." It also could name suspects, and the coroner could direct that they be arrested. Following the decision of a coroner's jury, the matter passed to a grand jury, which examined the evidence against the suspects and decided whether the case should go to trial and what charges should be brought.

The coroner's jury began its work by visiting the sites associated with the murder and then hearing from eighty-two witnesses. There was enormous interest in these proceedings—journalists and members of the public scrambled to gain access to the courtroom, causing a crush at the entrance on the first morning of testimony. Column after column in the Chicago newspapers was filled with reports gleaned from the testimony. Many papers published extra editions in order to get the stories out ahead of their rivals.

Those called to testify included Cronin's friends and family: Mrs. Conklin, Frank Scanlan, and Cronin's brother, John. Other witnesses included Pat Dinan, Jonas Carlson, John A. Mahoney (who had introduced O'Sullivan to Cronin), employees of A. H. Revell & Co., and John F. Beggs, the Senior Guardian of Camp 20. Some witnesses established that there had been suspicious activity around the Carlson cottage on the night of May 4; others testified to the discord within Clan na Gael that provided the motive for the murder. Much of the evidence gave weight to the conspiracy theory, with particular attention paid to Camp 20, as its members included Alexander Sullivan, Dan Coughlin, and Patrick O'Sullivan.

Beggs took the stand on June 6. Like Sullivan, he was a lawyer with a checkered past who had attracted police attention before Cronin's murder. In 1879 he had been found guilty of embezzling the funds of a seventeen-year-old girl and spent sixteen months in the Ohio State Penitentiary. While awaiting trial he had boarded with the family of a close friend, Patrick McNamara, in Cleveland. There he began a relationship with McNamara's daughter, Kitty. She became pregnant, and the couple were married while Beggs was in prison. When their daughter was born, Beggs was granted early release on the condition that he supported his wife and daughter, but within a month he abandoned them and fled to Chicago. In Chicago Beggs remarried and found a job with the law firm Boutell and Waterman. In the fall of 1887 he joined the Clan, and at the end of January 1889 he was appointed Senior Guardian of Camp 20.

During his testimony, Beggs "assumed a jaunty and defiant attitude. He posed as a defender of the persecuted and the smiter of the quarrelsome and loud-mouthed clansmen," though later he somewhat disingenuously dismissed the Clan's influence, claiming that the organization was intended to "keep alive Irish national spirit, and nominally to aid in the liberation of Ireland. In reality, I could not see it amounted to anything. On meeting nights we got together, listened to speeches and songs and then adjourned to some saloon, afterwards going home." Few had heard of Beggs before his testimony, but his behavior at the coroner's jury ensured that he was not quickly forgotten. His nonchalance, his dismissal of the Clan's importance, and his dissipated appearance all led to speculation that he had been drunk on the stand. This impression was reinforced when, four days after his testimony, he interrupted proceedings upon his arrival at court, "unsteady from whiskey and evidently still smarting from the coroner's innuendoes. . . . Spreading his arms in a martyr-like gesture he cried out to the court: 'I am here, I am here! Now use me as you like!'" Beggs was swiftly removed, though his earlier testimony meant that the police kept a close eye on his movements.

Many witnesses admitted Clan membership, and during the first few days of the coroner's jury they revealed much about the inner workings of the organization. But by June 7, the *Tribune* observed that some of the Clan witnesses who supported Sullivan "were becoming circumspect and cautious . . . those who have been loquacious with the reporters before yesterday when placed on the stand pretended to have little knowledge . . . of the organization. . . . The whisper of silence has passed around. The grip has been given." For the remainder of the coroner's jury and throughout the trial that followed in the fall and winter, an "amnesia epidemic" appeared to sweep through the Clan. Minds were conveniently blank, memories impaired, and paper records certainly destroyed. Two days after Cronin's body was discovered, Edward Spelman, district officer of the Clan, arrived in Chicago from Peoria, Illinois, claiming to want to "aid in the detection of the murderers of Dr. Cronin and incidentally vindicate Clan-na-Gael." Spelman's method of vindicating the Clan was to disband Camp 20 and burn all its files. As the *Inter Ocean* observed, "Mr. Spelman seems to be more a success as vindicator than as a detector."

A number of witnesses, including Patrick McGarry and John Sampson, testified that Cronin had believed his life to be in danger. Some witnesses were more credible than others. McGarry, a friend of Cronin and senior figure in the Ancient Order of Hibernians, had recently returned from searching for Cronin in Canada. He proved a "very dramatic witness" when he convincingly testified that Cronin was certain of Sullivan's masterminding attempts to kill him. According to the *Daily News*, the "audience 'rose to him' as actors say, and when he denounced Alexander Sullivan there was a noticeable thrill of excitement and a faint applause." Witnesses refuted the allegation that Cronin favored the use of dynamite in furthering the nationalist cause—a tale that appeared to originate with Le Caron. In an interview with the London *Evening News and Post* days after Cronin's body was found, Le Caron had claimed that the doctor was an "ardent advocate of the dynamite policy, and owing to his scientific attainments, he was appointed and acted as . . . an instructor in the use and handling of explosives." Any association with dynamite would remove public sympathy from Cronin, especially in the aftermath of the Haymarket bombing. Refuting this charge, Tom F. O'Connor, a Clan member and friend of Cronin, testified that when he was asked to take part in a dynamite mission he was dissuaded from doing so by Cronin, who "did not believe in the dynamite policy."

As the conspiracy theory revolved around Alexander Sullivan the coroner's jury paid close attention to the feud between him and Cronin. Sullivan's letter of 1888 denouncing Cronin was read by the jurors alongside Cronin's imagined interview where he outlined his grievances against Sullivan. Given Cronin's allegations against the Clan leader they spent much time considering Sullivan's finances. Evidence was produced showing that shortly after his return from Paris, Sullivan had sent the Land League money to his law firm. This money briefly rested in Sullivan's personal bank account in the Traders' Bank of Chicago before being withdrawn to pay the stockbrokerage J. T. Lewis & Co., which invested it at the Chicago Board of Trade, trading primarily in railroad and telegraph shares. The investments were not a success, and by June 1883 Sullivan had lost all but $5,000 of the Land League funds. Whether he had been speculating with Clan funds for Clan purposes or for personal gain was a matter of conjecture. Either way, the money was gone.

Toward the end of the coroner's jury, Luke Dillon, a Cronin supporter and former dynamiter, took the stand. He and John Devoy were two of Cronin's staunchest defenders. Dillon was popular within the Clan and greatly respected by many ordinary members on both sides of the divide. On the day of his testimony, hundreds attempted to gain access to the courtroom. Dillon was quite striking in person, "broad shouldered . . . square cut face and well moulded features. His dark blonde hair receded slightly from his forehead; while a full

blonde moustache of lighter hue shaded his firm compressed lips."
His attack on Alexander Sullivan was devastating. He reported that
Cronin had repeatedly said that Sullivan would murder him, that he
had "no more blood in him than a fish." He acknowledged that Sullivan's formal connections with the Clan and the National League
had been broken in 1884, but was adamant that "when he resigned
he did not cease to rule." He claimed Sullivan was at least indirectly
responsible for Cronin's death. His most damning charge was that
Sullivan was a "professional patriot, sucking the life-blood out of the
organization." Being thought a spy was the worst that could be said
of a member of the Clan, but close behind it was being accused of using the Clan to further personal political ambition. If Dillon was to
be believed, then whether or not the legal system would charge Sullivan with a crime was almost irrelevant. If Sullivan was considered a
"professional patriot," his power and influence were lost.

By the time Foreman Critchell read the verdict of the coroner's
jury at ten o'clock the evening of June 11, the panel had amassed
eleven hundred typewritten pages of evidence. It concluded that
Cronin had died "not from natural causes but from violent results,"
and the "evidence shows conclusively . . . that a plot or conspiracy
was formed . . . for the purpose of murdering . . . Cronin." The jury
found that "Daniel Coughlin, Patrick O'Sullivan, [and] Alexander
Sullivan . . . were either principals, accessories, or had guilty knowledge of the . . . conspiracy to murder Dr. Cronin . . . and they should
be held to answer to the grand jury." Moreover, it was convinced that
"other persons were engaged in this plot, or had guilty knowledge
of it." Although they had not been provided with sufficient evidence
to name these men, the jurors expressed hope that they too would
be apprehended. The verdict concluded with criticism of both the
police force and the secret societies. All secret societies, including
Clan na Gael, were found to be "injurious to American institutions,"
and the jury expected that "future vigor and vigilance by the police
force will more than compensate for past neglect by a portion of the
force in this case."

Coughlin and O'Sullivan were already in custody; despite the late
hour, police were dispatched to 378 Oak Street (now 37 East Oak
Street) to arrest Alexander Sullivan. With considerable arrogance,

Sullivan requested that Detective Harry Palmer, the arresting officer, stay overnight and take him into formal custody the following
morning. His request was denied and he was taken to the county jail.
According to Margaret Sullivan, her husband's arrest was carefully
orchestrated in conjunction with journalists. She claimed that on
the afternoon of June 11,

> the chief of police told Mr. Windes [Sullivan's law partner] . . . that
> there was no intention of arresting him. Mr. Windes said . . . "he will
> come to your office and accept arrest if you wish." The offer was de-
> clined. . . . Mr. Windes intimated that of course since Mr. Sullivan was
> at his office all day, if arrest occurred at any future time, it would be
> by day and not at his home by night. This was promised. . . . The ar-
> rest occurred *that night* with every circumstance of gratuitous brutal-
> ity, and that there was a compact between the Chief and the morn-
> ing newspaper sensation mongers was proven by the fact that within
> three minutes of Mr. Sullivan's leaving the house, the boys met the
> carriage with Extras [extra editions] . . . announcing that the arrest had
> taken place. . . . A dozen cabs accompanied the officers to the house.
> They contained reporters who had been, you see, notified. Not one of
> them was permitted by Mr. Sullivan to cross the threshold and every
> incident they narrated was imaginary.

There may have been some merit in Margaret Sullivan's accusation of
collusion between the police and the press, as some papers reported
that Sullivan had embraced his wife before departing for prison.
Given that she was among the American press delegation at the Paris
Exposition when the arrest was made, they were certainly fabricat-
ing that "fact."

Sullivan's arrest sent ripples from Chicago across the Atlantic
Ocean. On the afternoon of June 12, Sullivan, flanked by attorneys
Trude, Windes, and McArdle, made his first court appearance before
Judge M. F. Tuley at the Cook County Circuit Court. His defense team
requested his release on bail, and after two days of deliberation Tuley ordered that Sullivan was to be freed on $20,000 bail (approxi-
mately $525,000 in today's dollars). The judge concluded that there
was no evidence that Sullivan had been involved in organizing Cro-

nin's murder, nor did he believe that "Cronin was in possession . . . of any facts that would die with him," which suggested that the motive was not to silence Cronin but to punish him. Tuley believed that the coroner's jury had been "largely influenced by hearsay evidence," and while he acknowledged that there was little love lost between Sullivan and Cronin, this was not sufficient to "deprive a man of his liberty, if he is entitled to it under the law, . . . on the grounds that more evidence may be produced to show him guilty." The bail money was put up by four prominent and respected citizens of Chicago, including Fernando Jones, one of the city's wealthiest men, who had "great confidence in Aleck and small respect for popular clamor about his being connected in any way with the Cronin case. . . . He is no fool. Do you suppose any man of his caliber in full possession of his faculties would be foolish enough to engage in such a plot?"

While Margaret was in Paris and London the Sullivans communicated via telegrams, which provide some insight into both their relationship and Alexander's mindset in the weeks after Cronin's body was discovered. When word reached Margaret that Cronin's body had been found, she sent a telegram to her husband to see if he wanted her to return home. He replied, "No sense returning or fretting." Following his arrest, Sullivan telegraphed his wife: "Don't be alarmed. . . . Arrested. Will promptly notify *habeas corpus* result tomorrow. Don't think of coming." Margaret remained in Europe, cabling her husband: "Judgment against immediate return. Am with friends. All send assurance, affection. Be firm. Real nature of attack on you understood. It will be completely exploded. Your vindication will compensate for temporary injustice."

At least outwardly, Margaret Sullivan appeared unperturbed by the storm around her husband. From Paris she traveled to London, where she spent time with Michael Davitt and other figures in Irish political life, attended the Parnell Commission, and also mixed with poets and artists such as the young W. B. Yeats, Sydney Prior Hall (whose drawings of the Parnell Commission combined Margaret's love of politics and art), and the artist Sarah Purser. Yeats was quite taken with her, and wrote to his friend the poet and novelist Katharine Tynan, "I have seen a good deal of Mrs. Alexander Sullivan. She is looking much better than when I wrote last and seems to have quite recovered her spirits. . . . She is not yet sure he [Cronin] is dead. . . . A spy has no rights. There! You will be very angry with me for all these dreadful sentiments. I may think the other way tomorrow." Tynan was not so impressed, complaining that Mrs. Sullivan "certainly had a personality, but I found it a tiresome one." She was skeptical of Margaret Sullivan's behavior in London, noting that upon hearing of her husband's predicament,

> we were all sympathetic and set out to be very conciliatory, but after the first she brightened up so much that we concluded she knew everything and believed that he would soon be released, which he was. I think she had the deliberate intention at that time of appearing everywhere she could and meeting as many people—of facing the music, so to speak, and confuting by her presence those who might have believed her husband guilty.

While in London Margaret Sullivan made a rare incursion into reporting on Irish affairs when she filed stories about the Parnell Commission for Charles Dana's *New York Sun*. She was far from being a disinterested observer, as revelations at the commission potentially had repercussions for her husband. She noted, "The court is now devoted to ascertaining why Ireland and England, which God did not join together, should not be prevented from separating." Membership in Clan na Gael was restricted to men, but Margaret Sullivan was just as devoted as her husband was to a radical solution to Ireland's connection with Britain, and Charles Stewart Parnell thought her capable of great violence. While on a visit to London in 1886 she had visited the Ladies Gallery in the House of Commons, and when Parnell saw her there he was convinced that she would throw a bomb into the house. The proprietor of the *Chicago Daily News*, Melville Stone, thought her motive less violent, if no less sinister. He alleged that Margaret Sullivan had brought with her to the Commons a "courtesan of surpassing beauty" who had been engaged to seduce and blackmail Parnell. There is no evidence to sustain either story, but it is interesting that both Parnell and Stone thought Margaret

Sullivan capable of such acts. If either account was true, it seems that she was as determined as her husband to pursue violence over parliamentary efforts to secure Irish independence.

><del>+<)+<del>-O-<(>-+-<</del></del>

The arrest of Sullivan caused difficulties for the Catholic Church in Chicago. Archbishop Patrick A. Feehan came under pressure from newspapers, some Clan camps, and members of the church to address the issues of his tolerance for the Clan, his support for Father Maurice Dorney, and his own friendship with Sullivan. P. W. Dunne, a friend of Cronin, eagerly spoke to the press about Dorney, and described him as

> the earnest, consistent and willing tool and co-partner of Alexander Sullivan, standing at his shoulder from day to day during the passing years and furnishing him with a certificate of honesty, trustworthiness and respectability. . . . I believe that next to Alexander Sullivan no man in America is so much to blame today as Father Dorney for the unfortunate condition of affairs in Irish organizations and I hold him morally responsible for the blood of poor Cronin.

Such was the coverage of Cronin's murder that Feehan was obliged to produce a long report about the "criminal acts of Clan na Gael" to Cardinal Giovanni Simeoni, the Prefect of the Propaganda of the Faith and an official of the Roman Curia. In response, Pope Leo XIII was reported to have instructed that "the facility be granted to the Archbishop to take whatever means he may deem opportune to declare the Clan na Gael in opposition to the Church." Sullivan's supporters dismissed the report about the pope's instructions, pointing to the fact it had first appeared in the *London Standard*, a paper with an anti-Irish bias. They were confident that Feehan would not condemn the Clan, for as far as they were concerned, it had done nothing to merit censure.

Pro-Cronin Clan members wrote to Feehan, asking him to remove Dorney from ministry at St. Gabriel's, a move the *Tribune* correctly thought "a little cheeky" and one that the archbishop might interpret as an attempt "to run the religion of Chicago as well as its political force and its politics." The papers anticipated that Feehan would publicly condemn the Clan, announce that all members would be refused burial in a Catholic cemetery, and dispatch Dorney to some country parish where his "opportunities for scandalizing the church will be far less." The archbishop did none of these things. He remained resolutely silent on the matters of his friendship with Sullivan, Father Dorney, and Cronin's murder.

Other members of the Catholic Church hierarchy did criticize the Clan. Archbishop Patrick J. Ryan of Philadelphia wrote to Cardinal James Gibbons of Baltimore to suggest that the church authorities "consider the formal condemnation of the 'Clan na Gael' as a secret society. There can be little doubt that it is one, and that it is doing much evil amongst our people. The Cronin murder in Chicago will bring out some of the worst features." No immediate action was forthcoming, but the church watched the developments in Chicago with interest.

>─┼─◆)─•─○─•─(◆─┼─<

As the investigation progressed, the police added several new names to their growing list of suspects: John J. Maroney, Charles McDonald, Martin Burke, and Pat "the Fox" Cooney. All were members of the Clan, all were connected to Camp 20, and all had apparently fled Chicago following Cronin's murder. Some commentators believed this was to escape the attention of the Chicago police force; others, fearing a conspiracy, thought they had moved on to carry out further murders of Cronin allies—John Devoy, Luke Dillon, and Peter McCahey. If that was indeed their intent, they had blundered, for Devoy, Dillon, and McCahey were in Chicago regularly in the months after Cronin's death. In fact Devoy arrived in Chicago just after Cronin's body was discovered, and stayed for almost five years. Through the summer of 1889, he was regularly warned by pro-Sullivan Clan members to "shut up about Sullivan and go back to New York . . . that if I didn't go back voluntarily I might go in a coffin." Devoy armed himself with a revolver in case he met with Sullivan or his more radical supporters. But Devoy's and Sullivan's paths rarely crossed, though Devoy recalled one tense encounter in a basement restaurant at the corner of Adams and Clark Streets. He had been dining with Edward M. Lahiff, a reporter from the *Chicago Herald*, when Sullivan arrived with friends. In Devoy's version of events he immediately paid his bill, "walked towards Sullivan's table, turned towards the door and passed in front of him. . . . I had my right hand on the revolver in my overcoat pocket, as I walked slowly past him looking him in the eye. . . . I knew he always carried a revolver handy, and if he had made a motion to draw it I would have shot him before he could reach his hip pocket."

The day after Cronin's disappearance, his friends had organized a "general committee for assisting in the capture and punishment of the murderers of Dr. Cronin." The committee, which included Luke Dillon as chairman and W. P. Rend as treasurer, was determined to help the "authorities in the search for the assassins." In an attempt to avoid accusations of being involved in the Clan feud, members included an American and a German. One of the first tasks of the committee was to liaise with the Pinkerton detectives assigned to investigate Cronin's disappearance. At least fourteen Pinkertons pursued suspects around Chicago and New York; based on their findings, on June 11 John J. Maroney and Charles McDonald were arrested in New York. Devoy, Dillon, and the Chicago police were certain that Maroney was the "Simonds" who had rented the flat on Clark Street, and McDonald was the agitated man who had collected Cronin from his home and driven him to the Carlson cottage on the night of May 4. Following their arrest, Governor Joseph W. Fifer of Illinois requested Governor David B. Hill of New York to extradite both men. Hill denied the application on two grounds; first, it had not been accompanied by an indictment, and second, he was not convinced by the evidence provided by the Chicago police. The *Inter Ocean* believed the governor refused because he was "afraid to ignore the demand of a faction strong in New York City politics and he finds an excuse for ignoring the demand of the State of Illinois." There may have been something in that assessment, for in August 1889 Hill was asked to address a pro-Sullivan gathering in Chicago. He didn't attend, but the fact that he was invited was enough to convince many that he was in the pocket of the Triangle.

The police failed to locate Pat "the Fox" Cooney, who they believed had been in the Carlson cottage on May 4 and had taken part in the assault on Cronin. Originally from County Mayo, Cooney had worked as a laborer in Chicago, and in the month leading up to Cronin's death he had been heard to denounce Cronin in saloons on Market Street (now Wacker Drive). But by the time he became a suspect, he had left the city. Police sent a circular throughout the nation with a description of Cooney, "wanted" for the murder of Dr. Cronin. Part of the description was telling. Cooney was thought to be missing a finger, for in the bloodied cotton batting found alongside Cronin's body was a finger that was not Cronin's. The police were convinced that it was Cooney's, as none of the other suspects were missing a finger.

Martin Burke was caught on the run in Canada. Like Cooney, Burke was originally from County Mayo. He had arrived in Chicago in 1886 and joined Camp 20. With the assistance of Beggs and Sullivan, he found work in the city sewer department and was firmly on the Sullivan side of the Cronin-Sullivan feud. By early 1889, however, Burke was unemployed, though he appeared to have a considerable amount of money to spend in the saloons around Market Street. There he broadcast the fact that he had a girlfriend in Lake View, so when Cronin's body was found there some tongues began to wag within the Irish community, just as Inspector Frederick Ebersold had predicted. Soon Burke's name came to the attention of John Collins, one of the few Irish American members of the force allowed to remain on the case because, as a member of Camp 20 himself, he knew many of the suspects. A photograph of Burke was shown to the Carlsons and Mortensen, and both identified him as the "Frank Williams" who had rented the Carlson cottage. Over the course of the following week, the police discovered that Burke frequently used a number of aliases, including "Martin Delaney," "Frank Williams," and "W. J. Cooper."

Burke was tracked to Winnipeg when, posing as W. J. Cooper, he raised the suspicions of a railway ticket agent. Cooper wanted to travel from Winnipeg to Montreal, but would only take a train that ran exclusively through Canada because he had been in trouble in the United States. The railway official contacted John C. McRae of the Winnipeg police, who arrested Burke as he boarded the train. McRae recognized Burke from the description circulated by the Chicago police, and immediately telegraphed Police Chief Hubbard:

"Martin Burke . . . arrested here on suspicion of complicity in the
Cronin case. He was boarding the *Atlantic Express*, and had a ticket for
Liverpool, England." John Collins, armed with an extradition warrant
signed by President Benjamin Harrison, was dispatched to Winnipeg
to ensure Burke's return to Chicago. Upon his arrival, Collins identified Burke as the suspect and went with Chief McRae to see Judge
John F. Bain, where he formally requested Burke's extradition. Burke,
an unskilled laborer with no income, had legal representation at his
extradition hearing which indicated that there were others with a
vested interest in keeping Burke away from Chicago. Evidence was
presented, including testimony from Charles Carlson, who traveled
to Winnipeg to identify Burke, and on July 10 Bain agreed to the extradition. Burke appealed but lost, and the warrant of extradition
was issued on August 3. Collins, Hubbard himself, and several other
officers accompanied Burke back to Chicago—an indicator of the importance attached to his repatriation. Crowds gathered at every station en route in the hope of catching a glimpse of him, while police
hitched empty carriages to the train to confuse anyone who might
attempt to rescue the prisoner.

>-+-<>-+-O-+<>-+-<

While Burke's extradition was being pursued in Canada the grand
jury was active in Chicago. State's Attorney Joel Longnecker was determined to "place additional evidence against the men under arrest
before the jury." Longnecker argued that the murder conspiracy orig-
inated in Camp 20, and that it had been prompted by information
that came via Henri Le Caron and the Parnell Commission. It seemed
reasonable to suspect that the camp leader would have been aware
of it, so John Beggs was called to testify. Though not drunk this time,
his answers to the questions were inconsistent, and his correspondence with Clan district officer Spelman was damning—it implied
that if Spelman didn't take action against Cronin, others would.

The Chicago police were now satisfied that they had identified all
the key players in the conspiracy, and on June 29 the grand jury presented a general indictment against Martin Burke, John F. Beggs, Dan
Coughlin, Patrick O'Sullivan, Pat Cooney (in absentia), and a sixth

man named John Kunze. Without any eyewitnesses to the murder, and in an age (just) before the use of fingerprinting and blood analysis, the prosecution's best hope of a conviction lay in the Merritt Conspiracy Bill. This bill, passed in the aftermath of the Haymarket bombing, stated that anyone who "had conspired to perform an act of force or violence dangerous to human life, person or property was liable, even if not party to the accomplishment [and] could be punished." The grand jury recommended that all the accused be tried together, as had happened in the Haymarket trial. Otherwise, it would be almost impossible to prove the conspiracy charge.

Surprisingly, Sullivan was not charged, though there had been widespread anticipation he would be. The editorial in *Life* magazine on June 27, 1889, hoped that he would be charged with murder, because

> there are suggestions . . . that he waded through arson and embezzlement as well as man-killing to the presidency of the Land League and the head-devilship of the Clan na Gael. There might be something that this journal would like to say about him, but it does not do to free the mind absolutely about a man who has a habit of gunning in the street. It is time enough to be frank about such a person when his neck has been stretched.

The *New York Times* argued that "Dr. Cronin's persistent and fearless exposures of the misuse of the funds of the Clan na Gael . . . make it plain in what interest his 'removal' was effected. . . . The man most deeply involved and most seriously menaced by his exposures . . . is Alexander Sullivan." Cronin's supporters were convinced that he had instigated the murder, and Sullivan's business partner Thomas G. Windes had testified that Coughlin frequently visited their office, despite Sullivan's claims that he barely knew the detective. When Sullivan wasn't indicted, there was much speculation that he had bribed his way out of a charge.

Almost equal surprise met the indictment of John Kunze. Kunze, "a small dudish looking German with a vacuous countenance," was a petty crook who had no connection with Cronin, Sullivan, or the

Clan. He was a criminal associate of Coughlin, and many believed his arrest was a case of mistaken identity, or that he had been blackmailed by Coughlin to become involved. The other men were all connected by their membership in Clan na Gael, and specifically Camp 20, Alexander Sullivan's camp.

Although the men were kept in separate sections of the jail while they awaited trial, they were permitted to meet with one another. The *Tribune* firmly believed that the inmates should be isolated in the hope that one might decide to turn state's evidence. Meetings meant that "the stronger minded can brace up the weaker one and . . . they may more easily cook a plausible defense." Beggs and O'Sullivan were the two the papers expected to turn state's evidence. It was generally believed that O'Sullivan's involvement in the crime was limited, and that he should be encouraged to testify against his co-accused in return for a lighter sentence. The *Tribune* thought that

> what "squealing" is done should be by subordinates. If any one is allowed to turn State's evidence it should be the one whose hands have the least blood on them. Therefore it is O'Sullivan rather than Burke who should go on the witness stand if any one does. . . . Whether it will be possible to get back to the carefully concealed principals remains to be seen. The police can be reasonably sure of but one thing, that they too were Chicagoans, Irishmen and Clan-na-Gael men.

The men had a number of visitors in the days before the trial began. Beggs's wife, "a large blonde, apparently older than her husband," visited three or four times a week bringing delicacies, Maggie Coughlin brought her husband his meals, and O'Sullivan's food was provided by his sister. Matt Danahy, the owner of a saloon at the corner of Clark Street and Chicago Avenue that was favored by the supporters of the accused, arranged for Burke's meals to be supplied by a restaurant. Kunze alone remained isolated, with no visitors.

The accused were represented by a plethora of attorneys led by William S. Forrest, a "bright, sharp and rasping" lawyer with a "clear, logical and judicial mind." O'Sullivan and Kunze were defended by Dan Donohoe, "one of the most energetic and talented of the bright legal galaxy," and Burke by William B. Kennedy. William Foster, one of Beggs's attorneys, had represented the Haymarket anarchists and was regarded as "well read and a forcible speaker." R. W. Wing and M. E. Ames completed the defense team. The quantity and quality of the defense attorneys sparked much comment. With the exception of Beggs, none of the accused could afford expensive counsel, so it was assumed that their lawyers' fees, estimated at $20,000 (approximately $525,000 in today's dollars), were being paid by the Clan. Cronin's supporters believed that the lawyers were being paid indirectly by Sullivan, who was determined that the full story behind the murder not be revealed. Others saw the defense counsel as evidence that the Clan looked after its own, whether or not the men were guilty. Who paid for them was shrouded in secrecy, and the lawyers themselves claimed they didn't know where their compensation came from. They were paid through Forrest, who had received the money from Patrick W. Fitzpatrick, the proprietor of a bookstore. Forrest understood that Fitzpatrick was the treasurer of a fund made up of "subscriptions from persons living in all parts of the world."

Yet although he scrupulously avoided "any communication with the attorneys interested in the trial," Sullivan seems to have been heavily involved in paying for the defense team. He and his wife were a wealthy couple, with a combined annual income estimated to be between $13,200 and $18,000 ($345,000–$470,000 in today's dollars). Nonetheless, the day after the trial began, Sullivan sold his house to his lawyer A. S. Trude for $7,000. Three months later, he asked Davitt to secure a loan of $10,000 for him. Margaret Sullivan maintained that her husband's law firm had been "gravely injured" by his association with the Cronin murder, but even allowing for a substantial reduction in clientele, he could not have needed such financial bolstering for personal use within six months of Cronin's death. The only reasonable explanation for his urgent desire for large quantities of cash at this time was to pay the defense lawyers' fees.

>─┤◆>─◦○◦─<◆├─<

Through the summer of 1889, public interest in the Cronin case did not wane. Newspapers kept it on their front pages, and in Chicago both the nationalist and the republican sides of the Irish community were eager to find friendly journalists. Thousands flocked to festivals organized to raise money for the defense or the prosecution while others attended protest meetings and concerts to campaign for the suppression of secret societies. For some Chicagoans, Cronin's murder was further proof that the Irish could never assimilate and become fully American. The nativist American League held a Fourth of July celebration where those who waved two flags were condemned: "We want no flag . . . but the one our forefathers loved . . . the red flag [associated with the radical Left] has nearly vanished, the green will follow."

Those who supported Cronin were keen to enlist the backing of Americans and other non-Irish groups. They were determined to prove that being an Irish republican was not incompatible with being a US citizen. The invitations to the meetings they organized were couched in inclusive terms, calling on all "law-abiding citizens" to attend and assuring the authorities "of our earnest moral support in their efforts at bringing the guilty parties to justice." At a Cronin Memorial Meeting held on June 28, the stage was decorated by two large American flags, with some small Irish and American flags hung around the speakers' stand. Speaking to the three thousand people gathered in the Central Music Hall, W. P. Rend was keen to distance the vast majority of the Irish from those who murdered Cronin. He argued,

> Natives of other countries who have become American citizens should take an interest in the welfare of the land of their birth. They should work for the welfare and prosperity of their countrymen left behind. It is not right, however, for men to unite in secret and plot against the lives of others against whom they bear enmity. They are not patriots; they are conspirators; they are murderers; and as such should be punished.

At the same meeting, Robert Lindblom of the Chicago Board of Trade expressed American concerns: "We have come here to emphasize our rights as men and as American citizens and to protest against those rights being dominated by foreign influences and conspiracies."

In addition to the public meetings, the Irish community held its own events aimed primarily at an Irish audience. In 1876 Clan na Gael and other Irish American associations had established the United Irish Societies of Chicago to act as an umbrella group for organizing celebrations of Irish holidays. When the UISC was founded, some Irish societies feared that it would simply be a front for the Clan, and of the forty-four Irish societies known to be in Chicago in 1876, only twenty-three became involved with the UISC at the outset, and almost all of those were affiliated with the Clan. But it became increasingly difficult to run successful events without its support; within a decade, because of the growing influence of the Clan, eighty Irish societies were members of the UISC.

As the Feast of the Assumption celebration of August 15 loomed it became clear that the UISC annual picnic at Ogden's Grove would not pass without controversy. At a meeting in McCoy's Hotel on the corner of Clark and Van Buren Streets, a heated discussion ensued, with several speakers arguing that the picnic should be canceled in light of Cronin's death. John Finerty, editor of the *Citizen*, founder of UISC, and ally of Sullivan, thought that cancellation of the event was nonsense; he claimed that "Irish Americans are not made of the kind of stuff that wilts under fire." Finerty wanted the gathering to avoid assuming "the form of triumph of one class of Irish American citizens over another," and believed it should be "held for the benefit of the Irish cause and the honor of the Irish race." But supporters of Cronin split from the UISC and formed the Confederated Irish Societies. They organized rival demonstrations on the same key dates, and much of the money raised went toward the prosecution of those charged with Cronin's murder.

In August 1889 those who backed Cronin met at Cheltenham Beach, twelve miles south of the city center, while those who supported Sullivan met at Ogden's Grove. The events were similar in style, with the usual musical and sporting entertainments, food and beer tents, and speechifying in the evening. *America* was dismissive of both gatherings, claiming they represented traditions brought from the "old country" which allowed the Irish "an opportunity to indulge in their natural pastimes of drinking whiskey, cracking heads and raising funds."

Despite Finerty's claim that the Ogden's Grove event would be a unifying spectacle, the speeches at that picnic supported Sullivan and those accused of Cronin's murder, emphasized Irish loyalty to the United States, and attacked newspaper coverage of the investigation. Speaking from a platform decorated with an American flag and a harp of Erin, David Sullivan of the UISC declared,

> We stand here the denounced of the Chicago daily press (hisses)—we stand here the focus of British hatred; . . . but we stand here with the banner of the Republic above us and the banner of the old land we left. . . . Rebels at home, as we ought to be . . . we have been loyal here—loyal with our inmost souls, and with the best blood of our hearts.

John Finerty challenged any critic

> to point to a field of battle fought for the foundation or maintenance of this Union where Irish blood has not been generously poured out. . . . There is but one murder organization in modern politics, and that is the British Government. . . . The gallows is red with Irish blood, the English dungeons are red, the battlefields are red—and shall mere newspaper clamor do what these failed to accomplish?

The speeches were "not so remarkable for what was said as they were for the way in which they were received. Every mention of the Cheltenham demonstration was drowned in a cyclone of hisses. Every allusion, however slight, to 'Parnell's trusted lieutenant [Alexander Sullivan]' was taken up in an explosion of cheers." Sullivan didn't attend the Ogden's Grove celebrations despite being "strongly urged by friends"; according to his wife, he was determined "to give no one cause for bitterness." As darkness fell there was a firework display, the most impressive of which "were a harp, the star-spangled banner, a pyramid and a Maltese cross displayed all at one time. . . . Dancing continued until nearly midnight with the band playing a mix of American and Irish music including 'God Save Ireland' and 'The Star-Spangled Banner.'"

Cheltenham Beach—billed as the "Coney Island of the West" and consisting of a hundred-acre park, a beach with a long pier, beer gardens, restaurants, and a resort hotel—hosted the Confederated Irish Societies crowd of between 12,000 and 20,000. The entertainments and speeches mirrored those at Ogden's Grove. Speakers praised Cronin and attacked Sullivan, and all those involved in the Ogden's Grove event. P. W. Dunne criticized the Ogden's Grove meeting as a "factional display . . . intended to endorse the foulest and most barbarous murder ever recorded in the annals of human crime." Father J. B. Toomey called for the death penalty. He wanted the perpetrators of the crime to "dance upon nothing." The speakers were frequently interrupted by chants of "Sullivan, Sullivan" and "Hang him, hang him."

The picnics were substantial fund-raisers. Finerty claimed that over $2,000 (approximately $52,000 today) was raised for the Irish Tenants' Defense fund, while it was estimated that between $2,000 and $5,000 was collected at Cheltenham Beach—a combination of a fifty-cent entry fee and donations earmarked for assisting the prosecution at the Cronin trial.

The next significant annual event in the Irish republican calendar was November 23, the anniversary of the execution of the Manchester Martyrs. Supporters of Cronin planned to hold a benefit on that night, which outraged Finerty. In his view, an event raising money for the prosecution was "simply indecent." He believed Cronin's supporters had "no right to use names sacred to Ireland . . . in connection with a blood money fund of any description. It is a scandalous piece of impertinence on their part." Cronin's friends responded by claiming that Sullivan's supporters were using their considerable influence in politics and the church to ensure the acquittal of the accused. They claimed that both politicians and the Catholic Church were too weak to take action against the Clan, and believed that Archbishop Feehan "is tottering to his grave under the weight of this thing and can hardly walk the street because of the terrible burden that is upon him."

The twenty-second-anniversary celebration of the Manchester Martyrs was an opportunity for Cronin's supporters to publicly add Cronin's name to the pantheon of Irish martyrs, and they pressed ahead with the event. On that evening, P. W. Dunne charged members of the Triangle with being the instigators of the murder, and claimed that the men on trial were dupes and hired assassins.

Through the fall and winter of 1889 as the murder trial continued, both sides aired their differences through speeches, picnics, and fund-raisers. The fissures within Irish republicanism were laid open for all to see—and for a secret society this was a disaster.

CHAPTER EIGHT

"TRUTH IN ESSENTIALS,
IMAGINATION IN NON-ESSENTIALS"

The Press and Public Entertainment

Newspapers reveled in the disintegration of Clan na Gael and laid bare its internal wranglings. Personal animosity, corruption, embezzlement, and violence permeated the tales that daily filled columns in Chicago, throughout North America, and across the Atlantic Ocean in Britain. One commentator, undoubtedly guilty of hyperbole, claimed that Cronin's murder "may be said to rank with the assassinations of Presidents Lincoln and Garfield" while others referred to it as "the crime of the century." The story had everything an editor could want: conspiracy, theft, dynamite, betrayal, and murder. All it lacked was the "proverbial 'Woman' in the case."

The newspaper business was booming, like the country itself: between 1870 and 1900, the urban population of the United States tripled at the same time that the number of daily newspapers quadrupled and the copies sold increased sixfold. Although residents shared urban space, they navigated that space in the company of strangers. The speed of urban expansion meant what had once been familiar became strange and suspicious. Neighborhoods, once full of friends and acquaintances and familiar buildings, were transformed as new city dwellers poured in, bringing with them a fresh range of cultures, languages, and expectations.

Chicago was expanding at a much faster pace than any other city in the United States: between 1880 and 1890 the population grew by 118%, while that of New York rose by 26% and Philadelphia by 24%. This expansion, together with increasing literacy levels, drove the newspaper boom. Cities quickly became too large for the individual to comprehend without a guide, and residents became reliant on newspapers to educate and inform them on all matters local, national, and international. By 1880 the rapid growth of the newspaper industry was hardly equaled "by any other phase of industrial development in the United States." The 1880 census recorded 971 daily newspapers and 8,633 weekly papers across the nation, figures that rose to 1,731 and 12,721 respectively by 1890. At the time of Cronin's death, at least a dozen daily English-language newspapers in Chicago were competing for sales.

Newspapers were published to suit the demands of the market. Evening papers bought on the way home from work outnumbered morning papers by about two to one in 1890, and many papers also had a Sunday edition, which often had the largest circulation. In 1886 the *Chicago Daily News* claimed to have the largest daily circulation in America, with average daily sales of 160,000. It reckoned that the *Chicago Times* sold 30,000 copies, the *Tribune* more than 25,000, the *Inter Ocean* 18,000, and the *Chicago Herald* 20,000 per day. However, some papers counted circulation figures by the number of papers printed, not the amount sold, which may have been far fewer than the print run. Papers competed on price as well, and in 1889 the *Chicago Times* dropped its price from five cents to three—a move followed by all the main papers with the exception of the *Daily News*, which could be bought for two cents. Aimed at the general market, most Chicago papers were low-priced and visually appealing, with illustrations and headlines designed to catch the eye. Yet despite this intense competition for sales, editors also considered themselves the moral guardians of their readership. Newspapers, particularly metropolitan papers, began to employ campaigning journalists. The editor did not replace the minister as "as the conscience of the community," but he did stand alongside him as a figure of influence and authority in the urban landscape.

Morality-driven stories served a community need, but more important they were profitable, as they often boosted circulation. To maximize profits, in covering the Cronin case the *Chicago Times*, the *Journal*, the *Tribune*, and the *Inter Ocean* pooled their resources to purchase the Western Associated Press trial reports, leaving their own reporters free to write editorial, color, and comment pieces about

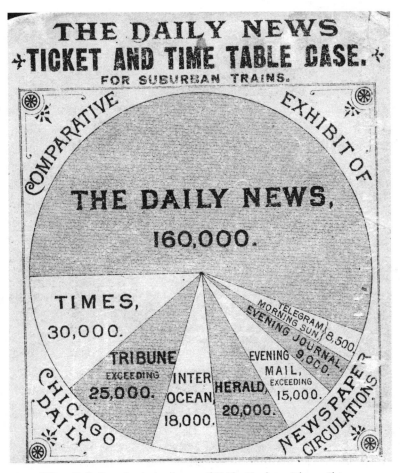

Chicago Daily News circulation figures, 1886. The Newberry Library, Chicago.
Call number MMS Field Enterprises, series 1, subseries 5, folder 417.

the trial. Similarly, journalists from different publications engaged in "combination reporting," sharing their information so that their articles were more detailed. Almost all the journalists knew one another, if not from one of the several press clubs in the city, then as former colleagues. The life of a journalist was a very fluid one, with reporters constantly flitting between newspapers. A colleague one week was often a rival the next.

Newspapers commonly had affiliations to political parties in the nineteenth century, and a paper's survival was thus tightly bound to the fortunes of the party. The *Chicago Times* was established in 1854 as a Democratic Party paper, while the *Tribune*, with Joseph Medill in control beginning in 1855, was a powerful organ of the Republican Party. By 1891 the *Tribune* was regarded as "by far the richest, most ably conducted and the best newspaper property in the West." Then the content of many papers was altered by the arrival of "new journalism" newsmen, such as Melville E. Stone and Wilbur F. Storey. In the main, new journalism was characterized by editorial independence, campaigns and investigations, and an emphasis on high-quality prose. Such papers may have been free from political influence, but their stories were not necessarily more reliable: in a highly competitive, increasingly profit-driven environment, the papers often prioritized dramatic details over complex analysis or principled polemic. But by 1889, all the Chicago papers bore some of the hallmarks of new journalism.

Revenue from advertisements and increasing sales delivered a degree of financial independence, and by 1889 all the Chicago dailies (except the fervently Republican *Inter Ocean*) wore their political affiliations lightly, if at all. Newspapers were fickle, as the cartoonist Art Young (writing of his arrival in Chicago in the late 1880s) observed:

> When I came from the country I had a strong belief that the newspapers of the big cities were oracles, beacon lights. I still clung to that belief, though a bit shakily. . . . I knew their policies were inconsistent, but perhaps that couldn't be helped. . . . In one election a Chicago daily would thunderingly assail some candidate and a year later would be lauding him. . . . The press blew hot and cold at will. I was often bewildered.

Referring to the Cronin case, the *Tribune* expressed astonishment that potential jurors in the murder trial might have been influenced by newspaper articles; it argued, slightly disingenuously, that "to know the views or opinions of any paper a reader had to have in his hand the latest edition."

As Theodore Dreiser recalled, in the late nineteenth century Chicago was in "the heyday of its newspaper prestige," playing host to innovative newspapermen such as Melville E. Stone, Wilbur F. Storey, Victor F. Lawson, Joseph Medill, and William Penn Nixon. Storey, owner and editor of the *Chicago Times*, and Stone, founder and editor of the *Daily News*, joined Medill of the *Chicago Tribune* as the dominating forces. From the 1860s to the 1890s they, as much as Joseph Pulitzer and Charles A. Dana, influenced a new generation of reporters, many of whom covered the Cronin murder.

Storey's motto was "to print news and to raise hell," and that he did. The *Times* was, as David Paul Nord puts it, "sensational, irreverent, diverse in content, and quick in news coverage." It managed to be both shocking and successful, and by the late 1880s it was the paper with the "most impact on local politics." It was perhaps best known for its headlines, the most famous being "Jerked to Jesus," which accompanied a story about the hanging of four murderers. Storey's organization of the newspaper was much emulated. He appointed a managing editor who, assisted by a city editor, looked after the editorial content and selected the news stories. Subeditors were employed to write features, reports, and reviews, and a business manager and his assistants oversaw the compositors, the pressroom, and advertising. A circulation manager made sure that the paper's distribution was extensive—for the *Times*, as for every other newspaper, murders sold copies. A key part of the distribution was the deployment of newsboys, who stood on street corners loudly hawking the paper.

Melville Stone's *Daily News* was "a crusading reform paper which appealed to all classes . . . because of its penny price and its short punchy articles," and in 1889 it claimed that its daily average circulation was 222,745. Stone was an advocate of what he termed "detective journalism," and by the late 1880s all newspapers in Chicago, to a greater or lesser degree, could be said to follow the tenets he laid out in 1879: to print news, to guide public opinion, and to provide entertainment. The Cronin case provided the papers with a perfect opportunity to achieve all three objectives.

Irish American newspapers were important for the Irish American community, for as the *Boston Pilot* observed, "even papers that are 'friendly to the Irish' are constantly led into misunderstanding and misrepresentation"; the paper greeted both the establishment of John Devoy's *Irish Nation* in New York in 1881 and John Finerty's

Chicago Daily News newsboy, 1886. The Newberry Library, Chicago. Call
number MMS Field Enterprises, series 1, subseries 5, folder 417.

weekly paper, the *Citizen*, in Chicago in 1882 with enthusiasm. Finerty
was a Galwayman with journalism and republicanism in his blood:
his father, M. J. Finerty, had been editor of the *Galway Vindicator*.
In 1863 the junior Finerty left Ireland for America after a series of
radical speeches that attracted the attention of the authorities. He
joined the Union army, fought in the Civil War, and later settled in
Chicago, where he was a journalist for a number of newspapers, most
notably the *Chicago Times*. As military correspondent for the *Times*
in the latter half of the 1870s, Finerty traveled with the US Army and

covered the war against the Sioux Indians. His dispatches from the front met with great acclaim, and he later published an account of that period, *War-Path and Bivouac*. In 1882 John O'Boyle Reilly described him as "an experienced and accomplished journalist, and a gentleman who has and deserves the personal respect and admiration of all who have ever known him."

The *Chicago Times* appointed Finerty its Washington correspondent in 1881, and his time in the nation's capital gave him the notion that he would make a fine congressman. In 1883 he tried and failed to secure the Democratic nomination, and ran as an Independent Democrat for Illinois. To the surprise of many he was victorious at the election, defeating Henry F. Sheridan, a Democrat and Clan member who was supported by Alexander Sullivan. Finerty proved to be an enthusiastic but largely ineffective congressman. Whitelaw Reid, editor of the *New York Tribune*, described him as "the member from Illinois elected to represent Ireland in the Congress," while Finley Peter Dunne, writing as "Mr. Dooley," recalled the time "me friend Jawn Finerty came out 'iv th' House iv Riprisintitives an' whin some wan ast him what was goin' on, he says, 'Oh nawthin' at all but some damned American business.'"

The first edition of the *Citizen* loudly proclaimed its intent to present "to the public in a faithful manner the status of the Irish and [afford] Irish Americans a wider opportunity to express sympathy with the cause of the motherland." The paper's motto was emblazoned across its front page: "Europe, not England, is the Mother Country of America." Finerty regarded himself as an American patriot and also an Irish republican, and he saw no contradiction in this dual allegiance. This was an argument he repeated time and again, verbally and in print. By the mid-1880s and despite Finerty's defeat of Sheridan, which must have irked Sullivan, the newspaper had become the mouthpiece for the Sullivan wing of the Clan. Throughout the Cronin murder trial, the *Citizen* remained loyal to Sullivan and continually (if rather naively) hopeful that the Clan would be reunited soon.

Curiously, newspapers in Ireland paid limited attention to the Cronin murder. His death was regretted, but the papers declared it the actions of individuals rather than the result of a conspiracy.

Cronin's supporters believed that there were "influences at work in Ireland, preventing the Irish press from placing the American side of the question before the people," so the Cronin Committee wrote a lengthy letter for publication in Irish newspapers. "To the People of Ireland" criticized Alexander Sullivan and condemned those who labeled Cronin a spy. The letter asked all Irish readers to "let the clear current of your judgment flow down the pure stream of justice and righteousness in favor of American law, now, as it has been in the past."

>–⊢◆⟩–○–⟨◆–⊢–◅

A fine line existed between Melville Stone's "detective journalism" and interference in police investigations. In their scramble to get a story, journalists occasionally overstepped ethical, if not legal, boundaries. It was not unusual for them to take on aliases, don disguises, steal evidence, or secure witness testimony with bribes in order to trump rival publications. Though not taking such drastic measures, Finley Peter Dunne was one of several newspapermen who, desperate for a scoop, "could think of nothing else but the Cronin case. I slept with it, I ate with it," and in an attempt to get a story, "drew on the cashier of our struggling newspaper for what he considered enormous sums to pay the expenses of reporters lodging in the same houses with scores of persons under suspicion." When Pat Dinan's white horse was identified as connected to the case, Charles Beck of the *Chicago Times* hired the same rig and drove it north in the vain and ridiculous hope that the animal would recall the route it had taken between Cronin's residence and the Carlson cottage. Less ethical methods were employed, including tampering with evidence. Twice the cottage was broken into by journalists. On the first occasion no evidence was touched, but on the second three reporters entered late at night and smeared the walls and floor with animal blood—something they later dismissed as a joke.

Many reporters were writing "on space," and so every word counted—and sensational stories required many words. When the British Foreign Office tracked down a journalist who had reported on the "Fenian Ram" to seek clarification of story details, he admitted that the story was exaggerated, because he was writing "on space, and made the most of the incident." In 1890 Charles Howard Shinn, writing in the *Writer* (a "monthly magazine to interest and help all literary workers"), complained that "among the evils with which the young journalist has to contend none . . . are more dangerous and insidious than the growing evil of space work. . . . Let us write less, but let us put more writing upon the writing we do. It may not bring in so much money . . . but it will . . . lead to results in every way more satisfactory and honorable." Shinn may have been correct, but many journalists adhered to Edwin Schuman's mantra of "truth in essentials, imagination in non-essentials." For some journalists and their readership, the Cronin case was as exciting a murder mystery as any novelist could imagine, and there was no harm in taking a little liberty with the truth. Fictional murder mysteries were one thing, but the real thing was even more fascinating—it played on public fears, ghoulish curiosity, and the desire to see the perpetrators punished and the victim avenged.

Journalists and newspapers "subscribed concurrently to the ideals of factuality and of entertainment," but it was often difficult for them to balance the two. Newspapers frequently drove the story for their own financial ends: after the Haymarket bombing, Mary Harris "Mother" Jones wrote that "the city went insane and the newspapers did everything to keep it like a madhouse." The press both manipulated and articulated public reaction to the bombing, and was quick to point a finger at the alleged perpetrators. In the Cronin case, some papers could be said to have done the same as they raced to target Alexander Sullivan. Jeffory A. Clymer, writing about the explosion at the Haymarket, has noted the "long-standing American fascination with conspiracies," which, when combined with newspapers' ability to "reproduce images, reports and testimonials again and again for an audience that did not directly experience the bombing," made the event all the more terrifying. To some extent the Cronin case had a similar impact: conspiracies, foreign allegiances, spies, corruption, and violence all fueled the dailies. Many of the papers that commented on the Cronin murder and the trial slipped into "entertainment" when it came to adding detail, comment, and analysis about the case.

A cartoon, "The Modern Editor and His Boss" by Frederick Opper,

THE MODERN EDITOR AND HIS BOSS.

Frederick Opper, "The Modern Editor and His Boss," *Puck*, Jan. 1, 1890.
The Newberry Library, Chicago. Call number A5.7634.

published in *Puck* in 1890 illustrates the pressure newspaper editors were under to publish the most sensationalized news possible. A soberly dressed, careworn editor sits at his desk while an enormous carnivalesque monstrosity of a "boss" looms over him. With cymbals clanging, drums beating, and horns tooting, the boss, whose motto is "Much Noise and Large Profits," demands lurid stories in his newspaper. Covering the giant boss's body are pages of imagined scandal sheets, including the *Daily Yell*, the *Noise*, the *Weekly Wildfire*, and the *Daily Howl*, to inspire and encourage the beleaguered editor.

>⋅┥⟩⋅○⋅⟨┝⋅┥⋖

The daily newspapers and the illustrated weeklies produced hundreds of "news illustrations" of people, places, and things associated with the Cronin case. Most of these images were not credited, but two artists who in many simple, often stylized sketches illustrated the main characters and scenes from the case were W. W. Denslow (later famous for his illustrations of L. Frank Baum's *The Wonderful Wizard of Oz*) and Charles Lederer. Both men were employed by the *Chicago Herald*, though their illustrations appeared in many other newspapers and books published about the murder.

While some Chicago papers condemned the accused in words, they did not attempt to demonize them through satirical or unflattering portraits. Instead, faithful likenesses of the victim, his friends, the accused, witnesses at the trial, the jury, and the legal counsel were regularly produced and often accompanied by detailed written descriptions. The most accurate portrait of Cronin, for instance, was based on a recent photograph (p. 20). The public still found it acceptable that newspapers took some artistic license when creating images of the murder or the discovery of the body, but was less tolerant of "imagined" portraits; therefore, published engravings of individuals had "from a daguerreotype," "from a recent photograph," or "from life" printed below them to assure the reader that they were authentic likenesses. Despite John Finerty's criticism of Chicago newspapers' attempts "to belittle [Irish Americans] in idiotic woodcuts [which] only makes the vile authors of those misrepresentations appear in their true colors as bigots and fools," most images relating to the Cronin case were informative rather than politicized.

Denslow & Kratzner, "The Discovery of the Body." *Chicago Herald;*
reproduced in Hunt, *Crime of the Century,* 131. Collection of the author.

Illustrations in newspaper articles, dime novels, illustrated week-lies, and books about the murder offered various scenarios of what had happened in the Carlson cottage. In John T. McEnnis's book *The Clan-na-Gael and the Murder of Dr. Cronin,* a well-dressed and un-suspecting Cronin is attacked from behind by two men dressed in laborer's clothes. The *National Police Gazette,* seemingly inspired by Jacques-Louis David's *The Death of Marat* and many paintings of Christ's body being taken down from the cross, shows a naked Cro-nin being lifted by two men into a trunk while other conspirators hover in the shadows. In the *Gazette*'s illustrations (and in black and white illustrations used by other publications), an extreme contrast between light and dark seemingly lends a more sensational, lurid aspect to the scene as well as heightens the division between good and evil.

Accuracy was not prioritized in all illustrations; the more imagina-tive ones often appeared in non-Chicago-based publications, whose readership was unlikely to be familiar with the locations pictured. Denslow and Kratzner's depiction of the discovery of Cronin's body, which they drew for the *Chicago Herald,* typifies a number of images published in Chicago newspapers, and is likely to be a realistic repre-sentation. The illustration shows several employees of the Board of

"The Tragedy in the Carlson Cottage." In McEnnis, *Clan-na-Gael*, 177.
Collection of the author.

Public Works examining the sewer catch basin where Cronin's body was found. It's an isolated, almost rural scene, complete with a number of small, scrubby bushes (p. 142).

The *National Police Gazette* published a very different and inaccurate version of the same scene; in it Cronin's naked body is being pulled feetfirst from a sewer in an urban environment, with several

"How Dr. Cronin Was Found," *National Police Gazette*, June 8, 1889.
Collection of the author.

townhouses visible in the background. For illustrated papers like the *Police Gazette* and most of their audience, a sensationalized approximation of reality was sufficient. The *Police Gazette*, based in New York and owned by the Irish-born journalist Richard K. Fox, was obsessed with the sensational and bizarre. As the historian Frank Luther Mott put it, the weekly "featured crime, as well as scandals, hangings and weird 'news' along with pictures of burlesque queens in tights, ring news . . . racing, cock-fighting and so on. It was not offered for sale at the more reputable newsstands, but it was to be found at practically every barroom and barber shop in America."

In the latter half of the nineteenth century, the press on both sides of the Atlantic frequently portrayed the Irish as apelike figures. Accordingly, the coverage of the Cronin murder included a number of illustrations depicting the Irishman as not fully evolved, though this treatment was restricted to the generic Irishman rather than anyone directly associated with the case. Political cartoons or "cartoons of opinion" remained the preserve of illustrated weeklies such as *Puck*, *Life*, *America*, and *Judge*. These all published satirical drawings that condemned the alleged activities of Clan na Gael. As L. Perry Curtis has noted, while many illustrations used the "simian simile,"

> the cartoonists of *Puck* and *Judge* were not blind to the existence of decent and even human qualities in many Irishmen. Like their English counterparts, these comic artists represented the soul of Ireland as a beautiful, dark-haired, and wide-eyed woman, usually labeled Erin or Hibernia. . . . Some of New York's cartoonists, in particular Gillam, occasionally drew handsome Irish faces. . . . Although some effort was made to discriminate between good and bad Irish Celts, it is fair to say that the politicized apes far outnumbered the apolitical angels.

Puck and its rival *Judge* both used lithography to produce color illustrations relating to the Cronin murder. In June *Puck* published a famous cartoon by C. J. Taylor: "The Mortar of Assimilation—And the One Element That Won't Mix." In it, a weary Lady Liberty dejectedly uses her spoon of "equal rights" to stir a bowl full of foreigners who are seeking citizenship. On the edge of the bowl, a simian Irishman brandishing a bloody knife and clasping a Clan flag dances defiantly, refusing to blend with the other immigrants determined to become Americans.

That same month, *Judge* devoted its front page to a Bernhard Gillam illustration of Cronin's murder, "Under False Colors" (p. 147). Gillam drew a masked simian Irishman standing over the body of a handsome and respectable-looking Dr. Cronin. The creature holds a dagger dripping blood and a green flag with a gold harp emblazoned with the motto "Freedom for Ireland"; a green sash across his stomach reads "Assassination League." In the background are two more corpses and a small sign indicating that the bodies are in "Phoenix Park." What is remarkable about this image is that it links the Phoenix Park murders of 1882, in which two senior figures of the British administration were murdered in Dublin, with the murder of Cronin in Chicago seven years later. In reality there was little to connect the two events, but for readers of *Judge* the illustration implied the existence of a transatlantic assassination society.

Thomas Nast, the most influential cartoonist of his generation, had been drawing anti-Catholic and anti-Irish images since

PUCK.

C. J. Taylor, "The Mortar of Assimilation—And the One Element That Won't Mix,"
Puck, June 26, 1889. The Newberry Library, Chicago. Call number A5.7634.

the 1860s for *Harper's Weekly*; at the time of Cronin's murder he was
based in Chicago working for *America*. Over the course of the investigation and trial, Nast and "Junius" produced cartoons almost every
week attacking the Clan, the Irish, and the Catholic Church. Several
referred to the trinity of "Rum, Rome, and Rebellion" and connected
all three to the Clan and the Triangle. Others, such as "No Upright

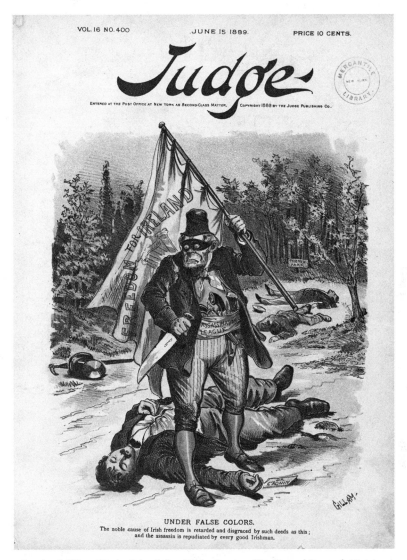

VOL. 16 NO. 400   JUNE 15 1889.   PRICE 10 CENTS.

Judge

ENTERED AT THE POST OFFICE AT NEW YORK AS SECOND-CLASS MATTER.   COPYRIGHT 1889 BY THE JUDGE PUBLISHING CO.

UNDER FALSE COLORS.
The noble cause of Irish freedom is retarded and disgraced by such deeds as this; and the assassin is repudiated by every good Irishman.

Bernhard Gillam, "Under False Colors," *Judge*, June 15, 1889. General Research Division, The New York Public Library, Astor, Lenox and Tilden Foundations.

Judge," show a man brandishing a pistol and holding a scroll relating to the Cronin case. His gun is pointed at Justice, who stands blindfolded, with her arms raised in surrender and her scales of justice and her sword tumbling to the floor. Around her, men are fleeing the courtroom. Many of *America*'s illustrations mocked the jury se-

Thomas Nast, "No Upright Judge," *America*, July 25, 1889.
The Newberry Library, Chicago. Call number A5.03.

lection process and the close connection between the Clan and the judiciary.

Many of the cartoons about the Cronin case relied on their viewers' familiarity with the case, though not necessarily with the individuals involved. A number featured imagined representations of Cronin, but only *America* attempted to present accurate portraits (and it confined these to Alexander Sullivan). In general, publications resorted to stereotypical images of the Irish, illuminating the prejudices and preoccupations of the press in a way that words sometimes struggled to do.

>─┼─◆>─○─<◆─┼─<

Although the testimonies given to the coroner's jury and at the trial itself were reported almost verbatim by most Chicago newspapers, the editorial content of the papers varied considerably. The Chicago press generally agreed that Cronin's murder was carried out by an anti-Cronin element within the Clan, but differed as to which aspects of the case to prioritize. The key bone of contention was whether Cronin's murder was the result of a conspiracy based in Camp 20, and if so, to what extent Alexander Sullivan was involved. Of all the city's newspapers, the *Tribune* functioned the most consistently as a mouthpiece for the Cronin faction of the Clan, because Cronin's friends fed their version of the feud to its reporter James Sullivan (no relation to Alexander Sullivan). Margaret Sullivan, who was an editorial writer and art critic for the *Tribune* until mid-1889, complained vigorously that the paper and others were biased against her husband. She was so incensed that she returned an advance the *Tribune* had given her, insisting that "until it makes some reparation for its brutality I will not write a line for it." She claimed that no paper was being fair to her husband, and that the best the couple could hope for was that some of the papers were "not offensive."

Margaret Sullivan was not entirely accurate. The *Citizen,* one of the few Irish American papers to comment in detail on Cronin's murder, regularly defended Alexander Sullivan's reputation. Finerty frequently used editorials to take potshots at Cronin's supporters, arguing that they weakened the Irish cause by publicly highlighting divisions. He excoriated the other Chicago papers for what he regarded as their increasingly biased and inaccurate reporting. *America*, the *Daily News*, and the *Inter Ocean* were the publications that most often felt Finerty's wrath. He rejected *America* as an "Anglo-knownothing pamphlet," and complained of the "editorial venom and impertinence" of the *Daily News* and the "bile" produced by the *Inter Ocean*. He dismissed William Penn Nixon, managing editor of the *Inter Ocean*, as anti-Irish, imagining "every Irish American who does not join in a bloodhound cry for premature conviction . . . is therefore engaged in a conspiracy . . . to shield the murderers." Devoy, on the other hand, praised Penn Nixon's paper for making itself "practically our organ" during much of 1889. W. P. Rend, a vocal supporter of Cronin, disregarded Margaret Sullivan's complaints and argued that several papers were publishing anti-Cronin articles which showed "evidence of having being 'fixed' by the parties at whose instigation Dr. Cronin was made away with." He thought "[some] reporters have been unduly influenced," and though "the general public might pass these things over, Irishmen familiar with the details of the American working of Irish concerns can perceive the ear-marks of those who have furnished something more than news."

America approached the case from an anti-Irish perspective. In an editorial in 1888, it summed up its position succinctly:

> The sentiment of Americanism which to the consternation of politicians is at present spreading over the land, is not against all immigration, good or bad, nor against foreign-born citizens. No tinge of Knownothingism dilutes or impairs its patriotism. It merely revolts at the dumping upon our shores of the off-scourings of Europe and rebels against the political foreigner from whatever land he may come.

The weekly regarded all Irish as "off-scourings of Europe." In words and images, it attacked the Irish as un-American and argued that the Irish in America could never be patriotic citizens while their primary focus remained Irish independence. Slason Thompson, its talented editor, reveled in painting the Irish as little more than savages, claiming that they had brought "to this continent the wild and lawless system of assassination that has made the civilization of Ireland a hissing and a reproach in the ears of history for the past 300 years."

The extremes of Irish republicanism were rarely praised in the pages of mainstream American newspapers, but more moderate nationalism received considerable support. Michael Davitt recalled that "the American press . . . almost without exception lent its approval to the work [of the Land League] and encouraged the propaganda of the Irish leaders for free government and free land." James Hayes Sadler, the British consul in Chicago, noted with regret that the press in the city generally took an "antagonistic tone . . . on the measures of Her Majesty's Government with regard to Ireland," though he observed a growing feeling "which reprobates American interference in the internal affairs of another country." In 1887 the *Chicago Times* published an editorial criticizing "Offensive Foreigners" who, "living under the protection of our laws and flag," made themselves "offensive either to this republic or to a friendly foreign state." Criticism of those who took on US citizenship to protect themselves from prosecution if caught breaking laws abroad increased in Chicago through 1889, with the Cronin case prompting considerable debate about the duties of American citizens. With the exception of *America*, no newspaper in Chicago specifically targeted the Irish as a community, though every paper was prepared to risk the loss of a portion of its readership who disagreed with its editorials.

>—⋅◆⋅⋅○⋅⋅◆⋅⋅—◁

For Chicagoans, the idea of using dynamite to terrorize a city was not an abstraction. The Haymarket bombing that had taken place exactly three years before Cronin's murder heavily influenced the reaction of police, politicians, and the public to the rift within the Clan. For the wider public, the dispute between Cronin and Sullivan hinged on the Clan's "Dynamite War" of the mid-1880s. At the time, this "war" attracted limited attention outside the Irish American community, but in the aftermath of the Haymarket explosion it took on a new significance.

Many regarded that violent episode as a crystallization of all the ills of urbanism—the city (any city) was a squalid, sordid place lined with vice-ridden streets and filled with poverty and lawlessness. The explosion drew out middle-class fears of the immigrant, the unions, and radical politics, whatever its purpose and nature. In the immediate aftermath of the bombing, leading Irish Americans were quick to comment. Alexander Sullivan, closely associated with the Dynamite War, distanced himself from the Haymarket violence, claiming that Irish radicals were "always lawful" and people should "have no fear of the Irish flag, or Irish arms, or of Irish muscle, unless they join the enemies of the [American] Nation or of the [American] state." Days after the explosion, Finerty wrote:

> Chicago during the current week has been a theater of great sensa-
> tions. The moral conflict between capital and labor has been taken ad-
> vantage of by a few hare-brained extremists . . . to throw dynamite
> bombshells into the ranks of the protectors of the city's peace, with
> inevitable murderous effect meets with the unstinted condemnation
> of all good citizens. . . . The ballot must decide the struggle. . . . Anarchy
> can never do it.

For a supporter of the dynamite campaign to make such a statement
seems disingenuous; yet he observed that in the United States the
ballot could be used to achieve change, whereas in Ireland, Britain
ensured there was limited political freedom, necessitating extreme
measures. In the *Irish World* Patrick Ford echoed Finerty's argument:
"For any member of a community to endeavor by violence to resist
the government and overturn the laws of that community after
the manner of the Chicago anarchists . . . I hold it to be altogether
wrong. . . . But dynamite employed in the direction given to it by Irish
patriotism was never intended for anarchical purposes. It was not
a war against society. It was *a war between two nations*." Finley Peter
Dunne (as Mr. Dooley) in many ways reflected the Irish American
perspective when he commented,

> I see . . . that anarchy's torch do be uplifted an' what th' 'ell it means,
> I dinnaw. But this here I knaw . . . , that all arnychists is inimies iv
> governmint an' all iv thim ought to be hung up be th' nick. What are
> they anny how but furiners an' what r-right have they to be holdin'
> tor-rch-light procissions in this land iv th' free an' home iv th' brave?
> Did ye iver see an American or an Irishman an arnychist? Naw, an' ye
> niver will.

Haymarket altered the public perception of Clan na Gael's activi-
ties. To casual observers, the modus operandi if not the aims of the
Clan was almost identical to that of anarchists or nihilists. Lionel
Sackville West, the British ambassador to the United States, believed
that "the conviction of the Anarchists . . . is a severe blow to the Ultra-
Irish faction in America." Although the Dynamite War had been sus-

pended in 1885, the Clan remained committed to achieving Irish freedom by using violence, and the British government remained alert to the prospect of attacks, fearing the importation from the United States of an explosive known as "Rack-Rocket," a version of which had been used extensively during blasting at Hell Gate in New York in 1885. In 1887 additional security was placed on British ports, as the authorities believed that the major threat to Britain came from the Irish in America. At the same time the Clan, particularly in Chicago, was desperate to distance itself from the use of dynamite. When William Fitzpatrick, a firm supporter of the Dynamite War, carried a bundle of fliers advocating the use of dynamite into a nationalist meeting in Chicago, he was arrested. As he was being hauled out he yelled, "Won't England rejoice when it reaches that country that an Irishman was locked up in Chicago for preaching dynamite."

Clan rhetoric distancing the movement from the anarchists failed to affect public opinion. *Life* published a cartoon on July 4, 1889, that both personified and clearly linked Anarchy, the Italian Vendetta (or feud), and Clan na Gael (p. 154). In the cartoon three sticks of dynamite are placed carefully around a triangle (clearly meant to represent Sullivan), and the caption reads, "Wouldn't it be a glorious fourth indeed if we could only 'fire' the above triangle of foreign manufacture." The front cover of *Judge* for July 6 carried a similar message (p. 155). In an illustration titled "Fooling with Fireworks," a young boy is seated on a barrel of dynamite. In one hand he holds several firework rockets, in the other a bunch of dynamite sticks. In his hair are three feathers representing "Socialism," "Anarchy," and "Clan na Gael." The image echoed a famous *Punch* cartoon of 1867, "Fenian Guy Fawkes," and Thomas Nast's cartoon "The Usual Irish Way of Doing Things," which was published in *Harper's Weekly* in 1871.

The anarchists were largely without influence, but the same could not be said of the Irish. If Cronin could be killed on the order of Alexander Sullivan, then what else might be possible? Much of the outrage over Cronin's murder was not personal. It was a determination to show that justice would be served despite the tentacles of the Irish; law and order would prevail. An editorial in *America* articulated one of the more extreme views:

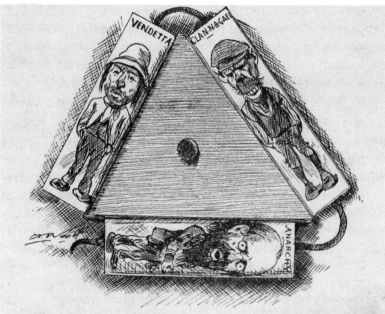

WOULDN'T IT BE A GLORIOUS FOURTH INDEED IF WE COULD
ONLY "FIRE" THE ABOVE TRIANGLE OF FOREIGN MANUFACTURE.

"Glorious Fourth," *Life*, July 4, 1889. The Newberry Library, Chicago. Call number A5.51.

[Chicago Justice] has now to grapple with an organization of assassination more direful, more deadly, and more desperate than anything
dreamed of in the fanatical minds of Herr Most, August Spies and
their associates. The Anarchists were a pestilential brood flung upon
this community from the rushing tide of European immigration. They
were without wealth, without political power, without social connections. . . . But in the conspiracy responsible for Dr. Cronin's murder,
American justice and American patriotism grapples with an entirely
different enemy. Entrenched in every community where an exile or
fugitive from Irish misery or English justice has found a home in this
beneficent land, the Clan na Gael and its affiliating societies have their
devoted adherents and apologists. The ramifications of these Irish
societies permeate our whole political system. They reach up to the
Presidential chair and down to the janitorship of the Chicago City
Hall.

Hamilton, "Fooling with Fireworks," *Judge*, July 6, 1889. General Research Division, The New York Public Library, Astor, Lenox and Tilden Foundations.

In 1889 the *New York Times* compared the anarchists to the Clan when it observed, "The Anarchists were almost friendless, at least they were without friends whose assistance could be of any value to them. They had no social influence nor any political 'pull' and their crime was detested and the effects of it feared by everyone not of their own number." The same could not be said of the Irish, whose influence was felt in the corridors of power be they in police stations, city halls, or courthouses.

The Cronin case was a cultural—as well as a social and political— sensation across Chicago. The city newspapers developed and fed a demand for information that they could not always meet; dime museums incorporated paraphernalia associated with the murder into their collections; the Carlson cottage became a tourist attraction; and thousands attended protest meetings and concerts to campaign for the suppression of secret societies.

The Carlsons were quick to capitalize on the infamy surrounding their cottage. On May 24, the day the cottage was identified as the murder site, a real-estate agent, W. J. Lukens, promised the couple that he could rent it out for up to $100 per month. Given that they had received $12 a month from Williams, they readily agreed. However, Captain E. H. Wing of the Lake View police insisted that the cottage was evidence, and agreed to pay the Carlsons $12 a month while the investigation continued. By early June the police no longer required the cottage, and had returned possession of it to the Carlsons. Almost immediately, a dime museum offered them $8,100 for the property so it could be dismantled and rebuilt as an exhibit. The Carlsons rejected the offer, and on June 14 the cottage was opened to the public. It rapidly became "the Mecca of the sensation-seeker" as thousands paid a dime to visit. For an additional dime, visitors could take with them a souvenir of a chip of wood from the floor (by June 23, 1889, over half a cord of wood had been removed; few were aware that the floor was a replica, as the police had taken away the original).

The success of the Carlson cottage attraction did not go unnoticed by Lake View officials. Keen to line their pockets in the weeks before the annexation vote that might render them unemployed, they informed the Carlsons of a permit costing $25 for "maintaining a place of public entertainment." Chicago's police chief, George W. Hubbard, proclaimed the permit requirement "stupid village bureaucracy," while city mayor Cregier thought "the Carlsons have a right to enjoy what little recompense they can obtain for their great misfortune." As a result of public outrage, the permit was revoked. A guest register taken on Sunday, June 17, listed visitors from Texas, Ohio, Washington, DC, Oregon, and England, and hundreds from Illinois. Anxious not to miss an opportunity to make money, the Carlsons made it clear that they would sell the cottage when the flow of visitors ceased. The *Tribune* believed that "it might offer a fine field for the experiments of the Psychical Research Society if there be a member of that body strong-nerved enough to try the experiment of sleeping in that pleasant front room."

Dime museums provided an opportunity for the public to get close to the Cronin murder. They were popular throughout the nineteenth century, but were at their zenith between 1880 and 1900. For a dime, visitors entered a world of dioramas, taxidermy, freaks, wax figures, theater, and chambers of horror, where they were educated, entertained, amused, and terrified. In a city such as Chicago, full of immigrants, the dime museum performed a function that the newspapers could not. Fluency in English, or indeed literacy, was not a prerequisite, and for a proportion of the visitors the museum provided images of the story they had previously only heard about. The tableaux on display at the dime museums "functioned like popular newspapers of a sort: celebrities, well-known actors, famous musicians, and local murderers—the headliners of their day—were presented as important stories." The Stanhope and Epstean Dime Museum had grandiose ideas about its objective:

> to open a Temple of Art, Instruction, Music and Drama, combined with a first-class Museum, at a price of admission which should make it accessible alike to the poor and middle classes as well as to the wealthy. . . . Within the walls of their monster Museum, every clime beneath the sun is represented, either by animal, bird, insect, work of art or freak of nature.

Both the Stanhope and Epstean Dime Museum and the Eden Musée had exhibits on display by Sunday, June 2.

At the Stanhope and Epstean, amid the "specimens of taxidermy . . . the invisible lady . . . the left foot of a human female (Irish)" and the representations of, among others, Bismarck, Cleopatra, and Alexander II, was Dr. Patrick Henry Cronin. His murder dominated the "Chamber of Horrors," where the curious could see a "magnificent life-size figure of the late Dr. Cronin" alongside Dinan's white horse and buggy that had transported Cronin to the Carlson cottage. At the Eden Musée, visitors saw a "realistic representation of the finding of the body in the catch basin," wax reproductions of several of the accused, "a trunk, blood-stained as the original," and a portrait of Cronin. The Eden Musée catalog gave few details, since "the particulars of this foul murder are too well known to need special mention," though it took pains to point out that the trunk which formed part of the tableaux was a "perfect facsimile of the one found by the police." Wax reproductions of the murdered and the accused were a considerable financial investment in the case, as such figures could cost up to $250 each. Most of the wax reproductions at Chicago's Eden Musée were manufactured in New York under the supervision of Constant Thys, the museum's chief wax artist.

In addition to the newspaper reports, the wax figures, and the visits to the Carlson cottage, those interested in the Cronin murder could delve into fictional accounts in both prose and poetry. In the summer of 1889, months before the murder trial proper began, two dime novels about the case were published. *Who Killed Doctor Cronin?* by Old Cap Lee was produced as part of the New York Detective Library series, and *Who Murdered Dr. Cronin?* by Old Cap Collier was the latest addition to the Old Cap Collier Library. The books offered barely fictionalized accounts. In both, a plucky pair of detectives (in one a father and son, in the other an uncle and nephew) tracked down Cronin's murderers and along the way found themselves donning disguises, narrowly escaping death, and being rescued by mysterious women before ultimately exposing the true criminals. Each novel relied heavily on newspaper accounts, and didn't shy from using the real names of people involved, such as Patrick O'Sullivan and Henri Le Caron. It's likely that both novels had been written by journalists covering the murder investigation. Both reproduced many illustrations that that had been previously published in the newspapers, though both used original drawings for their cover. The front page of *Who Killed Dr. Cronin?* shows a naked Cronin being dumped into the

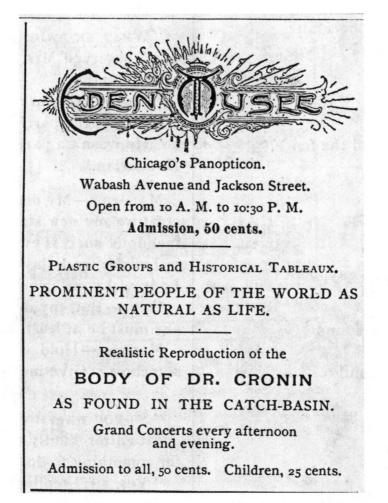

Advertisement for the Eden Musée, 1889. Collection of the author.

sewer by two sinister-looking men, while the compound image on the cover of *Who Murdered Dr. Cronin?* shows the heroes in a series of dramatic and violent situations as they pursue Cronin's murderers.

Cronin was memorialized in a number of poems, at least five of which were published in 1889. "The Murder of Dr. Cronin," an anonymous work, was sold at the Cronin Memorial Meeting held on June 28 at the Central Music Hall to raise money for the prosecution. "Cronin" was the title of two poems—one by Robert H. Vickers, the other

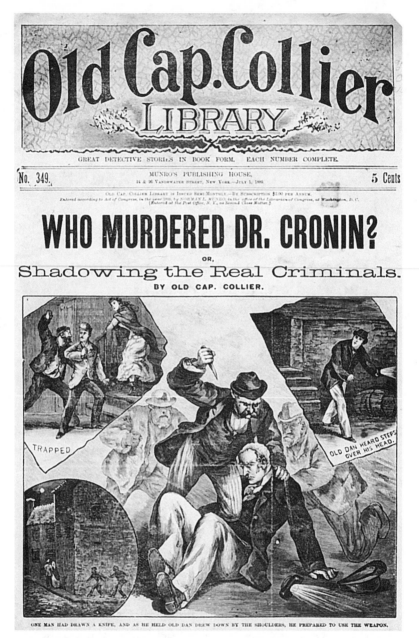

Front cover of *Who Murdered Dr Cronin?* (Munro's Publishing House, July 1889), detail. Chicago History Museum, ICHi-QF38UD011.

by James Newton Matthews. Vickers's poem decried Cronin's murder over six stanzas that were divided into three sections: "Physician," "Corpse," "Martyr?" Matthews, a doctor and friend of Cronin from their student days, bemoaned the loss of Cronin as a "Victim of the bold / Unblushing villainy that waits, / Red-handed, at old Erin's gates / And barter Irish blood for gold." The panegyrics in praise of Cronin called for justice for the dead man, but at least one poem— "Martin, Pat and Dan"—was written in support of those accused of Cronin's murder. This poem blamed the London *Times* for the predicament in which Martin, Pat, and Dan found themselves, because the newspaper had apparently conspired to wreak havoc in the Chicago Clan to avenge the fact that Father Dorney had brought copies of letters to the Parnell Commission. These letters helped prove that Richard Pigott had forged the letters purportedly written by Parnell which approved the Phoenix Park murders, a revelation that ultimately secured Parnell's victory:

> The London *Times* assumed the task of pulling Parnell down
> The downfall of the patriot would elevate the Crown;
> But the Irish of Chicago played havoc with the plan,
> And that's what brought misfortune to Martin, Pat and Dan.

Somehow, none of the poems entered Irish nationalism's pantheon of ballads and poems. There was one further poem that appears to refer, albeit obliquely, to Cronin's murder. In late 1889 Rudyard Kipling wrote "Cleared," an attack on Parnell's exoneration at the Parnell Commission. He intended it for the London *Times*, but the paper, not wishing to be reminded of its failure at the commission, rejected it. But in March 1890 it appeared in the *Scots Observer* in Edinburgh. Kipling had spent part of the summer of 1889 in Chicago, and was doubtless aware of the Clan split, Cronin's murder, and the trial; sections of the poem appear to reference these events. Kipling criticizes the Parnellites for accepting dollars from the "blood-dyed Clan na Gael" and scorns those that "that 'lost' the League accounts." In what can be read as an attack on Le Caron's testimony and the rumors claiming Cronin was a spy, Kipling wrote:

Their sin it was that fed the fire—small blame to them that heard
The "bhoys" get drunk on rhetoric, and madden at a word
They knew whom they were talking at, if they were Irish too,
The gentlemen that lied in Court, they knew, and well they knew . . .
. . . If words are words, or death is death, or powder sends the ball,
You spoke the words that sped the shot—the curse be on you all.

Though they mocked dime museums and the Carlson cottage attraction as the "Mecca of the sensation-seeker," journalists reveled in their own macabre interest in violent crime. The Whitechapel Club, established by Finley Peter Dunne and Charlie Seymour of the *Chicago Herald* in the summer of 1889, was inspired by the Cronin murder and the Jack the Ripper murders in London. The club rules were based on the rules of Clan na Gael, complete with code words, secret gestures, and numbers rather than names for members. The theme of the club was sensational crime, and the club rooms were decorated with macabre memorabilia from hangings, murders, and other violent crimes. The journalists effectively created their own personal, private dime museum: coffins served as tables and skulls as lampshades, while the walls were covered with the paraphernalia of crime and justice—chief among these were handcuffs used by Martin Burke, shards of wood taken from the Carlson cottage, and bloodstained cotton from the trunk that held Cronin's body.

Nonetheless, newspaper reporting was moving into an era of modernization. Journalism was becoming a profession: college courses were being developed for it, and within a few years, training a cub reporter simply by having him tail an old hack would no longer be acceptable. But in 1889 it was still deemed ethically sound for journalists to collect memorabilia (or evidence) from cases they covered—and to tamper with the scene of a crime and dismiss it as a joke.

CHAPTER NINE

"A THEATER OF GREAT SENSATIONS"

O n August 26 the Cronin murder trial began under the watchful eye of Judge Samuel P. McConnell. However, no evidence would be heard for almost two months as lawyers for both the prosecution and the defense squabbled daily over the selection of a jury. Between August 30 and October 22, 1,115 men were interviewed as potential jurors—at the time the longest jury selection process in American judicial history. As the weeks passed, the London *Times* mused that the defendants were "doomed," for "if they do not die by verdict of jury they are in a fair way of dying of old age before a jury is chosen." Over nine hundred prospective jurors were excused by the court "for cause" (where they showed a clear bias or other specified reason), while the remainder were removed by peremptory challenges (where a potential juror could be dismissed without cause) from either the defense or the prosecution lawyers.

The process proved as controversial as it was lengthy. Potential jurors were asked questions to ascertain whether they had prejudices against Catholics or Irishmen, and whether they had already formed an opinion about the case. The defense argued, quite plausibly, that thanks to the intense press coverage, there were few Chicagoans not already intimately acquainted with the case. Moreover, since 1874, Illinois accepted that "it shall not be a cause of challenge that a juror has read in the newspapers an account of the commission of a crime with which the prisoner is charged, if such juror shall state, on oath, that he believes he can render an impartial verdict, according to the law and the evidence." The *Tribune* took a dim view of the process. In its cartoon "The Devolution of a Jury," potential jurors appear more and more apelike as supposedly intelligent men are overlooked in favor of the pliable candidates.

The newspapers rarely alluded to the fact that it was their comprehensive coverage of the case that made it virtually impossible to find twelve men who were not already convinced of the guilt of those accused of Cronin's murder. In one article, "How Newspaper Reports Are to Be Read," the *Tribune* defended the press from any charge that newspaper reports might prejudice the trial. The paper was at pains to point out that as evidence changed, the papers too changed their opinions: "Intelligent men read the newspaper accounts of the Cronin case merely as the best information then at hand, and any opinions formed were subject to any modifications or change which further evidence might prove necessary." With staggering audacity, the paper concluded that despite the enormous amount of press coverage, the defendants would get an impartial trial.

William S. Forrest and the rest of the defense team were convinced that both Irish Americans and Catholics were being deliberately filtered out by those selecting the jury pool. The defense certainly believed that their chance of securing acquittals would be strengthened with some Irish on the jury, while the prosecution and the police agreed that anyone with an Irish or a Catholic connection was more predisposed to find the men not guilty, and were more open to intimidation and bribery. In an attempt to ensure a representative jury, Forrest approached Judge McConnell and proposed a series of ten questions to test the prejudices of potential jurors. McConnell dismissed half of Forrest's list but approved these five:

1. Have you formed an opinion as to whether or not the alleged murder of Dr. Cronin was in pursuance of the action or finding of a secret committee appointed by Camp 20 of the so-called Clan na Gael society, or its officers, or any of them, to try Dr. Cronin for the supposed offense?
2. Have you formed an opinion as to whether or not Dr. Cronin was taken to the Carlson Cottage by the horse and buggy engaged by Daniel Coughlin from Dinan, the liveryman?
3. Have you formed an opinion as to whether or not Martin Burke, one of the defendants, was a tenant of the Carlson Cottage?
4. Have you formed an opinion as to whether or not Dr. Cronin was killed in pursuance of a conspiracy?
5. Have you formed an opinion as to whether or not any of these defendants was concerned in said conspiracy, or was a member of said conspiracy?

In the absence of eyewitnesses, proving a conspiracy rather than establishing precisely who was responsible for the fatal assault on Cronin was crucial to the prosecution. In some ways this mirrored the Haymarket trial, which was concerned with the conspiracy to throw the bomb rather than the identity of the bomb thrower. While jury selection was ongoing, the defense counsel attempted to split up the case and have O'Sullivan tried separately from Beggs, Burke, and Coughlin. If granted, it was expected that Coughlin and Burke would petition for separate trials; if this was allowed, then the conspiracy element of the prosecution's case would disappear, and acquittals would be very likely.

The People of the State of Illinois were represented by a phalanx of attorneys led by State's Attorney Joel Longnecker. The rest of prosecution team was formed by Luther Laflin Mills, former state's attorney; William J. Hynes (who had defended Sullivan in the Hanford case); George C. Ingham, who had been part of the prosecution team at the Haymarket trial; and Kickham Scanlan, nephew of Cronin's friend John Scanlan. A contemporary publication, *Bench and Bar of Chicago*, regarded some of the prosecutors very highly: Ingham "excels at cross-examination . . . at once fluent, forcible, entertaining and convincing," and Hynes was "able and brilliant."

At the outset of the trial, even before the selection of jurors began, there was considerable grumbling about the prosecution lawyers. The defense counsel objected to Hynes, Laflin Mills, and Ingham, because their fees were being paid by the Cronin Committee, which meant they "received either money or the promise of money from . . . parties [that] . . . are solely activated by a desire to secure the conviction of the defendants." *America* articulated another perspective. The journal felt that there should have been no need for privately paid attorneys, for the state ought to have provided adequate representation:

> This county is rich enough to bear the expense of the prosecution and conviction of all the conspirators in this villainous case. But it should be willing to bankrupt itself before acknowledging that its means were inadequate to cope with the resources and villainies of the Clan na Gael.

Despite the defense team's objections, Hynes, Laflin Mills, and Ingham remained part of the prosecution team.

>—⊢◀▸•—○—•◂▸⊢—◃

It came as little surprise when jury selection was halted because of an alleged attempt to bribe jurors—bribery was rife in the Illinois judicial system. On October 11, Mark Salamon, a court bailiff, was accused of trying to bribe George Tschappatt, a potential juror, to find the defendants "not-guilty." Within a day six men, including Salamon, another bailiff, and several men with Clan connections, were charged with conspiracy to interfere with the administration of justice—in essence jury bribing. The newspapers latched on to this story, emphasizing that one of the men charged was a clerk in the office of A. S. Trude (Sullivan's lawyer), and that Sullivan's stenographer had been arrested (though not charged). Though Sullivan himself was not on trial, this was far from the first time that his name had been mentioned in connection with jury bribing, and it would not be the last.

For the papers, this development breathed new life into the murder case, which had stagnated somewhat while the jury selection dragged on. *America* marked the occasion of the attempted jury bribery charges with a series of illustrations by Thomas Nast and "Junius," along with several strongly worded editorials:

> Just now the authorities of Cook County hardly know whom to trust. If they turn to the police force they find its ranks polluted with the poisonous virus of the Clan na Gael. One half of the force owes its employment to the recommendation of the politicians who have been as wax in the hands of this desperate society. The disclosures of this week show that the tentacles of the Clan na Gael conspiracy reach into the Sheriff's office and have fastened their slimy folds about the officers of the court itself.

"The State of Illinois vs. the Clan-na-Bribe" by "Junius" showed Justice shackled to a rock and guarded by a dragon, "Jury Bribery." Poised at the dragon's head with his sword of "Popular Vengeance" raised stands the heroic figure of "Illinois." It appears at first glance that Illinois, aided by Popular Vengeance, will be successful, though the

Junius, "The State of Illinois vs. the Clan-na-Bribe," *America*, Oct. 17, 1889.
Collection of the author.

caption underneath suggests that "Clan-na-Bribe" will ultimately triumph: "There is a popular superstition that the strong arm of the law is powerful to destroy all the iniquitous monsters that may arise. In truth, the real situation isn't half so cheerful as depicted above."

>-!-<>-•-O-•-<>-!-<

On October 22 a jury of twelve men was finally sworn in. Despite Forrest's efforts to secure Irish American jurors, the jury was not representative of the population of Chicago. Juries generally fell far short of that ideal, but this panel wasn't even representative of the jury pool. Of the twelve men, there were no Catholics, nor any with an Irish surname. All had been born in the United States—ten of them of American parents, while one had parents from England and another had a Scottish mother. Ten were Protestant, while the other two were of no religion. The men were between twenty-nine and fifty-eight years old, and all but two were married. A jury representative of those eligible for jury service would have been four Catholics, two Protestants, and six of no religious affiliation. Such was its perceived bias against the defendants that there was much discussion of this at the time, and the defense argued that the jury resulted from deliberate collusion between the prosecution and the state authorities.

On the morning of October 23, the trial began in the Chicago Criminal Court. Five thousand people scrambled to get into a public gallery that could accommodate two hundred. The newspapers went to considerable expense to ensure that the public appetite for news about the Cronin trial was satisfied, and alongside their editorials many also published extensive transcripts. The *Inter Ocean* printed 461 columns of stenographic reports, while the *Tribune* published 210, the *Chicago Times* 279, and the *Journal* 140. Detailed descriptions of how the courtroom was arranged were provided as well: the prisoners were seated in a row of five armchairs, with bailiffs seated behind them; their lawyers sat around a table in front. To the right of the prisoners was a long table, which extended toward the judge's rostrum. Around that were gathered a number of journalists. The jury sat to the left of the prisoners, and the state's attorney at a table in front of the jury.

According to the *Tribune*, the courthouse on the north side of the Chicago River was an "expensive ruin which was constructed in the hey-day of Cook County local politics, when taxpayers existed for the benefit of politicians." It was connected to the county jail by a bridge known locally as the "Bridge of Sighs." The London *Times* was shocked by the informality with which the prisoners sauntered across the bridge . . . accompanied by bailiffs, all chatting together. . . . Each prisoner is faultlessly dressed in a new suit of clothing with immaculate collar and cuffs so that in attire they have a decided advantage over the shabbier clothes of their custodians; and in fact, they look more as if they were going to a holiday gathering than a trial for their lives.

The newspapers were anxious to maintain momentum with the Cronin case. Every rumor, every scrap of related information was published, sometimes embellished, occasionally created. Papers tried to give a sense of the atmosphere in court; occasionally this spilled over into a mawkish sentimentality, such as when the *Tribune* reported on October 16 that

through the open windows of the courtroom the notes of a cornet could be heard in the distance. As the sound floated in on the darkening twilight the strains of familiar Irish melodies could be distinguished. Martin Burke . . . appeared to be the first to recognize the airs of his native land. The distant notes momentarily dispelled the hard look that his face habitually wears, and it was evident that for the moment his memory went back to the old country. The deep scowl on Iceman O'Sullivan's face gave place to a look of sadness as he likewise mentally followed the notes of the cornet with the cords of "The Minstrel Boy" and "The harp that once through Tara's halls." John F. Beggs's pale blue eyes became almost tearful as he gazed wistfully through the window, and Dan Coughlin's head drooped lower and lower.

The London *Times* marveled at the attention and detail lavished on the murder trial by Chicago papers:

[They] devote pages to reporting the proceedings in elaborate detail, with every adjunct and theory copiously treated. Some of them illustrate their reports with pictures, usually laughable cartoons and caricatures, showing the various aspects of jurymen and lawyers and the attitudes of the prisoners. These pictures are at times quite amusing and are sketched in the court.

Soon after the jury bribing incident faded from the front pages, a story published in the *Daily News* suggested that a plot was being hatched to rescue Burke and Coughlin. The paper reported that one of their journalists had seen suspicious-looking strangers signaling to Coughlin while another man in the public gallery was busy drawing plans of the courtroom. The reporter later shadowed two men to a train station, where they inquired about tickets to Vancouver before returning to the court; there they made contact with Burke. The *Daily News* claimed that the Clan had decided that both men had to be "saved at all hazards in order to prevent their confessing and implicating men whose necks are thought to be worth much more to the Clan." But there was no evidence to support this rescue plan, and it may well have been hatched in the imaginations of the *Daily News* staff.

Desperate to satisfy demand, newspapers competed to provide details on every aspect of the lives of the accused and the jury. They provided lengthy descriptions of the men in the dock. Even the London *Times*, which had mocked the Chicago papers for their obsessive attention, joined in. The paper thought Beggs looked "like a man of great determination and slight scruple" whose "face betrays evidence of dissipation." The *Chicago Times* described O'Sullivan as having "the eye of the eagle and the glare of the serpent," while Coughlin was "physically a splendid specimen of a man, tall and straight as an arrow . . . sinewy and strong as an ox." It dismissed Kunze as "one of those small men, who think it is manly to smoke cigarettes and be tough." The *Tribune* considered Burke a "gaunt, strong figure, typical of the County Mayo, roughly cut animal face," with "eyes that would kill with their glittering darkness."

The jurors were also subject to intense scrutiny. For the duration of the trial, they resided at the Commercial Hotel at the corner of Lake and Dearborn Streets. The hotel was "well managed and respectable," and intended "for the accommodation of country merchants and unpretentious visitors." The papers reported that the jurors' evenings were occupied playing cribbage and whist, while some read the Bible and others books by Charles Dickens, H. Rider Haggard, and Wilkie Collins. Newspapers were supplied, but not before all information relating to the trial had been clipped out. Even the food eaten by the jurors was of interest, with the *Tribune* reporting on one breakfast which included "eggs in half-dozen different styles, ham, beefsteak, bacon, potatoes, bread and butter, buckwheat cakes and coffee" and a lunch of "mock turtle soup, baked whitefish, boiled mutton, corned beef and cabbage, roast spring chicken, sweetbreads, macaroni, pineapple fritters, mashed potatoes, squash, string beans, plum pudding, mince and apple pie, fruit cake and coffee." Clearly there was no likelihood of any juror going hungry.

>—+—+>—+O—+<>—+—<

There is no doubt that all the participants in the trial were aware of the attention focused upon them. While the guilt or innocence of the accused in the Cronin case was the primary focus, there were secondary debates (often played out in the press) relating to issues of religion, nationalism, patriotism, and the legal system. State's Attorney Joel Longnecker finally opened the prosecution's case on October 23, and over the next seven weeks 190 witnesses took the stand. Longnecker's opening speech outlined the conspiracy to murder Cronin, beginning with Coughlin's denunciation of Cronin as a spy, the meetings held at Camp 20, and Cronin's long-standing dispute with the Triangle. He assured the jurors that the State of Illinois had sufficient evidence

> to prove it a murder as the result of a conspiracy. . . . That same hidden hand that worked and moved this conspiracy, that concocted this scheme, was . . . working in this community to lead people to believe that Dr. Cronin was still alive. . . . Not content with having beat out his life, not content with having him laid to rest in a sewer, the same conspirators that brought it about were again at work for the purpose of blasting the character and reputation of the man they had murdered.

It was vital that the prosecution prove the conspiracy charge, and on several occasions during the trial the lawyers for the People took pains to ensure that the charge was made crystal clear to the jury. George Ingham, for the prosecution, offered a clear and concise summary of the law:

The law of this state on the subject of conspiracy is that where men conspire to do an illegal act, and any one of the conspirators in pursuance of the object of the conspiracy does an illegal act, all are equally guilty. So under that law, if these defendants conspired together, either alone . . . or with others . . . , and on the night of the 4th of May some one or more of these conspirators engages in that fatal act, then all are guilty no matter whether one of them was at home in his bed asleep. . . . If they had assisted, aided, advised and encouraged that murder they are as actually guilty under the law as the man who . . . struck the fatal blow.

Despite the fact that Alexander Sullivan was neither a witness nor a defendant at the trial, he was regularly referred to by both prosecution and defense, and newspapers continually linked him to the murder, prompting an exasperated Margaret Sullivan to exclaim, "We have a fine assortment of stupids writing now for the Chicago press." She was also outraged that

Longnecker, after failing to find any evidence upon which to indict Mr. Sullivan, had the brutality and cowardice to drag him into his opening speech. Of course not being in the indictment Mr. Sullivan cannot appear in court, either in person or by counsel. On the other hand the lawyers defending these men will be compelled in justice to them to assail him, also; certainly to repudiate him and claim that his sins are not to be opened on the head of their clients. Thus he will be attacked by both counsel. And under the law he cannot defend himself against the assaults of either.

During the trial, *America* published two cartoons by "Junius" that clearly identified Sullivan as key to the conspiracy. In "The Great Clan-na-Gael Triangle Puzzle (?)," a large drawing of Sullivan's head in profile is placed in the center of a triangle (p. 173). Weaving around his head are a number of simian Irishmen brandishing flags and bloody daggers. One of the flags reads "Dynamite Plot." A second illustration, "Not So Welcome a Visitor as Edward Spelman," shows Sullivan sitting in an armchair. The ghost of Justice stands behind him with one hand on his shoulder, the other wielding a

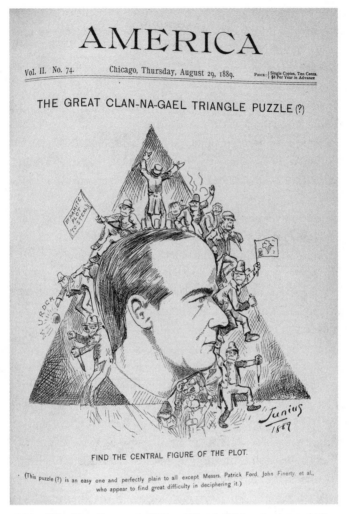

AMERICA

Vol. II. No. 74.   Chicago, Thursday, August 29, 1889.   Price: { Single Copies, Ten Cents. $3 Per Year in Advance }

THE GREAT CLAN-NA-GAEL TRIANGLE PUZZLE (?)

FIND THE CENTRAL FIGURE OF THE PLOT.

* (This puzzle (?) is an easy one and perfectly plain to all except Messrs. Patrick Ford, John Finerty, et al., who appear to find great difficulty in deciphering it.)

Junius, "The Great Clan-na-Gael Triangle Puzzle(?)," *America*, Aug. 29, 1889.
The Newberry Library, Chicago. Call number A5.03.

sword above his head. Spelman's visit to Chicago had resulted in the destruction of all papers relating to Camp 20; Justice might not be so helpful a visitor.

A wide range of witnesses provided testimony, including policemen, journalists, members of Camp 20, friends of Cronin, residents of Lake View, and medical experts. The state witnesses can be placed in seven categories:

1. Witnesses, including Captain Francisco Villiers of the Lake View Police, who provided information about the discovery and identification of Cronin's body.
2. Medical experts, including Drs. Egbert and Moore, who testified about the cause of death.
3. Witnesses, including Pat Dinan, who provided evidence that linked O'Sullivan and Burke to Cronin's murder.
4. Members of Camp 20, including Andy Foy and Tom F. O'Connor, who testified about the content of the meetings held by the camp in February.
5. Witnesses, including Theo Conklin and Frank Scanlan, who testified that Cronin believed his life was in danger.
6. Witnesses, including Hakon Mortenson and Pauline Hoertel, who provided evidence relating to the Clark Street flat and the Carlson cottage.
7. Witnesses who testified to the links between the defendants.

The prosecution case focused primarily on the roles played by Beggs, O'Sullivan, and Coughlin. Little attention was paid to Kunze, because the prosecutors believed he had been manipulated by Coughlin and should not be "ranked with the others in terms of guilt."

The prosecution devoted considerable time to quizzing witnesses about two meetings that were held in Camp 20 during February 1889. They argued that a meeting on February 8 marked the beginning of the conspiracy to murder Cronin. According to the prosecution, this meeting, held three days after Le Caron began his dramatic testimony at the Parnell Commission, resulted in the establishment of a secret committee to investigate reports of spies in the Chicago Clan. Andy Foy, a member of Camp 20, admitted that he may have been agitated when he called for the expulsion of all spies at the camp meeting, though he denied mentioning Cronin by name. In his testimony, Tom F. O'Connor, recording secretary for Camp 20 and an "intimate and devoted friend" of Cronin, recalled that there was much criticism of Cronin's continuing attacks on Sullivan and the Triangle, particularly since the Trial Committee of 1888 had found the Triangle largely "not guilty." Following the meeting, John Beggs wrote to the district officer, Spelman, asking him to investigate Cronin's activities. In lines that would become key to his defense, Beggs claimed that he was inclined to take no action against Cronin and "would let it pass if I could. Personally I think it better not to notice such things, but I am only one . . . a day of punishment will come. I am very much discouraged at the present outlook but hope no trouble will result." Spelman refused to investigate Cronin, insisting that he had no authority to do so; two days later the Clark Street flat was rented.

The prosecution contended that as Spelman would not act, members of Camp 20 had taken matters into their own hands, and a secret committee which included Coughlin, Burke, Beggs, and O'Sullivan began to make plans to murder Cronin. To ensure support, it was necessary that many believed Cronin to be a spy; at a meeting of Camp 20 on February 22, he was heavily criticized, prompting Cronin's friend (and member of Camp 20) Patrick McGarry to remark to the Camp that it was "very well to talk of unity . . . but that there could not be unity while the members of this organization would meet in back alleys and dark corners to vilify and abuse a man that had the courage to stand out and attack the treachery and robbery of the Triangle." As it had been at the coroner's jury, McGarry's testimony was delivered with "all the power of a cyclone. . . . The audience was electrified, the prisoners winced and squirmed and even their counsel were chilled."

Several witness testified that Cronin believed his life to be in danger. Others claimed they had been asked to kill or injure the doctor. John Garrity, a teamster, testified that two years before Cronin's murder, he had been approached by Coughlin to "do up" Cronin, while Detective Robert Bruce said Alderman John McCormack (a Clan member) had given him $100 with the promise of $500 more if he would "take care" of Cronin. However, the defense convincingly argued that most of those who alleged they had been asked to assault Cronin were unreliable witnesses with grudges against Coughlin.

Other witnesses, including Pauline Hoertel, a German woman who gave her evidence through a translator, testified to suspicious activity at the Carlson cottage on the night of May 4. Mrs. Hoertel recalled that she saw a man leap from a horse and buggy and enter the cottage. As soon as the door slammed shut behind him, she heard cries of "Oh God, Oh Jesus," followed by the sound of someone falling. William Mertes also claimed to have seen a man entering the Carlson cottage that evening. However, cross-examination of both witnesses highlighted inaccuracies in their recollections regarding the men they saw, and the time they saw them. This was a setback for the prosecution but not hugely damaging, as their focus was on proving the conspiracy to murder, rather than who carried out the murder.

Medical evidence was provided by a series of physicians. The most memorable was Dr. James Egbert, assistant to the Cook County physician, who arrived at court carrying the contents of Cronin's stomach in a jar filled with alcohol. In his testimony he said that the contents (maize, cabbage, and carrots) indicated that Cronin had been killed within three hours of eating. He thought that loss of blood rather than any single wound had caused death. Egbert's view was disputed by Dr. Charles Perkins, who had assisted at the autopsy and argued that any one of several blows to the head could have killed Cronin. The testimony of Dr. D. G. Moore, who was also present at the autopsy (and a pallbearer at Cronin's funeral), noted that the cause of death was in itself unremarkable; this view proved problematic when Moore admitted he had read Egbert's testimony in the previous day's newspapers. The defense wanted Moore's evidence struck from the record. McConnell ruled against the defense, observing that "if it were possible for me to ask proprietors of newspapers not to publish these accounts I should unquestionably do that, but of course no such request would be respected in this day of wide newspaper circulation and verbatim reports." In a prescient comment, the *Tribune* noted, "Of course when the case is appealed to the Supreme Court, as it will be if there is a conviction, the lawyers for the defense will make this one of their chief 'errors.'"

Blood and hair samples were produced as evidence. Walter Haines, professor of chemistry at Rush Medical College, testified that he had conducted tests on a chip of wood with a reddish stain, a piece of cotton similarly marked, and stained paper, all from the inside of the trunk that had been discovered in a Lake View ditch on May 5. He declared himself absolutely certain that these stains had been caused by blood. However, chemical tests could not tell if the blood was animal or human. Professor Tolman, a microscopist, examined similar specimens, and while he admitted that he could not swear that it was human blood, he believed it was. For the defense, Professor Marshall D. Ewell of Northwestern University stated that there was no value in examining bloodstains, and no way to prove they were human blood. Ewell was correct: despite the fact that in 1887 Sherlock Holmes had devised a test to distinguish human from animal blood, in real life such a test would not be developed until 1891.

Dr. John F. Williams testified that he had been Patrick O'Sullivan's physician for several years. His office was based a mile and a half from the iceman's home, and he estimated that there were at least a dozen doctors whose practices were located within a mile of O'Sullivan's address—circumstances which made O'Sullivan's arrangement with Cronin seem distinctly odd.

Circumstantial evidence was presented that highlighted the suspicious behavior of the defendants, and showed they were actively hostile to Cronin. Harry Planskie, a shirt salesman, testified that on the morning of May 5, Pat "the Fox" Cooney and Martin Burke bought new shirts at his business. Both declined to take off their coats to be measured, however, leading Planski to suspect retrospectively that the shirts they were wearing were bloodstained. The following day, a man matching Burke's description called at Klahre's hardware store on Clark Street. As Burke waited for Gustav Klahre to solder a tin box the men discussed Cronin's disappearance, and Burke exclaimed, "The son-of-a-bitch is a British spy and ought to be killed."

On November 8, toward the end of the prosecution case, startling new evidence was produced. Cronin's bloody clothes, surgical instruments, business cards, and prescription book were discovered in a sewer catch basin at the corner of Broadway (then Evanston) and Buena Avenues, one block from where the trunk had been discovered and just over a mile southeast from where the body had been found. Although dramatic, the finds added little to the prosecution case, since nothing directly connected the accused to the crime. The next day John Kunze wrote to the *Chicago Abend Post* to deny rumors that he was going to turn state's evidence and testify. As an innocent man, he maintained, he knew nothing of the murder—though he believed Burke was "one of the miscreants," because when Cronin's clothes were brought into the court "he trembled violently which is proof of his guilt," and he thought the others "white as snow."

More damaging evidence against Dan Coughlin appeared just

before the closing arguments began when Detective Barney Flynn approached Chief Hubbard and produced two pocket knives that he had confiscated from Coughlin the night he was arrested. According to his testimony, he placed them in a safety deposit box and forgot about them until his wife reminded him. Theo Conklin confidently identified the knives as Cronin's, though Coughlin's defense team was adamant that they were the detective's.

The defense began its case on November 16, and while much of the case rested on providing alibis for the accused, Forrest, who led the defense team, attacked the prosecution case on a number of key points:

1. The cause of death had not been proved
2. The place of death had not been proved
3. Most of the prosecution witnesses were unreliable
4. It wasn't proved that Dinan's horse was the one that took Cronin away.

A key part of the defense was the parade of witnesses who swore that the defendants were nowhere near the Carlson cottage on the night of May 4. To some extent such testimony was unnecessary, as the charge faced by the accused was "conspiracy to murder." As a result, whether or not they were in the Carlson cottage that evening was irrelevant, though if they could all prove they were elsewhere, a conviction would be very difficult to obtain.

In his closing argument for the prosecution, Hynes dismissed the alibi defense, arguing that "the only defense they set up is that of the commonest criminal: 'We'll get someone to swear we weren't there.' There is not a habitual criminal in Chicago that could not set up as strong a defense—an alibi." On November 28 *America* published a double-page cartoon, "Features of the Trial," mocking the defense case. A list of increasingly implausible alibis is suggested for the accused: "On the night of May 4 Dan Coughlin was teaching a Bible class, Pat O'Sullivan was taking the frost out of his ice, Bourke [*sic*] was playing poker with Geo. Pullman, Beggs shaking hands with Prest. Harrison, . . . Kunze had just arrived at Castle Garden."

Forrest attempted to dismiss the testimony of both Dinan and the Carlsons, arguing that they had cause to provide evidence to back

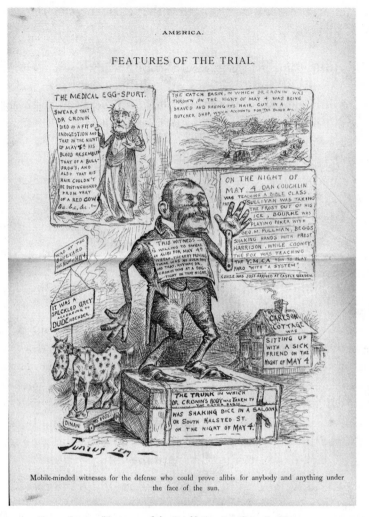

Mobile-minded witnesses for the defense who could prove alibis for anybody and anything under the face of the sun.

Junius, "Features of the Trial," *America*, Nov. 28, 1889.

up the prosecution case because they were gaining financially from it. He pointed to the fact that Dinan was receiving $100 (approximately $2,600 in today's dollars) weekly from the Stanhope and Epstean Dime Museum, where his white horse and wagon were on exhibit, while the Carlsons were making money by charging admission to their cottage.

The allegations of jury bribing refused to go away, and as the pros-

ecution steadily built its case against the defendants the *Herald* marveled that

> [the] defendants and their counsel do not exhibit the discouragement
> and alarm which would be natural to them under the circumstance.
> The battering down of their flimsy alibis . . . the opportune discovery
> of Cronin's clothing, the still more opportune discovery of Cronin's
> pocket knives . . . and above all the fact that not one of them has dared
> to take the witness-stand . . . is enough to plunge the whole gang into
> despair. But evidently it does not . . . what produces the equanimity?
> Evidently these men are counting on something which is not in sight
> to the general public.

This was a common trope throughout the trial, a belief that something would happen to ensure that the accused would be released, be that through a "rescue," the bribing of the jury, or some other method.

Toward the conclusion of the trial, most of the Chicago papers reported on a further attempt to bribe the jury. Juror Charles C. Dix discovered an envelope in the pocket of his overcoat. Inside was a letter and a necktie. The letter indicated that there would be "plenty of stuff in it" for him if he voted for acquittal, and that he should wear the necktie to indicate that he was "in." Rather than don the tie, he informed the court that an attempt had been made to bribe him, and he gave the tie and letter to State's Attorney Longnecker.

>⊶⊷⊙⊶⊷⊰

Closing arguments began on November 29 and concluded on December 12. Three lawyers spoke for the prosecution and five for the defense, with Forrest's speech running over three and a half days. Observers were impressed by the oratorical skills shown by all the attorneys. Even the *Citizen* (which sided with the defendants) found much to praise on both sides, observing that while Longnecker "attempted nothing ornate . . . he put forward his arguments clearly." John Finerty thought that Foster "used his oratorical rapier to good purpose," and that Forrest's speech was "keen as a surgeon's knife." He found Hynes eloquent, though, "like most Irishmen, he is a better de-

fender than prosecutor," but his greatest praise was reserved for Luther Laflin Mills, whom he regarded as "the Hotspur of the Chicago bar. . . . His elocution is superb and his sarcasm withering." Finerty concluded, "Chicago may well pride herself on the display of learning and eloquence made in this case by half a dozen of her lawyers—not one beyond middle age. This is about the only good that has come out of the Cronin trial."

For many observers the trial was pure theater. Never was it more apparent than during Dan Donohoe's closing speech, where his good looks generated more chatter in the public gallery than his legal prowess. One commentator called the day "Ladies Day," because the gallery was packed with women keen to see the handsome defense attorney. Some of the ladies arrived "with their fans and vinaigrettes [containing smelling salts], others with lunch baskets, but all prepared to be deeply moved, hugely entertained, and to enjoy a treat which they wouldn't have missed for anything in the world."

Longnecker's closing speech reminded the jurors that the murder trial was a serious matter, and that for justice to be done they should find the defendants guilty. The state's attorney argued,

> If you want to boil it down, if you want to write the history of the case, you are to write "I contracted for medical services"—Patrick O'Sullivan . . . "I contracted for your life"—Patrick O'Sullivan. "I contracted for the horse and buggy to drive you to your death"—Daniel Coughlin. "I rented the cottage in which to strike out your life"—Martin Burke. Write again "The committee reports to the senior guardian [Beggs] alone."

Hynes, in his summing-up, damned the accused men, though he was soft on Kunze. Like many observers, he thought Kunze was simply a tool who believed "it was a great thing be on intimate terms with a smart man like Coughlin."

Forrest's closing speech for the defense began on Saturday, December 8, and concluded on Wednesday, December 11, and from "the first to the last he held the attention of the jury with an attraction that never wavered, by sheer force and ingenuity of his argument." Forrest attacked the witnesses for the state, wryly observing that

"they had the most prodigious memories. They had eagle eyes for every circumstance. They were like the owl—they saw better by night than by day." Like the prosecution, the defense invoked the name of Alexander Sullivan, though he was not on trial. Forrest claimed that Beggs was on trial simply because he admitted a friendship with Sullivan: "Alexander Sullivan has been arrested in this case . . . he has been discharged . . . by one of the ablest . . . jurists that sits upon the bench . . . He is a free man. Now . . . will they ask you to convict my client because he is a friend of another man they despise but against whom they cannot prove any criminal act. Hang him for his friends!"

>→+◦→+○→+◦→+<

Under Illinois law, the jury had the power to decide both the law and the facts. Jurors were legally entitled to ignore any instructions given to them by the judge, and it was their "duty to reflect whether, from their habits of thought, their study and experience, they are better qualified to judge the law than the court. If, under these circumstances, they are prepared to say that the court is wrong in its exposition of the law, the statute has given them that right." On the evening of December 12, Judge McConnell delivered his instructions to the jury and informed them that if any of the defendants were found guilty, they must be sentenced to a minimum of fourteen years, but the jurors had freedom to decide on the exact length of sentence beyond that—or they could choose to sentence the guilty to death. Then the jury retired to the jury room at the top of the Criminal Court building, where they remained for four nights and three days until they reached their verdict. Observers had anticipated a swift verdict, but as the hours, then days, passed, the air around the courtroom became "as smoky as an Indian summer landscape," and there was increasingly frenzied speculation (encouraged by information leaked by a bailiff) that one juror, John Culver, was holding firm and refusing to agree to a guilty verdict.

Popular opinion, certainly outside the divided Irish American community, was that the accused were guilty and should hang, but such expectations were unlikely to be met. Between 1875 and 1920 only 36 percent of those who faced murder charges in Chicago were convicted; many murders never resulted in any charges in the first

place. Of those convicted between 1870 and 1930, less than one percent were executed. In the 1880s only five murder trials resulted in both guilty verdicts and death sentences, and a total of ten men were executed. The fact that the man who many newspapers had named as the instigator of the crime had not even been charged, allied to the fact that there were no witnesses to the murder, led many seasoned observers of Chicago courts to suspect that the defendants would emerge as free men.

>-!-+>-+-O-+-<+-!-<

From 4:15 on Friday afternoon until two o'clock on Monday afternoon, the jurors deliberated. Failure to reach a swift verdict led to frustration in the jury room, and newspapers reported that jurors had actually come to blows while debating the verdict. A bailiff told a journalist for the *Tribune* that juror John Culver had been assaulted, and that he "did not resent the blow nor the words used, but rose to his knees and offered up a prayer." The papers reported that the other jurors called Culver "a crank," "a lunatic," a "pigheaded Scot," and a "chucklehead." His neighbors in Evanston assured journalists that there would be no verdict delivered on Sunday, for that would be against his Methodist beliefs.

The press was desperate for a verdict, so much so that the *Chicago Times* decided to beat its opposition by publishing a scoop. Its headline on Monday morning, December 16, was "All Found Guilty," a remarkable claim given that the jury had not yet delivered its verdict. The accompanying article claimed that the verdict would be Coughlin—death sentence; O'Sullivan—death sentence; Burke—death sentence; Beggs—imprisonment for life; Kunze—imprisonment for twenty-five years.

That morning it became apparent that a verdict was indeed imminent, and a huge silent crowd gathered outside the courthouse in the fine rain. At the county jail "waiters brought in five good breakfasts consisting of beef steaks, eggs, potatoes, coffee, bread and butter and oatmeal and each man did ample justice to the meal except O'Sullivan who partook of little food." By the time the accused reached the courtroom, it was crowded with journalists, police, and family and friends of the dead and the accused. The newspapers described the prisoners as they waited: "Burke who was already pale became waxen and his face was moist with cold perspirations while O'Sullivan chewed on his moustache," "no longer malignantly defiant; no longer cruel to the sight, he was completely bowed and broken." Coughlin, "serious, but easy and comfortable . . . sat with neck thrust out and eyes staring from under his square beetling forehead." Beggs, chewing on some tobacco, "went white, except for two red spots in his cheek," while Kunze was fearful; "the muscles of his face twitched, he twisted and turned . . . and grew ashen white and dejected beyond description."

At two thirty Clerk Lee read the verdict. Coughlin, O'Sullivan, and Burke were found guilty and sentenced to life imprisonment, Kunze was found guilty and given a three-year prison sentence, and Beggs was acquitted. At this news "the crowd which had been leaning forward in expectant attitude started up and gasped as though they had been dashed with cold water. . . . Coughlin, O'Sullivan and Burke turned deathly pale while Kunze started suddenly from his seat and a moment later dropped his head upon his breast and burst into tears. Beggs' face was luminous with joy," and he immediately went over to the jurors to thank them. William Hynes "the big Irish lawyer . . . appeared as absolutely stunned as though he had been struck with a sandbag. Mr. Longnecker took it almost as badly," though they later agreed that a compromise was better than a retrial.

The crowd waiting outside the courthouse heard the verdict almost as soon as the prisoners themselves, because dozens of messenger boys raced from the courtroom and began shouting the judgment as they headed for their newspaper offices. Within minutes the verdict was posted on the windows of the *Chicago Tribune*; among the crowd outside the newspaper offices, there seemed to be only one opinion on the decision: it was too lenient. The men should hang. Reporters busied themselves interviewing men on the street. On the streets, if not in the courtroom, talk turned to Sullivan, and there was general agreement that even if the defendants had been sentenced to death, the real culprit remained at large. One man "dressed like a merchant" thought they "should have hung the whole lot," while "Mike," an Irishman wearing mud-stained overalls and holding a dinner pail, said, "I shouldn't be surprised to see 'em go down to the jail and pull them murderers out and string 'em up to a lamp-post or a telegraph pole. I'd be with 'em if they want."

John Culver was identified as the juror who refused to sentence the guilty men to death, and he was subjected to considerable public opprobrium. Immediately after the verdict was delivered, Culver attempted to walk from the courthouse to the Commercial Hotel. However, a hostile crowd numbering about two hundred had gathered outside the courthouse. They demanded that he explain why he refused to vote for the death penalty. When no answer was forthcoming, they began to chant, "Throw him off the Bridge." A police escort was required to ensure Culver's safe passage.

A week after the trial concluded, the *Tribune* published a letter from Culver to the paper. In it he defended his decision to refuse to agree to a death sentence, vowed that he would not be forced from his home, and provided several examples of the abusive letters he had received. One, from J. Irving Pearce, encouraged him to "go hang yourself and save the outraged public from doing it for you" while another accused him of being "an old hypocrite, you ought to be hung by the heels until bibles would run out of your mouth. . . . The jury ought to have thrown you out of the window and mashed your disguised religious head on the pavement for your mockery in defeating justice. . . . YOU VILLAIN!!!" Echoing aspects of the Clan na Gael split, a letter from the sinisterly named "Committee of 10" warned Culver that it had "decided to rid the county of Cook of a hypocrite perjurer, and a general scoundrel," and that if he did not leave the area by January 7, 1890, the "penalty would be death." Despite his assertions that he would not be forced to move, the *Tribune* reported on December 23 (a mere week after the trial verdict had been delivered, and a day after the paper published his letter) that Culver's house was for sale.

Theo Conklin was quick to talk to the press. Although dissatisfied with the verdict, particularly with the release of Beggs, he thought it "better than a disagreement. Nobody on the Cronin side . . . cares to go through the ordeal of another trial, the sleepless nights, the weary days, the annoyance . . . let the matter rest as it is." Cronin's brother John was disappointed with the verdict, though "not because of any desire for vengeance. I don't think the law has been sufficiently vindicated by the verdict. The murder was most foul and brutal . . . the punishment is not sharp enough and the guiltiest man, in my judgment, escapes," and by that he did not mean Beggs. John Devoy was more recalcitrant, refusing to tell journalists what he thought, because "you would not print what I would say about the verdict. It would be too emphatic." Cronin's friend John F. Scanlan was adamant that "the verdict is a miscarriage of justice."

While the newspapers articulated a variety of opinions on the verdicts, the overwhelming one was that they were unsatisfactory— most felt that Coughlin and Burke, at the very least, ought to have been sentenced to death. For the *Chicago Herald* the outcome of "one of the most sensational cases known in the history of American criminal law . . . was a disappointment." The *Chicago Times*, the *New York Times*, *America*, and the *Boston Advertiser*, among many others, believed that the guilty should have been executed. The *Chicago Times* found the verdict "a grievous disappointment," and believed that O'Sullivan, Coughlin, and Burke "ought to have been sent to the gallows" but for the "obstinacy of one man." It was widely suggested that Culver bore the sole responsibility for the fact that the convicted men were not sentenced to death. Many papers, including the *Chicago Inter Ocean*, the *Chicago Tribune*, and the London *Times*, thought the verdict too lenient but took solace from their belief that the verdict would have a detrimental effect on secret societies.

Charles Cameron, an assistant city attorney, was convinced that "under the shadow of the gallows some of those men would have told all." He was certain that the verdicts of life imprisonment rather than execution were the result of corruption and mused, "We ought to [take] down the stars and stripes and [hang the flag] of Ireland over the court house." The fact that no one's life was at stake meant there was little likelihood of any of the convicted men coming forward to confess to save their neck. The *Chicago Weekly Journal* thought that the life sentences meant that the true story of the murder would not be told, and "those who planned the murder and employed the tools are now secure."

Irish American papers generally praised the verdict. The *Citizen* reported the acquittal of John Beggs with some relief. The fact that he, as Senior Guardian of Camp 20, had been found not guilty proved, as far as Finerty was concerned, that the Clan had not conspired to kill Cronin. This was echoed by Patrick Ford of the *Irish World*, who believed it an "honest verdict. . . . I am glad . . . that there was no conspiracy proved and that no connection was found between Dr. Cronin's murder and the Clan na Gael. That is what the verdict of the jury virtually amounts to." But Finerty and Ford's analysis of the judgment was one that only the most blinkered supporter of Alexander Sullivan could accept. Although the Senior Guardian of Camp 20 had been acquitted, three members of the camp had been found guilty of conspiracy to murder. Their motive for murder was to silence a critic of Sullivan (who was also a member of Camp 20). Clan na Gael was certainly implicated.

British newspapers had watched the case with interest. Most had continued to report that Cronin was in favor of the Dynamite War that had terrified sections of Britain during the early 1880s, despite considerable evidence indicating that he had opposed this controversial strategy. However, the papers were correct when they reported that Cronin, like all members of the Clan, supported securing Irish freedom from Britain using violent means. The London *Times*, still smarting from its humiliation at the Parnell Commission, was unsurprisingly dismissive of both Cronin and the verdict, arguing that

> Dr. Cronin, the victim of a foul murder plot, was by no means deserving personally of the sympathies of Englishmen. He seems to have come into conflict with the other leaders of the Clan-na-Gael not at all because he objected to dynamite outrages but because he protested against the diversion of funds subscribed for the patriotic purpose of blowing up London to the private use of Mr. Alexander Sullivan's clique.

Another London paper, the *Morning Post*, claimed that "if the case shall result in a thorough awakening of public opinion in the United States to the real character of the Clan-na-Gael then Cronin's life was not sacrificed wholly in vain." The London *Graphic* reminded readers that Cronin was anti-English, and opined on the trial's significance: it had thrown

[a] lurid light . . . upon the inner working of the societies which, pretending to the most exalted patriotism, are but instruments to give power. . . . There is nothing clearer than the fact that Dr. Cronin was sentenced to death by his colleagues because he had detected their wholesale misappropriation of the funds. . . . He was, that is, a trifle more sincere as a dynamiter than they were. His conception was that the whole funds should be spent on the massacre of innocent English people; theirs, that a large portion should be expended on their own luxurious living and in procuring the assassination of any colleague who thwarted that purpose.

In the immediate aftermath of the verdict, Judge McConnell was pressed for his opinion. Speaking "as a citizen," McConnell suggested that the verdict resulted from "a probable objection of some of the jurors to the death penalty on circumstantial evidence. . . . You will probably find that Mr. Culver was not the only man upon the jury who was opposed to the hanging of the three principal defendants." It seemed that McConnell was correct. Almost two weeks after the conclusion of the trial, some jurors revealed what had occurred in the jury room.

Over the course of the deliberations, about forty ballots had been taken. Unanimous verdicts had to be recorded. The first vote was 11–1 in favor of a guilty verdict for all, with Culver the juror who voted against. Discussion then turned to individual defendants. Eight jurors thought Kunze guilty of murder, but when Judge McConnell assured the jury they could find him guilty of the lesser charge of manslaughter, a unanimous vote declared him guilty, and they swiftly agreed to a sentence of three years in prison. The first vote on Beggs found seven in favor of a guilty verdict, but after much discussion and several further ballots he was found not guilty.

Deliberation continued about the fate of Coughlin, Burke, and O'Sullivan. Eventually, it was agreed to find the three men guilty, but there was division over their sentence. Eleven jurors (Culver excepted) wanted the death penalty for Burke and Coughlin, while ten voted for the death penalty for O'Sullivan. A series of votes took place and the jury was deadlocked, with seven in favor of life in prison and five voting for the death penalty. Ultimately, the five who voted for

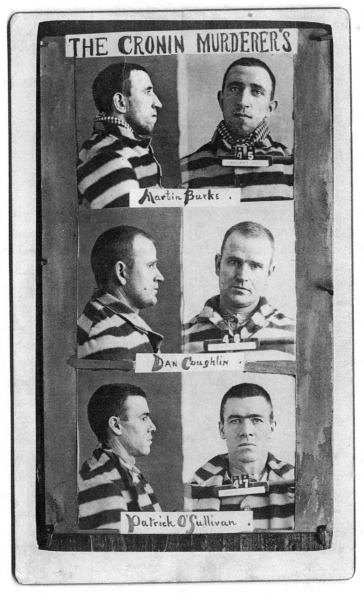

Martin Burke, Dan Coughlin, and Patrick O'Sullivan.
Chicago History Museum, ICHi-QF38KC88.

the death penalty were persuaded to agree to the sentence of life in prison.

Culver, a devout Methodist who spent time every day reading his Bible, had been immovable in his refusal to sentence the guilty men to death. His wife, when approached by Associated Press reporters during the jury deliberations, assured them that "Mr. Culver is a very determined man, and if he believed he was right he would stick it out in spite of the whole world." Coughlin, Burke, and O'Sullivan owed their lives to Culver's determination.

>-!-+>-·O-·<+-!-<

Following the verdict the four guilty men were taken back to the county jail, where they remained as Judge McConnell considered their motions for a new trial. The newspapers had little interest, for the Illinois Supreme Court had already established that if the men were tried for the same offense, a second jury could find the defendants not guilty, or it could decrease but not increase the sentence imposed at the first trial. In essence Coughlin, Burke, and O'Sullivan risked nothing by petitioning for a new trial, because the death sentence could not be given. On January 13, 1890, McConnell rejected the submissions of Coughlin, Burke, and O'Sullivan, though he did grant Kunze's petition. Kunze was released on $5,000 bail and promptly employed as a "freak" at the Stanhope and Epstean Dime Museum.

Coughlin, Burke, and O'Sullivan were handcuffed together and transferred to the Illinois State Penitentiary at Joliet to begin their life sentences. Before boarding the train to Joliet, the three men spoke to reporters. O'Sullivan and Coughlin loudly protested their innocence, with O'Sullivan claiming he had been "convicted by prejudice, by perjury, by newspaper report and by popular clamor." Upon arrival at Joliet the three men were issued prison uniforms, photographed, and set to work: Coughlin in the stone yard, O'Sullivan as a cobbler, and Burke in the cooper shop. It seemed the Cronin case was closed.

CHAPTER TEN

"REMEMBER CRONIN"

L ooking back on the events of 1889, John Devoy claimed that Cronin's murder "did more harm to the Irish cause than any single incident for many generations and put obstacles in the way of its success that were not fully overcome until the sacrifice of Easter Week, 1916 gave the Irish Race at home and abroad a new outlook and brought back the Soul of Ireland." Devoy may have exaggerated, but only a little, for the repercussions of Cronin's death were felt in Chicago, across the United States, and in Irish republican circles in Ireland and Britain for many years.

>–⊷–O–⊶–◅

The reputation of the Chicago police force was severely damaged by the Cronin case; decisive action was required to regain public trust, though Dan Coughlin was in prison and Michael Schaack had been dismissed. Within two days of the verdict, eight additional members of the force (all members of Sullivan's wing of the Clan) were discharged for conduct unbecoming of a police officer and neglect of duty. Those dismissed included Detective Barney Flynn, who had failed to surrender the knives he had found on Coughlin; Detective Harry Palmer, who had given information to the defense; and Station-Keeper Peter Kelly, who had hung around the courthouse deriding and jeering the officers involved in the case. On January 1, 1890, Mayor Cregier appointed Frederick H. Marsh, the US State Marshal for Northern Illinois, to the position of chief of police. Cregier outlined his vision for the police in a letter to Marsh:

Intelligence, integrity, and industry constitute the tripod of a safe police force. And so the reputation and usefulness of the police depart-

ment of our city will materially depend on the zeal and diligence with
which the members of it obey their instructions and devote themselves to their exacting and important duties.

The new police chief made sweeping changes, shuttling policemen across Chicago, splitting the city into five divisions, and adding
thirty-four new precincts. In part Marsh was simply taking account
of the expanded city limits that resulted from the annexations of
1889, but the changes were also a reaction to criticisms of the force
that had been leveled during the Cronin case. Five police inspectors
were appointed, including Frederick Ebersold and George Hubbard,
while Herman Schuettler was promoted to captain in recognition of
his work on the Cronin case. Known members of Clan na Gael were
moved to districts with small Irish populations, and many partner-
ships were split up. Yet for all the changes, by June 1890 the *Tribune*
was disillusioned. It complained that Marsh had failed to improve
discipline within the force and that "his orders are laughed at. . . .
Marsh is the mere creature of . . . an inefficient, foresworn, truckling
mayor."

For Captain Schuettler there was a violent postscript to the Cronin case. A month after the trial ended, he went with several friends
to Vogelsang's Restaurant at 178 Madison Street, famed for its "Bohe-
mian Lunches." Among the patrons that day were several members
of the Clan, including Alderman John McCormack, Bob Gibbons, and
Redmond McDonald. All three were connected to the murder case:
McCormack had been accused of soliciting men to assault Cronin,
Gibbons had provided an alibi for Burke, and McDonald was one of
the patrolmen dismissed in the aftermath of the trial. Witnesses reported that as Schuettler left the restaurant the Clan men became
abusive; a scuffle ensued, during which Schuettler fired his gun. Gibbons was hit in the lung and died of his injuries several days later. Chicago's German-language newspaper *Illinois Staats-Zeitung* was quick
to jump to Schuettler's defense, claiming that he had acted "bravely
and rightly." It noted that

among all honest people there is general regret that Gibbons departed
alone. They would have been glad to give him his comrade, McCor-

mack, for a companion for the other world. The assault on Captain Schuettler was an infamous aftermath to the assassination of Cronin, and every participant in it deserved to be shot down like a dog.

No charges were brought against Schuettler—at the inquest into Gibbons's death, Schuettler's claim that he had acted in self-defense was accepted.

>—+—+>—+—O—+<—+—+—<

From Cronin's disappearance to the conclusion of the trial, the Chicago newspapers regularly praised themselves for their coverage of the case and the assistance they gave to the police. They were not alone in this: Reverend F. M. Bristol, pastor of Chicago's Trinity Methodist Church, described the press as

> "The Silent Policeman" working alongside, and occasionally ahead of, the police investigation. . . . Of course the papers published some false reports, yet they were working for the public good and did not know that the reports were inaccurate at the time. After seeing their zeal and enthusiasm the people will say "Well done, good and faithful servants!" For they know that earnest efforts to detect and expose crime do much to prevent it.

So convinced was the *Tribune* that the newspapers had been the most powerful force in the investigation of the murder of Dr. Cronin that it printed an editorial from the *Adrian (Michigan) Times and Expositer* which praised the paper for aiding the prosecution:

> The Cronin trial is over, and here it is proper to note the great work that has been done in connection with it by the Chicago papers, notably *The Tribune*. . . . No work has been too arduous, no expense has been too great for this great newspaper to undertake in its efforts to bring to justice the murderers of Dr. Cronin. Its alert and active reporters have led the way and unearthed evidence far in advance of the professional detectives, some of whom *The Tribune* has fearlessly unmasked and shown them to be in sympathy with the suspects. It was great work well done.

John McEnnis, journalist and author of *The Clan-na-Gael and the Murder of Dr. Cronin* (1890), echoed the sentiments of many contemporaries when he declared,

> There probably never was a mystery more magnificently handled by the press of any city than was the Cronin murder by the Chicago newspapers. From first to last it was the press that made the case. The police were distanced in the race for news, and surprise after surprise was scored morning after morning in the columns of one journal or the other. It was the reporters of Chicago who uncovered the conspiracy and really wound the chain of evidence around the prisoners in the dock.

Undoubtedly, newspaper coverage drove the murder investigation forward. Journalists subjected the police to intense scrutiny, and exposed irregularities and unearthed serious weaknesses within the department. Press coverage contributed to the debate on jury bribing and on a jury's right to decide on the appropriate sentence. However, the papers, like the police force they criticized, were also flawed. The newspapers' rush to print, their inclination to sensationalize a story, and their loose association, at times, of fact and supposition ultimately weakened the prosecution case. Reporters often prioritized the sensational elements over the newsworthy and on occasion (as in the Carlson cottage) interfered with both evidence and witnesses. Though editors were largely free from political interference, this did not make them genuinely independent, and their angles on the case were heavily influenced by lobbying from Cronin's supporters and, to a lesser extent, Sullivan's. In many ways newspaper coverage of the Cronin case mirrored the richness, complexities, and fragmented reality of late nineteenth-century urban life, with all its flaws and promises.

>─┤─◆〉─◦─O─◦─〈◆─├─◄

The impact of the case on Irish republicanism was, as Devoy suggested, immediate and devastating. Press coverage of the Cronin case forced Clan na Gael from the shadows into the limelight, and after such public exposure, the society's ability to act as an effective fund-raiser for Irish republicanism was greatly diminished. Many Irish in Chicago had joined the Clan not because they had any overriding interest in Irish nationalism but because they saw membership as a way of securing a good job; they were primarily interested in what the Clan could do for them, not what they could do for Ireland. Cronin's murder forced them to make a decision, and large numbers walked away from involvement in any form of Irish nationalism. Such was the disillusionment among the Irish in Chicago that there was no St. Patrick's Day parade in 1890. However, there was one Clan camp that expanded after the Cronin case had concluded— Camp 20. It had been nominally disbanded by Edward Spelman before the murder trial began, but as soon as the trial concluded it re-formed; within three weeks of his release, John Beggs was reappointed Senior Guardian. Given that Camp 20 was Alexander Sullivan's power base within the Clan, it seemed that even if the Clan's strength was diminished, Sullivan himself might bounce back, just as he had so many times before.

A decade after Cronin's death, Patrick Ford of the *Irish World* told Michael Davitt that there was little point in approaching any "of our 'Irish Irishmen' in the United States," as they "must not be expected to do anything that will not repay themselves, and with interest." The impact of this attitude was felt in Ireland and Britain, because funding for Irish nationalist and republican movements had virtually dried up. This was not simply because of the Cronin murder; the Parnell Commission also had a significant negative impact on the Clan in America. Although Parnell was exonerated, the Clan had been exposed, for much of its secret underbelly had been revealed through the inclusion of secret memoranda, letters, and the Clan constitution as evidence at the commission. By the time the commission and the Cronin murder case had concluded, there was little that remained secret about the secret society.

After the conclusion of the murder trial, neither side of the Clan was inclined to try to unite it and so the division continued, exacerbated by the sensational O'Shea divorce case of November 1890, when Charles Stewart Parnell's adulterous relationship with Katherine O'Shea was made public. Parnell's position as leader of the Irish Parliamentary Party became untenable, but he refused to leave without a fight. Both constitutional nationalists and those of a more radical mind were divided on this matter, although Irish Americans generally took Parnell's side. In almost every sense, the American movement had already fallen asunder, and support for Parnell had been one of the very few things both sides of the Clan agreed on. In the wake of the divorce scandal, however, even that disappeared. Devoy feared that if Parnell departed the stage, it would completely "destroy [the] American movement," for "no other man or men can keep it together." Grasping at straws, Devoy offered to act as a broker between the two sides of the Irish Parliamentary Party, but nothing came of his peace plan. When Parnell died on October 4, 1891, he left behind a divided political party that would never regain the influence it enjoyed in the mid- to late 1880s.

The Clan wasn't the only secret society that came under additional scrutiny following Cronin's murder. Many others were subjected to unwanted attention from civic and church authorities. As the *Inter Ocean* observed at the close of the Cronin trial, "Everybody now knows that no creatures or serfs of any secret league can do murder in America at the bidding of their infamous masters and go unscathed of justice." Although Archbishop Feehan, the Catholic Church's most senior figure in Illinois, remained silent on the issue of the Clan, other senior clergymen were more forthcoming. As the first anniversary of Cronin's death approached, Bernard McQuaid, bishop of Rochester, complained to Archbishop Michael Corrigan of New York: "It [Clan na Gael] is reviving after the shock occasioned by the Cronin murder has begun to pass away. Yet nothing is being done. Some priests belong to it." Corrigan and McQuaid were opposed to revolutionary Irish republicanism, and were determined to ban Catholics from membership in the Clan. At a meeting of Catholic bishops in Boston in July 1890, Clan na Gael was the focus of debate. Formal criticism of the Clan was resisted by Archbishops James Gibbons of Baltimore, John Ireland of St. Paul, and, unsurprisingly, Feehan. As Archbishop Frederick Katzer of Milwaukee reported to the Vatican, "The decision reached was that it is best to refrain from any special condemnation of them." In Chicago few Irish Americans were bothered whether or not the Clan was banned by the Catholic Church. As Alderman John Powers observed, with some justification, of his largely Irish electorate, they "are a people that are governed by saloons—not by the church—not by the press."

For several years after Cronin's death, Devoy remained in Chicago, where he worked on the *Chicago Herald*. One of his colleagues was Margaret Sullivan. Devoy disliked her just as much as he disliked her husband. He complained that she used her charm to turn people against him, though he admitted (in what amounted to a backhanded compliment) that she "was a very clever woman (or man in petticoats)." When Devoy finally left Chicago, he blamed her for his departure, claiming that he was forced to resign because of a campaign she had launched against him at the paper. However, his return to New York was actually a response to a request from Luke Dillon, who wanted Devoy to become secretary of the Clan and work to reunite it.

Devoy's efforts to reunite the Clan were initially met with hostility on both sides, but he was resolute in the face of rejection. On September 28, 1894, a Clan convention representing Cronin's side took place in Philadelphia. The meeting was intended to develop a strategy whereby a united Clan would be reorganized on a thoroughly revolutionary basis. When Cronin's death came under discussion, the gathering declared that although the men who took part in the planning or execution of Cronin's death were "honest dupes," they would remain excluded from a reunited Clan. The men considered to have been the chief instigators of the murder had their names sent to every branch and were declared "outlawed by the Irish race." Newspaper reports implied that Sullivan and Coughlin were the names circulated.

Slowly, over the next five years, hostilities lessened (at least partly because the Clan's influence in America was reduced, and with that, competition for senior positions); by the end of the century, it seemed a united Clan was a possibility. Five representatives of each side met in Philadelphia on September 4, 1899, to discuss their desire to "weld both into one compact body." They agreed to issue a joint circular to every Camp which read,

> Inasmuch as the death of Dr. P. H. Cronin and the events preceding that unfortunate occurrence have been chiefly instrumental in keep-

ing the [Sullivan wing] and the [Devoy wing] apart, the Conference
Committee hereby declare that . . . the [Sullivan wing was not] in any
way responsible for or connected with the death of Dr. P. H. Cronin
and the members of the [Sullivan wing of the Conference] Committee affirm as their belief and the members of the [Devoy wing of the
Conference] Committee state as a fact that Dr. Patrick H. Cronin was
a faithful member of the Organization, an upright and honorable Patriot, and that attacks upon his memory are unwarranted.

It is remarkable that almost twenty years after Sullivan took control
of the Clan at the Chicago convention of 1881, an event which led to
the split in the organization, the document designed to reunite both
sides of the Clan was concerned solely with Cronin. Cronin may have
exacerbated the divisions within the Clan, but he was not the cause.
Perhaps it was easier to fixate on Cronin's murder than to address the
complex issues raised by the Triangle's deeply questionable behavior.

The first convention of the reunited organization took place in
Atlantic City, New Jersey, in July 1900. There the delegates agreed
to move forward in a united movement rededicated to achieving an
Irish Republic through force of arms. For the newly united and rein-
vigorated Clan, the new century dawned bright.

>–·–·–O–·–·–<

In the courts, several cases connected to the Cronin murder rum-
bled on. The trial of those accused of attempting to bribe potential
jurors at the Cronin trial took place in February 1890. Of the seven
accused, only one man, Jeremiah O'Donnell, faced the court. Of his
fellow defendants, one had fled Chicago, one had charges against
him dropped, and the other four turned state's evidence and testified against him. O'Donnell was found guilty and sentenced to three
years in prison for conspiracy to "pack" a jury in favor of the defendants in the Cronin case.

The verdict at the Cronin trial was not the first to prompt discussions about jury power in Illinois. During the 1880s the Illinois
State Bar Association regularly debated the role of juries at its annual
meetings, with some members calling for an end to the situation in
which juries could decide the law and others arguing that the sys-

tem was a good one that offered much-needed flexibility. Following the Cronin trial, a number of newspapers (primarily those outside Chicago) criticized what they saw as the excessive power of the jury. Papers, including the *Boston Advertiser*, found fault with "a system which puts it into the power of one man to annul the judgment of eleven men and either to bring them to his terms or render the law of no avail." The *Spectator* in London observed that in Illinois, jury power meant that "deliberate and cruel murder in the interest of a secret society is . . . not a capital offence. . . . The justice . . . is as inherently absurd as it is undemocratic; absurd because it permits a twelfth of the court . . . to nullify all its proceedings; undemocratic because it enables one man to override eleven."

Strong arguments were made which claimed that granting extensive powers to jurors who had no real knowledge of the law meant that emotional decisions often trumped logical ones. Juries—coroner's, grand, and trial—frequently acquitted killers on very broad grounds of self-defense. As Jeffrey S. Adler has pointed out, jury "verdicts in homicide cases, at every level of the criminal justice system, indicated that they believed that men must be allowed to be men, that the law should not interfere in affairs of honor, and that residents assumed risks when they engaged in particular kinds of behavior."

The necessity for a jury to return a unanimous verdict also generated many complaints, and formed part of a debate that continued for many years. Despite many misgivings, jurors maintained the power to decide both the law and the facts until 1931. More remarkably, juries in Illinois continued to set the sentences for those found guilty until the 1980s, and it remains a requirement in that state that verdicts in criminal trials be unanimous.

John Culver, the juror who held out against the death penalty, sued the *Herald* for $25,000 damages because of allegedly libelous articles. He believed that all the newspapers had victimized him, but thought the *Herald* the most offensive. The paper dismissed his challenge: "If Culver imagines that by such action he is to silence the press on the subject of his disgraceful performance in the jury-room he is making a mistake. . . . John Culver is crazy or he is corrupt. He is a fool, or he has been bought." The *Inter Ocean* was inclined to agree, and it pointed out that "the newspapers have been far more charitable than the general public. . . . Outside the circle of his immediate personal friends, the people at large are free to express an opinion which is anything but complimentary." Given that few knew anything about Culver before he became a juror, it could be convincingly argued that public opinion about him was directed by press coverage. *Culver vs. Herald* finally came before the court in May 1891. William Hynes, who had been one of the prosecution lawyers in the Cronin case, represented the *Herald*. The jury found against Culver, a verdict that delighted all the Chicago papers.

As expected, Dan Coughlin, Patrick O'Sullivan, and Martin Burke appealed their original conviction. Their case for a new trial rested heavily on the argument that the original trial had been unfair because several of the jurors were biased, but neither O'Sullivan nor Burke lived long enough to discover if a new trial would be granted. Both men died of tuberculosis in prison in 1892. O'Sullivan's body made one last trip to his home on Bosworth Avenue, where he was waked before being buried at his family plot in Argyle, Wisconsin. In May 1896, on the fourth anniversary of his death, five hundred people (including twenty-five from Chicago) attended the unveiling of a large monument, complete with Celtic cross, over his grave. Burke too returned to Chicago, where before his burial at Mount Olivet Cemetery he was waked at his cousin John Conway's house. A crowd of more than two hundred people queued to pay their respects and drink some of the twelve cases of beer that were allegedly supplied by Sullivan's wing of the Clan.

In January 1893 Coughlin's case for a new trial came before the Illinois Supreme Court. In his "writ of error," Coughlin's counsel, William S. Forrest, highlighted forty-six flaws in the original case, and according to the Justices of the Illinois Supreme Court, "filed exceedingly . . . and needlessly voluminous arguments." The justices dismissed most of the alleged errors and focused on the issue of the bias, or otherwise, of the original trial jury. Coughlin's counsel argued that as a result of biased newspaper coverage, at least two jurors, Elijah J. Bontecou, a salesman, and Benjamin F. Clark, a real estate agent, had decided on his guilt before the trial began. Coughlin's legal team had objected to both Bontecou and Clark when they were selected for the jury, but their objections had been overridden by the court because they had no peremptory challenges left. When questioned by the court before his selection, Bontecou admitted that he believed Burke, Coughlin, and O'Sullivan were guilty and had a prejudice against members of Camp 20, but was convinced that with his "own knowledge of my own mental and moral make-up, that, if sworn as a juror, I could render a fair and impartial verdict in this case based exclusively upon the law and the evidence." Clark told the court, "I am strongly prejudiced . . . [but] if I was serving on this jury, I certainly shall try to throw aside prejudice and give my decision on the law and the evidence as presented to me." On January 19, 1893, a divided Supreme Court reversed the decision of the Cook County Court and set a new trial in motion.

The smug self-satisfaction of the Chicago newspapers after the first trial was conspicuous by its absence this time. The press had congratulated itself on the role it played in helping to identify the conspirators, yet the newspapers' collective obsession with finding the accused guilty before the trial, along with a flawed jury selection process, contributed to nullifying the original verdict. The Illinois Supreme Court decision also had consequences for the men found guilty of the Haymarket bombing, for it formed one of the primary reasons why Governor John Peter Altgeld decided to pardon Samuel Fielden, Oscar Neebe, and Michael Schwab, the surviving "bombers." Altgeld made much of the Supreme Court justices' comments regarding the competency of jurors in the Cronin trial. They had observed that "it is difficult to see how, after a juror has avowed a fixed and settled opinion as to a prisoner's guilt, a court can be legally satisfied of the truth of his answer that he can render a fair and impartial verdict." Altgeld applied the Supreme Court judgment to the Haymarket case, concluding, "It is very apparent that most of the jurors were incompetent because they were not impartial."

Coughlin's new trial began in December 1893 and lasted until March 1894, and for most newspapers it was unheralded and largely unreported. There were several reasons for this. Because the new trial could not impose a harsher sentence than the original, there was no prospect of Coughlin being sentenced to death. Second, the press largely regarded the trial as a sham. There were few who did not think Coughlin was guilty, just as there were few who did not think he would have his conviction overturned. Moreover, the press was convinced that the jury chosen for the retrial had been bribed by Coughlin's supporters. Third, much of the evidence presented at the second trial repeated what had been reported in the first, though there were fewer witnesses to call—at least twelve people associated with the case had died in the intervening four years.

People talked of the "curse of the Cronin case." Many in Chicago were afraid to use white horses, because one had taken Cronin to his brutal death. The press speculated that the Triangle had organized the deaths of Spelman, Beggs, Burke, and O'Sullivan (and several others) in order to ensure that "mouths [were] closed forever." Newspapers claimed that O'Sullivan died of "consumption" just as "he was on the point of making a statement of his knowledge of the murder." It seems unlikely that Sullivan was behind the string of deaths—his reputation had been destroyed, and arranging the assassination of those associated with the Cronin case would do nothing to enhance it. Schuettler acknowledged that "the mortality in the case is somewhat remarkable," but didn't think there was "anything mysterious in it." And apparently the dead didn't disappear entirely: in 1896 the Brennan family who lived in O'Sullivan's former home fled because they believed the house was haunted by his ghost.

One witness, Elizabeth Foy, did attract the attention of the newspapers. Lizzie Foy was the wife of Andy Foy, a member of Camp 20 who, at the first trial, admitted he had spoken out against Cronin. Mrs. Foy maintained that beginning in March 1889, her husband and Coughlin regularly met in the Foys' home at 91 Locust Street (now 308 West Locust Street). After one meeting she found a letter from Michael Davitt to Alexander Sullivan that included the phrase "remove all hazards, but use your discretion with it." After Cronin was killed, Mrs. Foy took the letter to have been a command from Davitt to Sullivan.

It is improbable that Davitt wrote such a letter. Though his claim that he had never heard of Cronin until after his death is implausible, and though he was friends with the Sullivans, there is nothing to suggest that he was involved in the Cronin-Sullivan feud. Davitt's friends believed that the letter was a forgery by Dan Coughlin which he used to persuade others to join his conspiracy. Davitt responded to Lizzie Foy's accusation in an open letter to the Associated Press in which he denied any involvement with the Cronin murder, suggesting that the letter was a "monstrous fabrication." It would be "just as true," he wrote, "to charge me with having advised the removal of Julius Caesar or Abraham Lincoln."

Lizzie Foy testified in court that Andy had told her he had helped to "remove another Le Caron." He explained that the men had drawn lots to decide who would kill Cronin. He had been selected, though the burden was taken from him: he was married with children, while some of the others were single men. However, he told his wife, "I did my share and I am ready to take my punishment." Mrs. Foy revealed that contrary to newspaper and police speculation, the weapon used to murder Cronin was not an ice pick but Foy's stonemason's chisel. She testified that after the body was discovered, M. E. Ames, one of the defense lawyers, had visited the Foy house several times to brief Andy on what to say if arrested. When asked why she had not come forward at the first trial, Mrs. Foy claimed that she didn't know what to do, but that her conscience now prompted her to testify. She added that three of her children had died since Cronin's murder: Robert Emmet drowned in Lake Michigan, while Maria (a year old) and Heloise (nine months old) both died suddenly. She believed that these deaths were God's punishment for both her husband's involvement in the murder and her silence.

Andy Foy was called to rebut his wife's testimony. Press reports commented on his calm and relaxed demeanor on the witness stand. He rejected his wife's statement and maintained that he was at home on the night that Cronin was murdered. He claimed that his wife was crazy, and she had accused him not only of Cronin's murder but also of throwing the Haymarket bomb. Few took Lizzie Foy's testimony seriously. In court she was ridiculed as a "crazy, wild-eyed dreamer," and it was implied that the death of her children had rendered her mentally unstable, though the *New York Times* thought her evidence compelling. Coughlin's lawyer attacked Lizzie Foy's motive for testifying, and produced three letters that she had written to Coughlin. Forrest interpreted the letters as indicators that she was prepared to sell her silence. However, there was nothing in them to substantiate this interpretation—they simply asked Coughlin to intervene with her husband, as he "had become a drunkard and an outcast since the murder."

On March 8, 1894, the jury delivered its anticipated verdict: not guilty. There had been an air of ennui about the newspaper coverage of the retrial. It was, as Finley Peter Dunne observed, "a farcical trial, a farcical judgment." In addition to Coughlin, one man had cause to celebrate that day—John Culver, who believed that the new verdict vindicated his decision to refuse to vote for a death sentence in the original trial. On the day Coughlin was released, someone placed a wreath of lilies bearing the inscription "Vindicated" on the grave of Martin Burke.

With his name apparently cleared, Dan Coughlin returned to Chicago and opened a saloon at 123 Clark Street (now 326 North Clark Street). For five years little was heard of him, but in 1899 he and his saloon partner, William Armstrong, were indicted for attempting to bribe a juror, James F. Taylor, in a lawsuit against the Illinois Central Railroad. Coughlin and Armstrong were arrested, and released on a bail of $30,000 (approximately $870,000 in today's dollars). Upon his return to his saloon, Coughlin announced to a customer, "I don't like indictments. . . . I don't like trials, you never know how they are going to come out." Later that afternoon, both men fled the city. Coughlin remained on the run for eight years before he was arrested in Mobile, Alabama, where he had been living as "Jim Davis." While awaiting extradition to Illinois, Coughlin engineered an escape and boarded a tramp steamer to Central America. He settled in Honduras and found work on a banana plantation. There, in San Pedro in the winter of 1910, he died.

>—⋅◄►⋅•O•⋅◄►⋅—◄

The Cronin case broke Alexander Sullivan; whether he was guilty or not, many members of the Clan, and of Chicago's political and legal elite, thought he had been instrumental in organizing the killing and the attempted cover-up. Despite strong support from a section of the Clan, Sullivan had become such a divisive figure that he was obliged to lie low for several years. He was never charged in relation to Cronin's murder, but the public and the press had convicted him. However, in 1895 he made a comeback in front of cheering crowds at the St. Patrick's Day parade, where he rode in an open carriage. In September of that year, he spoke at an event honoring Robert Emmet, and was regularly interrupted as the audience "broke out into applause again and again." However, such apparent acceptance was largely illusory. The parade had been boycotted by supporters of Cronin, and at an opposition event marking Emmet's birthday in Apollo Hall, the names of Coughlin, Sullivan, and others were vilified.

In the summer of 1896, Sullivan took a two-month trip to Europe; he spent time in Carlsbad, apparently to get relief from stomach trouble. His trip coincided with an alleged dynamite expedition led by Patrick J. Tynan, a member of the Invincibles, the organization responsible for the Phoenix Park murders. Before Tynan reached Britain he was intercepted at Boulogne, France, and the plot was foiled. There was no evidence to connect Sullivan to Tynan's supposed plot, but there were many who were prepared to believe it.

Upon his return to Chicago, Sullivan made a final attempt to reclaim some political influence. In 1897, when Carter H. Harrison II announced his candidacy for mayor, Sullivan attempted to do with the son what he had done with the father. He proposed a deal whereby he would support Harrison if he pledged that Sullivan could choose the next police chief and effect the removal of a number of policemen who had been active in securing the conviction of Coughlin and the others. Harrison refused. As he later recalled, Sullivan's face was "a picture, for once, all its impassiveness was obliterated; the one word to accurately describe his expression would be flabbergasted." Harrison's rejection of Sullivan's overtures was the clearest sign that Sullivan's power and influence had ebbed away. Such a divisive figure could no longer deliver the Irish vote en masse.

Rumors that Sullivan, like Coughlin, was an inveterate jury briber dated to the Hanford murder case in 1876, though no charges had ever been brought against him. However, in 1901 Sullivan was charged with "conspiracy to abet a fugitive from justice" as part of a jury bribing case. The murky story behind this trial ultimately brought an end to Sullivan's legal career. In 1898 a bailiff, John J. Lynch, was arrested, charged with jury bribing, and freed on bail. He then fled to Canada (as Burke had done before him), where he remained for more than two years before resurfacing in Chicago. He claimed that Sullivan had paid him $4,000 (approximately $120,000 in today's dollars) to leave, along with a monthly stipend of $150 (approximately $4,500 today), until September 1901. When the money dried up, Lynch returned to Chicago armed with the tale Sullivan was desperate to keep quiet.

Lynch also alleged that during 1897 and 1898, Sullivan had paid him close to $6,000 to bribe jurors. This in itself was scandalous, but the truly sensational element of Lynch's evidence was his allegation that Sullivan's partner in jury bribing was the former detective Dan Coughlin. Ever since Cronin's disappearance in May 1889, Sullivan had repeatedly denied he had anything but a passing acquaintance with Coughlin, and yet it now appeared that their close working relationship had lasted well over a decade. Sullivan had to weather this storm alone, as Coughlin had gone on the run the previous year over the Illinois Central Railroad bribery case. At the trial, senior figures in the Chicago legal scene, including John P. Altgeld, William J. Hynes, Joel Longnecker, and C. H. Aldrich, lined up to testify against Sullivan. He was found guilty and fined $2,000.

Many of Sullivan's peers thought his punishment too light, and they took action to disbar him in 1904. The Illinois Supreme Court ruled that there was insufficient evidence to do so. However, despite the court finding in his favor, Sullivan's legal career never recovered. The collapse of his business may not have been entirely bound up with the court cases, however. In 1903 his wife, Margaret, died of a stroke, and Sullivan was reportedly grief-stricken.

Alexander Sullivan died on August 21, 1913. In his will he left everything to his loyal friend and supporter Father Maurice J. Dorney. So divisive was Sullivan, even in death, that his former law partner Thomas G. Windes, now a judge, was reduced to merely stating the facts of their relationship rather than offering anything that might be construed as praise of the deceased: "He was a student in my law office. He began practice in 1878 and a year later became my partner. We were in partnership until I was chosen to a bench in the circuit court in 1892." James O'Shaughnessy, the founder of the Irish Fellowship Club, remembered Sullivan as a "man of polish, self-control and the most infinite good humor." Father Dorney recalled for a *Chicago Tribune* story that Sullivan "was looked upon as a ruling factor here in Irish societies and was in the vanguard of the Irish National League of America." He reminded readers that Parnell valued Sullivan's opinion and "always communicated with him before [he] took any steps in the Irish cause in the United States." This was an exaggeration, though the two men were certainly in contact when Sullivan was at the helm of the National League.

Despite the brief campaign to have him removed from St. Gabriel's in 1889, Father Dorney remained in the parish he founded until his death in March 1914. After Sullivan's fall from grace, Dorney also withdrew from Clan activity and concentrated on parish work. In 1908 the *Tribune* commented that "Father Dorney is one of the best known, best loved, and most influential priests in Chicago. . . . He has interested himself deeply and sympathetically in every activity of his parishioners, and their pride in, and love for, their pastor is widely known." Newspaper obituaries made no mention of Dorney's association with the Clan, but much was made of his concern for the poor and his determination to provide all the children of his parish with a good education. On the day of his funeral, "hundreds of automobiles blocked the streets around St. Gabriel's and beside them stood the wagons of peddlers, and truckmen from the yards who had abandoned work for the day to pay tribute to the dead priest." Thousands, including Mayor Harrison, attended, and all businesses in the parish of St. Gabriel's closed between nine and three o'clock. At the time of his burial, all the packinghouses in the area suspended work for five minutes. Dorney attracted support from every sector of society, and so on the day of his funeral Archbishop Quigley of Chicago was the chief celebrant at the Requiem Mass, and Bishop Peter J. Muldoon (who had presided over Cronin's funeral twenty-five years earlier) preached the sermon as requested by Dorney.

>─┼─◆>─○─<◆─┼─<

And what of Dr. Patrick Henry Cronin? His coffin remained in the public vault at Calvary Cemetery for a year while a public subscription raised money for a tombstone that would be a fitting memorial. His supporters chose a prominent plot at the easternmost edge of the cemetery, close to Lake Michigan and visible to all who passed along Sheridan Road. However, even the formal interment of Cronin's remains was not without controversy. The Trustees of South Evanston had prohibited burial within nine hundred feet of the lake as a sanitary measure. The Cronin plot fell within the prohibited territory, and so, rather than a grand public burial, early on the morning of Wednesday, April 30, 1890, a small group of Cronin's friends removed his coffin from the vault, placed it in his grave, and covered it with concrete and a stone slab to prevent the authorities from reburying the body. On Sunday, May 4, the first anniversary of Cronin's death, two specially hired trains took friends and supporters from Chicago to the cemetery, where Father Muldoon conducted a graveside service. Later that day Cronin's memory was further honored with speeches, music, and song at an event at the Central Music Hall.

The Cronin Monument Association aimed to raise $5,000 (approximately $131,000 in today's dollars) to erect a memorial over Cronin's grave. The proposed monument was a fifty-foot plain granite shaft incorporating a bronze bust of the murdered man. A number of fund-raisers took place, including a picnic at Burlington Park in August 1891. However, no such extravagant memorial was ever erected. The association had reserved the right to use money raised for the monument to help secure convictions for Cronin's murder, and so the funds had been spent, fruitlessly, on assisting the prosecution during Coughlin's second trial. Today a small granite stone, lying flat on the grass, marks the site of Cronin's grave.

>─┤─◆>─◯─<◆─┤─<

What, in the end, was the true story of the Cronin murder? Did the first trial get to the truth? Just after that trial concluded, an anonymous member of Sullivan's branch of the Clan spoke to John McEnnis, a journalist and fellow member. McEnnis's source claimed that the majority of men in Camp 20 believed that Cronin, if not a spy, was a "dangerous firebrand" and, with John Devoy, an "obstacle to unity and harmony in the Irish ranks." Cronin's determination to continue to assail Sullivan's good name after the 1888 trial produced a further "schism," and "hot-heads" in Camp 20 had lured the doctor to the Carlson cottage, where they planned to assault but not murder him. The Clan man maintained that things got out of hand when Cronin, "a fearless man and a combative man," defended himself

Cronin's grave, Calvary Cemetery, Evanston, Illinois. Author's photograph.

vigorously. As evidence that only an assault was planned, the source observed that "men who were about to commit murder would have been provided with weapons. A quick thrust of a dagger would have ended the man with less noise and less chance for defense than clubs or the broken arm of a chair." Deliberate assassins would also have had a coherent plan to dispose of the body, and he claimed there was no evidence of this in the Cronin case. McEnnis's source concluded, "It was murder certainly, and murder the result of a conspiracy, but it was not the result of a conspiracy to murder."

There is much that is plausible in this explanation, though if Cronin did put up a fight it is strange that none of the physicians who examined his corpse found any defensive wounds, suggesting that he was struck from behind and killed almost as soon as he had entered the Carlson cottage. This indicates that there was no intention to try to persuade Cronin to end his vendetta against Sullivan. Additionally, the evidence suggests that those who killed Cronin planned to take his body out into Lake Michigan and dump it overboard. The fact that his clothes had been removed implies that they anticipated that the body might at some later stage wash up on the lakeshore, so they took steps to minimize the chance of its being identified. They may also have intended to send the clothes to London as part of a plan to frame Cronin as a spy.

Patrick O'Sullivan's arrangement with Cronin and the renting of both the Clark Street flat and the Carlson cottage indicate that there was a conspiracy to lure Cronin to the cottage. The evidence suggests that the plan was led by Coughlin and Andy Foy. For all the weaknesses in Lizzie Foy's testimony, her overall argument rings true, and it seems that it was Foy that the police should have arrested rather than John Kunze, who bore a striking resemblance to Foy. Coughlin and Foy had planned the attack and persuaded O'Sullivan, Burke, Pat "the Fox" Cooney, and several others to become involved. Burke, Coughlin, and Foy were in the Carlson cottage on the night of the murder, though it seems likely that O'Sullivan was not. There was no convincing evidence to indicate that Beggs knew of the plan. His actions as Senior Guardian did not discourage an attack on Cronin, but there is little to suggest that he took an active part in the conspiracy.

Was Sullivan the mastermind behind Cronin's murder? There is no doubt that Cronin was murdered by supporters of Sullivan, but no evidence to suggest that Sullivan played any role. He was well capable of violence and deeply corrupt, but if he wanted Cronin dead he would have organized it more professionally. Also, as Judge Tuley observed, Sullivan did not benefit from Cronin's death. The fact that Sullivan's fingerprints were everywhere in the aftermath of the murder, funding the defense and interfering with jury selection, does not mean that he ordered the killing, merely that his inclination was to defend the men who thought they were helping to rid him of a problem. He was loyal to those who killed Cronin, including his friend Coughlin, but did not orchestrate the murder.

Sullivan's wife, Margaret, probably knew much more about the murder than she admitted. She was closely involved in all her husband's activities, and perhaps more committed to the Irish cause than he was. As one contemporary observed, "Alexander Sullivan never takes an important step without first consulting his wife. She is every bit as much a diplomat as he." In fact, had more attention been paid to the women in the case, much more might have been uncovered. Cordelia

Conklin was often overlooked in favor of her husband, and although her testimony was occasionally problematic, she could identify the man who lured Cronin away. Even so, the primary focus of lawyers on both sides was on her ability to identify a specific white horse while watching from an upstairs room. Lizzie Foy was dismissed as an over-emotional woman, and Margaret Sullivan, while acknowledged as a brilliant journalist, was never questioned about any aspect of the case despite her own political activity. In this trial, as in so many others, as Patricia Cline Cohen has observed, "male privilege . . . was built into the ways that most men and women thought about who has power and authority, whose word counts more, and who is more highly valued." In the Cronin case, at every stage, women's involvement was given much less credit than men's, and their testimony at the trial always subjected to an analysis of their emotional state (which was often deemed to negate their testimony) in a way that was never replicated with their male counterparts.

What prompted Cronin's determined and relentless campaign against Sullivan? There is no doubt that Sullivan used Clan money for his own purposes, and that he made a series of failed investments at the Chicago Board of Trade. Cronin was likely motivated by a desire to prevent Clan money from being put to personal use, and there was some truth in Luke Dillon's charge that Sullivan was a "professional patriot" who used the Irish movement as a tool for financial gain and to secure influence in American political life. Financial gain was not the motive of either Cronin or Devoy. Neither man sought to remove Sullivan from power to make money for themselves. Cronin did not profit from his association with the Clan—indeed, it may have been his lack of financial security that prompted him to agree to O'Sullivan's business proposition, a move that ultimately led to his murder. Following his death, Theo Conklin filed an inventory of Cronin's estate in the probate court which stated that Cronin owned no property and left behind a library full of medical texts, biographies, and travel and history books valued at $300, and surgical instruments valued at $100. This is not the legacy of a man on the make.

Still, there is no doubt that Cronin was ambitious. In addition to opposing Sullivan's financial recklessness and his use of the Clan for personal political gain, Cronin saw himself as a potential leader of the Clan in Chicago if Sullivan could be ousted from power. His rise from warehouse porter to professor of eye and ear diseases at the St. Louis College of Physicians and Surgeons points both to his ability and to his determination. The proximity of the two men undoubtedly made the feud a great deal more personal. Cronin disagreed with the "active policy" pursued by Sullivan, and he believed that links with the Irish Republican Brotherhood should be strengthened rather than weakened. The only way Clan policy would change was with a change of leadership, and Cronin was certain that he could play a significant role in a Clan that was not dominated by Sullivan. A further factor in encouraging Cronin's campaign was the support of Devoy, who undoubtedly encouraged him to take on Sullivan. It is possible that Devoy felt some responsibility for Cronin's death, for he threw himself wholeheartedly into the hunt for his killers. Above all, we can be certain that Cronin was not a spy. If he was, then, like Henri Le Caron, he would have engineered a close relationship with Sullivan, not pushed himself far away from the center of power by embarking on a bitter feud.

>·─·‹›·─·❍·─·‹›·─·❮

Well into the twentieth century, newspapers continued to make mention of the Cronin case. As press attention turned from what one journalist had called "Celtic Carbonari" to other illegal movements in Chicago, there were several occasions when comparisons were made, linking "one underground stream of corruption" to the other. The parallels were easy to draw. In 1904 Natoli Selafani was beaten to death and his body taken to the lakeshore in a wagon, and in 1911 the body of another Italian, Salvatore Costanza, was found in a sewer. His throat had been slashed. In 1912 the *Tribune* noted that "Remember Cronin" was still being used as a threat on the street, and observed that "nothing in Naples or Sicily under the Camorra and the Mafia is more dastardly than these secret hatreds which plot in the darkness and strike without shame or mercy."

In Chicago folklore, the Italian American mob killings of the 1920s quickly superseded the intrigues of Clan na Gael, but the memory of the murder lingered. In 1900 the *Tribune* published a map of Chi-

cago's wards that showed "places and things of historic and present interest." The Carlson cottage was given the most substantial
entry. In 1904 the paper recalled that Cronin was "the most talked
about man ever in Chicago in any period of its existence." Until the
late 1920s, whenever the Cronin case was mentioned in the press, no
background to the story was provided. Clearly there was an expectation that the readership would still be sufficiently familiar with the
case. A letter from "CST" to the *Tribune* in 1927 recalled that

> in the years immediately following the Cronin murder . . . we Chicago-
> ans used to take our country cousins out on Sundays and show them
> where Dr. Cronin was murdered; where the assassins laid in wait for
> him in an office building on Clark Street; where O'Sullivan the iceman
> kept his horses and then we took a North Clark Street car and piloted
> them to . . . the catch basin where the body was found.

Writing in the late 1940s, the journalist Robert Casey remembered
visiting his grandparents in Lake View as a young boy. His grandfather claimed special knowledge of the case, and brought him to see
the Carlson cottage:

> Grandpa was never quite pleased that his midnight visit to the Carlson
> Cottage had received so little acclaim from the community. He had
> seen a buggy drawn by a white horse driven by one man. He had seen a
> bay horse drawing a wagon which in all probability carried the body of
> Dr. Cronin. He had seen three men on the wagon's front seat. He had
> seen a lighted lamp and other signs of tenancy in the Carlson Cottage.
> But, a canvass of the district seems to show, so had everybody else in
> Lake View, although Grandpa sniffed at that suggestion. He thought
> he had been silenced by a sort of conspiracy. "I saw what I saw and I
> know what I know," he said. "They were trying to protect somebody
> and they were afraid of what I might say."

Newspapers published articles on the Cronin murder until the
1950s. In 1929, on the fortieth anniversary of Cronin's murder, the *Tribune* held a competition where readers were asked to "solve the mystery of the case" in order to win $500. In October 1932 the radio sta-

tion WGN broadcast "Headline of Other Days," which included a feature on the Cronin case. The *Tribune* published a lengthy article on the Cronin murder by Delos Avery in 1946, while in 1952 Charles Collins, its veteran reporter, wrote "The Slaying of Dr. Cronin" as part of the paper's Famous Chicago Crimes series. The story was briefly retold by June Sawyers in the *Tribune* in 1988.

Cronin made at least two fictional appearances in twentieth-century novels. In Sherwood Anderson's *Winesburg, Ohio*, published in 1919, the mysterious Dr. Parcival suggests to the young George Williard that he might in fact be one of the men who murdered Cronin:

> "I was a reporter like you here," Doctor Parcival began. "It was in a town in Iowa—or was it in Illinois? I don't remember and anyway it makes no difference. Perhaps I am trying to conceal my identity and don't want to be very definite. Have you ever thought it strange that I have money for my needs although I do nothing? I may have stolen a great sum of money or been involved in a murder before I came here. There is food for thought in that, eh? If you were a really smart newspaper reporter you would look me up. In Chicago there was a Doctor Cronin who was murdered. Have you heard of that? Some men murdered him and put him in a trunk. In the early morning they hauled the trunk across the city. It sat on the back of an express wagon and they were on the seat as unconcerned as anything. Along they went through quiet streets where everyone was asleep. The sun was just coming up over the lake. Funny, eh—just to think of them smoking pipes and chattering as they drove along as unconcerned as I am now. Perhaps I was one of those men. That would be a strange turn of things, now wouldn't it, eh?"

In 1992 the journalist Mary Maher published *The Devil's Card*, a novel based on the murder. What makes Maher's book particularly interesting is that she is the great-granddaughter of Andy and Lizzie Foy.

John Devoy maintained that "the brutal murder of Dr. Patrick Henry Cronin . . . shocked the entire country and created a worldwide sensation." This was true for a while, and as late as the 1940s, tours were conducted around the sites associated with the murder. Today little remains of those places—unless you know where to look.

ACKNOWLEDGMENTS

There are a myriad of people and institutions to thank. This book could not have been completed without the support of the Fulbright Commission, the Newberry Library, the Cushwa Center at the University of Notre Dame, and IES Abroad, who made it possible to travel to libraries and archives in Ireland, Britain, and the United States. I would like to thank all the librarians and archivists who assisted me in Chicago (Newberry Library, Harold Washington Library, Chicago History Museum, Illinois Regional Archives Depository, Cook County Archives), New York (New York Public Library), Springfield (Illinois State Archives, Abraham Lincoln Presidential Library and Museum), St. Louis (Pius XII Memorial Library, St. Louis University; Bernard Becker Medical Library, Washington University at St. Louis), London (National Archives, British Library), Dublin (National Library of Ireland, University College Dublin Archives, Trinity College Dublin, St. Patrick's College, Dublin City University), and Liverpool (Liverpool John Moores University, University of Liverpool).

The Newberry Library has been my Chicago "home" since 2006. It's been the most welcoming of havens, and much of the research and writing of the book took place there. I am grateful to all the employees of the library, but special mention has to be made of several current and former staff members who encouraged and supported this project from the outset: Jim Grossman, Diane Dillon, and Danny Greene. I spent six months at the Newberry in 2009 as a Fulbright Scholar, and I was privileged to be part of a cohort of supportive and inspiring Fellows. I would like to thank in particular Sarah Burns, Kristin Huffine, Carmen Nocentelli, Holly Crawford Pickett, and Sam Truett. I am especially grateful to Sarah for reading sections of the book and for providing stellar advice and encouragement. Others in Chicago also provided great company and friendship; I would like to thank Heather Ahrenholz, Sean Farrell, Bryan and Cara Fenster, Danny Fenster, Jill Gage, Jonathan Heller, Leila Porter, Julie and Jeff

Stauter, Margaret Storey, and Frank Valadez. In New York, Michael Staunton and Jane Folpe provided both support and accommodation.

Sections of this book have been presented at conferences and public lectures, and I'm grateful to Marie Coleman, Diane Dillon, Sean Farrell, Shane Kenna, Eileen Reilly, and Mary Trotter for allowing me to air parts of the story of the murder of Dr. Cronin in Dublin, Belfast, Madison, Chicago, and New York. I am grateful to both the anonymous and the acknowledged readers of the manuscript for their comments and suggestions on the text. Many scholars and friends gave freely of their time and advice, and their input has undoubtedly improved this book. Particular thanks go to Richard D. Barrett, Mimi Cowan, John Corrigan, R. Perry Duis, Charles Fanning, Leon Fink, Kate Haldane, Carla King, Mary Maher, Finola O'Kane, Niamh O'Sullivan, David Wilson, and Katie Wink. A special mention must go to Ellen Skerrett, whose knowledge of Irish Chicago is rivaled only by her knowledge of the streetscape of the nineteenth-century city.

At the University of Chicago Press, I would like to thank Robert Devens, who first took the project under his wing, and Tim Mennel, who has been a supportive and encouraging editor. I am also grateful to Nora Devlin, Sandra Hazel, and Lauren Salas, who have been a pleasure to work with.

Colleagues past and present have supported me throughout this project. Some of my oldest debts are to Tom Bartlett and Marianne Elliott, who have been my guiding lights for many years. I am also thankful to Katherine Harbord, Jimmy Kelly, Dáire Keogh, Steve Lawler, Marian Lyons, Seona MacReamoinn, Alex Miles, Daithí Ó Corráin, Deaglán Ó Donghaile, Matthew Stout, and David Tyrer, who have supported this project. Many friends have tolerated my obsession with the Cronin murder and provided excellent company and entertainment to drag me away from the archives. For that and many other things, I am grateful to (among others) the Skerries girls, the badminton gang, my FitzGerald "family," Ania Anderssen, Stephen Kearns, Regina Fitzpatrick, Jude McCarthy, and Stephen McMahon.

This book was written in Chicago, London, Liverpool, Whitstable, Skerries, and Ballygriffin. For allowing me the time and space to write by the banks of the Blackwater, only a few miles from where Cronin was born, I am indebted to my wonderful and inspiring aunt, Frances Crowe, and all at the Nano Nagle Centre (especially the late Sister Paula Buckley and Karen O'Shea). Philip and Lynn kindly provided a Kentish retreat while, in my "London home," Alice and Spike provided the best of company, friendship, and family.

My greatest thanks go to my family. My parents, Annette and John, have been constant cheerleaders, and have encouraged and supported me in anything I set my mind to. My brothers, Barry and Gavin; their partners, Niamh and Janice; my nephew, Jack; and my nieces, Abbey and Lucy, have been amusing, entertaining, and very welcome distractions from the world of nineteenth-century murder.

Finally, this book is for my husband, Alistair Daniel. Without his eye for a fine phrase, and his love, support, good humor, kindness, and unsurpassed editing skills, *Blood Runs Green* would never have been completed.

NOTE ON SOURCES

E very book is a collaboration. All those who have written about the subject and related topics contribute in some way to the next book, and *Blood Runs Green* is no exception. The story of the murder of Dr. Cronin is a multifaceted one. It is a tale of identity and belonging, of striving to make a new life in a new world. It is also a story of corruption, deception, and conspiracy. At its most basic it is a murder mystery. To write *Blood Runs Green* required an understanding of the United States, Britain, and Ireland in the late nineteenth century. In Ireland and America the sense of loss, guilt, and anger about the Great Potato Famine and Britain's continued control of Ireland found form with the establishment of secret republican societies: the Fenians and later Clan na Gael. Some of their members fought using dynamite, others through land agitation, still others through constitutional means. Many Irish in America avoided the politics but retained the culture, choosing to socialize, live, and work among their own but remain apart from Irish nationalist and republican movements.

The story of Cronin's murder is also a story of Chicago, a city where many Irish immigrants flourished. Arriving in the early years of the city, they faced less hostility than their brethren did in more established cities such as New York and Boston, where there was a Protestant ruling class in situ. In the aftermath of the Great Fire, Chicago provided an opportunity for Irish Catholics to rise alongside the city.

This book would have been much poorer without the input of generations of historians who have written about Irish America, Irish republicanism, Chicago, immigration, the growth and development of the newspaper industry, and much more. I have deliberately avoided engaging in historiographical debates, but the text has been enhanced by them. My intention was to tell the story of a murder that received international coverage in its day, and to examine its causes and consequences. Although I do not explicitly discuss his-

219

toriography, my book reflects the latest scholarship on Irish nationalism, identity, and late-ninteenth-century Chicago. The books and
articles addressing the complex issues associated with Irish America
and enriching this book include Thomas N. Brown, *Irish-American
Nationalism* (1966), Lawrence J. McCaffrey, *The Irish Catholic Diaspora
in America* (revised edition 1997), Kerby A. Miller, *Emigrants and Exiles*
(1985), Timothy J. Meagher, *Columbia Guide to Irish American History*
(2005), Kevin Kenny, *The American Irish* (2000), James R. Barrett, *The
Irish Way* (2012), and David M. Emmons, *The Butte Irish* (1990), among
many others. There has been a tendency for books about the Irish in
America to focus on the East Coast, but Chicago has its champions
too, beginning with Michael Funchion's *Chicago's Irish Nationalists*
(1976). This book's great strength lies in its development of the political significance of the Clan in Chicago, but its brevity means that
the social, cultural, religious, and economic history of the Irish in
Chicago are largely ignored. However, Funchion's baton was taken up
by historical and literary scholars, including Charles Fanning, Ellen
Skerrett, and Lawrence J. McCaffrey.

On the other side of the Atlantic, a number of books and articles
have been published in recent years that have explored the activities of the Fenians, the Clan, and the Irish Republican Brotherhood.
Notable among these are Shane Kenna's *War in the Shadows* (2014)
and Owen McGee's *The IRB* (2007), which build on K. R. M. Short's
impressive *Dynamite War* (1979). Sean McConville's immense *Irish
Political Prisoners 1848–1922* (2005), Mathew Kelly's *The Fenian Ideal
and Irish Nationalism* (2006), and edited collections such as Ferghal
McGarry and James McConnell's *Black Hand of Republicanism* (2009)
have also been enlightening. Niall Whelehan's *Dynamiters* (2012) is
excellent; it adds a new layer to our understanding of the Fenian and
Clan na Gael movements in their international context. He is particularly informative about how radical movements in Russia, France,
and Italy influenced Irish republican thinking in the latter half of the
nineteenth century.

There are a range of histories of Chicago, and many have been invaluable for this book, beginning with Bessie Louise Pierce's mon-
umental multivolume *History of Chicago* (1937, 1940, 1957). William
Cronon's *Nature's Metropolis* (1991), Dominic A. Pacyga's *Chicago* (2006),

and Donald A. Miller's *City of the Century* (1999), alongside the immense *Encyclopedia of Chicago* (2004), edited by James R. Grossman, Ann Durkin Keating, and Janice L. Reiff, were among those that provided content and context for this book. More immediately relevant were Carl Smith's *Urban Disorder and the Shape of Belief* (1995), Richard Schneirov's *Labor and Urban Politics* (1998), Louise Carroll Wade's *Chicago's Pride* (1987), Jeffrey Adler's *First in Violence, Deepest in Dirt* (2006), and Elizabeth Dale's *The Great Trunk Mystery* (2011). Works by Dale, Mark Haller, Sam Mitrani, and others on the police and the judiciary were also enlightening.

On the history of journalism, newspapers, and periodicals, Frank Luther Mott's work, particularly *American Journalism* (1962), is still the place to start. Other books that proved particularly useful include Joshua Brown's *Beyond the Lines* (2002), Karen Roggenkamp's *Narrating the News* (2005), and Michael Trotti's *The Body in the Reservoir* (2005). However, discussions of the press often overlook Chicago and focus on two New York–based newspaper publishers, Charles A. Dana and (to a much greater extent) Joseph Pulitzer, and their two newspapers, the New York *Sun* and the New York *World*. There are exceptions to this, including Hugh Daziel Duncan, *The Rise of Chicago as a Literary Center from 1885 to 1920* (1964) and David Paul Nord's *Newspapers and New Politics* (1979) and *Communities of Journalism* (2001).

With the exception of an article by Elizabeth Dale, little has been published about the Cronin murder since 1890. It is mentioned in a lot of secondary literature, but rarely merits more than a paragraph. Yet at the time, in addition to the newspaper accounts, the case generated a flurry of other publications: five books, two dime novels, and a pamphlet. Such was the interest in the Cronin case that some books on the topic were published even before the trial had begun. Two lightly fictionalized dime novels appeared in the summer of 1889 alongside a pamphlet, *The Assassination of P. H. Cronin*, and two books, *The Great Cronin Mystery* and *Murder Will Out*, which both purported to tell the real story of the murder. Within days of the guilty verdicts, a further three books about the murder were published: *The Clan-na-Gael and the Murder of Dr. Cronin* by John McEnnis, *The Crime of the Century* by Henry M. Hunt, and *The Cronin Case* by Duke Bailie. Both Hunt and McEnnis were journalists who had covered the case for Chicago newspapers. A member of Clan na Gael, McEnnis knew many of those involved. He was also closely associated with the police force, as he had cowritten Michael Schaack's *Anarchy and Anarchists*. Theodore Dreiser, who worked with McEnnis at the *Chicago Globe* in 1892, regarded him as "a truly brilliant writer whose sole fault was that he drank too much."

Bailie's, McEnnis's, and Hunt's books relied heavily on court transcripts, Clan documents, and newspaper reports, and all three came to quite different conclusions about the Cronin case. McEnnis was convinced that Sullivan had nothing to do with the murder, and his account was, unsurprisingly, dismissed by Devoy, who commented that "its only use was that it gave dates and documents correctly." Bailie, a severely disabled Civil War veteran, sat through every day of the trial and concluded that Sullivan was behind the conspiracy to murder Cronin, while Hunt, an Englishman, proffered no opinion on Sullivan but was convinced that all the accused men were guilty of Cronin's murder. Hunt's book was endorsed by Joel Longnecker, the state's attorney and chief prosecutor at the trial.

Secondary material has been invaluable for writing about Clan na Gael in 1880s America, but I found the real essence of the story in the wide variety of primary source material available. It is daunting to embark on writing a book whose many main characters are members of a secret society. Such organizations rarely keep an archive, and Clan na Gael was no exception. John Devoy is the only significant individual in *Blood Runs Green* who left a large collection of correspondence, notes, and diaries. Despite such challenges, a wide range of relevant primary material exists in libraries and archives across Ireland, Britain, and the United States. Devoy's extensive papers are held in the National Library of Ireland; in addition to much relating to his own perspective, it also houses many documents relating to the Clan, including copies of its constitution, memoranda, and letters. Devoy corresponded with hundreds of Clan members, and many of the letters written to him are in the collection. The transcript of the murder trial, which runs to over seven thousand pages, is in the Illinois State Archives in Springfield. In the book, I have (in general) referenced newspapers rather than the original transcript for several reasons, but the primary one is that the original documentation is confusing, and the referencing is hard to follow. Newspapers' transcripts of the trial, in almost every instance, match the official transcripts; on the few occasions when the official document does not match the newspapers' version, I have referenced the official account.

The Chicago History Museum holds an eclectic mix of information relating to the murder, from photographs of the suspects to dime novels. Between them the Newberry Library and the Harold Washington Library in Chicago, the New York Public Library, the British Library in London, and the National Library of Ireland hold copies of almost all the newspapers used in this study. The National Archives in London has a treasure trove of papers and reports relating to Fenian and Clan activity in the United States, Ireland, and Britain. The digitization of newspapers and other archival material has also been extremely useful. Chronicling America (Library of Congress), Trove (National Library of Australia) and the California Digital Newspaper Collection (CDNC) (University of California, Riverside) contains, among many other things, a wealth of newspapers and magazines, while the Catholic University of America has digitized its Fenian Brotherhood and O'Donovan Rossa Collection and Villanova University has a collection of Fenian Brotherhood papers. Northwestern University's website "Homicide in Chicago 1870–1890" is also a very useful resource.

The voices of Patrick Henry Cronin, Alexander Sullivan, John Devoy, Luke Dillon, Theo Conklin, Joel Longnecker, and others can be heard in *Blood Runs Green* because of extant letters, newspaper articles, and trial transcripts, while those of historians emerge in the notes and the bibliography. Both are vital collaborators in any attempt to understand past events, and to assess their significance at the time and subsequently.

PROLOGUE

1n1 **"It strikes me, doctor":** Patrick Cronin, *Is It a Conspiracy?*, pamphlet published by Cronin and distributed within Clan na Gael. The final section of the pamphlet is an imagined conversation between Cronin and a journalist. Quoted in Henry M. Hunt, *The Crime of the Century; or, The Assassination of Dr. Patrick Henry Cronin* (Chicago: H. L. and D. H. Kockersperger, 1889), 59.

1n2 **Chicago hadn't seen its like:** *Chicago Herald*, May 25, 1889.

1n3 **The crowd represented all classes and all ages:** *Chicago Tribune*, May 27, 1889; Thomas N. Brown, *Irish-American Nationalism 1870–1890* (New York: J. B. Lippincott, 1966), 175.

1n4 **The body was too decomposed:** *Chicago Daily Inter Ocean*, May 25, 1889; *New York Times*, May 27, 1889; Duke Bailie, *The Cronin Case: The Assassination of Dr. Patrick Henry Cronin* (Chicago: Rhodes and McClure, 1890), 66; *Chicago Tribune*, May 26, 27, 1889; *Times* (London), June 13, 1889; John T. McEnnis, *The Clan-na-Gael and the Murder of Dr. Cronin* (Chicago: F. J. Schulte and J. W. Iliff, 1890), 202.

2n1 **At 10.45 a.m. the casket was carried:** Pallbearers included representatives from the Ancient Order of Hibernians, the Catholic Order of United Workmen, and the Ancient Order of United Workmen, alongside aldermen; senior police officers; wealthy businessmen, including mine owner W. P. Rend; representatives of Clan na Gael, including Luke Dillon and John Devoy; and friends of the dead man, including Frank Scanlan. The majority of the pallbearers were Irish or Irish American, but there were also Germans and American Indians. [Anon.], *The Great Cronin Mystery; or, The Irish Patriot's Fate: By One of America's Most Famous Detectives* (Chicago: Laird and Lee, 1889), 169; *Gaelic American* (New York), "The Story of Clan na Gael," Feb. 28, 1925.

2n2 **Several carriages filled with friends and family:** Behind the Hibernian Rifles came a platoon of policemen and Clan na Gael guards in gray uniform and tricolored plumes. *Chicago Evening News*, May 27, 1889; *New York Times*, May 27, 1889.

2n3 **The funeral route was crowded:** "To the solemn music of the bands the men marched with slow and measured step," and the procession wound its way slowly up Michigan Avenue toward Holy Name Cathedral on State Street. "Four bands played funeral dirges while six drum corps beat time with muffled drums. Over 7,000 took part in the procession, many of them carrying flags and banners edged with black crepe." *Chicago Tribune*, May 27, 1889; *New York Times*, May 27, 1889; *Times* (London), May 28, 1889; *The Great Cronin Mystery*, 171.

2n4 **Inside Holy Name Cathedral:** The capacity of the cathedral was twenty-three hundred seated, but it could hold a congregation of four thousand on "extraordinary occasions." *Chicago Tribune*, "Dedications," Nov. 21, 1875. I am grateful to Ellen Skerrett for this reference.

2n5 **The Chicago Evening News reported:** *Chicago Evening News*, May 27, 1889.

2n6 **Several priests concelebrated:** Father Muldoon, only twenty-six, was at the time chancellor and secretary to Archbishop Feehan (see Rocco Facchini and Daniel Facchini, *Muldoon: A True Chicago Ghost Story; Tales of a Forgotten Rectory* (Chicago: Lake Claremont Press, 2003), 98. Muldoon later became Bishop of Rockford. Father Muldoon's eulogy quoted in Hunt, *Crime of the Century*, 230. The other concelebrants were Father Agnew, Father Mooney, and Father Perry.

3n1 *At the conclusion of the funeral mass:* Chicago Tribune, May 27, 1889.

3n2 *It was, as one newspaper editor put it:* Chicago Weekly Journal, "The Ghastly Cronin Crime," May 29, 1889.

CHAPTER ONE

4n1 *"That astonishing city":* Mark Twain, *Life on the Mississippi* (Boston: James R. Osgood, 1883), 593.

4n2 *In the spring of 1873:* John T. McEnnis, *The Clan-na-Gael and the Murder of Dr. Cronin* (Chicago: F. J. Schulte and J. W. Iliff, 1890), 140; Federal Writers Project, "The Case of Dr. Cronin" (unpublished manuscript, n.d. [probably 1936]), 1; Abraham Lincoln Presidential Library and Museum, Springfield, Illinois.

4n3 *Dressed in his trademark black suit:* Terry Golway, *Irish Rebel: John Devoy and America's Fight for Irish Freedom* (New York: St. Martin's Griffin, 1998), 155.

4n4 *Huge swaths of Chicago:* Dominic A. Pacyga, *Chicago: A Biography* (Chicago: University of Chicago Press, 2009): 77.

4n5 *Faced with disaster:* The city's population leapt from 298,977 in 1870 to 503,185 in 1880 to 1,099,850 in 1900. The Home Insurance Building, at the corner of Adams and LaSalle Streets, was the nation's first skyscraper and was built in 1885. Campbell Gibson, *US Census Bureau Population of the 100 Largest Cities and Other Places in the United States: 1790–1990* (June 1998), http:// www.census.gov/population/documentation/twps0027 /twps/00027.html.

5n1 *As the trains slowed:* Theodore Dreiser, *Sister Carrie* (unexpurgated edition, London: Penguin, 1986 [orig. pub. New York: Doubleday, Page, 1900]), 10. Dreiser moved to Chicago in 1883 at the age of twelve. Carrie arrives in Chicago in 1889.

5n2 *Aside from Alexander Sullivan:* Carl Smith, *Urban Disorder and the Shape of Belief: The Great Chicago Fire, the Haymarket Bomb and the Model Town of Pullman* (Chicago: University of Chicago Press, 1995), 105. Like the man who shared his surname, Alexander Sullivan saw Chicago as a place of possibility, an opportunity to rise phoenix-like from the ashes, and he would have echoed Louis's account of his arrival into the city: "[I] tramped the platform, stopped, looked toward the city, ruins about [me]; looked at the sky and as one alone, stamped [my] foot, raised [my] hand and cried in full voice: THIS IS THE PLACE FOR ME!" Louis H. Sullivan, *The Autobiography of an Idea* (New York: Press of the American Institute of Architects, 1924), 197.

5n3 *Always clean-shaven:* Quoted in Thomas Power O'Connor and Robert M. MacWade, *Gladstone-Parnell and the Great Irish Struggle* (Philadelphia: Hubbard Bros., 1886), 661–62.

5n4 *William O'Brien:* William O'Brien, *Evening Memories* (Dublin: Maunsel, 1920), 142.

6n1 *Born in 1848 in Amherstberg:* Sullivan's birthplace was disputed with some, including Devoy, believing that Sullivan had been born in Amherstberg, Ontario, while Sullivan himself claimed to have been born in Waterville, Maine. Maine is listed as his place of birth in the 1870 and 1880 census returns and also in the Cook County Death Index. Sullivan's probate record lists surviving family of four half-siblings. Three of these siblings lived in Amherstberg. Archives of the Clerk of the Circuit Court of Cook County, Alexander Sullivan probate record. D. C. Lyne and Peter M. Toner, "Fenianism in Canada, 1874–84," *Studia Hibernica* 12 (1972): 51; McEnnis, *Clan-na-Gael*, 144; *Clinton Sunday News*, "Sullivan and the Irish Movement in 1884," June 23, 1889. The issue of where Sullivan was born became important when he decided to pursue a career in American politics.

6n2 **Accused of arson:** "Alexander Sullivan's Record," written in Devoy's handwriting, n.d.; NLI, Devoy Papers, MS 18142(1).

7n1 **His career in the press was brief:** Michael Funchion, *Chicago's Irish Nationalists 1881–1890* (New York: Arno, 1976), 45.

7n2 **Having secured a good job:** McEnnis, *Clan-na-Gael*, 144; Federal Writers Project, "Case of Dr. Cronin," 12.

7n3 **Like Sullivan, Buchanan was of Irish stock:** Margaret Buchanan was born in County Tyrone in 1847 and in 1851 moved with her recently widowed mother to Michigan, where they joined other family members. *New York Times*, "Noted Woman Writer Dead," Aug. 29, 1903.

8n1 **The editor, C. H. Ray:** Willis J. Abbot, "Women in Chicago Journalism," *Review of Reviews* 11, no. 65 (June 1895): 664.

8n2 **Margaret Sullivan was regarded:** *Gaelic American* (New York), Feb. 21, 1925; O'Brien, *Evening Memories*, 124.

8n3 **She was on the editorial staff:** W. J. Abbot, "Chicago Newspapers and Their Makers," *Review of Reviews* 11, no. 65 (1895): 664; *Good Housekeeping* 7 (1888): 238.

8n4 **In an anonymous letter:** Colvin had been elected by a coalition of Germans and Irish who had come together partly because the incumbent, *Tribune* owner Joseph Medill, had bowed to pressure from temperance movements to enforce a long-neglected Sunday drinking ban. This ban impacted most heavily on German and Irish laborers, whose only free day was Sunday. Smith, *Urban Disorder*, 103. The City Council was then known as the Common Council.

8n5 **He claimed that she had used her influence:** On the Catholic Church and public schools see Timothy Walch, "Catholic Social Institutions and Urban Development: The View from Nineteenth-Century Chicago and Milwaukee," *Catholic Historical Review* 64, no. 1 (Jan. 1978): 16–32; Walch, "The Catholic Press and the Campaign for Parish Schools: Chicago and Milwaukee 1850–1885," *U.S. Catholic Historian* 3, no. 4 (Spring 1984): 254–72.

8n6 **After trials in October 1876:** In the first trial, the jury failed to reach a unanimous verdict. Professor David Swing, a well-known preacher and friend of Mary Todd Lincoln, widow of the president, was certain that the killing of Hanford would destroy Sullivan's life: "Let us pity tenderly the widow and the fatherless, and pity also the hearthstone of Alexander and Margaret Sullivan. The ruin of their home, founded only last spring, seems complete." *Chicago Tribune*, "What Prof. Swing Thinks of the Homicide," Aug. 20, 1876.

8n7 **According to a contemporary commentator:** For detail on the Hanford Murder see Charles H. Wood, "The Sullivan Trial," *American Law Register* (1852–91), 25, no. 7, n.s., vol. 16 (July 1877): 384–92; Isaac E. Adams, *Life of Emery A. Storrs* (Chicago: G. L. Howe, 1886), 548–65; *Thirteenth Annual Report of the Board of Public Works to the Common Council of the City of Chicago for the Municipal Fiscal Year Ending March 31 1874* (Chicago: J. S. Thompson, 1874), 23. Funchion, *Chicago's Irish Nationalists*, 26–29. The *Philadelphia Press* noted that Judge McAllister and Thomas A. Moran (one of Sullivan's attorneys) were elected at the next judicial hearing. Charles Reed, the prosecutor in the case, was not. This "immense change of votes from one party to the other showed the current of popular sympathy." *Philadelphia Press*, "Who Is Sullivan," April 1883; copy in TNA (UK), FO 5/1961.

8n8 **At the second trial:** McEnnis, *Clan-na-Gael*, 144.

9n1 **The board had responsibility:** *Thirteenth Annual Report of the Board of Public Works to the Common Council of the City of Chicago*.

9n2 **He set his sights on a legal career:** The college was a department of the now defunct Chicago University, and the city's first law school. It was established in 1859 and in 1891 became part of Northwestern University.

9n3 *However, by 1879:* Federal Writers Project, "Case of Dr. Cronin," 21, 46. Sullivan's probate record states that he was a lawyer from 1873 to 1913, which is untrue. Alexander Sullivan probate record, Cook County Archives.

9n4 *Soon after his admission to the bar:* Daniel E. Sutherland, *The Confederate Carpetbaggers* (Baton Rouge: Louisiana State University Press, 1988), 107.

9n5 *Once again, Sullivan proved adept:* "Alexander Sullivan's Record." Le Caron suggests that Sullivan was involved with the Fenians while he was in Chicago, but there is little evidence for this. However, it is very likely that Sullivan cultivated useful friendships and would have known many members. [Thomas Miller Beach], *Twenty-Five Years in the Secret Service: The Recollections of a Spy by Major Henri Le Caron* (London: William Heinemann, 1892), 63–64.

9n6 *The official name of Clan na Gael:* "Constitution of the 'V.C.' [United Brotherhood]" (1881), article 1; NLI, Devoy Papers, MS 18015/16.

10n1 *The first Clan "camp" in Chicago:* Funchion, *Chicago's Irish Nationalists*, 8–9, 26–29; Funchion, "Irish Chicago: Church, Homeland, Politics and Class—The Shaping of an Ethnic Group, 1870–1890," in *Ethnic Chicago, ed.* Melvin G. Holli and Peter d'Alroy Jones (Grand Rapids, MI: William B. Eerdmans, 1981), 9. In 1850 the Irish made up 20 percent of the population of Chicago. In 1870 the almost 40,000 Irish-born residents of Chicago made up 28 percent of the foreign-born population and 13 percent of the total population. By 1890 there were 70,000 Irish-born residents in the city, accounting for 16 percent of all foreigners and almost 6.5 percent of the total population.

10n2 *If residents with at least one Irish-born parent:* Funchion, *Chicago's Irish Nationalists*, 9; Funchion, "Irish Chicago," 10. Funchion's own figures vary by over 13,000. In *Chicago's Irish Nationalists* he suggests 170,000; in "Irish Chicago" the figure given is 183,844. Carl Smith has suggested that as the city's population increased, the percentage of Irish-born in Chicago declined. In 1870 27.66 percent of all foreign-born Chicagoans were Irish; by 1890 this had dropped to 15.54%. See Smith, *Urban Disorder*, 373n.

10n3 *After the fire of 1871:* Bessie Louise Pierce, *A History of Chicago*, vol. 3, *The Rise of a Modern City, 1871–1893* (New York: Alfred A Knopf, 1957), 19, 35; Eileen M. McMahon, *What Parish Are You From?: A Chicago Irish Community and Race Relations* (Lexington: University Press of Kentucky, 1996), 8.

10n4 *By the early 1880s, the* **Chicago Tribune:** *Chicago Tribune*, quoted in Richard Schneirov, *Labor and Urban Politics: Class Conflict and the Origin of Modern Liberalism in Chicago 1864–97* (Urbana: University of Illinois Press, 1998), 104, 106n; Donald L. Miller, *City of the Century: The Epic of Chicago and the Making of America* (New York: Simon and Schuster, 1996), 442.

11n1 *Like many others:* Sullivan was a member of AOH Div 8, Chicago, but was suspended for nonpayment of dues. In 1883 he used his AOH connections to help secure his election as president of the Land League of America, an action that ultimately precipitated a split in the AOH in America and its relationship with its sister organization in Ireland. See the Ancient Order of Hibernians official website: http://www.aoh.com/pages/aoh_history.html.

11n2 *His initial attempt to join:* Members cast white and black balls in membership elections. If no black and white balls were available, a paper ballot was taken.

11n3 *Sullivan rose quickly:* "Alexander Sullivan's Record"; Alexander Sullivan to Michael Davitt, Nov. 9, 1891, TCD, Davitt Papers, MS 9432/2956; Funchion, *Chicago's Irish Nationalists*, 30.

12n1 *As one contemporary journalist:* Quoted in McEnnis, *Clan-na-Gael*, 140.

12n2 *Through the 1880s, Sullivan's influence:* Funchion, *Chicago's Irish Nationalists*, 26–29.

12n3 *Yet despite this unpromising background:* Parnell's speech on the Peace Preservation (Ireland) Bill; Hansard, House of Commons Debates, April 26, 1875, vol. 233, cols 1644–45.

13n1 *Parnell's trip was a risky one:* Quoted in R. Barry O'Brien, *The Life of Charles Stewart Parnell*, vol. 1 (New York: Harper and Brothers, 1898), 198.

13n2 *He appealed to Americans:* New York Times, Nov. 8, 1869. Parnell traveled with fellow MP John Dillon, but Dillon was repeatedly overshadowed by Parnell, particularly when it came to media coverage.

13n3 *Parnell's tour was initially intended:* Resolutions of the Irish National Land League, 1879; cited in D. B. Cashman, *The Life of Michael Davitt with a History of the Rise and Development of the Irish National Land League* (Boston: Murphy and McCarthy, 1881): 180–81.

13n4 *However, these aims were rapidly overtaken:* Alan O'Day has estimated that five times more money was raised by Parnell and Dillon for famine relief than for the Land League during their American tour. See Alan O'Day, "Media and Power: Charles Stewart Parnell's 1880 Mission to North America," in *Information, Media and Power through the Ages*, ed. Hiram Morgan, Historical Studies, 22 (Dublin: UCD Press, 2001), 212.

13n5 *Parnell's trip was a whirlwind tour:* NLI, Devoy Papers, MS 18041 (2), list of meetings that CSP attended in the United States, January–March 1880; Michael Davitt, *The Fall of Feudalism in Ireland; or, The Story of the Land League Revolution* (London: Harper and Brothers, 1904), 193–205; Donal McCartney, "Parnell and the American Connection," in *The Ivy Leaf: The Parnells Remembered*, ed. Donal McCartney and Pauric Travers (Dublin: UCD Press, 2006), 48. Funchion, *Chicago's Irish Nationalists*, 60. Both Funchion and McCartney suggest sixty-two cities, but I can find no evidence to support this.

13n6 *His excursion included:* O'Brien, *Life of Charles Stewart Parnell*, 1:201.

14n1 *In Cleveland:* Quoted in F. Hugh O'Donnell, *A History of the Irish Parliamentary Party— Butt and Parnell—Nationhood and Anarchy. The Curse of the American Money*, vol. 1 (London: Longmans, 1910), 446.

14n2 *It was in Chicago that Parnell met with the most support:* Alexander Sullivan, "Parnell as a Leader," *North American Review* 144 (June 1887): 613; Davitt, *Fall of Feudalism*, 204; Ely M. Janis, "Anointing the 'Uncrowned King of Ireland': Charles Stewart Parnell's 1880 American Tour and the Creation of a Transatlantic Land League Movement," *German Historical Institute Bulletin*, suppl. 5 (2008): 23, 32; Federal Writers Project, "Case of Dr. Cronin," 40; A. T. Andreas, *History of Chicago: From the Earliest Period to the Present Time*, vol. 3, *From the Fire of 1871 until 1885* (Chicago: A. T. Andreas, 1886), 866. The Exposition Building was built in 1872 on the site of the present-day Art Institute. It was demolished in 1892. The Key to the City was called "The Freedom of the City" in 1880.

14n3 *As Michael Davitt later recalled:* Davitt, *Fall of Feudalism*, 208; NLI, Devoy Papers, MS 18142 (11), Typescript of Poem— *The Irish Famine of 1880*; Alexander Sullivan to John Devoy, March 5, 1880, NLI, Devoy Papers, MS 18012 (17).

15n1 *Finally, Parnell rose to speak:* Alexander Sullivan to John Devoy, March 5, 1880, in *Devoy's Post-Bag*, ed. William O'Brien and Desmond Ryan, vol. 1 (Dublin: C. J. Fallon, 1948), 497; McCartney, "Parnell and the American Connection," 48; *Chicago Tribune*, Feb. 24, 1880; Davitt, *Fall of Feudalism*, 208. Conversion values here and elsewhere in text have been calculated using www.measuringworth.com and have been based on the Consumer Price Index (CPI).

15n2 *Alexander Sullivan accompanied Parnell:* The other organizers were Hynes and Finerty. John McDonald, *Diary of the Parnell Commission: Revised from The Daily News* (London: T. Fisher Unwin, 1890), 131. At the Parnell Commission, Parnell denied that the Clan had been involved—"I am absolutely convinced that the arrangements for my tours were in nobody's hands. We had to complain most strongly of the want of any organization to receive us or arrange for our tours." Sullivan, "Parnell as a Leader," 613.

15n3 *However, he concluded:* Sullivan, "Parnell as a Leader," 613.

15n4 *Irish Catholics received a significant boost:* Feehan grew up in Ireland and entered the seminary at Maynooth in 1847. Prior to his ordination, he was transferred to the Archdiocese of St. Louis, Missouri, where he was ordained in 1852. In 1865 he was appointed bishop of Nashville, and in 1880 he became the first archbishop of Chicago, a position he held until his death in 1902. Cornelius James Kirkfleet, *The Life of Patrick Augustine Feehan: Bishop of Nashville, First Archbishop of Chicago, 1829–1902* (Chicago: Martre, 1922), 19–21; 34, 79. Charles Ffrench, *Biographical History of the American Irish in Chicago* (Chicago: American Biographical Publishing, 1897), 5.

16n1 *However, Archbishop Feehan:* Kirkfleet, Feehan's biographer, maintained that Feehan had a close family connection to the Young Irelander Thomas Francis Meagher, and it could be argued that Feehan's attitude toward physical-force republicanism mirrored Meagher's. Kirkfleet, *Life of Patrick August Feehan*, 2.

16n2 *He sympathized with the aspirations:* Ibid., 277.

16n3 *In an 1882 address:* The address was given at the Moore Annual Celebration held at the Central Music Hall. Quoted in ibid., 281.

16n4 *Perhaps this awareness of oppression:* Occasionally, the establishment of national parishes caused huge controversies, such as the one that wracked the Polish St. Hedwig Parish in the 1880s and 1890s. Edward R. Kantowicz, "Polish Chicago: Survival through Solidarity," in Holli and Jones, *Ethnic Chicago*, 183–84.

16n5 *Following Feehan's death:* John Finerty, spokesman for the United Irish Societies, July 1902, quoted in Kirkfleet, *Life of Patrick Augustine Feehan*, 294. Clan na Gael guards marched in Feehan's funeral procession in 1902 (ibid., 345).

17n1 *Within a decade he had transformed St. Gabriel's:* Louise Carroll Wade, *Chicago's Pride: The Stockyards, Packingtown, and Environs in the Nineteenth Century* (Urbana: University of Illinois Press, 1987), 274–75, 294.

17n2 *Cronin was "a fine-looking":* McEnnis, *Clan-na-Gael*, 129.

17n3 *According to the journalist:* Eugen Seeger, *Chicago: The Wonder City* (Chicago: Geo. Gregory Printing, 1893), 275.

19n1 *He enrolled at the Missouri Medical College:* Catalog of the *St. Louis University* (St. Louis, MO: Ev. E. Carreras); *Thirty-Eighth Annual Announcement of Missouri Medical College, 1878–1879*, 12. I am grateful to Alice Hubbard of Pius XII Memorial Library, St. Louis University, and Mark Peterson of the Bernard Becker Medical Library, Washington University at St. Louis, for helping me locate this information.

19n2 *Cronin was an ambitious:* The college had been established in 1869, and was reorganized and reopened by Cronin and his associates in 1879.

19n3 *He was sufficiently embedded: Report of the United States Commissioners to the Paris Universal Exposition 1878*, vol. 1 (Washington, DC: Government Printing Office, 1880), 58. The state commissioners were appointed to represent the interest of their state at the exposition, but were not entitled to either pay or expense accounts.

19n4 *However, Cronin soon established:* Cronin and the Conklins lived at 351 North Clark Street (now 1000 North Clark Street, at the corner of Oak and Clark) before moving to the Windsor Theatre Building (at the northwest corner of Clark and Division Streets) in late 1887. Conklin was the proprietor of a large saloon underneath the Windsor Theatre Building, and also owned one at 81 North Clark Street. *Chicago Globe*, "Trunk Mystery," May 6, 1889; *The Lakeside Annual Directory of the City of Chicago* (Chicago: Chicago Directory Company, 1889), 412; *Chicago Tribune*, "Burlingham Is Back," Oct. 27, 1889.

19n5 *He was a prominent member: Chicago Tribune*, "She Is Still Looking for Dr. Cronin," March 18, 1894.

19n6 *He regularly sang: Chicago Tribune*, Sept. 7, 1884.

CHAPTER TWO

20 **Then in 1867 uprisings began:** Maureen Hartigan, Alan O'Day, and Roland Quinault, "Irish Terrorism in Britain: A Comparison between the Acts of the Fenians in the 1860s and Those of Republican Groups since 1972," in *Ireland's Terrorist Dilemma*, ed. Yonah Alexander and Alan O'Day (Dordrecht: Martinus Nijhoff, 1986), 52–53. William Allen, Michael Larkin, and Michael O'Brien were executed, while Edward O'Meagher Condon and Patrick Melody were imprisoned and eventually exiled.

21n1 **William Gladstone:** Lawrence J. McCaffrey, "Components of Irish Nationalism," in *Perspectives on Irish Nationalism, ed.* Thomas E. Hachey and Lawrence J. McCaffrey (Lexington: University Press of Kentucky, 1989), 12. Alongside the removal of state support for the minority church, disestablishment also dispensed with the last remnants of the hated tithe system, which had forced Catholics and Protestants alike to pay for the upkeep of a church that ministered to a small minority of the population.

21n2 **John Devoy:** John Devoy, *Recollections of an Irish Rebel* (New York: Charles D. Young, 1929), 250. Gladstone saw the actions of the Fenians (he described Fenianism as "a foul disease afflicting society") as a consequence of mismanagement of Ireland. Indeed it was not, as the Amnesty Association claimed, the case that "the Prime Minister of England has repeatedly and distinctly avowed that it is to the boldness of your conduct that Ireland owes the passing of those remedial measures to which English statesmen point as concessions to the Irish people." Whatever his motivation, concessions were made, and as is often the case, it is what was believed rather than what was most important. Seán McConville, *Irish Political Prisoners, 1848–1922* (London: Routledge, 2003), 224 (Gladstone speech at Southport, Dec. 19, 1869); ibid., 223, quote from *Freeman's Journal*, Jan. 10, 1871; Niall Whelehan, *The Dynamiters: Irish Nationalism and Political Violence in the Wider World, 1867–1900* (Cambridge: Cambridge University Press, 2012), 73.

21n3 **These victories were still some way off:** O'Sullivan Burke, like Thomas J. Kelly, Timothy Deasy, and Michael O'Brien, had fought in the Union army in the American Civil War.

21n4 **Five men and one woman:** K. R. M. Short, *The Dynamite War: Irish-American Bombers in Victorian Britain* (Dublin: Gill and Macmillan, 1979), 10–11; Hansard, House of Commons Debates, March 9, 1868, vol. 190, cols. 1215–18. Barrett's execution on May 26, 1868, was the last public hanging in England.

22 **James J. O'Kelly, senior Clan man:** James J. O'Kelly, Berlin, to John Devoy, Oct. 24, 1882, in *Devoy's Post-Bag*, ed. William O'Brien and Desmond Ryan, vol. 2 (Dublin: C. J. Fallon, 1953), 155.

23n1 **Gestures were also used:** X [Luke Dillon] to Devoy, [n.d.; ca. March 15, 1887], in ibid., 2:303.

23n2 **The Revolutionary Directory:** "Constitution of the 'V.C.'" (1881), article 4; NLI, Devoy Papers, MS 18015/16. The Executive Committee was reduced to five members by Sullivan in 1881.

23n3 **At a state level:** Ibid., article 2. In 1881 there were Districts from A to P; Thomas N. Brown, *Irish-American Nationalism 1870–1890* (New York: J. B. Lippincott, 1966), 66.

24 **However, these lists were often incomplete:** "Constitution of the 'V.C.,'" article 11.

25n1 **Picnics, balls, and fairs:** Circular issued by Executive Committee of the Clan, May 5, 1883, quoted in *Report of the Special Commission on Parnellism and Crime*, vol. 12 (London: Her Majesty's Stationery Office, 1890), 102.

25n2 **However, their primary focus:** John Corrigan, "United Irish Societies of Chicago," in *Irish-American Voluntary Organizations*, ed. Michael Funchion (Westport, CT: Greenwood Press, 1983), 278; Charles Fanning, "Robert Emmet and Nineteenth-Century Irish America," *New Hibernia Review* 8, no. 4 (Winter 2004): 76–77. Cronin and Sullivan appeared at the same event honoring Emmet in 1884.

25n3 **Most popular of all:** T. D. Sullivan, *Recollections of Troubled Times in Irish Politics* (Dublin: M. H. Gill and Son, 1905), 178.

25n4 **T. P. O'Connor:** T. P. O'Connor, *The Parnell Movement* (new and revised ed., London: Ward & Downey, 1887), 137.

25n5 **At the St. Patrick's Day celebration:** *Chicago Tribune*, "The Green Flag Waved," March 18, 1888.

25n6 **From 1876 onward:** Corrigan, "United Irish Societies of Chicago," 276. Ann Durkin Keating, *Chicagoland: City and Suburbs in the Railway Age* (Chicago: University of Chicago Press, 2005), 123. Ogden's Grove was established as a family picnic ground in 1879 by members of the Krieger Verein, a German veteran's association that was primarily a social club.

25n7 **As "Mr Dooley":** ["There's one thing about the Irish of this town . . . they give picnics that does beat all. By heavens if Ireland could be freed by a picnic, it would not only be free today, but an Empire."] Finley Peter Dunne, *Mr. Dooley and the Chicago Irish: The Autobiography of a Nineteenth-Century Ethnic Group*, ed. with a new introduction by Charles Fanning (Washington, DC: Catholic University of America Press, 1987), 286.

26n1 **There was Irish dancing:** *Chicago Tribune*, "Disappointed Irishmen," Aug. 16, 1889.

26n2 **Further evidence of Irish Americans':** *Chicago Tribune*, "The Green Flag Waved," March 18, 1888.

26n3 **An elaborate ceremony:** John Devoy, "The Story of Clan na Gael," *Gaelic American* (New York), Nov. 29, 1924. Unsurprisingly, former prisoners such as John Devoy disliked this element of bondage. Over the course of several years, the more extreme rituals were abolished or modified.

26n4 **It was essential that the Senior Guardian gave a stirring performance:** "Ritual of the United Brotherhood," (1890), 3–4, 6, NLI, Devoy Papers, MS 18015/15.

27 **The new member then swore:** Ibid., 11–12, 13–14, 15–16.

28n1 **Central control of finances:** "Constitution of the 'V.C.,'" articles 18, 12, 10.

28n2 **All camps had their own code:** Ibid., article 10.

28n3 **Every camp meeting closed:** "Ritual of the United Brotherhood," 24.

29n1 **Writing of Devoy, he noted:** John Dillon, M.P., to Devoy, Aug. 6, 1891, in O'Brien and Ryan, *Devoy's Post-Bag*, 2:320.

29n2 **It highlighted the dire conditions:** McConville, *Irish Political Prisoners*, 220; Padraic Kenney, "'I Felt a Kind of Pleasure in Seeing Them Treat Us Brutally': The Emergence of the Political Prisoner, 1865–1910," *Comparative Studies in Society and History* 54, no. 4 (2012): 873–78. See Jeremiah O'Donovan Rossa's account of his time in prison, *O'Donovan Rossa's Prison Life: Six Years in English Prisons* (New York: P. J. Kennedy, 1874). Isaac Butt, the barrister and founder of the Home Rule movement, was president of the Amnesty Association.

30n1 **Upon his arrival:** Quoted in Short, *Dynamite War*, 24.

30n2 **Alongside men such as Jerome Collins:** Brown, *Irish-American Nationalism*, 65.

30n3 **The Catalpa, captained by George S. Anthony:** Philip Fennell and Marie King, eds., *John Devoy's Catalpa Expedition* (New York: New York University Press, 2006), introduction, 20–24.

31n1 **The outrageous and daring rescue:** Dr. William Carroll ["H"] to [Patrick Mahon], June 13, 1876, in *Devoy's Post-Bag*, ed. William O'Brien and Desmond Ryan, vol. 1 (Dublin: C. J. Fallon, 1948), 181. The escaped prisoners were Thomas Darragh, Martin Horgan, Michael Harrington, Henry Hassett, Robert Cranston, and James Wilson. See Freemantle Prison, http://www.fremantleprison.com.au/Pages/Convict.aspx.

31n2 **As John Boyle O'Reilly:** John Boyle O'Reilly to John Devoy, June 10, 1876, in O'Brien and Ryan, *Devoy's Post-Bag*, 1:174.

31n3 **Therefore, the timing of his meeting:** R. K. Morris, *John P. Holland: Inventor of the Modern Submarine* (Annapolis, MD: United States Naval Institute, 1966), 22; R. K. Morris, "John P. Holland and the Fenians," *Journal of the Galway Archaeological and Historical Society* 31, no. 1 (1964): 25–38.

32n1 **One of the more outlandish propoals:** *Irish World*, Dec. 4, 1875, and June 9, 1877, quoted in Whelehan, *Dynamiters*, 138, 235.

32n2 **Few knew the precise details:** Dr. William Carroll to John Devoy, February 1, 1877, quoted in Morris, *John P. Holland*, 26.

32n3 **Blakely Hall:** Lionel Sackville West, Washington, DC, to Lord Grenville, July 14, 1883, TNA (UK), FO 5/1862; Denis Donohoe, Baltimore, to Grenville, October 1883, TNA (UK), FO 5/1862.

32n4 **Most of the construction work:** Morris, *John P. Holland*, 37–38.

32n5 **Much of the Skirmishing Fund:** "Account of money spent by the Skirmishing Fund," n.d., NLI, Devoy Papers, MS 18016 (10); Brown, *Irish-American Nationalism*, 73. The account indicates that $25,000 was spent on the Fenian Ram, and a further $2,090 was paid to J. J. Breslin as watchman, while $2,000 was spent on O'Mahony's funeral. An additional $16,000 was loaned to Clan na Gael, and $165 was spent on a reception for Parnell.

33n1 **This fund was controlled:** Whelehan, *Dynamiters*, 81–82.

33n2 **One night in July 1883:** Lionel Sackville West, Washington, DC, to Lord Grenville, July 17, 1883, TNA (UK), FO 5/1862; Robert Charles Clipperton, HM Consul, Philadelphia, to Grenville, Sept. 27, 1883, TNA (UK), FO 5/1862; Denis Donohoe, Baltimore, to Grenville, Oct. 18, 1883, TNA (UK), FO 5/1862. Morris, *John P. Holland*, 46–47, suggests that this happened in November, but evidence from the Foreign Office Papers indicates that July is more accurate. Holland complained to John Devoy about the theft but received no response: "No official explanation was ever made to me concerning it. As a result, I never bothered again with my backers, nor they with me." Holland to ___, [n.d], quoted in Morris, *John P. Holland*, 47.

34n1 **A growing number:** Clan circular, April 19, 1880, quoted in *Report of the Special Commission*, 12:102.

34n2 **In a letter to Devoy in September:** Sullivan to Devoy, Sept. 4, 1880, in O'Brien and Ryan, *Devoy's Post-Bag*, 1:549–60.

35n1 **On August 3:** Clan na Gael circular, NLI, Devoy Papers, MS 18015 (3).

35n2 **They also voted for significant changes:** Printed copy of the "Constitution of the 'V.C. [United Brotherhood]'" (1881), 1, NLI, Devoy Papers, MS 18015/16.

35n3 **Then the convention promptly voted:** Michael F. Funchion, *Chicago's Irish Nationalists 1881–1890* (New York: Arno, 1976), 68, 83.

35n4 **There was an element of Greenhorns versus Narrowbacks:** Timothy J. Meagher, "'Irish All the Time': Ethnic Consciousness among the Irish in Worcester, Massachusetts, 1880–1905," *Journal of Social History* 19, no. 2 (Winter 1985): 273–75.

36n1 **By 1884 the Clan leadership:** Duke Bailie, *The Cronin Case: The Assassination of Dr. Patrick Henry Cronin* (Chicago: Rhodes and McClure, 1890), 23.

36n2 **As William O'Brien:** William O'Brien, *Evening Memories* (Dublin: Maunsel, 1920), 141.

36n3 **Sullivan observed:** Sullivan to Devoy, October 13, 1880, in O'Brien and Ryan, *Devoy's Post-Bag*, 1:556.

36n4 **Shortly after he became chairman:** "Alexander's Record," written in Devoy's hand, n.d., NLI, Devoy Papers, MS 18142 (1).

37n1 **The British consul in New York:** E. M. Archibald, New York, to Lionel Sackville West, Jan. 16, 1882, TNA (UK), FO 5/1816. In 1882 $100,000 was the equivalent of £20,000 and many of the primary and secondary sources about this transaction refer to the sterling amount.

37n2 **Devoy was horrified:** Terry Golway, *Irish Rebel: John Devoy and America's Fight for Irish Free-dom* (New York: St. Martin's Griffin, 1998), 144.

37n3 **Egan resented:** "Alexander's Record," written in Devoy's hand, n.d., NLI, Devoy Papers, MS 18142 (1); Christy Campbell, *Fenian Fire: The British Government Plot to Assassinate Queen Victoria* (London: HarperCollins, 2002), 106; *Gaelic American* (New York), Nov. 17, 1923.

37n4 **Despite Devoy's growing antipathy:** See for example Sullivan to Devoy, July 14, 1882; Sullivan to Devoy, Oct. 12, 1882; Sullivan to Devoy, Oct. 19, 1882, in O'Brien and Ryan, *Devoy's Post-Bag*, 2:128–29, 153–56.

38n1 **Devoy was a prickly character:** Sullivan to Devoy, Sept. 2, 1882; in ibid, 137–38.

38n2 **Reflecting on the early 1880s:** "Alexander's Record," written in Devoy's hand, n.d., NLI, Devoy Papers, MS 18142 (1).

38n3 **At its proceedings:** Clan na Gael circular, April 19, 1880, in *Verbatim Copy of the Parnell Commission Report* (Dublin: Irish Loyal and Patriotic Union, 1890), 124.

38n4 **Many attended in response to a letter:** Copy of secret circular from the leaders of Clan na Gael to members, sent to Harcourt, April 30, 1883, TNA (UK), HO 144/1537/1.

38n5 **From April 1883:** As president of the National League, Sullivan embarked on an exten-sive lecture tour through over forty cities in fifteen states while writing a series of articles and giving interviews, all aimed at furthering the National League's agenda—promoting Home Rule and demanding additional reforms for Ireland. Sullivan's tour was a resounding success. Thomas Power O'Connor and Robert M. MacWade, *Gladstone-Parnell and the Great Irish Struggle* (Philadelphia: Hubbard Bros., 1886), 593–94.

39n1 **Sullivan's involvement with both the Clan and the League:** *Chicago Times*, "Alexander Sul-livan," June 13, 1889.

39n2 **As president of the National League:** Quoted in O'Connor and MacWade, *Gladstone-Parnell*, 659.

CHAPTER THREE

40n1 **There were a few explosions in Britain:** Translated letter, Anonymous to Consul at Leg-horn, Oct. 17, 1881; in A. P. Inglis, acting consul, Leghorn, Oct. 21, 1881, to A. Paget, Rome, TNA (UK), HO 144/84/a7266; Niall Whelehan, *The Dynamiters: Irish Nationalism and Political Violence in the Wider World, 1867–1900* (Cambridge: Cambridge University Press, 2012), 85, 273–74; Shane Kenna, *War in the Shadows: The Irish-American Fenians Who Bombed Victorian Britain* (Dublin: Merrion Press, 2013), 132.

40n2 **The first significant bombings:** Whelehan, *Dynamiters*, 110; K. R. M. Short, *The Dyna-mite War: Irish-American Bombers in Victorian Britain* (Dublin: Gill and Macmillan, 1979), 205–8; Draft Reply to the Secretary of State from Commissioners of Police, Jan. 25, 1885, TNA (UK), MEPO/3/3070.

40n3 **The Irish World celebrated:** *Irish World*, Feb. 7, 1885, quoted in Niall Whelehan, "Skir-mishing, *The Irish World*, and Empire, 1876–1886," *Éire-Ireland* 42 (Spring–Summer 2007): 196.

41n1 **By commandeering the Land League funds:** On May 6, 1882, Cavendish and Burke were killed by a hitherto largely unknown Irish republican secret society, the Invincibles, and stories circulated suggesting that Parnell both knew and approved of the killings.

41n2 **The debate was not just a political one:** Niall Whelehan, "'Cheap as Soap and Common as Sugar': The Fenians, Dynamite and Scientific Warfare," in *The Black Hand of Repub-licanism: Fenianism in Modern Ireland*, ed. Ferghal McGarry and James McConnell (Dub-lin: Irish Academic Press, 2009), 111–12.

41n3 **Cronin told a close friend:** Tom O'Connor, quoted in John T. McEnnis, *The Clan-na-Gael and the Murder of Dr. Cronin* (Chicago: F. J. Schulte and J. W. Iliff, 1890), 150. Le Caron claimed that Cronin was an ardent advocate of the dynamite policy and was a chief instructor in the use and handling of explosives. There is no evidence that this was the case. [Thomas Miller Beach], *Twenty-Five Years in the Secret Service: The Recollections of a Spy by Major Henri Le Caron* (London: William Heinemann, 1892), 223; *Chicago Times*, "Spy Le Caron's Story," May 26, 1889.

41n4 **Devoy had great respect:** Devoy, quoted in Short, *Dynamite War*, 48.

42n1 **Lomasney was strongly in favor:** Lomasney to Devoy, quoted in ibid., 49; ibid., 48; McConville, *Irish Political Prisoners*, 228, n56. Lomasney had his play, a patriotic drama titled *Irish Hearts*, put on in Chicago in the early 1880s. It was not a success. *Chicago Tribune*, June 6, 1889.

42n2 **As he told Devoy:** Lomasney to Devoy, February 1881, quoted in Michael F. Funchion, *Chicago's Irish Nationalists 1881–1890* (New York: Arno, 1976), 67.

42n3 **In February 1881 there were explosions:** Lomasney ["Charles Waldron," "K"] to Devoy, Feb. 23, 1881, in *Devoy's Post-Bag*, ed. William O'Brien and Desmond Ryan, vol. 2 (Dublin: C. J. Fallon, 1953), 44.

42n4 **As the men prepared to row away:** Robert Anderson to Under Secretary of State, Home Office, Dec. 14, 1891, TNA (UK), HO144/145/a38008; Short, *Dynamite War*, 200; The character of Zero in Robert Louis Stevenson's 1885 novel *The Dynamiter* is loosely based on Lomasney. Deaglán Ó Donghaile, *Blasted Literature: Victorian Political Fiction and the Shock of Modernism* (Edinburgh: Edinburgh University Press, 2011), 38.

43n1 **Sullivan believed that "the mystery":** Clan na Gael circular, Dec. 23, 1885, in *Verbatim Copy of the Parnell Commission Report* (Dublin: Irish Loyal and Patriotic Union, 1890), 143.

43n2 **Between 1881 and 1885:** Funchion, *Chicago's Irish Nationalists*, 83–86; Henry M. Hunt, *The Crime of the Century; or, The Assassination of Dr. Patrick Henry Cronin* (Chicago: H. L. and D. H. Kockersperger, 1889), 66.

43n3 **The British authorities placed the blame:** McEnnis, *Clan-na-Gael*, 65. On the impact transatlantic terror had on the Anglo-American relationship, see Jonathan Gannt, *Irish Terrorism in the Atlantic Community, 1865–1922* (London: Palgrave Macmillian, 2010), 128–86.

43n4 **The British government believed:** John Y. Simon, ed., *The Papers of Ulysses S. Grant*, vol. 21, *Nov. 1, 1870–May 31, 1871* (Carbondale: Southern Illinois University Press, 1998), 221–26. See for example O'Donovan Rossa to Ulysses S. Grant, March 18 and April 24, 1871; Rutherford B. Hayes to Grant, Sept. 23, 1872; Thomas Condon to Grant, [n.d]. O'Meagher Condon was pardoned in 1878.

43n5 **Back in June 1881, Edward Thornton:** Edward Thornton, Washington, DC, to Early Granville, June 27, 1881. Confidential. TNA (UK), FO 5/1863.

44n1 **The attacks at the very heart:** Kenna, *War in the Shadows*, 214–17. "A Bill to Prevent and Punish Crimes Committed by Means of Explosive Compounds," 48th Congress, 2nd Session, quoted in ibid., 215.

44n2 **Then, in a State of the Union address:** Lionel Sackville-West to Marquis of Salisbury, Dec. 8, 1885, TNA (UK), HO/144/133/a340707c.

45n1 **In August 1886:** Report of Committee of U.B. Appointed at the Chicago Convention 1888 to Examine Charges Brought by John Devoy against Alexander Sullivan, Michael Boland, and Denis Feely, NLI, Devoy Papers, MS 18018.

45n2 **Mitchel, himself an exile:** John Mitchel, *The Last Conquest of Ireland (Perhaps)* (London: R. and T. Washbourne, 1860), 139. Mitchel was exiled to Van Diemen's Land (now Tasmania) and later escaped to America, arriving there in November 1853.

46n1 **From the Society of United Irishmen:** Theobald Wolfe Tone, "Memoirs I, Youth and Early Political Career 1763–1792," in *Life of Theobald Wolfe Tone*, ed. Thomas Bartlett (Dublin: Lilliput Press, 1998), 46.

46n2 **By 1880 there was an acute awareness:** Sullivan to Devoy, October 13, 1880, in *Devoy's Post-Bag*, ed. William O'Brien and Desmond Ryan, vol. 1 (Dublin: C. J. Fallon, 1948), 556.

47n1 **And yet the Clan thrived:** E. M. Archibald to Lionel Sackville West, Jan. 16, 1882, TNA (UK), FO 5/1816.

47n2 **As a result of that organization:** Thomas N. Brown, *Irish-American Nationalism 1870–1890* (New York: J. B. Lippincott, 1966), 66; Short, *Dynamite War*, 29; Lawrence J. McCaffrey, "Forging Forward and Looking Back," in *The New York Irish*, ed. Ronald H. Bayer and Timothy J. Meagher (Baltimore: Johns Hopkins University Press, 1997), 224; McEnnis, *Clan-na-Gael*, 80; Owen McGee, "Irish Republicanism in the Age of Parnell: The Irish Republican Brotherhood, 1879–1893" (PhD thesis, University College Dublin, 2003), 1:231. The figure of 40,000 is likely to be an exaggeration, and if accurate certainly includes both factions of the Clan.

47n3 **The city was:** Louis H. Sullivan, *The Autobiography of an Idea* (New York: Press of the American Institute of Architects, 1924), 200–201.

48n1 **By 1883 the Irish dominated:** Funchion, *Chicago's Irish Nationalists*, 42.

48n2 **Even his critics conceded:** William O'Brien, *Evening Memories* (Dublin: Maunsel, 1920), 142.

48n3 **Walter Wellman:** Walter Wellman, *Daily True American* (Trenton, NJ), "Notes from the Capital," June 12, 1889.

48n4 **But for years the flood:** Gaelic American (New York), "The Story of Clan na Gael," Jan. 10, 1925; Funchion, *Chicago's Irish Nationalists*, 46.

48n5 **Devoy complained that under Sullivan's control:** Gaelic American (New York), "The Story of Clan na Gael," Jan. 10, 1925.

49n1 **The Store was a saloon:** Daily Argus (Crawfordsville, IN), April 5, 1887.

49n2 **But he was not content with wealth alone:** Fremont O. Bennett, *Politics and Politicians of Chicago, Cook County and Illinois* (Chicago: Blakely Printing, 1886), 525, 529.

49n3 **These he used to secure:** Other useful connections included Sullivan's brother, Florence, who was clerk in the Superior Court of Cook County (and later a journalist for the *Chicago Herald*), and his friend Timothy Crean, who was secretary of the Board of Election Commissioners. Funchion, *Chicago's Irish Nationalists*, 45. Harrison was reelected as mayor in 1893 but was assassinated later that year.

49n4 **Although some Irish found jobs:** In the 1880s the Irish comprised 28 percent of laborers, 65 percent of freight handlers, 29 percent of hod carriers, and 28 percent of lumber vessel unloaders. In 1884 the average annual earnings of an Irish head of household in an unskilled job were $362; those of a German were $351, while British unskilled workers earned $420 and Scandinavians $470. For a more detailed breakdown, see table 9: Occupational Structure by Nativity, 1870, 1880, 1890, and table 10: Earnings of Head of Household by Ethnic Group and Working-Class Sector, 1884, in Eric L. Hirsch, *Urban Revolt: Ethnic Politics in the Nineteenth-Century Chicago Labor Movement* (Berkeley: University of California Press, 1990), 92–93, 97; see also 118, 123–24.

50n1 **Few were as privileged:** Funchion, *Chicago's Irish Nationalists*, 14. Cronin was one of only 5 of the 161 physicians in the city who were of Irish Catholic origin (there were more than 161 physicians in Chicago, but only 161 were listed in Andreas, as explained below), while Sullivan was one of the 30 Irish or Irish American lawyers in a city of almost 500 lawyers. These figures are incomplete and do not include all members of the professions—only those distinguished enough to be listed in biographical histories such as A. T. Andreas, *History of Chicago: From the Earliest Period to the Present Time*, vols. 2, 3 (Chicago: A. T. Andreas, 1884, 1886). Foster in his closing speech to the jury indicated that in 1889 there were 2,100 lawyers in Cook County, which is likely to have been an exaggeration. McEnnis, *Clan-na-Gael*, 482.

50n2 **In the packinghouse:** Funchion, *Chicago's Irish Nationalists*, 46; Louise Carroll Wade, *Chicago's Pride: The Stockyards, Packingtown, and Environs in the Nineteenth Century* (Urbana: University of Illinois Press, 1987), 294. McInerney's funeral home (established 1873) is still in existence. On its promotional matchbox, it includes part of T. J. O'Donnell's poem: "Bring out the lace curtains and call McInerney; / I'm nearing the end of my life's pleasant journey. / Send quick for the priest, just tell him I'm dying / my last minutes on earth so swiftly are flying. / Tell dear Father Dorney I'm meeting my maker / (He's losing his old collection up taker) . . ." My thanks to Ellen Skerrett for alerting me to this.

50n3 **Dorney, along with other nationalist priests:** Richard Schneirov, *Labor and Urban Politics: Class Conflict and the Origin of Modern Liberalism in Chicago 1864–97* (Urbana: University of Illinois Press, 1998), 104–5ft, 121ft.

50n4 **One of the camps of that neighborhood:** Funchion, *Chicago's Irish Nationalists*, 46.

50n5 **Although the Irish often favored:** Schneirov, *Labor and Urban Politics*, 104.

50n6 **At the "Battle of the Viaduct":** James Green, *Death in the Haymarket: A Story of Chicago, the First Labor Movement and the Bombing That Divided Gilded Age America* (New York: Pantheon Books, 2006), 74–80; Schneirov, *Labor and Urban Politics*, 75.

50n7 **The Irish were also heavily involved:** Hirsch, *Urban Revolt*, 56, 135. Membership of the Knights of Labor in Chicago peaked at 27,000 in 1886, but began to collapse by the end of the year, at least partly because they were involved in the hog butcher strike that failed to achieve its aims. James R. Barrett, *Work and Community in the Jungle: Chicago's Packinghouse Workers, 1894–1922* (Urbana: University of Illinois Press, 1987), 122–26.

50n8 **In the early 1880s:** Bruce C. Nelson, "Revival and Upheaval: Religion, Irreligion, and Chicago's Working Class in 1886," *Journal of Social History* 25, no. 2 (Winter 1991): 247. By 1904 Irish involvement in the unions had increased significantly. Local unions in the packinghouses whose members were classified by nationality had 57% Irish membership when they made up only 25% of the workforce. Barrett, *Work and Community*, 140.

50n9 **But for most Irish workers:** Hirsch, *Urban Revolt*, 117.

51n1 **Seven men were indicted:** Schneirov, *Labor and Urban Politics*, 112n.

51n2 **He stood down as president:** Extract from *The United Irishman* (New York) in *The Abiline (Kansas) Reflector*, "The Irish Bolt," Oct. 23, 1884.

51n3 **When those negotiations broke down:** The newspaper suggested, though it seems unlikely, that Sullivan and Blaine had discussed Sullivan's possible candidacy for vice president. *Chicago Tribune*, "Sullivan Dead," Aug. 22, 1913.

51n4 **Sullivan promised the Irish American vote:** *New York Times*, "Kerwin and the Clan na Gael," July 17, 1894; "Alexander Sullivan Dead," Aug. 22, 1913; *Clinton Sunday News*, "Sullivan and the Irish Movement in 1884," June 23, 1889; James R. Barrett, *The Irish Way: Becoming Irish in the Multiethnic City* (New York: Penguin, 2012), 209.

51n5 **Devoy later claimed:** *Gaelic American* (New York), "The Story of Clan na Gael," Dec. 1, 1923.

52n1 **At the time, however:** Terry Golway, *Irish Rebel: John Devoy and America's Fight for Irish Freedom* (New York: St. Martin's Griffin, 1998), 151.

52n2 **Critics of Sullivan:** [Beach], *Twenty-Five Years in the Secret Service*, 293; Joseph P. O'Grady, *Irish-Americans and Anglo-American Relations, 1880–1888* (New York: Arno Press, 1976), 94; Kenna, *War in the Shadows*, 145.

52n3 **The convention that took place:** *Gaelic American* (New York), "The Story of Clan na Gael," Nov. 10, 1923.

53n1 **The constitution was altered:** Letter from the FC [Executive Directory] of the VC [United Brotherhood] to the "Officers and Members of the VC [United Brotherhood] of the US [United Sons]," Sept. 15, 1885. The letter comes from the anti-Triangle section of the Clan and is addressed to Clan members who remained in Sullivan's Clan. At this point Devoy and Hynes were out, but Cronin was still within Sullivan's Clan. Letter reproduced in Hunt, *Crime of the Century*, 70–76.

53n2 **Questions were raised:** Funchion, *Chicago's Irish Nationalists*, 87.

53n3 **Writing of the Land League:** Devoy in *Irish Nation*, Dec. 17, 1881, and March 11, 1882, quoted in Eric Foner, "Class, Ethnicity, and Radicalism in the Gilded Age: The Land League and Irish America," in *Politics and Ideology in the Age of the Civil War* (Oxford: Oxford University Press), 167–68.

53n4 **Sullivan, on the other hand:** Alexander Sullivan, "The American Republic and the Irish National League of America," *American Catholic Quarterly Review*, 9 (1884): 42.

53n5 **His criticisms may have been grounded:** Funchion, *Chicago's Irish Nationalists*, 88; Sullivan to Devoy, Jan. 13, 1885; Sullivan to Devoy, April 2, 1885; Sullivan to Devoy, April 7, 1885, in O'Brien and Ryan, *Devoy's Post-Bag*, 2:260–63. Through the early months of 1885, there were a series of touchy letters between Sullivan and Devoy that had little to do with the crisis in the Clan and more to do with the financial requirements of Devoy's paper, and Sullivan's determination to get Devoy to repay $350 he had loaned him. Devoy's *Irish Nation* was published between 1881 and 1885. Philip Fennell and Marie King, eds., *John Devoy's* Catalpa *Expedition* (New York: New York University Press, 2006), 174.

53n6 **The Triangle took immediate action:** NLI, Devoy Papers, MS 18016 (4), "Statement by the Triangle," Jan. 15, 1885; *Gaelic American* (New York), "The Story of Clan na Gael, Nov. 17, 1923.

54n1 **The offense was not a significant one:** *Gaelic American* (New York), "The Story of Clan na Gael," Nov. 10, 1923.

54n2 **Devoy recalled that so many were opposed:** *Gaelic American* (New York), "The Story of Clan na Gael," Nov. 17, 1923; [Beach], *Twenty-Five Years in the Secret Service*, 219–20.

54n3 **William Hoare:** W. R. Hoare, New York, to Marquess of Salisbury, May 20, 1887, TNA (UK), FO 5/2044.

54n4 **The circular implied:** Clan circular [issued by the Triangle], April, 26, 1885, in O'Brien and Ryan, *Devoy's Post-Bag*, 2:234.

55 **Indeed, John Boyle O'Reilly:** John Boyle O'Reilly to John Devoy, May 3, 1886, in ibid., 280–18.

CHAPTER FOUR

56n1 **Though they were members:** People of the State of Illinois v. Daniel Coughlin, Patrick O'Sullivan, Martin Bourk et al., Supreme Court of Illinois, RS # 901.001, Illinois State Archives, vol. 25939; Evidence of T. T. Conklin, October 25, 1889, 4:475; Evidence of Michael J. Kelly, Junior Guardian of Camp 20, 4:115; Evidence of Thomas F. O'Connor, 4:37; Evidence of Patrick McGarry, 4:57. Sullivan lived on Oak Street, while Cronin lodged with his friends the Conklins at 351 Clark Street, on the corner of Clark and Oak Streets, and later at 470 North Clark between Division and Goethe, in the Windsor Theatre Building. Cronin was a member of Camp 96 (later called Camp 234), publicly known as the Columbus Club, which met regularly in Phoenix Hall on Division Street. Sullivan was a member of Camp 20, publicly known as the Columbia Club, which met at Turner Hall. Cronin had established Camp 96 in 1885. Le Caron ([Thomas Miller Beach], *Twenty-Five Years in the Secret Service: The Recollections of a Spy by Major Henri Le Caron* [London: William Heinemann, 1892], 299) suggests that Cronin's camp was the Columbia Club and Sullivan's the Columbus, but testimony at the trial indicates the reverse.

56n2 **He was Senior Guardian:** The 18th Ward League was then known as the Banner League of Chicago. Cronin remained as president of the 18th Ward until 1888. [Beach], *Twenty-Five Years in the Secret Service*, 223–25.

56n3 **In addition, he was a member:** John T. McEnnis, *The Clan-na-Gael and the Murder of Dr. Cronin* (Chicago: F. J. Schulte and J. W. Iliff, 1890), 184; Eugen Seeger, *Chicago: The Wonder City* (Chicago: Geo. Gregory Printing, 1893), 274; *Chicago Daily Inter Ocean*, "Is Cronin Murdered?," May 6, 1889. Royal Arcanum (founded Boston 1877), Catholic Foresters (founded Chicago 1883), and Independent Order of Foresters were Catholic fraternal insurance societies. Cronin was also the deputy Grand Regent of the Royal Arcanum and had been a commander of the Knights of Pythias.

56n4 *By 1884 his prominence:* Chicago Tribune, "City Intelligence," Nov. 25, 1884.

56n5 *He also suspected him of embezzling:* Thomas P. O'Connor and Robert M. MacWade, *Gladstone-Parnell and the Great Irish Struggle* (Philadelphia: Hubbard Bros, 1886), 598–602; Patrick W. Ettinger, *Imaginary Lines: Border Enforcement and the Origins of Undocumented Immigration, 1882–1930* (Austin: University of Texas Press, 2009), 24.

57n1 *In June 1883, Sullivan:* Alexander Sullivan, Henry L. Hoguet, James Lynch, James Reynolds, and Patrick Smith, *Emigration versus Enforced Emigration: Addresses to Chester A. Arthur, President of the United States,* pamphlet (n.p.) of speeches delivered at the White House, June 23, 1883.

57n2 *He produced the standard Narrowback argument:* Terry Golway, *Irish Rebel: John Devoy and America's Fight for Irish Freedom* (New York: St. Martin's Griffin, 1998), 156; Kirby A. Miller, *Emigrants and Exiles: Ireland and the Irish Exodus to North America* (Oxford: Oxford University Press, 1985), 510–11.

57n3 *In 1882, as a new resident:* Sullivan to Devoy, Oct. 19, 1882, in *Devoy's Post-Bag,* ed. William O'Brien and Desmond Ryan, vol. 2 (Dublin: C. J. Fallon, 1953), 154.

57n4 *Unsurprisingly, Dorney reported:* Dorney claimed that Sullivan's wealth was generated by the shipment of cattle from a vast estate bequeathed to him in New Mexico and from a real estate deal he had made with Mike McDonald. *Chicago Tribune,* "P. W. Dunne on Dorney," June 16, 1889.

57n5 *Dunne was tried:* This was not the first time Dunne had difficulties with republican leadership. In 1865 Dunne and P. J. Meehan were dispatched to Ireland by the Fenian leadership. They carried with them secret documents, which had mysteriously disappeared upon their arrival in Dublin. The lost papers found their way into the hands of the British authorities and were used to secure the convictions of several senior Fenians. Meehan and Dunne were accused of treason, found guilty, and expelled, though both later persuaded the Clan that they were not guilty of the charge. Michael F. Funchion, *Chicago's Irish Nationalists* (New York: Arno, 1976), 89; McEnnis, *Clan-na-Gael,* 105.

58n1 *A contemporary observer noted:* Seeger, *Chicago,* 275.

58n2 *Documents circulated by Cronin:* Circular read by Cronin to his camp, quoted in *Chicago Tribune,* Dec. 21, 1889.

58n3 *In fact Cronin's actions backfired:* Federal Writers Project, "The Case of Dr. Cronin" (unpublished manuscript, n.d. [1936?]); Abraham Lincoln Presidential Library, Springfield, Illinois.

58n4 *The Clan constitution listed eleven offenses:* Camp 20 had nearly four hundred members. In addition to Sullivan the trial committee consisted of Henri Le Caron, Dan Coughlin, James J Cunnen, John Dwyer, John F. O'Malley, Lawrence Buckley and Frank Murray. "Constitution of the 'V.C.'" (1881), article 16, NLI, Devoy Papers, MS 18015/16; Duke Bailie, *The Cronin Case: The Assassination of Dr. Patrick Henry Cronin* (Chicago: Rhodes and McClure, 1890), 76; Henry M. Hunt, *The Crime of the Century; or, The Assassination of Dr. Patrick Henry Cronin* (Chicago: H. L. and D. H. Kockersperger, 1889), 69.

59n1 *Cronin refused to accept his dismissal:* [Beach], *Twenty-Five Years in the Secret Service,* 226.

59n2 *In September 1885 he was one of the authors:* Letter from the FC [Executive Directory] of the VC [United Brotherhood] to the "Officers and Members of the VC [United Brotherhood] of the US [United Sons]," September 15, 1885. Letter reproduced in Hunt, *Crime of the Century,* 70–76.

60n1 **As the dispute raged on:** William O'Mulcahy to Devoy, Feb. 28, 1886, in O'Brien and Ryan, *Devoy's Post-Bag*, 2:274.

60n2 **When he took the witness stand:** *New York Times*, "Cronin's Bitter Enemies," May 24, 1889.

61n1 **Convinced that the court cases:** Cronin to [Devoy], 1887, quoted in McEnnis, *Clan-na-Gael*, 159–61.

61n2 **He was convinced that Sullivan would rachet up his harassment:** Federal Writers Project, "Case of Dr. Cronin," 83–84. Evidence given by R. S. Iles at the Coroner's Inquest.

61n3 **The following year, his old school friend:** *Chicago Daily Inter Ocean*, May 24, 1889; *Chicago Evening News*, May 25, 1889.

61n4 **In a letter to Clan members:** Sullivan's letter of objection to Cronin's place on the committee, quoted in McEnnis, *Clan-na-Gael*, 130–31. Sullivan claimed there was a record at Buttevant, County Cork, that showed Cronin had been baptized on April 20, 1844. I have checked with the parish, and it has no record of anyone that could be Cronin having been baptized there around that time. Sullivan also claimed that Cronin said that after moving to Canada, he had remained there until after Lincoln's assassination in 1865 (which would make him either nineteen or twenty-one), and he argued that Cronin was a British citizen and a member of No. 2 Company, Nineteenth Battalion of the Canadian militia. Sullivan maintained that at most he could have been two years in the United States, and that more likely he was over twenty-one when he moved from Canada to the United States. Cronin's birth year is given variously as 1844 or 1846. His tombstone reads 1846–1889. Some census records indicate 1844, some 1846. The 1861 census of Canada lists Cronin's age as 17 next birthday, implying that 1844 is the correct year. See the Census Returns of 1861 for Canada, St. Catharines, Lincoln, Canada West, Roll C-1049, 20; Library and Archives Canada, Ottawa, Ontario. In this census, Cronin's father is listed as shoemaker, his mother Margaret is 53, sister Ellen is 20, and brother John is 27 (however, in the census of 1871 his sister Ellen is 28 rather than 30, casting doubt on the accuracy of the information).

61n5 **But the cross-examinations failed:** As a result of the Act of May 26, 1824, immigrants who were minors upon arrival in the United States had to wait two years to file their declaration of intent.

62n1 **As Devoy rather crudely put it:** Devoy speech at Central Music Hall, Chicago, 1889 quoted in *Gaelic American* (New York), "The Story of Clan na Gael," Jan. 17, 1923.

62n2 **Stories also circulated:** *Gaelic American* (New York), "The Story of Clan na Gael," Jan. 25, 1923.

62n3 **Devoy listed four specific charges:** Report of Committee of U.B. Appointed at the Chicago Convention 1888 to Examine Charges Brought by John Devoy against Alexander Sullivan, Michael Boland, and Denis Feely, NLI, Devoy Papers, MS 18018.

62n4 **A six-man jury:** The other committee members were Peter McCahey, P.A. O'Boyle, C.F. Byrnes, James J. Rogers and J.P. McMahon.

63n1 **Sullivan laid out several grounds:** Alexander Sullivan to P. A. O'Boyle, Sept. 15, 1888; NLI, Devoy Papers, MS 18018; *Chicago Tribune*, June 8, 1889.

63n2 **James apparently found the case:** Henry James, London, to Charles Eliot Norton, March 25 [1889], in *Henry James Letters*, ed. Leon Edel, vol. 3 (Cambridge, MA: Harvard University Press, 1890), 251–54. Oscar Wilde attended some of Le Caron's evidence testimony (his brother William was a journalist reporting the trial). Colm Toibín, "Outsiders in England and the Art of Being Found Out," in *Ford Madox Ford: Literary Networks and Cultural Transformation*, ed. Andrzeu Gasiorek and Daniel Moore (New York: Rodopi, 2008), 75.

63n3 **The first sessions of the Clan trial:** Christy Campbell, *Fenian Fire: The British Government Plot to Assassinate Queen Victoria* (London: HarperCollins, 2002), 305.

64n1 **In October 1888, Egan and Sullivan:** Algar Labouchere Thorold, *The Life of Henry Labou-*

chere (New York: G. P. Putnam's Sons, 1913), 280, 374; Labouchere in *Truth*, the periodical he founded, quoted in the *Advertiser* (Adelaide), April 15, 1889, National Library of Australia, http://trove.nla.gov.au/ndp/del/article/24474118; Labouchere to Pigott, Jan. 26, 1889, TNA (UK), HO/144/1538/8; McEnnis, *Clan-na-Gael*, 216.

64n2 *All the bitterness:* Quoted in Golway, *Irish Rebel*, 165. Devoy carried a revolver that had been given to him by Ricard O'Sullivan Burke.

64n3 *In contrast, Luke Dillon:* P. A. O'Boyle's report on the committee's deliberations, February 8, 1889, in NLI, Devoy Papers, MS 18018.

64n4 *Dillon managed to straddle both camps:* Owen McGee and Desmond McCabe, "Luke Dillon," *Dictionary of Irish Biography*, online at http://dib.cambridge.org/home.do.

65n1 *A number of witnesses came forward:* Niall Whelehan, *The Dynamiters: Irish Nationalism and Political Violence in the Wider World, 1867–1900* (Cambridge: Cambridge University Press, 2012), 184.

65n2 *Jury members C. F. Byrnes and J. D. McMahon:* J. D. McMahon to the United Brotherhood, Jan. 16, 1889. Report of Committee of U.B. Appointed at the Chicago Convention 1888 to Examine Charges Brought by John Devoy against Alexander Sullivan, Michael Boland, and Denis Feely, NLI, Devoy Papers, MS 18018; McEnnis, *Clan-na-Gael*, 237; Owen McGee, "Irish Republicanism in the Age of Parnell: The Irish Republican Brotherhood, 1879–1893" (PhD thesis, University College Dublin, 2003), 2:407.

65n3 *However, he reneged on this:* Peter McCahey [and Patrick Cronin], "To the FC of the UB," Jan. 15, 1889, NLI, Devoy Papers, MS 18018. The letter is in McCahey's handwriting, and at the end is added, in Cronin's handwriting: "I concur in the within and foregoing report as presented and signed by Dr. Peter McCahey and would recommend in strict fairness to all concerned and in justice to the entire organization that the evidence from which we deduce the foregoing be printed by the F.C. [Executive Directory], sent to each D.O. [District Officer] and by him read at general meeting of district over which he presides."

66n1 *His notes also formed the basis:* Quoted in *Chicago Tribune*, June 4, 1889; Hunt, *Crime of the Century*, 59.

66n2 *He told his friend Stephen Conley:* *Chicago Daily Inter Ocean*, May 24, 1889.

66n3 *Beggs despaired of Cronin's behavior:* John F. Beggs to Edward Spelman, Feb. 18, 1889, quoted in McEnnis, *Clan-na-Gael*, 126–27. Spelman was also a senior figure in the Whiskey Trust, a united group of distilleries in the Chicago area. {Ernest E. East, "The Distillers' and Cattle Feeders' Trust, 1887–1985," *Journal of the Illinois State Historical Society* 45, no. 2 (Summer 1952): 101. Spelman's testimony at the trial, see *People of the State of Illinois v. Coughlin et al.*, Supreme Court of Illinois, Illinois State Archives, 5:257.

67n1 *The ructions were no longer:* *Chicago Tribune*, Feb. 8, 1889.

67n2 *Le Caron was memorably described:* Quoted in John McDonald, *Diary of the Parnell Commission: Revised from* The Daily News (London: T. Fisher Unwin, 1890), 121.

67n3 *Le Caron began his testimony:* [Beach], *Twenty-Five Years in the Secret Service*, 10; Sir Robert Anderson, *The Lighter Side of My Official Life* (London: Hodder and Stoughton, 1910), chap. 10, 152–66; McEnnis, *Clan-na-Gael*, 62.

69n1 *Le Caron was a largely idle spy:* [Beach], *Twenty Five Years in the Secret Service*, 8–9; *Galignani's New Paris* (Paris: Galignani Library, 1883), end pages advertisement for Arthur & Co.; *Military Register of the Officers of the Irish Republican Army*, March 7, 1870, TNA (UK), HO 144/1538/7. Papers relating to Thomas Beach, 1867–94; Letterhead of Dr. H. Le Caron, Proprietor of Miner's Drug Store, Braidwood, Illinois, TNA (UK), HO 144/1536/5; Alexander Sullivan to Michael Davitt, Nov. 9, 1891, TCD, Davitt Papers, MS 9432/2956. There were three attempted invasions of Canada undertaken by the Fenians—in 1866, 1870, and 1871. All ended in humiliating disaster for the Fenians; *Chicago Times* sketch of Le Caron quoted in McEnnis, *Clan-na-Gael*, 113–14.

69n2 *For a time he supplemented his income:* Funchion, *Chicago's Irish Nationalists,* 31; Alexander Sullivan to Michael Davitt, June 2, 1889, TCD, Davitt Papers, MS 9432/2588.

69n3 *The number of bodies donated:* Few bodies were stolen that had family or friends to claim them, though in one famous case the body of Congressman John Harrison, son of President Benjamin Harrison, was found at the Medical College of Ohio in 1878. The first law allowing bodies to be donated to the medical schools was passed in 1789, when bodies of executed prisoners were allowed to be dissected by medical students. Beginning in Massachusetts in 1831, states began to pass anatomy acts that granted the bodies of the "unclaimed"—those who died in workhouses, asylums, prisons, and other institutions—to medical schools. In Illinois the Anatomy Act of 1885 allowed for the release of the body to medical schools or physicians if it was to be buried at public expense. D. C. Humphrey, "Dissection and Discrimination: The Social Origins of Cadavers in America, 1760–1915," *Bulletin of the New York Academy of Medicine* 49, no. 9 (September 1973): 822; Michael Sappol, *A Traffic of Dead Bodies: Anatomy and Embodied Social Identity in Nineteenth-Century America* (Princeton, NJ: Princeton University Press, 2002), 122–23.

69n4 *During his time on the stand:* Special Commission Act, 1888, Proof of Sir Robert Anderson, TNA (UK), HO 144/1538/5; Beach to Anderson, Dec. 31, 1889, TNA (UK), HO 144/1538/8; Le Caron's testimony at the Parnell Commission, quoted in McEnnis, *Clan-na-Gael,* 112–13.

69n5 *He was close to many senior Clan men:* Quoted in McEnnis, *Clan-na-Gael,* 115.

69n6 *Although Cronin had long been an enemy:* Le Caron interview in the *New York Herald,* Feb. 10, 1889, quoted in O'Brien and Ryan, *Devoy's Post-Bag,* 2:49.

70 *The ripples sent across the Atlantic:* Le Caron's testimony was sensational, and may well have brought the house of cards surrounding Parnell tumbling down but for the testimony of Richard Pigott a few weeks later. Pigott was exposed as a forger of letters purporting to be from Parnell, and while this did not clear Parnell of some of the charges against him, the impact of the discovery of Pigott's forgery was such that all other attacks on Parnell held little weight. Pigott and Le Caron were lumped together and vilified, with both men's statements in court largely dismissed, though Le Caron's testimony had far-reaching consequences in Irish America. Bernard Porter, *The Origins of the Vigilant State: The London Metropolitan Police Special Branch before the First World War* (London: Boydell Press, 1987), 93–95.

71n1 *Cronin addressed Le Caron's appearance:* Cronin's final editorial for *Celto-American,* quoted in *Chicago Herald,* "Dr. Cronin's Last Editorial," May 6, 1889.

71n2 *Back in 1883:* Triangle circular, Sept. 16, 1883, quoted in *Verbatim Copy of the Parnell Commission Report* (Dublin: Irish Loyal and Patriot Union, 1890), 12:113.

71n3 *Many Clan members in America:* Testimony of Henry O'Connor; Testimony of John M. Collins, *People of the State of Illinois v. Coughlin et al.,* Supreme Court of Illinois, Illinois State Archives, 4:748–59, 779–93.

CHAPTER FIVE

72n1 *Lake View began in the 1840s:* Ann Durkin Keating, ed., *Chicago Neighborhoods and Suburbs: A Historical Guide* (Chicago: University of Chicago Press, 2008), 189.

72n2 *Indeed, his doctor's bills:* *Times* (London), Sept. 24, 1889; Testimony of Michael Schaack; Testimony of Dr. John F. Williams, *People of the State of Illinois v. Coughlin et al.,* Supreme Court of Illinois, Illinois State Archives, 4:1668, 7:2114–19; *The Lake View Directory, 1889* (Chicago: R. R. Donnelley and Son, 1889), 550–52; George Ingram, summing up for the prosecution at the trial, quoted in John T. McEnnis, *The Clan-na-Gael and the Murder of Dr. Cronin* (Chicago: F. J. Schulte and J. W. Iliff, 1890), 441.

73n1 *His optimism was well founded:* *Sunday Herald,* "Probable Ice Famine," June 2, 1889;

Susanne Friedberg, *Fresh: A Perishable History* (Cambridge, MA: Harvard University Press, 2009), 26; Jonathan Rees, "The Natural Price of Ice in America," *Business and Economic History On-Line* 6 (2008): 2, http://www.thebhc.org/publications/BEHonline /2008/rees.pdf.

73n2 **Customers used some of their purchase:** Ice dealers flourished in parts of the United States from 1880 to 1910, particularly around Chicago, where in 1914 ice sales were five times what they had been in 1880. Friedberg, *Fresh*, 21.

73n3 **He had told friends of several occasions:** *Chicago Tribune*, May 6, 1889; *Chicago Daily News*, "Michael Morris Speaks," June 5, 1889; *Chicago Tribune*, "A North Side Tough Hired to Thrash the Doctor a Year Ago," May 23, 1889; *Chicago Pictorial West*, Nov. 20, 1889; *Chicago Daily News*, June 5, 1889. Evidence of Cronin's fear was also given by Joseph O'Byrne, who was Senior Guardian of Columbia Camp 366, and Patrick McGarry. Both men confirmed that Cronin believed that "Alexander Sullivan and Michael Boland [would] complete their murderous designs and kill him." *Chicago Tribune*, June 6, 1889.

75n1 **Mrs. Cordelia Conklin:** Cordelia (b. 1845) from West Virginia had married Theodore Conklin of New York (b. 1839) in 1869. "United States Census, 1900," index and images, *FamilySearch* (https://familysearch.org/pal:/MM9.1.1/MSQW-WNT), T T Conklin, ED 663 Precinct 4 Chicago City Ward 22, Cook, Illinois, United States; citing sheet 11B, family 228, National Archives and Records Administration microfilm publication T623, FHL microfilm 1240271.

75n2 **For several minutes:** Testimony of Sarah McNearney, October 28, 1889, Illinois State Archives, vol. 4—Supreme Court Case File 25939—continuation transcript of trial.

75n3 **When Cronin finally emerged:** McEnnis, *Clan-na-Gael*, 332; Henry M. Hunt, *The Crime of the Century; or, The Assassination of Dr. Patrick Henry Cronin* (Chicago: H. L. and D. H. Kockersperger, 1889), 17–22; [Anon.], *The Great Cronin Mystery; or, The Irish Patriot's Fate: By One of America's Most Famous Detectives* (Chicago: Laird and Lee, 1889), 19–22; *Chicago Globe*, "Trunk Mystery," May 6, 1889.

75n4 **The Conklins knew that Cronin lived in fear:** Testimony of T. T. Conklin, Oct. 25, 1889, *Abstract of Record*, 2:9, Supreme Court of Illinois, RS # 901.001, 35/13B/65 V# 25939, Illinois State Archives; *Chicago Tribune*, May 6, 1889.

75n5 **Theo Conklin feared the worst:** Hunt, *Crime of the Century*, 30.

76 **Immediately upon returning home:** Mícheál de Búrca, *The Life and Poems of Michael Scanlan, the Fenian Poet* (Killmalock: Abbey Printing, 1969), 3; *Gaelic American* (New York), "Michael Scanlan Obituary," March 29, 1917; Charles Ffrench, *Biographical History of the American Irish in Chicago* (Chicago: American Biographical Publishing, 1897), 366–72; Federal Writers Project, "The Case of Dr. Cronin" (unpublished manuscript, n.d. [1936?]), 120; Abraham Lincoln Presidential Library, Springfield, Illinois.

77n1 **The Pinkerton Agency:** Richard Slotkin, *Gunfighter Nation: The Myth of the Frontier in Twentieth-Century America* (New York: Atheneum, 1992), 140.

77n2 **In some respects the employment:** On the Molly Maguires see Kevin Kenny, *Making Sense of the Molly Maguires* (New York: Oxford University Press, 1998); Kenny, *The American Irish* (New York: Logman, 2000), 156–7l. The story of the Molly Maguires and the Pinkertons was the inspiration for Arthur Conan Doyle's Sherlock Holmes novel *The Valley of Fear*, published in 1915. See Lindsay Clutterbuck, "The Evolution of Counter Terrorism Methodology in the Metropolitan Police from 1829 to 1901, with Particular Reference to the Influence of Extreme Irish Nationalist Activity" (PhD thesis, University of Portsmouth, 2002), 266–68; McEnnis, *Clan-na-Gael*, 70–71.

77n3 **Cronin's friends had nothing more concrete than suspicion:** Conklin informed Captain Michael Schaack of the East Chicago Avenue Police Station that Cronin was missing at midday on May 5. Schaack was dismissive, and Conklin returned to the station at four o'clock that afternoon to tel him about the dispute between Sullivan and Cronin. Testimony of T. T. Conklin, *Abstract of Record*, 2:93–94; McEnnis, *Clan-na-Gael*, 181; Hunt, *Crime of the Century*, 31, 125.

77n4 **On May 8 his old school friend:** Thomas P. Tuite to John Devoy, Detroit, May 8, 1889 in *Devoy's Post-Bag*, ed. William O'Brien and Desmond Ryan, vol. 1 (Dublin: C. J. Fallon, 1948), 311.

78n1 **John Scanlan refused to speculate:** John F. Scanlan to Devoy, Chicago, May 10, 1889, in ibid., 1:312; *Chicago Tribune*, May 6, 1889.

78n2 **At around two o'clock:** Federal Writers Project, "Case of Dr. Cronin," 123.

79 **Bizarre sights were commonplace:** Emily Clark, "Moving Day," in *The Encyclopedia of Chicago*, ed. James Grossman, Ann Durkin Keating, and Janice L. Reiff (Chicago: University of Chicago Press, 2004), 548; Perry R. Duis, *Challenging Chicago: Coping with Everyday Life, 1837–1920* (Chicago: University of Illinois Press, 1998), 75; *Chicago Tribune*, 1880, quoted in Duis, *Challenging Chicago*, 85.

80n1 **Cronin's barber:** Hunt, *Crime of the Century*, 38–41.

80n2 **A local night watchman:** ibid., 43; Federal Writers Project, "Case of Dr. Cronin," 127.

81n1 **The Chicago Daily News complained:** *Chicago Daily News*, May 8, 1889.

81n2 **Mrs. Conklin later recalled:** Testimony of Cordelia Conklin, *Abstract of Record*, 2:76, *Daniel Coughlin vs. People of the State of Illinois*, Supreme Court of Illinois, RS # 901.001, 35/13B/65 V# 25939, Illinois State Archives.

81n3 **Alexander Sullivan was visited:** *Chicago Daily Inter Ocean*, "Is Dr. Cronin Murdered?," May 6, 1889; *Chicago Daily News*, "Is Cronin Alive?," May 6, 1889; Alexander Sullivan to Michael Davitt, May 28, 1889, TCD, Davitt Papers, MS 9432/2586.

82n1 **The Chicago Herald reported:** *Chicago Herald*, "Dr. Cronin's Circular," May 6, 1889.

82n2 **The Chicago Tribune quoted:** *Chicago Tribune*, "Is Cronin in New York?," May 7, 1889.

82n3 **The St. Louis Post-Dispatch hinted:** *St. Louis Post-Dispatch*, May 24, 1889, quoted in *Chicago Tribune*, June 4, 1889.

82n4 **Keen to do his duty:** *Chicago Tribune*, "Collier and Victoria," May 9, 1889; *Chicago Citizen*, Dec. 14, 1889.

83n1 **As Finley Peter Dunne:** Peter Dunne, ed., *Mr. Dooley Remembers: The Informal Memoirs of Finley Peter Dunne* (Boston: Little Brown, 1936), 74.

83n2 **So many rumors abounded:** Theo Conklin quoted in *Chicago Times*, "Is It Cronin's Hair?," May 7, 1889.

84n1 **She knew him well from their regular appearances:** *Chicago Tribune*, May 29, 1889; *Chicago Herald*, May 10, 1889; *Chicago Daily News*, May 6, 1889.

84n2 **Several miles from Lake View:** *Chicago Tribune*, "Lawyers for the State Protest," Oct. 27, 1889; Hunt, *Crime of the Century*, 196.

84n3 **Within weeks of his promotion:** Elizabeth Dale, *The Chicago Trunk Murder: Law and Justice at the Turn of the Century* (DeKalb: Northern Illinois University Press, 2011), 70. In August 1885 Mrs. Kledzic was brutally robbed and murdered in her home. The chief suspect was a man named Brunofski who had been living with the family. Schaack's investigation uncovered the fact that Brunofski was in fact Mulkowsky, who had come to America from Poland after serving twenty-two years there for murder. By using photographs of Mulkowsky's sister, who looked similar to him, Schaack tracked down his man, who was later found guilty of murder.

84n4 **But as Dinan entered the station:** Hunt, *Crime of the Century*, 202–4.

84n5 **Armed with this suspicious development:** Schaack's evidence at the inquest, in McEnnis, *Clan-na-Gael*, 185–86; *Chicago Tribune*, "Officer Coughlin Hires a Rig," May 26, 1889.

85n1 **He had little interest in the Cronin case:** *Chicago Daily News*, May 11, 1889; *Chicago Tribune*, "What Capt. Schaack Has to Say," May 23, 1889.

85n2 **Woodruff, dressed in cheap clothes:** *Chicago Tribune*, "Woodruff Regrets Having Talked," May 11, 1889; McEnnis, *Clan na Gael*, 193–95.

86n1 **The police thought the body:** *Times* (London), May 13, 1889; *Chicago Tribune*, May 11, 1889.

86n2 **As the Chicago Police Chief:** *New York Times*, May 12, 1889, quoted in *Chicago Daily Inter Ocean*, "No Tidings of Cronin," May 14, 1889.

86n3 **Detective Dan Coughlin:** Dunne, *Mr. Dooley Remembers*, 76.

86n4 **He already had a criminal record:** *Chicago Tribune*, June 12, 1889.

87n1 **He told a reporter from the Tribune:** *Chicago Tribune*, May 11, 1889. Woodruff was charged in connection with the Cronin murder, but the general consensus was that he had nothing to do with it and was merely a petty thief with a vivid imagination. He was granted a separate trial, but it never took place, as the police in Chicago had no evidence to tie him to the Cronin murder. Instead, they sent him to Kansas, where he was wanted for horse stealing.

87n2 **Long reported that he had bumped into Cronin:** C. T. Long telegram to Chicago newspapers May 10, 1889; C. T. Long account of interview with Cronin, May 11, 1889, in McEnnis, *Clan-na-Gael*, 187–88, 191.

87n3 **If Long's tale was to be believed:** *New York Times*, May 11, 1889.

87n4 **Theo Conklin issued a statement:** By 1889 Starkey was living in Toronto, having fled Chicago because of alleged association with jury bribing. *New York Times*, "Cronin's Bitter Enemies," May 24, 1889; T. T. Conklin statement to the press, May 1889, in McEnnis, *Clan-na-Gael*, 192–93.

87n5 **No record of his stay:** Patrick McGarry, letter written as a statement and furnished to the press, Toronto, May 14, 1889, quoted in McEnnis, *Clan-na-Gael*, 193; *Chicago Daily Inter Ocean*, May 14, 1889. Long refused to retract his story, and following the discovery of Cronin's body, he refused to talk about his alleged interview with him.

88 **All speculation as to the whereabouts of Dr. Cronin:** Hunt, *Crime of the Century*, 128.

CHAPTER SIX

89n1 **He had been badly beaten:** *Chicago Tribune*, May 23 1889. The *Tribune* reported that the body, "stark naked, was lying in the hole below. It was dirt begrimed and half floating in the dirty water of the sewer. The back was partially covered with cotton-batting and an old dirty towel was hanging about the neck. The body was lying face downward. . . . The face was half hidden in the dirt and water, and the hair was clotted with mud." On the injuries inflicted, the *Tribune* reported: "Over the left temple a cut four inches long, through the scalp and into the skull; over the left arietal bone a cut one and a half inches long, which also marked the skull; also a cut . . . over the frontal bone; a cut . . . through the scalp . . . a large bruise back of the forehead . . . bruises on the left leg and severe contusions, apparently made by a bludgeon on the forehead." The *Chicago Daily Inter Ocean* of May 23, 1889, was even more graphic in its description, commenting that "the body presented a horrible appearance. The skin which had been partially detached from the legs and arms while the body was being removed from the sewer hung in shreds about his feet and hands. The body and face were terribly bloated and the greater part of the moustache . . . had fallen off. . . . The eyelids were swollen to such an extent that they had forced each other partly open and the eyes were gazing staringly at the ceiling. The head was a mass of bruises and gashes. . . . There were about eight of these ghastly wounds, almost any of which would have caused instant death."

89n2 **Even before formal identification:** *Chicago Daily News*, "The Cronin Mystery," 6 p.m. Extra Edition, May 22, 1889.

89n3 **Police armed with batons:** *Chicago Tribune*, "Scenes at Lake View Station," May 24, 1889.

90n1 **His "baseball finger":** *Chicago Tribune*, "Cronin Is Murdered," May 23, 1889. Cronin's "baseball finger"—tendon damage meant that the middle finger of Cronin's right hand was permanently bent at the top joint; Henry M. Hunt, *The Crime of the Century*;

or, The Assassination of Dr. Patrick Henry Cronin (Chicago: H. L. and D. H. Kockersperger, 1889), 138–41. The papers were determined to find a "woman in the case," and reported that a "mysterious lady physician" came to view the corpse. There was little mystery to this—she was Sarah Hackett Stevenson, the first female member of the American Medical Association. *Chicago Daily News*, "Cronin's Body Found," May 23, 1889; *Journal of the Proceedings, the Élite Club Directory and Club List of Chicago, 1889–90* (Chicago: Elite Directory Company, 1889).

90n2 **As hordes gathered:** *Times* (London), June 13, 1889; Hunt, *Crime of the Century*, 198, 200.

90n3 **A reporter from the Chicago Tribune:** *Chicago Tribune*, "Cronin Is Murdered," May 23, 1889.

90n4 **Brandt concluded that the head:** Brandt was assisted by two local physicians, Gray and Porter, and observed by Walter V. Hayt, a city health inspector. Photographs were taken of the corpse. *Chicago Daily Inter Ocean*, May 23, 1889; *Chicago Tribune*, May 23, 1889.

91n1 **The autopsy took place:** The autopsy was organized by the county coroner, H. L. Hertz, and one of his deputies, Louis Eckhardt. The autopsy was observed by a deputy coroner Barrett, and Captain E. H. Wing and Lieutenant Spengler of the Lake View police. *Chicago Tribune*, "Scenes at Lake View Station" and "Swearing in the Coroner's Jury," May 24, 1889; Hunt, *Crime of the Century*, 146–48.

91n2 **Nicholas Birren was shocked:** *Chicago Tribune*, "Scenes at Lake View Station," May 24, 1889; *Chicago Times*, "The Body Lying in State," May 26, 1889; *A. N. Marquis and Co.'s Handbook of Chicago 1887–8* (Chicago: A. N. Marquis, 1887), 95. Hunt, *Crime of the Century*, 149.

91n3 **With his wife Ellen:** Hunt, *Crime of the Century*, 150–51. "Asthore" is an Anglicized version of "a stór," an Irish term of endearment that means "my love" or "my darling." Its direct translation is "my treasure."

92n1 **As the Daily News observed:** *Chicago Daily News*, "The Cronin Mystery," 6 p.m. Extra Edition, May 22, 1889.

92n2 **The Inter Ocean observed:** *Chicago Daily Inter Ocean*, "Dr. Cronin's Body Found," May 23, 1889.

92n3 **As the Evening News reported:** *Chicago Evening News*, May 29 1889.

93n1 **The crowd milling around:** *Chicago Tribune*, "Cronin Is Murdered," May 23, 1889.

93n2 **Speaking on behalf of Cronin's friends:** *Chicago Daily Inter Ocean*, "Dr. Cronin's Body Found," May 23, 1889.

93n3 **There was fevered speculation:** Hunt, *Crime of the Century*, 334–35; John T. McEnnis, *The Clan-na-Gael and the Murder of Dr. Cronin* (Chicago: F. J. Schulte and J. W. Iliff, 1890), 272.

93n4 **In New York, John Devoy:** *Chicago Daily Inter Ocean*, "A Bold Statement," May 23, 1889. However, Devoy swiftly backtracked, possibly fearful of linking Parnell, however tangentially, with the murder. He claimed that he had been misrepresented and he had meant to say that he was convinced that Cronin had been murdered by "by some Irish ruffians who are a disgrace to the Irish cause . . . the murder was the result of a conspiracy embracing only a few men and that they had him killed for purposes of private vengeance." *Chicago Tribune*, "What John Devoy Has to Say," May 24, 1889.

93n5 **The state's attorney, Joel Longnecker:** *Chicago Tribune*, "Scenes at Lake View Station," May 24, 1889.

93n6 **Most homicides in Chicago:** Jeffrey S. Adler, "'My Mother-in-Law Is to Blame, but I'll Walk on Her Neck Yet': Homicide in Late Nineteenth-Century Chicago," *Journal of Social History* 31, no. 2 (Winter 1997): 256. See also Adler, *First in Violence, Deepest in Dirt: Homicide in Chicago* (Cambridge, MA: Harvard University Press, 2006). Over 80 percent of those accused of murder in that period were unskilled or semiskilled workers. Drunken brawls accounted for more than 25 percent of all murders in the city between 1875 and 1900, a further 12 percent were spousal murders, and murders committed during robberies accounted for 5 percent of the total. Jeffrey S. Adler, "'It's His First Offense. We Might as Well Let Him Go': Homicide and Criminal Justice in Chicago 1875–1920," *Journal of Social History* (Fall 2006): 14.

94n1 **But in contrast to popular perception:** Christopher Thale, "Police," in *The Encyclopedia of Chicago*, ed. James Grossman, Ann Durkin Keating, and Janice L. Reiff (Chicago: University of Chicago Press, 2004), 626–27; Richard C. Lindberg, *To Serve and Collect: Chicago Politics and Police Corruption from the Lager Beer Riot to the Summerdale Scandal 1855–1960* (Carbondale: Southern Illinois University Press, 1998), 21–24; Sam Mitrani, "Reforming Repression: Labor, Anarchy, and Reform in the Shaping of the Chicago Police Department, 1879–1888," *Labor: Studies in Working Class History of the Americas* 6, no. 2 (2009): 79. The Bertillon system was designed by a French police officer, Alphonse Bertillon, in 1879. New York adopted the system in 1896.

94n2 **Throughout the 1880s the police force expanded:** Mitrani, "Reforming Repression," 79; Leigh B. Bienen and Brandon Rottinghaus, "Criminal Law: Learning from the Past, Living in the Present; Understanding Homicide in Chicago, 1870–1930," *Journal of Criminal Law and Criminology* 92, nos. 3–4 (2003): 445n; Michael Willrich, *City of Courts: Socializing Justice in Progressive Era Chicago* (Cambridge: Cambridge University Press, 2002), xxxi, table 1. It is worth noting that the city limits changed in 1889, when the City of Chicago incorporated the surrounding towns, including Lake View, thus quadrupling the city's acreage. See also Northwestern University, "Homicide in Chicago 1870–1890," homicide.northwestern.edu; Adler, *First in Violence, Deepest in Dirt*, 15. The population of the city doubled in the decade between 1880 and 1890, from 503,185 to 1,099,850, but the number of murders rose even more sharply, increasing from twenty-two in 1880 to fifty-six in 1890—a rise of 255%.

94n3 **In 1880 there had been one police officer:** *Chicago Herald*, "Comparative Police Statistics," Dec. 27, 1889. The police figures include members of the Lake View force who had joined the Chicago police after the town's annexation by the city (though not all 266 of the Lake View police pursued a career with the Chicago force). The paper estimated that there was 1 policeman for every 700 members of the public. By comparison it reckoned that London had 1 policeman for every 250 Londoners. In 1880 San Francisco had 1 policeman for every 658 people and Boston had 1 for every 527, while in New York in 1876 that ratio was was 1 to 435. R. A. Burchell, *The San Francisco Irish 1848–1880* (Berkeley: University of California Press, 1980), 23–24.

95n1 **The police chief was usually chosen:** Mark H. Haller, "Historical Roots of Police Behavior: Chicago, 1890–1925," *Law and Society Review* 10, no. 2 (Winter 1976): 306–7, 314–15; Mitrani, "Reforming Repression," 76–78.

95n2 **In 1897 the Illinois governor:** Governor Tanner, message to the legislature, Dec. 7, 1897; in *Senate Report on the Chicago Police System as Made by the Committee of Investigation, Appointed by 40th General Assembly Special Session 1897–98* (Springfield, IL: Philip Brothers, 1898), 3.

95n3 **By the middle of 1885:** Mitrani, "Reforming Repression," 81–85; James Green, *Death in the Haymarket: A Story of Chicago, the First Labor Movement and the Bombing That Divided Gilded Age America* (New York: Pantheon Books, 2006), 121–23.

96n1 **In the spring of 1886:** Art Young, *His Life and Times* (New York: Sheridan House, 1939), 76.

96n2 **By ten o'clock:** Green, *Death in the Haymarket*, 5–6, 134.

96n3 **A high-profile police investigation:** Ibid., 207; Mitrani, "Reforming Repression," 90–91.

97n1 **Frederick Ebersold was police chief:** Mitrani, "Reforming Repression," 84. Following the strike at the Chicago West Division Railway Company in 1885, Ebersold was promoted to police chief.

97n2 **"Captain Schaack has a lot of gall":** Quoted in Young, *His Life and Times*, 76.

97n3 *Whatever his methods:* Lindberg, *To Serve and Collect*, 63.

97n4 *"it would be a false delicacy":* Michael J. Schaack, *Anarchy and Anarchists* (Chicago: F. J. Schulte, 1889), 183.

97n5 *"It was my policy to quiet matters":* Quoted in John P. Altgeld, *Reasons for Pardoning Fielden, Neebe and Schwab*, June 26, 1893 (Chicago, 1893), 51–52; Young, *His Life and Times*, 165.

98n1 *Chicago's citizens had considerable sympathy:* See for example *Chicago Tribune*, "Two More Dead Heroes," May 7, 1886; Mitrani, "Reforming Repression," 94.

98n2 *Under the management of James J. West:* Richard Schneirov, "Rethinking the Relation of Labor to the Politics of Urban Social Reform in Late Nineteenth-Century America: The Case of Chicago," *International Labor and Working-Class History* 46 (Fall 1994): 93–108; Bienen and Rottinghaus, "Criminal Law," 456.

98n3 *In early 1889 the paper ran:* See for example *Chicago Times*, "Bonfield's Crooked Work," Jan. 10, 1889; "The Act of a Sneak," Jan. 13, 1889; Schaack as Whitewasher," Jan. 19, 1889; "His Greatest Outrage," Jan. 28, 1889; "A Terrible Lesson," Jan. 28, 1889; "Typical Police Methods," Jan. 30, 1889. Elizabeth Dale, *The Chicago Trunk Murder: Law and Justice at the Turn of the Century* (DeKalb: Northern Illinois University Press, 2011), 117–18. Charles Fanning, *Finley Peter Dunne and Mr. Dooley: The Chicago Years* (Lexington: University Press of Kentucky, 1978), 10.

98n4 *The men were swiftly released:* Lindberg, *To Serve and Collect*, 96–98. *Chicago Daily Inter Ocean*, "Dr. Cronin's Body Found," May, 23, 1889; *Chicago Daily Inter Ocean*, June 14, 1889.

98n5 *For the* Times, *the timing of the Cronin case:* *Chicago Times*, "A Better Police Force Needed," May 27, 1889.

98n6 *As the murder investigation inched forward:* *Chicago Daily News*, May 25, 1889.

99n1 *In an editorial of May 27:* *Chicago Daily Inter Ocean*, May 27 1889.

99n2 *The* Omaha Republican *joked:* *Omaha Republican*, quoted in *Chicago Tribune*, June 5, 1889.

99n3 *A further difficulty for the case:* The Lake View Police Station and the East Chicago Avenue Police Station (on Chicago Avenue just west of Clark Street) were the two hubs of the investigation.

99n4 *The* Chicago Times *used the murder:* *Chicago Times*, "Annexation," May 24, 1889.

99n5 *As a result, the 266 officers:* A City Charter of 1875 allowed for the expansion of the city of Chicago under certain conditions, and between 1887 and 1889 towns such as Lake and Jefferson, villages such as Hyde Park, and the city of Lake View were the focus of campaigns both for and against annexation. *New York Herald*, "Chicago Gains Population," June 30, 1889. Raphael W. Marrow and Harriet I. Carter, *In Pursuit of Crime: The Police of Chicago; Chronicle of a Hundred Years, 1833–1933* (Sunbury, OH: Flats, 1996), 183.

100n1 *In the late 1880s, the Irish:* Haller, "Historical Roots," 304. The Irish-born and those of Irish parents accounted for 48% of the police force, while Germans accounted for 10%.

100n2 *Chicago wasn't unique in this:* Eric H. Monkkonen, "History of Urban Police," *Crime and Justice* 15 (1992): 547.

100n3 *In an editorial the* Inter Ocean *claimed:* *Chicago Daily Inter Ocean*, May 27, 1889.

100n4 *Slason Thompson:* *America: A Journal for Americans*, "Comment," May 30, 1889.

100n5 *Cronin's friends believed that there was reluctance:* *Chicago Daily Inter Ocean*, May 25, 1889.

101n1 *He maintained that "a portion":* *Chicago Tribune*, "What John Devoy Has to Say," May 24, 1889.

101n2 *At the time, De Witt Cregier:* Mayor De Witt Cregier's inaugural address, April 15, 1889, Chicago City Council, *Journal of the Proceedings*, 8–19. Accessed at http://www.chipub lib.org/cplbooksmovies/cplarchive/mayors/cregier_inaug_1889.php

101n3 *They called on him to carry out:* *Chicago Tribune*, "Devoy Scores Finerty," Oct. 28, 1889. Dr. P. Curran on Cregier.

101n4 *According to the police:* *Chicago Daily Inter Ocean*, May 25, 1889.

101n5 **Hubbard hoped to harness:** Quoted in Eugen Seeger, *Chicago: The Wonder City* (Chicago: Geo. Gregory Printing, 1893), 287.

102n1 **Inspector Ebersold also believed:** *Chicago Daily Inter Ocean*, "Dr. Cronin's Body Found," May 23, 1889.

102n2 **"I like you boys":** Quoted in *Chicago Daily Inter Ocean*, May 23, 1889.

102n3 **According to Inspector Ebersold:** Quoted in *Chicago Evening News*, "Tales of the Cronin Case," May 24, 1889.

102n4 **The Chicago Evening News mocked him:** Ibid., May 29, 1889.

102n5 **The Chicago Tribune reported that the iceman:** *Chicago Tribune*, May 23, 1889, "P. O'Sullivan Hears the News." James Clancy of the *New York Herald* was one of those who went to O'Sullivan's house. Testimony of James Clancy, *People of the State of Illinois v. Coughlin et al.*, Supreme Court of Illinois, Illinois State Archives, 7:2419–21, 8:474–75.

103n1 **Sullivan also dismissed Cronin:** *Chicago Tribune*, "Alexander Sullivan's View of It," May 23, 1889.

103n2 **A week later:** *Chicago Daily News*, May 31, 1889.

103n3 **The area around O'Sullivan's house:** Robert J. Casey, *Chicago Medium Rare—When We Were Both Younger* (Chicago: Bobbs-Merrill, 1949), 54–55.

103n4 **The Daily News reported that after speaking with O'Sullivan:** *Chicago Daily News*, May 23, 1889.

104n1 **As they approached the cottages:** Marrow and Carter, *In Pursuit of Crime*, 133; Hunt, *Crime of the Century*, 158–62.

104n2 **Seeing their opportunity:** *Chicago Daily Inter Ocean*, May 21, 1889; *Chicago Evening News*, May 24, 1889. Schuettler immediately suspended the officer in charge of securing the Carlson cottage. *Chicago Weekly Journal*, May 29, 1889. Edwin Jones of the *Chicago Evening News*, his brother Harry, and Robert M. Johnson were the journalists who entered the cottage. Newspaper reporters were not alone in trying to gain access to it. On September 9 attorneys representing those accused of Cronin's murder broke into the cottage and took away portions of the floor and wall. Duke Bailie, *The Cronin Case: The Assassination of Dr. Patrick Henry Cronin* (Chicago: Rhodes and McClure, 1890), 121, 303.

105 **The couple confessed that they knew:** Hunt, *Crime of the Century*, 169–70. Also there at the time was the Carlsons' son Charles and his wife Annie.

106n1 **On April 20, when Williams arrived:** *Chicago Daily Inter Ocean*, May 25, 1889.

106n2 **"My sister is low at present":** Quoted in Hunt, *Crime of the Century*, 174.

106n3 **In a significant development:** Hunt, *Crime of the Century*, 174–6.

107n1 **He concluded not only that it was human blood:** Ibid., 166–67. Brandt was accompanied by Dr. Hectone, and both men claimed they could tell that the blood was human by using a powerful microscope to examine the size of the corpuscles. But in 1889 there was no way to distinguish between human and animal blood—the Uhlenhuth test was not devised until 1891—so Brandt was simply making assumptions.

107n2 **Following the lead suggested by the furniture bill:** Testimony of W. P. Hatfield, *People of the State of Illinois v. Coughlin et al.*, Supreme Court of Illinois, Illinois State Archives, 5:878–85; Hunt, *Crime of the Century*, 177–86.

CHAPTER SEVEN

108n1 **Several people reported seeing suspicious activity:** Eugen Seeger, *Chicago: The Wonder City* (Chicago: Geo. Gregory Printing, 1893), 290; Henry M. Hunt, *The Crime of the Century; or, The Assassination of Dr. Patrick Henry Cronin* (Chicago: H. L. and D. H. Kockersperger, 1889), 191–92.

108n2 **Born in Michigan of Irish parents:** Hunt, *Crime of the Century*, 196, 274; *Chicago Herald*, "Charged with Murder," May 23, 1889; *Chicago Tribune*, "No Time Will Be Wasted," June 12, 1889.

108n3 *Moreover, Coughlin, known as the "Slugger of Market Street":* Chicago Weekly Journal, June 26, 1889.

109n1 *"We had on the paper one of those creatures":* Peter Dunne, ed., *Mr. Dooley Remembers: The Informal Memoirs of Finley Peter Dunne* (Boston: Little, Brown, 1936), 76–77.

109n2 *The article, "He Must Explain It":* Chicago Times, "He Must Explain It," May 25, 1889; Chicago Daily News, May 25, 1889.

109n3 *"In the Cronin case look to this man Coughlin":* Chicago Times, "Look to Coughlin," May 26, 1889.

109n4 *The detective's response:* Chicago Times, "He Must Explain It," May 25, 1889; "Coughlin Is Locked Up," May 26, 1889; Chicago Tribune, "Coughlin Is in a Fix," May 26, 1889.

110n1 *O'Sullivan was arrested:* Coughlin's partner, Detective Michael Whalen, was O'Sullivan's cousin. Testimony of Michael Whalen; Testimony of Tom Whalen, *People of the State of Illinois v. Coughlin et al.*, Supreme Court of Illinois, Illinois State Archives, 7:2617–29, 7:2769–81. Following Coughlin's arrest, Whalen was suspended from his duties. *Chicago Times,* "Whalen Also Suspended," May 26, 1889; Hunt, *Crime of the Century,* 212–13, 217–18.

110n2 *The Daily News thought the jurors:* Chicago Daily News, "The Coroner's Jury," May 28, 1889. The jurors were Justus Killian, Victor Sutter, R. S. Critchell, John H. Van Housen, H. A. Haugan, and Rudolf Seifert. *Chicago Times,* "Swearing in of Coroner's Jury," May 24, 1889.

110n3 *The panel would be responsible:* Judge Tuley, opinion on the granting of bail to Alexander Sullivan, quoted in John T. McEnnis, *The Clan-na-Gael and the Murder of Dr. Cronin* (Chicago: F. J. Schulte and J. W. Iliff, 1890), 239.

110n4 *Many papers published extra editions:* Chicago Daily News, "The Afternoon Session," June 7, 1889; *Chicago Times,* "Drawing in the Net," June 10, 1889.

111n1 *Beggs took the stand on June 6:* Chicago Tribune, "Why Beggs Was Silent," June 7, 1889. Rosa Zuckor, a seventeen-year-old, had been granted a small estate that was being managed by her guardian. In order to claim her inheritance at eighteen, she employed Beggs. She was to be awarded several small mortgages and a note for $500. Beggs never handed over the note and fobbed her off for eight months. Finally, it was discovered that he had spent the money a few days after receiving it. He was sentenced to two years in prison. Beggs's daughter was born on July 10, 1880.

111n2 *In Chicago Beggs remarried:* Testimony of Tom F. O'Connor, *People of the State of Illinois v. Coughlin et al.*, Supreme Court of Illinois, Illinois State Archives, 4:505–15; *Chicago Tribune,* "John F. Beggs Dead," April 6, 1892; Duke Bailie, *The Cronin Case: The Assassination of Dr. Patrick Henry Cronin* (Chicago: Rhodes and McClure, 1890), 116.

111n3 *During his testimony:* Quoted in New York Times, "The Cronin Case," July 1, 1889.

112n1 *This impression was reinforced:* Federal Writers Project, "The Case of Dr. Cronin" (unpublished manuscript, n.d. [1936?]), 202; Abraham Lincoln Presidential Library, Springfield, Illinois.

112n2 *But by June 7:* Chicago Tribune, "Trying the Gag Rule," June 7, 1889.

112n3 *For the remainder of the coroner's jury:* Federal Writers Project, "Case of Dr. Cronin," 202.

112n4 *Two days after Cronin's body was discovered:* Chicago Daily Inter Ocean, "Camp 20 Disbanded," June 26, 1889.

112n5 *He proved a "very dramatic witness":* Chicago Daily News, "EXTRA: Cronin's Prophecy," June 5, 1889.

113n1 *In an interview:* Evening News and Post (London), May 25, 1889, quoted in *Chicago Tribune,* "The Spy Le Caron on the Murder," May 26, 1889.

113n2 *Refuting this charge:* Chicago Tribune, "Trying the Gag Rule," June 7, 1889.

113n3 *Evidence was produced:* Hunt, *Crime of the Century,* 252–53; Margaret Sullivan to Michael Davitt, June 7, 1889, TCD, Davitt Papers, MS 9432/2601.

113n4 **Dillon was quite striking:** Hunt, *Crime of the Century*, 254–55.

114n1 **He acknowledged that Sullivan's formal connections:** Dillon in his evidence to the coroner's jury, June 7, 1889, quoted in Hunt, *Crime of the Century*, 256.

114n2 **By the time Foreman Critchell:** McEnnis, *Clan-na-Gael*, 230, 239; Hunt, *Crime of the Century*, 236–37; *Chicago Daily News*, "The Coroner's Jury," May 28, 1889.

114n3 **It concluded that Cronin had died:** *Chicago Tribune*, "Trying the Gag Rule," June 7, 1889; *Chicago Times*, "Their Verdict," June 12, 1889.

115n1 **His request was declined:** Cook County Coroner's Inquest Record Index, 1872–1911, vol. 20, p. 32, file 6/11/1889. Illinois Regional Archives Depository, Ronald Williams Library, Northeastern Illinois University.

115n2 **She claimed that on the afternoon of June 11:** Margaret Sullivan to Michael Davitt, Aug. 9, 1889, TCD, Davitt Papers, MS 9432/2589.

115n3 **Given that she was among the American press delegation:** *Chicago Times*, "Locked Up," June 12, 1889; Willis J. Abbot, "Chicago Newspapers and Their Makers," *Review of Reviews* 11, no. 65 (June 1895): 664; Kathleen Sprows Cummings, *New Women of the Old Faith: Gender and American Catholicism in the Progressive Era* (Chapel Hill: University of North Carolina Press, 2009), 49; Margaret Sullivan to Michael Davitt, May 31, 1891, TCD Davitt Papers, MS 9432/2600; *New York Times*, "Noted Woman Writer Dead," Aug. 29, 1903.

115n4 **His defense team requested his release:** Tuley's statement, quoted in the *Chicago Citizen*, June 22, 1889.

116n1 **The bail money:** *Chicago Daily Inter Ocean*, June 14, 1889. The other guarantors were Daniel Corkery, Michael W. Kirwin, and James W. Tuohy. *Broome Republican* (Binghamton, NY) "Sullivan Released," June 20, 1889. The bonds remained in force until November 8, when Sullivan returned to court before Judge Baker. "The bonds were declared canceled, and Alexander Sullivan, by reason of the failure of the grand jury to find sufficient evidence upon which he could be brought to trial, was legally declared innocent of all complicity in the crime." Hunt, *Crime of the Century*, 299–300.

116n2 **When word reached Margaret:** [Alexander Sullivan] to Mrs. S[ullivan], Paris, May 24, 1889; [Alexander Sullivan] to Mrs. S[ullivan], May 28, 1889; [Alexander Sullivan] to Mrs. S[ullivan], June 11, 1889; Mrs. S[ullivan], London, to Alexander Sullivan, June 13, 1889; Schedule and Transcripts of Cablegrams and Telegrams passing between AS, his wife, Michael Davitt, etc., March–June 1889, NLI, Devoy Papers MS 18058 (11).

116n3 **Yeats was quite taken with her:** W. B. Yeats, London, to Katharine Tynan, July 25, [1889], in *W. B. Yeats: Letters to Katharine Tynan*, ed. Roger McHugh (New York: McMullen, 1953), 98.

117n1 **Tynan was not so impressed:** Katharine Tynan, *Twenty-Five Years: Reminiscences* (London: Smith, Elder and Company, 1913), 184, 293.

117n2 **While in London:** Abbot, "Chicago Newspapers and Their Makers," 664; *Sheffield Independent*, June 21, 1889; *Northampton Mercury*, July 6, 1889. Margaret Sullivan rarely wrote about Ireland in her newspaper articles, but in 1881 she published a book, *Ireland of To-day: Causes and Aims of Irish Agitation*, and occasionally wrote political pieces for the *American Catholic Quarterly Magazine* in the 1870s and 1880s.

117n3 **"The court is now devoted":** *New York Sun*, July 28, 1889.

117n4 **While on a visit to London:** William O'Brien, *Evening Memories* (Dublin: Maunsel, 1920), 124; Terry Golway, *Irish Rebel: John Devoy and America's Fight for Irish Freedom* (New York: St. Martin's Griffin, 1998), 158.

117n5 **He alleged that Margaret Sullivan had brought with her to the Commons:** Melville E. Stone, *Fifty Years a Journalist* (London: Doubleday, 1921), 87.

118n1 **P. W. Dunne, a friend of Cronin:** *Chicago Tribune*, "P. W. Dunne on Dorney," June 16, 1889. Slason Thompson alleged that at a meeting of priests held in a small town in southern Illinois, Father Dorney had discussed the Cronin murder and "was said to have offered to bet $500 that not a name who is now under arrest for the crime would be convicted. Irrespective of the indecency of such a bet by a priest, there are reasons to suppose that if his bet had been taken Father Dorney would not have been above using his influence in this community to make certain of his winning." Thompson, "Short Notices," *America: A Journal for Americans,* July 25, 1889.

118n2 *In response, Pope Leo XIII:* Quoted in *Chicago Tribune,* June 24, 1880.

118n3 *Sullivan's supporters dismissed the report:* Daily Alta California (San Francisco), "The Cronin Mystery," June 26, 1889.

118n4 *Pro-Cronin Clan members:* Chicago Tribune, "After Dorney's Scalp," June 17, 1889; "Getting into Hot Water," June 18, 1889.

119n1 *The papers anticipated that Feehan:* Chicago Tribune, "Religious and Civil Relations of the Clan na Gael," June 25, 1889.

119n2 *Other members of the Catholic Church hierarchy:* Patrick J. Ryan to James Gibbons, June 9, 1889, in Fergus MacDonald, *The Catholic Church and Secret Societies in the United States* (New York: Catholic Historical Society, 1946), 162.

119n3 *Some commentators believed this was to escape:* Chicago Daily News, "The Situation in New York," May 28, 1889; *Philadelphia Times,* quoted in *Chicago Inter Ocean,* June 14, 1889; Seeger, *Chicago,* 280.

119n4 *Through the summer of 1889:* Gaelic American (New York), "The Story of Clan na Gael," Jan. 10 and 17, 1925.

120n1 *In an attempt to avoid accusations:* Col T. O'Leary was secretary. *Chicago Times,* "The Cronin Murder," May 30, 1889.

120n2 *At least fourteen Pinkertons:* Operatives "E.S.G." and "J.W.L.," June 7, 8, 9, 11, 1889, in reports to Luke Dillon from Robert Pinkerton, NLI, Devoy Papers, MS 18058 (4). Pinkerton Reports, June 10–July 11, 1889; Operative "J.H.F.," June 14, 1889, in Pinkerton Report to Luke Dillon, NLI, Devoy Papers, MS 18058 (5); Pinkerton Reports June 15–29, 1889.

120n3 *Following their arrest:* Fifer cited Article IV, section 2 of the US Constitution. However, the Kentucky v. Dennison case of 1861 had offered an interpretation of Article IV which meant that the "executive authority of the state [seeking extradition] was not authorized by the article to make the demand unless the party was charged in the regular course of judicial proceedings." Elizabeth Dale, *The Chicago Trunk Murder: Law and Justice at the Turn of the Century* (DeKalb: Northern Illinois University Press, 2011), 86; *Opinion of the Supreme Court of the United States, Kentucky v. Dennison,* 65 U.S. 66 (1861), www .law.cornell.edu/supct/historics/ussc_cr_0065_0066_zo.html.

120n4 *The Inter Ocean believed the governor:* Chicago Daily Inter Ocean, "Editorial—Extradition of Suspects," June 14, 1889; *America: A Journal for Americans,* "Irish Picnic to Collect Funds," July 25, 1889.

120n5 *The police failed to locate Pat "the Fox" Cooney:* Times (London), "The Fate of Dr. Cronin," May 25, 1889; Seeger, *Chicago,* 286. Cooney was mentioned in Nelson Algren's 1951 essay "City on the Make." John Devoy believed that it was Mike Gannon's finger. NLI, Devoy Papers, MS 18058 (2), Notes by Devoy on Murder of Cronin, January 31, 1893.

121n1 *Martin Burke was caught:* The area is near the junction of Wacker Drive and Orleans Street and in the vicinity of the Merchandise Mart. Hunt, *Crime of the Century,* 304.

121n2 *Soon Burke's name came to the attention of John Collins:* Collins later became chief of police (1905–7).

121n3 *A photograph of Burke:* Regina V. Burke, June 1889, *Reports of Cases Argued and Determined in the Court of Queen's Bench, Manitoba,* ed. John S. Ewart, vol. 6 (Winnipeg: Carswell, 1890), 121; *Chicago Tribune,* "Into Mother Earth," Dec. 11, 1892; McEnnis, *Clan-na-Gael,* 248.

122n1 *Evidence was presented:* Times (London), "The Cronin Case," June 22, 1889; *Life,* editorial,

June 27, 1889; The terms of Article 10 of the Webster-Ashburton Treaty of 1842 allowed for extradition between Canada and the United States of "all persons being charged with the crime of murder, or assault with intent to commit murder, or piracy, or arson, or robbery, or forgery, or the utterance of forged paper."

122n2 *It began immediately after the coroner's jury:* The members of the grand jury were J. H. Clough, D. B. Dewey, H. P. Kellogg, W. B. Forsythe, J. McGregor Adams, Jacob Gross, Francis B. Peabody, W. H. Beebe, J. F. Wollensak, Isaac Jackson, H. S. Peck, W. J. Quan, Henry Greenebaum, C. Gilbert Wheeler, C. J. Rhode, Geo W. Waite, Henry A. Knott, Wm. D. Kerfoot, D. A. Pierce, A. G. Lundberg, Louis Hasbrouck, John O'Neill, and A. P. Johnson. Bailie, *Cronin Case,* 111; Hunt, *Crime of the Century,* 359–61.

122n3 *The Chicago police were now satisfied:* Also Frank Woodruff, alias Black.

123n1 *Without any eyewitnesses:* Fingerprint evidence was first used by the Chicago Police Department in 1905. *People v. Jennings* in 1910 was the first case where it was used to secure a conviction. Thomas Jennings was convicted of the murder of Clarence Hiller largely because of prints that he had left on wet paint at the scene of the crime. Richard C. Lindberg, *To Serve and Collect: Chicago Politics and Police Corruption from the Lager Beer Riot to the Summerdale Scandal 1855–1960* (Carbondale: Southern Illinois University Press, 1998), 80; David E. Newton, *DNA Evidence and Forensic Science* (New York: Facts on File, 2008): 62–63.

123n2 *The grand jury recommended:* Bessie Louise Pierce, *A History of Chicago,* vol. 3, *The Rise of a Modern City, 1871–1893* (New York: Alfred A Knopf, 1957), 289; *New York Times,* "The Cronin Case," July 1, 1889.

122n3 *The editorial in* Life *magazine:* Life, editorial, June 27, 1889.

123n4 *The* New York Times *argued:* New York Times, June 16, 1889.

123n5 *Almost equal surprise met the indictment:* Times (London), Sept. 24, 1889.

124n1 *Although the men were kept in separate sections:* Chicago Tribune, Aug. 4, 1889. New York Times, "The Cronin Case," July 1, 1889.

124n2 *The Tribune thought that:* Chicago Tribune, June 23, 1889.

124n3 *The men had a number of visitors:* Testimony of Matt Danahy, People of the State of Illinois v. Coughlin et al., Supreme Court of Illinois, Illinois State Archives, 8:2938–63; Chicago Tribune, Aug. 4, 1889.

124n4 *The accused were represented:* McEnnis, Clan-na-Gael, 289–91; Bench and Bar of Chicago, 1883, 186–88.

125n1 *With the exception of Beggs:* Hynes's closing speech in McEnnis, Clan-na-Gael, 277; Hunt, Crime of the Century, 572–74. The financial cost of the trial to Cook County was significant. Including expenses incurred by prosecution witnesses, the jurors, additional security, lawyers' fees, and stenographers' wages, the estimated cost to the taxpayer was between $80,000 and $100,000 (between $2,090,000 and $2,610,000 in today's dollars). *America* concluded that "if the result is the rescue of the country from the domination of the Clan na Gael the prosecution will prove a most profitable investment." Chicago Tribune, Dec. 16, 1889. The *Chicago Inter Ocean* estimated that each juror cost $2 a day. *Chicago Inter Ocean,* Dec. 17, 1889; *America: A Journal for Americans,* "Editorial— The Cronin Verdict," Dec. 19, 1889; Hunt, *Crime of the Century,* 572–74.

125n2 *Who paid for them was shrouded in secrecy:* Federal Writers Project, "Case of Dr. Cronin," 236. It appears that Ames was paid separately.

125n3 *Yet although he scrupulously avoided:* Margaret Sullivan to Michael Davitt, Sept. 24, 1889, TCD, Davitt Papers, MS 9432/2599.

125n4 *He and his wife were a wealthy couple:* Sullivan's income was estimated to be between $8,000 and $10,000 annually, and his wife's between $5,200 and $8,000. By comparison a US senator or congressman earned $5,000 a year in 1889, and the average wage for a manufacturing worker was $427. Walter Wellman, *Daily True American* (Trenton,

NJ), "Notes from the Capital," June 12, 1889; *Los Angeles Times*, "Margaret Sullivan," June 4, 1893; Robin F. Bachin, *Building the South Side: Urban Space and Civic Culture in Chicago, 1890–1919* (Chicago: University of Chicago Press, 2004), 219.

125n5 **Nonetheless, the day after the trial began:** New York Times, "The Deed Tells a Tale," Aug. 29, 1890 (Trude asked for the deed to be suppressed from the press, and so the sale remained secret for a year. He claimed that the sale was kept secret to avoid embarrassing Mrs. Sullivan). Federal Writers Project, "Case of Dr. Cronin," 312. The FWP text claims that a county recorders' title entry shows that Sullivan had mortgaged his residence at Oak Street a few days before the opening of the Cronin trial. Margaret Sullivan to Michael Davitt, Dec. 5, 1889, TCD, Davitt Papers, MS 9432/2591. Sullivan assured Davitt that he would repay the loan within three years. There is no record of whether Sullivan received this money.

125n6 **Margaret Sullivan maintained:** Margaret Sullivan to Michael Davitt, Sept. 24, 1889, TCD, Davitt Papers, MS 9432/2599.

126n1 **Thousands flocked to festivals:** Times (London), June 29 and Sept. 7, 1889; Chicago Tribune, June 29, Aug. 16, Oct. 28, and Oct. 29, 1889; McEnnis, Clan-na-Gael, 268, 270.

126n2 **The nativist American League:** Quoted in Ellen M. Litwicki, "'Our Hearts Burn with Ardent Love for Two Countries': Ethnicity and Assimilation at Chicago Holiday Celebrations, 1876–1918," Journal of American Ethnic History 19, no. 3 (Spring 2000): 17.

126n3 **The invitations to the meetings:** Quoted in New York Times, "The Cronin Case," July 1, 1889.

126n4 **At a Cronin Memorial Meeting:** Chicago Tribune, "They Honor His Memory," June 29, 1889. Speakers included Father J. B. Toomey, Charles Barry, Congressman George E Adams, Judge Prendergast, Congressman Taylor, and Adolph Loob. In the audience were Judge Gresham, Joseph Kaufman, Victor Lawson, General M. Wallace, Judge Collins, and T. T. Conklin. H. E. Bartholemew read a poem, "Cronin." A number of speakers were from the Personal Rights League (Cronin had been a member).

126n5 **Robert Lindblom of the Chicago Board of Trade:** Quoted in Hunt, Crime of the Century, 376.

127n1 **In 1876 Clan na Gael:** John Corrigan, "United Irish Societies of Chicago," in Irish-American Voluntary Organizations, ed. Michael Funchion (Westport, CT: Greenwood Press, 1983), 278; Litwicki, "'Our Hearts Burn with Ardent Love for Two Countries,'" 15.

127n2 **John Finerty, editor of the Citizen:** Chicago Citizen, "The Coming Irish Demonstration," July 13, 1889.

127n3 **They organized rival demonstrations:** Corrigan, "United Irish Societies of Chicago," 276–82. The Confederated Irish Societies was much smaller than the UISC, and both organizations reunited in 1897 under the UISC banner.

127n4 **America was dismissive:** America: A Journal for Americans, "Irish Picnic to Collect Funds," July 25, 1889.

128n1 **David Sullivan of the UISC:** Quoted in Chicago Citizen, "Still She Lives," Aug. 16, 1889. America estimated the crowd as between 7,000 and 8,000, while the Boston Pilot thought that about 20,000 had attended, and Finerty claimed an attendance of 15,000. America: A Journal for Americans, "Editorial—The Two Irish Picnics," Aug. 22, 1889; Times (London), "Irish Faction in America," Sept. 7, 1889.

128n2 **John Finerty challenged any critic:** Finerty's speech at Ogden Grove, Aug. 14, 1889, quoted in McEnnis, Clan-na-Gael, 268–69. John Fitzgibbon, businessman and member of Camp 20, also spoke.

128n3 **The speeches were "not so remarkable":** Chicago Citizen, "Still She Lives," August 16, 1889.

128n4 **Sullivan didn't attend:** Margaret Sullivan to Michael Davitt, Aug. 9, 1889, TCD, Davitt Papers, MS 9432/2589.

128n5 **As darkness fell there was a firework display:** Chicago Tribune, "Disappointed Irishmen," Aug. 16, 1889.

128n6 **Cheltenham Beach:** F. M. Morris, The Stranger's Guide: Morris' Dictionary of Chicago with

Map (Chicago: F. M. Morris, 1891), 47; Perry R. Duis, *Challenging Chicago: Coping with Everyday Life, 1837–1920* (Chicago: University of Illinois Press, 1998), 177.

129n1 **P. W. Dunne criticized the Ogden's Grove:** Quoted in *Times* (London), "Irish Faction in America," Sept. 7, 1889. Other speakers included Congressman Foran and Frank Lawler. Ibid.

129n2 **The picnics were substantial fund-raisers:** *America: A Journal for Americans*, "Editorial— The Two Irish Picnics," Aug. 22, 1889; *Chicago Tribune*, "The Finerty Article," Oct. 29, 1889.

129n3 **He believed Cronin's supporters:** *Chicago Tribune*, "The Finerty Article," Oct. 29, 1889.

129n4 **They claimed that both politicians and the Catholic Church:** *Chicago Tribune*, "Devoy Scores Finerty," Oct. 28, 1889.

129n5 **On that evening, P. W. Dunne:** *Chicago Tribune*, Nov. 24, 1889.

CHAPTER EIGHT

131n1 **One commentator, undoubtedly guilty of hyperbole:** See for example Robert J. Casey, *Chicago Medium Rare—When We Were Both Younger* (Chicago: Bobbs-Merrill, 1949), 54; Henry M. Hunt, *The Crime of the Century; or, The Assassination of Dr. Patrick Henry Cronin* (Chicago: H. L. and D. H. Kockersperger, 1889), 15–16. As Michael Ayers Trotti has noted, sensational murder trials often were given this nomenclature; "Murder Made Real: The Visual Revolution of the Halftone," *Virginia Magazine and Biography* 111, no. 4 (2003): 384.

131n2 **All it lacked:** Question 11 of the Illinois State Penitentiary Admission Papers asked, "Was there the proverbial 'Woman' in the Case"? Illinois State Archives, 243.200, 1857–1916, files 41c–60c, Penitentiary Mittimus files, Joliet Penitentiary.

131n3 **The newspaper business was booming:** Edwin Emery, Michael Emery, and Nancy J. Roberts, *The Press and America: An Interpretative History of the Mass Media*, 9th ed. (Boston: Allyn and Bacon, 2000), 285. The percentage increase in daily newspapers between 1870 and 1900 was 1870–80 an increase of 69%, 1880–90 an increase of 66%; and 1890–1900 an increase of 38%. Figures in Ted Curtis Smythe, *The Gilded Age Press 1865–1900* (Westport, CT: Praeger, 2003), 98n.

131n4 **The speed of urban expansion:** Eric H. Monkkonen, *Police in Urban America: 1860–1920* (Cambridge: Cambridge University Press, 1981), 1; Gunther Barth, *City People: The Rise of Modern City Culture in Nineteenth-Century America* (Oxford: Oxford University Press, 1982), 49.

131n5 **Chicago was expanding at a much faster pace:** Between 1880 and 1890, the five largest urban centers in the United States grew rapidly. New York increased its population by 26% to 1,515,301; Philadelphia increased by 24% to 1,046,964; Brooklyn increased by 42% to 806,343; and St. Louis by 29% to 451,770. Chicago's population swelled by 118%: from 503,185 to 1,099,850. Campbell Gibson, *US Census Bureau Population of the 100 Largest Cities and Other Places in the United States: 1790–1990* (June 1998), https://www.census.gov/population/www/documentation/twps0027/twps0027.html

132n1 **By 1880 the rapid growth:** Barth, *City People*, 59.

132n2 **The 1880 census:** Ibid., 79, 84.

132n3 **At the time of Cronin's death:** F. M. Morris, *The Stranger's Guide: Morris' Dictionary of Chicago with Map* (Chicago: F. M. Morris, 1891), 15. In 1891 there were 24 dailies, 260 monthlies, 36 semimonthlies, 5 bimonthlies, and 14 quarterlies published in Chicago. Ibid., 97.

132n4 **In 1886 the Chicago Daily News:** *Chicago Daily News* advertising literature, 1886, Newberry Library, Midwest Manuscript Collection, Field Enterprises Records; David Paul Nord, "The Urbanization of American Journalism," *OAH Magazine of History* 6 (Spring 1992): 23.

132n5 **Papers competed on price:** Ted Curtis Smythe, "The Advertisers' War to Verify News-paper Circulation, 1870–1914," *American Journalism* 3 (1986): 171–73, 176.

132n6 **Aimed at the general market:** Emery, Emery, and Roberts, *Press and America*, 162–63.

132n7 **The editor did not replace the minister:** Barth, *City People*, 59. See also W. S. Lilly, "The Ethics of Journalism," *Forum* (July 1889): 505. Lilly, writing primarily about the British press, commented that "our journalists have succeeded to an important position in the functions which in by-gone days were discharged by the clergy," but he feared this was not the case for the American press.

132n8 **To maximize profits:** *Chicago Inter Ocean*, "Editorial—Reporting the Cronin Trial," Dec. 19, 1889; Ted Curtis Smythe, "The Reporter, 1880–1990: Working Conditions and Their Influence on Their News," *Journalism History* 7, no. 1 (Spring 1980): 6. See also Willis J. Abbot, "Chicago Newspapers and Their Makers," *Review of Reviews* 11, no. 65 (June 1895): 657.

133 **The life of a journalist was a very fluid one:** The career of Finley Peter Dunne is just one example of many. In 1887 he began his journalistic career with the *Chicago Daily News*, in 1888 he moved to the *Chicago Times*, in 1890 to the *Chicago Tribune*, in 1892 to the *Chicago Evening Post*, in 1897 to the *Chicago Journal*, and in 1900 he moved to New York to pursue his career there.

134n1 **The Chicago Times was established:** Morris, *Stranger's Guide*, 97–98. Medill was mayor of Chicago between 1871 and 1873, but resumed his involvement with the *Tribune* in 1874.

134n2 **In the main, new journalism was characterized:** Emery, Emery, and Roberts, *Press and America*, 162–63; see also Smythe, *Gilded Age Press*, chap. 5.

134n3 **Newspapers were fickle:** Art Young, *His Life and Times* (New York: Sheridan House, 1939), 81.

134n4 **Referring to the Cronin case:** *Chicago Tribune*, "How Newspaper Reports Are to Be Read," Sept. 6, 1889.

134n5 **As Theodore Dreiser recalled:** Theodore Dreiser, *A Book about Myself* (New York: Boni and Liveright, 1922), 36.

135n1 **Storey's motto:** David Paul Nord, *Communities of Journalism: A History of American News-papers and Their Readers* (Urbana: University of Illinois Press, 2001), 112.

135n2 **It managed to be both shocking and successful:** Richard Schneirov, "Rethinking the Re-lation of Labor to the Politics of Urban Social Reform in Late Nineteenth-Century America: The Case of Chicago," *International Labor and Working-Class History* 46 (Fall 1994): 100.

135n3 **It was perhaps best known:** *Chicago Times*, "Jerked to Jesus," Nov. 27, 1875; Bessie Louise Pierce, *A History of Chicago*, vol 3, *The Rise of a Modern City, 1871–1893* (New York: Alfred A Knopf, 1957), 413.

135n4 **Storey's organization:** Barth, *City People*, 88–89; John R. Brazil, "Murder Trials, Murder, and Twenties America," *American Quarterly* 33, no. 2 (Summer 1981): 163–84.

135n5 **Melville Stone's Daily News:** Victor Lawson to Messrs N. W. Ayer and Son, Times Build-ing, Philadelphia, Jan. 6, 1890, Newberry Library, Chicago, Midwest Collection, Vic-tory Lawson MS, box 30, folder 63; Morris, *Stranger's Guide*, 97.

135n6 **Stone was an advocate:** Stone believed journalists were at least as useful as the po-lice force in pursuing criminal investigations. Melville E. Stone, *Fifty Years a Journalist* (London: Doubleday, 1921), 52–53, 77, 92; Frank Luther Mott, *American Journalism: A History; 1690–1960*, 3rd ed. (New York: Macmillan, 1962), 465.

135n7 **Irish American newspapers:** *Boston Pilot*, quoted in *Nation*, March 18, 1882.

136 **Finerty was a Galwayman:** John F. Finerty, *War-Path and Bivouac; or, Conquest of the Sioux* (Chicago: Donohue and Henneberry, 1890).

137n1 **In 1882 John O'Boyle Reilly:** *Boston Pilot*, quoted in *Nation*, March 18, 1882.

137n2 **In 1883 he tried and failed:** Richard Schneirov, *Labor and Urban Politics: Class Conflict and* *the Origin of Modern Liberalism in Chicago 1864–97* (Urbana: University of Illinois Press, 1998), 134n.

137n3 **Finerty proved to be an enthusiastic:** ["my friend John Finerty came out of the House of Representatives and when someone asked him what was going on, he says, 'Oh nothing at all but some damned American business'"]. Charles Fanning, *Finley Peter Dunne and Mr. Dooley: The Chicago Years* (Lexington: University Press of Kentucky, 1978), 257; Michael F. Funchion, *Chicago's Irish Nationalists 1881–1890* (New York: Arno, 1976), 49. Finerty was a one-term congressman, and was replaced by another Irish nationalist, Frank Lawler, who had been president of the Ship Carpenter's Union, Schneirov, *Labor and Union Politics*, 53.

137n4 **The first edition of the Citizen:** The *Citizen* was not the first Irish newspaper in Chicago. A weekly, the *Irish Republic*, was established there in May 1867, but by April 1868 its publication had been moved to New York. Finerty's editorial in the first edition of the newspaper, quoted in Finley Peter Dunne, *Mr. Dooley and the Chicago Irish: The Autobiography of a Nineteenth-Century Ethnic Group*, ed. with a new introduction by Charles Fanning (Washington, DC: Catholic University of America Press, 1987), 257.

138n1 **Cronin's supporters believed:** "To the People of Ireland." The letter signed by James F. Boland and David P. Ahern on behalf of the Cronin Committee was published in at least one newspaper, but there is no indication in the scrapbooks as to whether it was an Irish or a Chicago paper. Chicago History Museum, Cronin case scrapbook, F38K. C88 folio.

138n2 **It was not unusual for them to take on aliases:** Smythe, "The Reporter," 7.

138n3 **Though not taking such drastic measures:** Peter Dunne, ed. *Mr. Dooley Remembers: The Informal Memoirs of Finley Peter Dunne* (Boston: Little, Brown, 1936), 75.

138n4 **When Pat Dinan's white horse:** This was a technique used by the police in 1904 in a case similar to Cronin's; see *Chicago Tribune*, Nov. 18, 1904.

138n5 **Less ethical methods:** *Chicago Daily Inter Ocean*, May 24, 1889; John T. McEnnis, *The Clan-na-Gael and the Murder of Dr. Cronin* (Chicago: F. J. Schulte and J. W. Iliff, 1890), 217–18; *Times* (London), Nov. 21, 1889; *Chicago Weekly Journal*, May 29, 1889.

138n6 **When the British Foreign Office:** Denis Donohoe to Lord Grenville, Oct. 18, 1883, TNA (UK), FO 5/1862.

139n1 **In 1890 Charles Howard Shinn:** Charles Howard Shinn, "The Evils of Newspaper Space-Work," *Writer* 4, no. 1 (January 1890): 5–6.

139n2 **Shinn may have been correct:** Edwin Schuman, *Steps into Journalism: Help and Hints for Young Writers* (Evanston, IL: Correspondence School of Journalism, 1894), 123.

139n3 **Fictional murder mysteries:** Karen Roggenkamp, *Narrating the News: New Journalism and the Literary Genre in Late Nineteenth-Century American Newspapers and Fiction* (Kent, OH: Kent State University Press, 2005), 56.

139n4 **Journalists and newspapers:** Michael Schudson, *Discovering the News: A Social History of American Newspapers* (New York: Basic Books, 1978), 88–90.

139n5 **Newspapers frequently drove the story:** Quoted in James Green, *Death in the Haymarket: A Story of Chicago, the First Labor Movement and the Bombing That Divided Gilded Age America* (New York: Pantheon Books, 2006), 9.

139n6 **The press both manipulated and articulated:** Ibid., 9.

139n7 **Jeffory A. Clymer:** Jeffory A. Clymer, "The 1886 Chicago Haymarket Bombing and the Rhetoric of Terrorism in America," *Yale Journal of Criticism* 15, no. 2 (Fall 2002): 317–18.

139n8 **Many of the papers that commented:** Schudson, *Discovering the News*, 88–90.

141n1 **The daily newspapers:** Joshua Brown, *Beyond the Lines. Pictorial Reporting, Everyday Life, and the Crisis of Gilded Age America* (Berkeley: University of California Press, 2006), 235. Also see Karen Halttunen, *Murder Most Foul: The Killer and the American Gothic Imagination* (Cambridge, MA: Harvard University Press, 1998), 84–85 and image section between 90 and 91. Gregory A. Borchard, Stephen Bates, and Lawrence J. Mullen, "Publishing Violence as Art and News: Sensational Print and Pictures in the 19th Century Press," in *Sensationalism: Murder, Mayhem, Mudslinging, Scandals, and Disasters in 19th-Century Reporting*, ed. David W. Bulla and David B. Sachsmann (Piscataway, NJ: Transaction Press, 2013), 53–74.

141n2 *Most of these images were not credited:* Illustrations were also reproduced by the Levy-type Company and the Binner Engraving Company. The reproduction of the same images in different publications was usually done without acknowledging the original source. Duke Bailie, *The Cronin Case: The Assassination of Dr. Patrick Henry Cronin* (Chicago: Rhodes and McClure, 1890), 64. Other sketches were done by Henry Savage Landor, *Graphic* (London), June 22, 1889. Clymer, "The 1886 Chicago Haymarket Bombing," 321.

141n3 *While some Chicago papers condemned:* Trotti, "Murder Made Real," 384, 389. See also Hugh Daziel Duncan, *The Rise of Chicago as a Literary Center from 1885 to 1920* (Totowa, NJ: Bedminster Press, 1964), 162; Michael Brown, "Discriminating Photographs from Hand-Drawn Illustrations in Popular Magazines, 1895–1904," *American Journalism* 17, no. 3 (2000): 15–30.

141n4 *The public still found it acceptable:* Trotti, "Murder Made Real," 387.

141n5 *Despite John Finerty's criticism:* Chicago Citizen, "Abuse of Irish-Americans," July 6, 1889.

142n1 *Illustrations in newspaper articles:* National Police Gazette, June 15, 1889.

142n2 *Denslow and Kratzner's depiction:* The image originally appeared in the *Chicago Herald* and was later reproduced in Hunt, *Crime of the Century*, 131.

143 *The National Police Gazette:* After the Haymarket bombing there were visual representations of the event, the most enduring being the one published by *Harper's Weekly* on May 15, 1889. It bore little resemblance to the real scene but became the accepted reality. Carl Smith, *Urban Disorder and the Shape of Belief: The Great Chicago Fire, the Haymarket Bomb and the Model Town of Pullman* (Chicago: University of Chicago Press, 1995), 125–26.

144n1 *As the historian Frank Luther Mott:* Frank Luther Mott, *A History of American Magazines*, vol. 2, *1856–1865* (Cambridge, MA: Harvard University Press, 1938), 334.

144n2 *Political cartoons:* Thomas Milton Kemnitz, "The Cartoon as Historical Source," *Journal of Interdisciplinary History* 4, no. 1 (Summer 1973): 82.

145n1 *As L. Perry Curtis has noted:* L. Perry Curtis, *Apes and Angels: The Irishman in Victorian Caricature* (New York: Smithsonian Institution Press, 1971), 65.

145n2 *That same month:* I am grateful to Mimi Cowan for alerting me to the existence of this image. *Judge* was not alone in associating the Phoenix Park murders with Cronin's. A number of newspapers, including the *Chicago Tribune* and the *Chicago Herald*, also linked the two, though they saw the Dublin murders as evidence that the Irish were prone to violence rather than making any direct connection between the two events. *Chicago Herald*, May 24, 1889; *Chicago Daily Tribune*, "Modern Secret Societies," July 17, 1889; *Chicago Citizen*, "The Cronin Mystery," May 18, 1889; *Citizen*, "The Great Tragedy" (editorial), June 1, 1889.

146 *Over the course of the investigation:* Tom Culbertson, "The Golden Age of American Political Cartoons," *Journal of the Gilded Age and Progressive Era* 7, no. 3 (July 2008): 279.

149n1 *The Chicago press generally agreed:* The variety of opinion spread across the Chicago papers was reflected across the United States and beyond. See for example the *New York Times*; *Philadelphia Public Ledger*; *New York Herald*; *Omaha Republican*; *St. Louis Republic*; *Boston Courier*; *Minneapolis Tribune*; *Cincinnati Enquirer*; *Toledo Blade*; *Dallas News*; *Atlanta Constitution*.

149n2 *She was so incensed:* Margaret Sullivan to Michael Davitt, Aug. 9, 1889, TCD, Davitt

Papers, MS9432/2589; Abbot, "Chicago Newspapers and Their Makers," 664; *Good Housekeeping* 7 (1888): 238.

149n3 *Finerty frequently used editorials: Chicago Citizen*, July 6, July 24, and Nov. 30, 1889.

149n4 *He dismissed William Penn Nixon: Chicago Citizen*, "An Unreasonable Editor," June 8, 1889.

150n1 *Devoy, on the other hand: Gaelic American* (New York), "The Story of Clan na Gael," Jan. 17, 1925.

150n2 *W. P. Rend, a vocal supporter: Chicago Daily Inter Ocean*, "Coughlin's Enmity to Cronin," May 27, 1889.

150n3 *"The sentiment of Americanism":* Quoted in Slason Thompson, *Way Back When: Recollections of an Octogenarian, 1849–1929* (Chicago: A. Kroch, 1931), 284. The Know-Nothing party (also known as the American Party) was anti-emigrant and anti-Catholic. It was at its strongest between the 1840s and the 1860s, but its name continued to be used long after it ceased to be a political force.

150n4 *Slason Thompson, its talented editor: America: A Journal for Americans*, May 30, 1889.

150n5 *Michael Davitt recalled:* Michael Davitt, *The Fall of Feudalism in Ireland; or, The Story of the Land League Revolution* (London: Harper and Brothers, 1904), 252.

150n6 *James Hayes Sadler:* J. Hayes Sadler, Chicago, to Marquis of Salisbury, May 25, 1887, TNA (UK), HO 144/471/x14187.

151n1 *In 1887 the* Chicago Times *published an editorial: Chicago Times*, "Offensive Foreigners," May 18, 1887.

151n2 *At the time, this "war":* Mimi Cowan, "Ducking for Cover: Chicago's Irish Nationalists in the Haymarket Era," *Labor: Studies in Working-Class History of the Americas* 9, no. 1 (2012): 53–76.

151n3 *Many regarded that violent episode:* Smith, *Urban Disorder*, 138–41, 258–63; Nord, "Urbanization of American Journalism," 23–25.

151n4 *The explosion drew out middle-class fears:* See Cowan, "Ducking for Cover," 55n6.

151n5 *Alexander Sullivan, closely associated with the Dynamite War:* Quoted in ibid., 72. Sullivan's speech was given at a meeting held in support of the Home Rule Bill.

151n6 *Days after the explosion:* John Finerty in *Chicago Citizen*, May 8, 1886, quoted in Eric L. Hirsch, *Urban Revolt: Ethnic Politics in the Nineteenth-Century Chicago Labor Movement* (Berkeley: University of California Press, 1990), 133.

152n1 *In the* Irish World *Patrick Ford echoed:* Patrick Ford in *Irish World*, Sept. 4, 1886, quoted in Niall Whelehan, *The Dynamiters: Irish Nationalism and Political Violence in the Wider World, 1867–1900* (Cambridge: Cambridge University Press, 2012), 292. Emphasis in original.

152n2 *"I see . . . that anarchy's torch":* ["I see that anarchy's torch do be uplifted and what the hell it means, I don't know. But this here I know, that all anarchists are enemies of government and all of them ought to be hung up by the neck. What are they anyhow but foreigners and what right have they to be holding torch-light processions in this land of the free and home of the brave? Did you ever see an American or an Irishman an anarchist? No, and you never will."] Quoted in Barbara C. Schaaf, *Mr. Dooley's Chicago* (New York: Anchor Press), 1977, 109.

152n3 *Lionel Sackville West:* Lionel Sackville West, Washington, DC, to Lord Iddesleigh, Aug. 25, 1886, TNA (UK), FO 5/1975.

152n4 *Although the Dynamite War:* Goodson [?], Custom House, London, Secret to Godfrey Lushington Home Office, July 9, 1887, TNA (UK), HO 144/196/a46866.

153n1 *In 1887 additional security:* Custom House, London, May 4, 1887, Pressing and Confidential, TNA (UK), HO 144/196/a46866.

153n2 *When William Fitzpatrick:* Quoted in Cowan, "Ducking for Cover," 53.

153n3 *Clan rhetoric:* Ibid., 55.

153n4 *The image echoed:* *Punch,* "Fenian Guy Fawkes," Dec. 28, 1867; *Harper's Weekly,* "The Usual Irish Way of Doing Things," Sept. 2, 1871.

153n5 **An editorial in America articulated:** *America: A Journal for Americans,* "Editorial—Giant Task for Chicago Justice," June 20, 1889.

155 **In 1889 the New York Times:** Quoted in *Chicago Tribune,* June 15, 1889.

156n1 *The Cronin case was a cultural:* See Halttunen, *Murder Most Foul,* on the crime of murder as a cultural event: chapter 3, "The Pornography of Violence," 60–90.

156n2 *The city newspapers:* *Chicago Tribune,* "At the Carlson Cottage," June 23, 1889; Federal Writers Project, "The Case of Dr. Cronin" (unpublished manuscript, n.d. [1936?]), 216; Abraham Lincoln Presidential Library, Springfield, Illinois, 216. See letters to the *Tribune,* Jan. 15, 1927; Nov. 17, 1935; *Times* (London), June 29 and Sept. 7, 1889; *Chicago Tribune,* June 29, Aug. 16, Oct. 28, and Oct. 29, 1889; McEnnis, *Clan-na-Gael,* 268, 270.

156n3 *However, Captain E. H. Wing:* The newspapers differed on the amount Lukens claimed he could charge, with some suggesting $50 a month, others $100. *Chicago Times,* "A Most Important Discovery," May 25, 1889; *Chicago Daily Inter Ocean,* May 25, 1889.

156n4 *Almost immediately, a dime museum:* *Chicago Tribune,* "At the Carlson Cottage," June 23, 1889.

156n5 *The success of the Carlson cottage:* Federal Writers Project, "Case of Dr. Cronin," 223–24; *Chicago Tribune,* "At the Carlson Cottage," June 23, 1889; *Times* (London), June 27, 1889; Raphael W. Marrow and Harriet I. Carter, *In Pursuit of Crime: The Police of Chicago; Chronicle of a Hundred Years, 1833–1933* (Sunbury, OH: Flats, 1996), 190.

157n1 *For a dime, visitors entered:* Andrea Stulman Dennett, *Weird and Wonderful: The Dime Museum in America* (New York: New York University Press, 1997), 5.

157n2 *The tableaux on display:* In 1890 Chicago had a population of 1,099,850, and the number of illiterate citizens was 39,046. For those literate in a language other than English, the city's newspapers were published in a dozen different languages in the late nineteenth century. Leigh B. Bienen and Brandon Rottinghaus, "Criminal Law: Learning from the Past, Living in the Present; Understanding Homicide in Chicago, 1870–1930," *Journal of Criminal Law and Criminology* 92, nos. 3–4 (2003): 445n20; Dennett, *Weird and Wonderful,* 7.

157n3 *The Stanhope and Eptstean Dime Museum:* *Catalogue of Stanhope and Epstean's New Dime Museum,* [n.d.], Chicago History Museum, F38RN N381.

157n4 *At the Stanhope and Epstean:* Morris, *Stranger's Guide,* 69; *Chicago Tribune,* May 29 1889; McEnnis, *Clan-na-Gael,* 335; Federal Writers Project, "Case of Dr. Cronin," 309. Louis Epstean paid Dinan $100 a week to exhibit his horse and buggy. *Times* (London), Dec. 11, 1889. In June 1889 one of the men named as a suspect in the case took Louis Epstean to the Superior Court of Illinois in an unsuccessful attempt to have the wax reproduction of him removed from the Cronin exhibit.

158n1 *At the Eden Musée:* *Chicago Tribune,* May 29, 1889; June 2, 1889; Aug.18, 1889; *Eden Musée Catalogue,* 1890, 1891, Chicago History Museum, F38QR E4 1890/1891. The Eden Musée in Chicago was part of the Eden Musée American Company, which had been established in 1882. Its primary location was on Twenty-Third Street between Fifth and Sixth Avenues in New York, where it had opened in February 1883. The museum's real strength was its wax figures, something the Chicago outlet also became famous for. Dime museums did not always charge a dime—Epstean's charged 10 cents, but the Eden Musée charged adults 50 cents and children 25 cents. Lyman B. Glover was the manager of the Eden Musée in Chicago. Dennett, *Weird and Wonderful,* 8.

158n2 *The Eden Musée catalog gave few details:* *Eden Musée Catalogue* (Chicago, 1890), Chicago History Museum, F38QR E4 1890.

158n3 *Wax reproductions:* Dennett, *Weird and Wonderful,* 109, 116.

158n4 *In the summer of 1889:* Michael Denning, "Cheap Stories: Notes on Popular Fiction and

Working-Class Culture in Nineteenth-Century America," *History Workshop* 22 (Autumn 1986): 9.

158n5 **Who Killed Doctor Cronin:** Old Cap Lee, *Who Killed Dr. Cronin? or, At Work on the Great Cronin Mystery*, New York Detective Library, June 15, 1889, Chicago History Museum, F38UD.B345-Y86; Old Cap Collier, *Who Murdered Dr. Cronin? or, Shadowing the Criminal*, Old Cap Collier Library, July 1889, Chicago History Museum, F38UD.011 no. 349.

159n1 *Cronin was memorialized:* "The Murder of Dr. Cronin," NLI, Devoy Papers, MS 18058 (13), Printed Circulars; Federal Writers Project, "Case of Dr. Cronin," 227.

159n2 *"Cronin" was the title of two poems:* Printed Circulars, NLI, Devoy Papers, MS 18058 (13).

161 *In late 1889 Rudyard Kipling:* Owen Dudley Edwards, "Kipling and the Irish," *London Review of Books* 10, no. 3 (February 1988): 22–23.

162n1 *The Whitechapel Club:* On the Whitechapel Club see George Ade Papers, Midwestern Manuscripts Collection, Newberry Library, box 9, folder 389; Whitechapel Club Papers; Charles H. Dennis Papers, Midwestern Manuscripts Collection, Newberry Library, box 12, folder 574, letters and articles from Wallace Rice; Larry Lorenz, "The Whitechapel Club: Defining Chicago's Newspapermen in the 1890s," *American Journalism* 15, no. 1 (Winter 1998): 83–102; Norman Howard Sims, "The Chicago Style of Journalism" (PhD diss., University of Illinois at Urbana-Champaign, 1979), 218.

162n2 *Journalism was becoming a profession:* See for example Schuman, *Steps into Journalism*; Charles A. Dana, *The Art of Newspaper Making: Three Lectures* (New York: D. Appleton, 1895); Brad Asher, "The Professional Vision: Conflicts over Journalism Education, 1900–1950," *American Journalism* 11, no. 4 (1994): 304–20.

CHAPTER NINE

163n1 *On August 26 the Cronin murder trial began:* McConnell was a Democrat. He was elected as a judge of the Circuit Court of Cook County in 1889. The 1848 Illinois Constitution allowed for elected judges, and this was retained in the 1870 state constitution, which lasted for ninety-four years. In addition to judges, the state's attorney, the chief prosecutor and the clerk of the county were also elected positions. Leigh B. Bienen and Brandon Rottinghaus, "Criminal Law: Learning from the Past, Living in the Present; Understanding Homicide in Chicago, 1870–1930," *Journal of Criminal Law and Criminology* 92, nos. 3–4 (2003): 462.

163n2 *Between August 30 and October 22:* John T. McEnnis, *Clan-na-Gael and the Murder of Dr. Cronin* (Chicago: F. J. Schulte and J. W. Iliff, 1890), 295–96; Henry M. Hunt, *The Crime of the Century; or, The Assassination of Dr. Patrick Henry Cronin* (Chicago: H. L. and D. H. Kockersperger, 1889), 391–97.

163n3 *As the weeks passed:* *Times* (London), Sept. 24, 1889.

163n4 *Over nine hundred prospective jurors:* The defense was entitled to twenty peremptory challenges and so was the prosecution, which meant that two hundred peremptory challenges were allowed. Elizabeth Dale, "*People v. Coughlin* and Criticism of the Criminal Jury in Late Nineteenth-Century Chicago," *Northern Illinois University Law Review* 28 (2008): 515–16.

163n5 *The process proved both lengthy and controversial:* Illinois Rev. Stat. ch. 78, 14 (1874), quoted in Dale, "*People v. Coughlin*," 517. One of the jurors, Benjamin Clark, said he read the *Tribune* daily, the *News* occasionally, and the *Times*, *Inter Ocean*, and *Herald* on Sundays. Benjamin Clark examination by Counsel for the People, 1889, from *Coughlin v. The People*, in *Reports of Cases at Law and in Chancery Argued and Determined in the Supreme Court of Illinois*, vol. 147 (Springfield: Journal Company, 1893), 156.

163n6 *The Tribune took a dim view:* *Chicago Tribune*, "The Devolution of a Jury," Sept. 4, 1889. This image is interesting because, as the prosecution would point out, none of those selected for jury service were of Irish extraction.

164n1 *In one article, "How Newspaper Reports":* Chicago Tribune, "How Newspaper Reports Are to Be Read," Sept. 6, 1889. A generation later, Clarence Darrow, writing of the Leopold and Loeb case, commented: "Truth is, when there is a public outcry against some defendant, all other business in the court is set aside for a criminal prosecution. The case must be tried at once while the haters are hating and hot on the trail. . . . Every prospective juror called into the box knows the case, and all its details, as presented by the press. He has all the bias of a partisan, and it is not possible for him to give the defendant a fair trial. Juror after juror is excused because of having an opinion." Clarence Darrow, *Story of My Life* (New York: Da Capo, 1932), 233.

164n2 *In an attempt to ensure a representative jury:* Dale, "People v. Coughlin," 519–20; Hunt, *Crime of the Century*, 387–88; 393. The court reduced the number of questions that could be asked of potential jurors to five.

164n3 *McConnell dimissed half of Forrest's list:* Quoted in Hunt, *Crime of the Century*, 388–89.

165n1 *While jury selection was ongoing:* Chicago Tribune, "Splitting Up the Cronin Case," Aug. 26, 1889.

165n2 *A contemporary publication:* Bench and Bar of Chicago: Biographical Sketches (Chicago: American Biographical, 1883), 271–73, 531–33.

165n3 *At the outset of the trial:* Transcript of Trial, People of the State of Illinois v. Daniel Coughlin, Patrick O'Sullivan, Martin Bourk et al., Supreme Court of Illinois, 1889, RS # 901.001, 25939, Illinois State Archives, 2:13; McEnnis, Clan-na-Gael, 285–86.

165n4 *The journal felt that:* America: A Journal for Americans, "Editorial—The Conspiracy to Corrupt Justice," Oct. 17, 1889.

166n1 *On October 11, Mark Salomon:* Chicago Tribune, Oct. 16, 1889. Henry Stoltenberg, Alexander Sullivan's stenographer, was questioned but not charged—something Margaret Sullivan believed was a blatant attempt to keep her husband connected to the case. Salomon implicated a second bailiff, A. J. Hanks, in the affair. Others indicted included men with Clan connections—Fred W. Smith, a hardware manufacturers' agent; Tom Kavanaugh, a contractor; Jeremiah O'Donnell, a US revenue gauger; Joseph Konen, fruit dealer (and the selected jury member who had agreed to take a bribe); and John Graham, a clerk in A. S. Trude's (Sullivan's lawyer's) law office. McEnnis, Clan-na-Gael, 301–9.

166n2 *America marked the occasion:* America: A Journal for Americans, "Editorial—The Conspiracy to Corrupt Justice," Oct. 17, 1889.

168n1 *Of the twelve men:* Hunt, Crime of the Century, 417–19.

168n2 *A representative jury:* Bruce C. Nelson, "Revival and Upheaval: Religion, Irreligion and Chicago's Working Class in 1886," Journal of Social History 25, no. 2 (Winter 1991): 234–35.

168n3 *According to the Tribune:* Chicago Tribune, "Matters Connected with Juries," Dec. 16, 1889; Times (London), Aug. 15 and Sept. 24, 1889.

168n4 *The London Times was shocked:* Times (London), Aug. 15, 1889.

169n1 *Papers tried to give a sense of the atmosphere:* Chicago Tribune, "The Past Recalled," Oct. 16, 1889.

169n2 *The London Times marveled:* Times (London), Sept. 24, 1889.

170n1 *The reporter later shadowed:* New York Times, "The Cronin Murder Case," Oct. 20, 1889.

170n2 *Desperate to satisfy demand:* Times (London), "The Cronin Murder Trial," Sept. 24, 1889; Chicago Times, "All Found Guilty," Dec. 16, 1889; Chicago Tribune, "Stripes for Four," Dec. 17, 1889; Chicago Tribune, Aug. 4 and Dec. 16, 1889; Chicago Daily News, Dec. 14, 1889.

170n3 *For the duration of the trial:* John J. Flinn, Chicago, the Marvelous City of the West: A History, an Encyclopaedia, and a Guide (Chicago: Flinn and Sheppard, 1891), 319.

170n4 *The papers reported that the jurors' evenings:* Chicago Tribune, "Their Appetites Do Not Suffer," Dec. 16, 1889. Books read by the jurors included Nicholas Nickleby, A Tale of Two Cities, King Solomon's Mines, and The Parisians.

171n1 **While the guilt or innocence:** Janice L. Reiff, "What's on Trial," *Labor: Studies in Working Class History of the Americas* 9, no. 3 (2012): 44.

171n2 **State's Attorney Joel Longnecker:** Transcript of Trial, *People of the State of Illinois v. Daniel Coughlin, Patrick O'Sullivan, Martin Bourk et al.*, Supreme Court of Illinois, RS # 901.001, 35/13B/65V#, 25939, Illinois State Archives. The bulk of the trial was spent on the prosecution, which closed its case on November 16. The defense put forward its case between November 17 and 25, and the prosecution countered with rebuttal evidence. Closing arguments were heard between November 29 and December 13.

171n3 **He assured the jury:** Longnecker's opening speech, quoted in McEnnis, *Clan-na-Gael*, 322.

171n4 **George Ingham, for the prosecution:** George C. Ingham, prosecutor, quoted in *Chicago Herald*, Dec. 4, 1889.

172n1 **Despite the fact that Alexander Sullivan:** Margaret Sullivan to Michael Davitt, Oct. 28, 1889, TCD, Davitt Papers, MS 932/2590.

172n2 **During the trial, America published two cartoons:** *America: A Journal for Americans*, "The Great Clan-na-Gael Triangle Puzzle (?)," Aug. 29, 1889; "Not So Welcome a Visitor as Edward Spelman," Nov. 7, 1889.

174n1 **The prosecution case focused primarily:** William J. Hynes's closing speech, quoted in McEnnis, *Clan-na-Gael*, 460, 464.

174n2 **The prosecution devoted considerable time:** Testimony of Andrew Foy, Oct. 29, 1889; Testimony of Tom F. O'Connor, *People of the State of Illinois v. Coughlin et al.*, Supreme Court of Illinois, Illinois State Archives, 4:558–76, 4:707–47; Beggs to Spelman, Feb. 16, 1889; Spelman to Beggs, Feb. 17, 1889, quoted in McEnnis, *Clan-na-Gael*, 125–26.

174n3 **Following the meeting, John Beggs:** John F. Beggs to Edward Spelman, Feb. 18, 1889, quoted in McEnnis, *Clan-na-Gael*, 126–27. Spelman was also president of the Whiskey Trust. Spelman's testimony at the trial: *People of the State of Illinois v. Coughlin et al.*, Supreme Court of Illinois, Illionois State Archives, 5:1238–54.

175n1 **To ensure support:** Testimony of Pat McGarry, *People of the State of Illinois v. Coughlin et al.*, Supreme Court of Illinois, Illinois State Archives, 5:795–820.

175n2 **As it had been at the coroner's jury:** Duke Bailie, *The Cronin Case: The Assassination of Dr. Patrick Henry Cronin* (Chicago: Rhodes and McClure, 1890), 230.

175n3 **John Garrity, a teamster:** *Chicago Weekly Journal*, June 12, 1889; *Chicago Daily News*, May 28, 1889; *Times* (London), Nov. 2, 1889; McEnnis, *Clan-na-Gael*, 225. "Bruce does not bear a savoury reputation and has been in numerous scrapes. The police do not place implicit reliance in his story." *Times* (London), June 29, 1889, claimed Bruce had been offered $1,000 to kill Cronin.

175n4 **Other witnesses, including Pauline Hoertel:** *Chicago Tribune*, Nov. 14, 1889; McEnnis, *Clan-na-Gael*, 338, 352–54; Bailie, *Cronin Case*, 279.

176n1 **Medical evidence was provided:** Testimony of Dr. Egbert, Oct. 25, 1889, *People of the State of Illinois v. Coughlin et al.*, Supreme Court of Illinois, Illinois State Archives, 4:162–87; *Times* (London), "The Cronin Murder Trial," Oct. 28, 1889.

176n2 **The testimony of Dr. D. G. Moore:** *Chicago Tribune*, "Lawyers for the State Protest," Oct. 27, 1889; *Times* (London), "The Cronin Murder Trial," Oct. 28, 1889.

176n3 **In a prescient comment:** *Chicago Tribune*, "A Scene in the Cronin Trial," Oct. 27, 1889.

176n4 **Blood and hair samples:** *Times* (London), Nov. 11, 1889; McEnnis, *Clan-na-Gael*, 380–86; John F. Fisher and Joe Nickell, *Crime Science: Methods of Forensic Detection* (Lexington: University Press of Kentucky, 1999), 193–94.

177n1 **His office was based a mile and a half:** Testimony of Dr. John F. Williams, *People of the State of Illinois v. Coughlin et al.*, Supreme Court of Illinois, Illionois State Archives, 6:2114–19.

177n2 **Harry Planskie, a shirt salesman:** Testimony of Gustav Klahre, *People of the State of Illinois* *v. Coughlin et al.*, Supreme Court of Illinois, Illinois State Archives, 7:2046–66; McEnnis, *Clan-na-Gael*, 350.

177n3 **On November 8:** *Times* (London), Nov. 11, 1889; Hunt, *Crime of the Century*, 336–40.

177n4 **The next day John Kunze wrote:** Kunze to *Chicago Abend Post*, November 1889, translation in Bailie, *Cronin Case*, 286–87.

177n5 **More damaging evidence:** McEnnis, *Clan-na-Gael*, 397–402.

178n1 **A key part of the defense:** William Neiman, owner of the saloon on the southeast corner of School Street and Ashland Avenue, testified that O'Sullivan was in his bar on the night of May 4. Defense provided evidence from Tom Whalen, his wife, and several of O'Sullivan's employees to prove that he was at home the entire evening. Testimony of William Nieman, *People of the State of Illinois v. Coughlin et al.*, Supreme Court of Illinois, 6:1800–816, Illinois State Archives; McEnnis, *Clan-na-Gael*, 391. Matt Danahy, owner of the saloon that became the unofficial headquarters of the defense, testified that Burke was in his saloon on the evening of May 4, while Michael Whalen provided an alibi for Coughlin. *People of the State of Illinois v. Coughlin et al.*, Supreme Court of Illinois, 7:2617–29, Illinois State Archives. McEnnis, *Clan-na-Gael*, 366–70.

178n2 **In his closing argument:** Hynes' closing speech, quoted in McEnnis, *Clan-na-Gael*, 461.

178n3 **On November 28 America published a double-page cartoon:** Between 1855 and 1890, Castle Garden was an immigration center at the very tip of Manhattan. George Pullman was a leading industrialist in Chicago. He was the owner of Pullman's Palace Car Company and the founder, in 1881, of the town of Pullman, a model industrial town, thirteen miles south of Chicago.

179 **The allegations of jury bribing:** *Chicago Herald*, "Those Cheerful Defendants," Dec. 1, 1889.

180n1 **Juror Charles C. Dix:** Bailie, *Cronin Case*, 408.

180n2 **Three lawyers spoke:** Federal Writers Project, "The Case of Dr. Cronin," (unpublished manuscript, n.d. [1936?]), 301; Abraham Lincoln Presidential Library, Springfield, Illinois.

180n3 **Observers were impressed:** *Chicago Citizen*, "Oratory at the Cronin Trial," Dec. 14, 1889.

181n1 **For many observers the trial was pure theater:** Quoted in Bailie, *Cronin Case*, 350–52.

181n2 **The state's attorney argued:** Longnecker's closing speech, quoted in McEnnis, *Clan-na-Gael*, 421.

181n3 **Hynes, in his summing-up:** Hynes's closing speech, quoted in ibid., 459.

181n4 **Forrest's closing speech:** Ibid., 491.

181n5 **Forrest attacked the witnesses:** Forrest's closing speech, quoted in ibid., 495.

182n1 **Like the prosecution:** Ibid., 488.

182n2 **Under Illinois law:** Juries were given the power to decide the law and the facts when it was put on the statute books in 1827 and confirmed by the Illinois Supreme Court in 1859. *Schnier v People*, 23, Ill., 17, 30 (1859), quoted in Elizabeth Dale, "Not Simply Black and White: Jury Power and the Law in Late Nineteenth-Century Chicago," *Social Science History* 25, no. 1 (Spring 2001): 13. Illinois was not the only state to confer great power on juries—in at least nine other states, juries had similar responsibilities. Dale, "*People v. Coughlin*," 528–29.

182n3 **On the evening of December 12:** McConnell's instructions to the jury, quoted in McEnnis, *Clan-na-Gael*, 513–14.

182n4 **Observers had anticipated a swift verdict:** *Chicago Daily News*, Dec. 14, 1889.

182n5 **Between 1875 and 1920:** Jeffrey S. Adler, "'It's His First Offense. We Might as Well Let Him Go': Homicide and Criminal Justice in Chicago 1875–1920," *Journal of Social History* (Fall 2006): 6–7.

183n1 **Of those convicted:** Derrel Cheatwood, "Capital Punishment for the Crime of Homicide in Chicago: 1870–1930," *Journal of Criminal Law and Criminology* 92, nos. 3–4 (2003): 853–55, table 2. There were 9,095 homicides in Chicago between 1870 and 1930. Of these, 114 (or 1.2%) were given a death sentence, and 87 (or 0.96%) executions were carried out. These figures are based on the Chicago Police Department Homicide Record Index, and the information contained therein is sometimes flawed. For example the Cronin case (record 335.1) records no verdict. Northwestern University, "Homicide in Chicago 1870–1890," homicide.northwestern.edu/database.

183n2 *In the 1880s:* Elizabeth Dale, *The Chicago Trunk Murder: Law and Justice at the Turn of the Century* (DeKalb: Northern Illinois University Press, 2011), 69, 137n22. The ten executed in Chicago between 1880 and 1890 were James Tracey, executed February 3, 1882, for the murder of Police Officer Huebner; Frank Mulkowski for the murder of Agnes Kledziak in 1884; Giovanni Azari, Agostino Gelardi, and Ignazio Silvestri for killing Filippo Caruso in 1885; August Spies, Albert Parsons, Adolph Fischer, and George Engel executed November 11, 1887, for the murder of Officer Mathias J. Degan during the Haymarket Riot May 1886; and Zephyr Davis, executed February 27, 1888, for the murder of Maggie Gaughan.

183n3 *A bailiff told a journalist:* Chicago Tribune, "Culver Assaulted," Dec. 16, 1889; Dale, "People v. Coughlin," 524.

183n4 *Its headline on Monday:* Chicago Times, "All Found Guilty," Dec. 16, 1889.

183n5 *That morning it became apparent:* Chicago Herald, "Crowds Kept Moving On," Dec. 16, 1889; *Chicago Evening News,* "How the Prisoners Feel," Dec. 14, 1889; *Chicago Tribune,* "Stripes for Four," Dec. 17, 1889; *Chicago Daily News,* "Four Men Guilty," Dec. 16, 1889; *Chicago Daily Inter Ocean,* "Four Men Guilty," Dec. 16, 1889; "How They Took the News," Dec. 16, 1889.

184n1 *At two thirty Clerk Lee:* Chicago Daily News, "Four Men Guilty," Dec. 16, 1889; *Chicago Tribune,* "Stripes for Four," Dec. 17, 1889.

184n2 *The crowd waiting at Dearborn Avenue:* Chicago Herald, "Escaped the Hangman," Dec. 17, 1889; *Chicago Tribune,* "What the People Think of It," Dec. 17, 1889.

184n3 *One man "dressed like a merchant":* Chicago Tribune, "What the People Think of It," Dec. 17, 1889.

185n1 *Immediately after the verdict was delivered:* Chicago Daily Inter Ocean, "Juryman Culver," Dec. 17, 1889; *Chicago Tribune,* "Juror Culver," Dec. 17, 1889.

185n2 *A week after the trial concluded:* Chicago Tribune, "Sample Letters to Mr. Culver," Dec. 22, 1889; "His House for Sale," Dec. 23, 1889.

185n3 *Although dissatisfied:* Chicago Tribune, "Opinion of Dr. Cronin's Friends," Dec. 17, 1889.

186n1 *For the* Chicago Herald: *Chicago Herald,* "Escaped the Hangman," Dec. 17, 1889.

186n2 *The* Chicago Times *found the verdict:* Chicago Times, "Editorial—The Cronin Verdict," Dec. 17, 1889; *America: A Journal for Americans,* "Editorial—The Cronin Verdict," Dec. 19, 1889.

186n3 *It was widely suggested:* Among those who believed that the verdict would smash the power of secret societies were the *Chicago Daily Inter Ocean, Chicago Times,* and *Chicago Tribune.* Many newspapers thought that the guilty should have hung: *Chicago Weekly Journal, America: A Journal for Americans, Philadelphia Public Ledger, New York Herald, New York Times, New York World, St. Louis Republic, London Morning Post, London Daily News, Boston Journal,* and the *Boston Advertiser,* among others. For the *New York Herald,* the verdict was "a compromise and a disappointment" while the *New York Times* claimed that "the verdict was . . . an outrageous miscarriage of justice." *New York Times,* editorial, Dec. 17, 1889. The *St. Louis Republic* and the *Globe-Democrat* were both dissatisfied with the verdict.

186n4 *Charles Cameron:* Quoted in *Chicago Daily News,* Dec. 16, 1889, also *Chicago Tribune,* "What the People Think of It," Dec. 17, 1889.

186n5 *The fact that no one's life:* Chicago Weekly Journal, "Aspects of the Cronin Verdict," Dec. 18, 1889. The *Tribune* concurred and observed, "It is believed in official quarters that if

P. O'Sullivan is left to himself he will tell the whole truth about his contract with Dr. Cronin. It is not believed that O'Sullivan actually participated in the murder. He was merely an accomplice before the fact." *Chicago Tribune,* "Explaining That Ice Contract," Dec. 18, 1889.

186n6 *Irish American papers generally praised the verdict:* Chicago Citizen, "The Cronin Verdict," Dec. 21, 1889; *Chicago Herald,* "What Is Said in New York," Dec. 17, 1889.

187n1 *The London Times, still smarting:* Times (London), "The Cronin Murder Trial," Dec. 17, 1889.

187n2 *Another London paper:* Quoted in *New York Times,* "English View of It," "Dissatisfied with the Result," Dec. 17, 1889; *Chicago Herald,* "Press Opinion of the Verdict," Dec. 17, 1889.

187n3 *The London* Graphic: London *Graphic,* Dec. 23, 1889 quoted in *Chicago Tribune,* Jan. 10, 1890.

188 *Speaking "as a citizen":* Quoted in *Chicago Daily News,* "Four Men Guilty," Dec. 16, 1889. McConnell may have been pleased that no death sentences were passed, for he had been part of the clemency movement that followed the Haymarket trial. Later, however, he conceded that "the hanging of these men did do away with the hysteria which had pervaded the body of the people." He concluded, "And, aside from the injustice of such an occurrence, perhaps it did not matter who was hanged provided the public was satisfied." McConnell, "The Chicago Bomb Case," *Harper's Monthly* (1934), quoted in Carl Smith, *Urban Disorder and the Shape of Belief: The Great Chicago Fire, the Haymarket Bomb and the Model Town of Pullman* (Chicago: University of Chicago Press, 1995), 344n46.

190n1 *Culver, a devout Methodist:* Chicago Daily Inter Ocean, "Juryman Culver," Dec. 17, 1889; *Chicago Tribune,* "Juror Culver," Dec. 17, 1889; "Cronin Jurors Explain," Dec. 29, 1889.

190n2 *The newspapers had little interest:* Chicago Daily Inter Ocean, "Through Pat Grant's Eyes," Dec. 17, 1889; *New York Times,* "The Cronin Verdict," Dec. 18, 1889.

190n3 *Kunze was released:* Louis Epstean put up Kunze's $5,000 bail and paid him £100 a week for a season of ten weeks to appear at the Stanhope and Epstean Dime Museum. *Chicago Times,* "Motion for a New Trial," Dec. 17, 1889; *Los Angeles Herald,* "He Will Pose as a Dime Museum Freak," Jan. 19, 1890. In 1900 Kunze was arrested in Milwaukee and later returned to Joliet Prison—he had been convicted of swindling and had skipped town while on parole.

190n4 *Coughlin, Burke, and O'Sullivan were handcuffed:* Chicago Citizen, "The Cronin Prisoners," Jan. 18, 1890; *Chicago Tribune,* "They Start for Joliet Prison," Jan. 15, 1890; Bailie, *Cronin Case,* 425.

CHAPTER TEN

191n1 *Looking back on the events:* John Devoy, "The Story of Clan na Gael," *Gaelic American* (New York), Jan. 31, 1925.

191n2 *The reputation of the Chicago police:* Michael Whalen (Coughlin's partner) had been suspended from the force when Coughlin was arrested, but was later cleared of any involvement. However, in his trial testimony Whalen said that despite his innocence he was formally discharged from the force on August 31, 1889. Others dismissed included Detective Michael J. Crowe, Patrol Sergeant John Stift, and Patrolmen Michael Ahern, Daniel Cunningham, and Redmond McDonald. Cunningham, a long-serving detective, had given information to the defense. Ahern spent much of his time criticizing the prosecution while neglecting his patrol duty. *Chicago Times,* "Whalen Also Suspended," May 26, 1889; Testimony of Michael Whalen, *People of the State of Illinois v. Coughlin et al.,* Supreme Court of Illinois, Illinois State Archives, 7:2617–29; *Chicago*

Tribune, "Weeding Out Clan na Gaels," Dec. 18, 1889; *Chicago Daily Inter Ocean,* "Triangle and the Star," Dec. 20, 1889. According to the *Inter Ocean,* "It is only fair to say . . . that not all Clan-na-Gael policemen are Trianglers. In fact there are several glowing examples to the contrary. . . . It is a fact though that a large majority of all the police force are Irishmen, and it is a further fact that the vast majority of those Irishmen who have received their appointments through Triangle scheming are wedded to the Triangle and bound to condone its murderous deeds. These men must go to a man." *Chicago Inter Ocean,* Dec. 19, 1889.

191n3 **Cregier outlined his vision:** Quoted in Richard C. Lindberg, *To Serve and Collect: Chicago Politics and Police Corruption from the Lager Beer Riot to the Summerdale Scandal 1855–1960* (Carbondale: Southern Illinois University Press, 1998), 85.

192n1 **Yet for all the changes:** *Chicago Tribune,* "Police Reorganization," Jan. 10, 1890; "Marsh Makes a Move," Jan. 21, 1890; "Superintendent Marsh," June 5, 1890.

192n2 **Chicago's German-language newspaper:** Translation from *Illinois Staats Zeitung* (Chicago), Feb. 1, 1890, in *Chicago Tribune,* Feb. 2, 1890.

193n1 **No charges were brought:** Joseph H. Heinen and Susan Barton Heinen, *Lost German Chicago* (Chicago: Arcadia, 2009), 81; *Chicago Tribune,* "It Was a Fatal Wound," Feb. 1, 1890; "Was Self-Defense," Feb. 2, 1890.

193n2 **They were not alone in this:** Rev. Bristol, quoted in *Chicago Tribune,* July 1, 1889.

193n3 **So convinced was the Tribune:** *Chicago Tribune,* Dec. 20, 1889.

194n1 **John McEnnis, journalist and author:** John T. McEnnis, *The Clan-na-Gael and the Murder of Dr. Cronin* (Chicago: F. J. Schulte and J. W. Iliff, 1890), 147.

194n2 **Press coverage contributed:** For further discussion of this see Elizabeth Dale, "Not Simply Black and White: Jury Power and the Law in Late Nineteenth-Century Chicago," *Social Science History* 25, no. 1 (Spring 2001): 7–27.

195n1 **Such was the disillusionment:** *Chicago Tribune,* "No Parade March 17," Feb. 17, 1890.

195n2 **A decade after Cronin's death:** Patrick Ford to Michael Davitt, Jan. 19, 1899, quoted in James R. Barrett, *The Irish Way: Becoming Irish in the Multiethnic City* (New York: Penguin, 2012), 241; Owen McGee, "Irish Republicanism in the Age of Parnell: The Irish Republican Brotherhood, 1879–1893" (PhD thesis, University College Dublin, 2003), 2:408.

196n1 **In the wake of the divorce scandal:** Devoy to James J. O'Kelly M.P., [Nov.–Dec.] 1890, in *Devoy's Post-Bag,* ed. William O'Brien and Desmond Ryan, vol. 2 (Dublin: C. J. Fallon, 1953), 316.

196n2 **As the Inter Ocean observed:** *Chicago Daily Inter Ocean,* "Editorial—The Verdict in the Cronin Case," Dec. 17, 1889.

196n3 **As the first anniversary:** Bernard McQuaid to Michael Corrigan, May 6, 1890, in Fergus MacDonald, *The Catholic Church and Secret Societies in the United States* (New York: Catholic Historical Society, 1946), 163.

196n4 **But at a meeting of Catholic bishops:** Michael F. Funchion, "Irish Chicago: Church, Homeland, Politics and Class—The Shaping of an Ethnic Group, 1870–1890," in *Ethnic Chicago,* ed. Melvin G. Holli and Peter d'Alroy Jones (Grand Rapids, MI: William B. Eerdmans, 1981), 21. The Fenians had been formally condemned by the Catholic Church in January 1870. In 1893 the church condemned the Independent Order of Good Templars, and the following year condemned the Odd-Fellows, Sons of Temperance, and Knights of Pythias. (Cronin had been a Commander of the Knights of Pythias.)

196n5 **As Archbishop Frederick Katzer:** Archbishop Frederick Katzer of Milwaukee to [anon.] Cardinal, Rome, Nov. 15, 1891, in MacDonald, *Catholic Church and Secret Societies,* 164.

196n6 **As Alderman John Powers observed:** Quoted in Philip Kinsley, *The Chicago Tribune: Its First Hundred Years,* vol. 3 (Chicago: Chicago Tribune, 1943), 159.

197n1 *For several years after Cronin's death:* Gaelic American (New York), "The Story of Clan na Gael," March 28, 1925; Terry Golway, *Irish Rebel: John Devoy and America's Fight for Irish Freedom* (New York: St. Martin's Griffin, 1998), 172.

197n2 *On September 28, 1894:* Times (London), Oct. 13, 1894.

197n3 *They agreed to issue a joint circular:* Articles of Union. Agreed to by the Conference Committee, representing the T.H. and the U.B., at the Sheares Club Rooms, Philadelphia, Sept. 4, 1899, Joseph McGarrity Collection, Villanova University, http://digital.library.villanova.edu /Item/vudl:135541. The signatories to the articles were John J. Teevens, John Revens, William Crossin, James C. Vaughan, John Devoy, O'Neill Ryan, Patrick J. Judge, Patrick O'Neill, James G. Fitzgerald, and John T. Keating.

198n1 *The first convention:* Golwoy, *Irish Rebel*, 179–80.

198n2 *Of the seven accused:* Chicago Tribune, "Must Remain in Prison," June 3, 1891; "It Was Squealers Day," Feb. 19, 1890; "Jerry O'Donnell 'Goes Down,'" May 18, 1890.

198n3 *During the 1880s the Illinois State Bar Association:* Dale, "Not Simply Black and White," 16.

199n1 *Papers, including the* **Boston Daily Advertiser:** Boston Daily Advertiser quoted in *Chicago Tribune*, Dec. 22, 1889.

199n2 *The* **Spectator** *in London observed:* Spectator (London), Dec. 21, 1889.

199n3 *As Jeffrey S. Adler has pointed out:* Jeffrey S. Adler, "'It's His First Offense. We Might as Well Let Him Go': Homicide and Criminal Justice in Chicago 1875–1920," *Journal of Social History* (Fall 2006): 18.

199n4 *Despite many misgivings:* Elizabeth Dale, "People v. Coughlin and Criticism of the Criminal Jury in Late Nineteenth-Century Chicago," *Northern Illinois University Law Review* 28 (2008): 527 including nn212–19; 533–35.

199n5 *John Culver, the juror who held out:* Chicago Herald, "Editorial—Juror Culver and the Herald," Dec. 21, 1889; *Chicago Daily Inter Ocean*, Dec. 20, 1889.

200n1 *The jury found against Culver:* Chicago Tribune, "Juror Culver's Suit for Damages," May 13, 1891; "No Damages for Culver," May 21, 1891; "Culver vs the Herald," May 22, 1891.

200n2 *Both men died of tuberculosis:* O'Sullivan died on May 5, Burke on December 9. *Times* (London), Dec. 12, 1892; *Chicago Tribune*, "Brought to Chicago," May 7, 1892; "Blessed in Spring Glory," May 6, 1896; "Into Mother Earth," Dec. 11, 1892. Dan Donohoe, O'Sullivan's lawyer, gave a speech at his graveside; Burke's funeral mass took place at St. Bridget's Church on Archer Avenue.

200n3 *Coughlin's counsel argued:* Coughlin v. The People, in *Reports of Cases at Law and in Chancery Argued and Determined in the Supreme Court of Illinois*, vol. 147 (Springfield, IL: Journal Company, 1893): 150–51.

200n4 *Coughlin's legal team had objected:* Ibid., 140–96.

201n1 *When questioned by the court:* Bontecou's examination by counsel, 1889, quoted in ibid., 151–56, 152.

201n2 *Clark told the court:* Clark's examination by counsel, quoted in ibid., January 1893, 156–61.

201n3 *The press had congratulated itself:* Ibid., 143–88. Not all the judges concurred with this decision. John Schofield and Benjamin D. Magruder dissented, with Magruder arguing that "nearly everybody who knows how to read, reads the newspapers. When a great crime is committed . . . there is scarcely a man who does not know of it, and read about it, and form some sort of an opinion in regard to it. If men, who read, and are affected by, newspaper accounts of the commission of crime, are excluded from the jury box, than trial by jury might as well be abolished." Ibid., 191. See Illinois State Archives, Joliet Prison Records, 243.200, 1857–1916, files 41c–60c, Penitentiary Mittimus files.

201n4 *The Illinois Supreme Court decision:* John P. Altgeld, *Reasons for Pardoning Fielden, Neebe and Schwab*, June 26, 1893 (Chicago, 1893), 30–35.

201n5 **Coughlin's new trial began:** The retrial took longer than the original trial—120 days compared with 107.

202n1 **The press speculated:** *San Francisco Call,* "Why Burke Died," Dec. 13, 1892.

202n2 **Schuettler acknowledged:** *Chicago Tribune,* "[Tom] O'Connor Takes His Life," Dec. 8, 1896. O'Sullivan and Burke died in prison; Edward Spelman fell from a ladder, "literally losing his head," while both John Beggs and Pat Dinan died in the spring of 1892; Agnes McNearney, who had been in Cronin's medical office the evening he disappeared, died soon after the first trial ended; Robert Gibbons was shot dead by Shuettler in January 1890, and three of Andy Foy's children died suddenly. Le Caron died in 1894. Beggs died at his home at 24 Chicago Terrace on April 5, 1892. He had been suffering from pneumonia after appearing at the St. Patrick's Day parade. Eugen Seeger, *Chicago: The Wonder City* (Chicago: Geo. Gregory Printing, 1893), 298–99. *Chicago Tribune,* "John F. Beggs Dead," April 6, 1892.

202n3 **And apparently the dead didn't disappear:** Brennan had been an employee of O'Sullivan and had testified on his behalf at the murder trial. He had bought the ice business from the Lincoln Ice Company, which had bought it from O'Sullivan. The story prompted a journalist, Miss Roscoe, to stay overnight at the home in the hope of getting an interview with O'Sullivan's ghost. No interview materialized. *Chicago Tribune,* "Sees O'Sullivan's Ghost," March 1, 1896; "Girls Go Ghost Seeing," March 16, 1896.

202n4 **One witness, Elizabeth Foy:** *New York Times,* "Mr. Davitt in the Cronin Trial," Dec. 17, 1893.

203n1 **Davitt responded to Lizzie Foy's accusation:** Michael Davitt to the Associated Press, Dec. 27, 1893, quoted in *San Francisco Call,* "Davitt's Answer," Dec. 29, 1893.

203n2 **Lizzie Foy testified in court:** Statement by Mrs. [Elizabeth (Lizzie)] Foy re: murder of Dr. Cronin, 59 typed pages, unsigned, NLI, Devoy Papers, MS 18058 (3). When Lizzie Foy discovered that the dead man was Cronin, she was horrified, for he was their family doctor and she liked him.

203n3 **Few took Lizzie Foy's testimony seriously:** *Chicago Tribune,* "Foy's Flat Denials," Feb. 7, 1894; *New York Times,* "Was a Sensational Witness," Dec. 23, 1893.

203n4 **However, there was nothing in them:** *Chicago Tribune,* "Resume of the Evidence Given," Feb. 10, 1894.

204n1 **It was, as Finley Peter Dunne observed:** Peter Dunne, ed., *Mr. Dooley Remembers: The Informal Memoirs of Finley Peter Dunne* (Boston: Little, Brown, 1936), 77.

204n2 **In addition to Coughlin:** *Chicago Tribune,* "John Culver Is Well Pleased," March 9, 1894; Lindberg, *To Serve and Collect,* 84.

204n3 **Upon his return to his saloon:** *Chicago Tribune,* "Cash for Coughlin Hunt," July 15, 1899; "Diamond in the Case," June 19, 1899; Robert J. Casey, *Chicago Medium Rare—When We Were Both Younger* (Chicago: Bobbs-Merrill, 1949), 61.

204n4 **Coughlin remained on the run:** *Chicago Tribune,* "Money Lavished to Aid Coughlin," June 7, 1907.

204n5 **There, in San Pedro:** *Chicago Tribune,* "Big Dan Knows Crime Secrets," Aug. 21, 1910; Raphael W. Marrow and Harriet I. Carter, *In Pursuit of Crime: The Police of Chicago; Chronicle of a Hundred Years, 1833–1933* (Sunbury, OH: Flats, 1996), 189–90. Convincing proof that Coughlin was dead came when his widow sold off much of the household furniture, as she was no longer receiving funds from her husband. *Chicago Tribune,* "Raffle Proves Coughlin Dead," Sept. 15, 1911. In 1923 the *Tribune* published a letter from James Garner in which he claimed to have met an American owner of a banana plantation who told him Coughlin had died in San Pedro of tuberculosis. *Chicago Tribune,* letters to the editor, April 29, 1923.

205n1 **However, in 1895 he made a comeback:** *Chicago Tribune,* "Resumes His Role," March 1, 1895; "Love of Erin's Hero," March 5, 1895; "Ghost of Dr. Cronin," March 17, 1895; Michael F. Funchion, *Chicago's Irish Nationalists 1881–1890* (New York: Arno, 1976), 40.

205n2 **In the summer of 1896:** Niall Whelehan, *The Dynamiters: Irish Nationalism and Political Violence in the Wider World, 1867–1900* (Cambridge: Cambridge University Press, 2012), 130–31. Attempts were made to extradite Tynan to Britain, but the entire case collapsed when it became apparent that most of those involved were British agents.

205n3 **Harrison refused:** Carter H. Harrison, *Stormy Years: The Autobiography of Carter H. Harrison, Five Times Mayor of Chicago* (New York: Bobbs-Merrill, 1935), 106–8.

205n4 **However, in 1901 Sullivan was charged:** Account of the case in *The People v. Alexander Sullivan*, Dec. 20, 1905, in *Reports of Cases at Law and in Chancery Argued and Determined in the Supreme Court of Illinois*, vol. 218 (Bloomington, IL, Pantagraph Printing and Stationery, 1906), 419–38.

206n1 **Lynch also alleged:** *San Francisco Call*, "Boy Unfolds Some Secrets," Dec. 8, 1901; account of the case in *The People v. Alexander Sullivan*, Dec. 20, 1905; *New York Times*, "Alexander Sullivan on Trial for Conspiracy," Nov. 30, 1901; *Chicago Daily Inter Ocean*, "Mr. Sullivan Is Not Sure," May 27, 1889; *Chicago Tribune*, "Fellow Lawyers Brand Sullivan," Dec. 20, 1901; *New York Times*, "Alexander Sullivan Guilty," Dec. 23, 1901.

206n2 **The Illinois Supreme Court ruled:** *The People v. Alexander Sullivan*, Dec. 20, 1905, 419–38.

206n3 **So divisive was Sullivan:** *Chicago Tribune*, "Sullivan Dead," Aug. 22, 1913; "Alexander Sullivan Left All to Father M. J. Dorney," Aug. 30, 1913.

207n1 **After Sullivan's fall from grace:** *Chicago Tribune*, "Fr. Dorney Taken by Death," March 16, 1914; "Priest Forgets His $68,000," May 30, 1908; "Hosts Pay Honor to Fr. Dorney," March 19, 1914; "Many Mourn for Fr. Dorney," March 17, 1914.

207n2 **And what of Dr. Patrick Henry Cronin?:** *Chicago Tribune*, "A Pretty Fight on Hand," May 2, 1890; "Over the Grave of Dr. Cronin," May 3, 1890; "Dr. Cronin's Memory Honored," May 4, 1890; "His Last Resting Place," May 5, 1890; *New York Times*, May 27, 1890.

208n1 **The Cronin Monument Association:** The secretary of state granted a charter to the Cronin Monument Association—James F. Boland, Frank T. Scanlan, Maurice Morris, and others were named as the incorporators. Boland said, "We felt the necessity before asking for contribution, of having a legal standing in the community." *Chicago Tribune*, "For a Cronin Monument," May 27, 1890; "Irish Society Picnic Program," Aug. 13, 1891; "They Honor Dr. Cronin," Aug. 16, 1891.

208n2 **Just after that trial concluded:** McEnnis, *Clan-na-Gael*, 162–64.

210 **As one contemporary observed:** Walter Wellman, *Daily True American* (Trenton, NJ), "Notes from the Capital," June 12, 1889.

211n1 **In this trial, as in so many others:** Patricia Cline Cohen, *The Murder of Helen Jewett: The Life and Death of a Prostitute in Nineteenth-Century New York* (New York: Alfred A. Knopf, 1998), 322.

211n2 **Theo Conklin filed an inventory:** Duke Bailie, *The Cronin Case: The Assassination of Dr. Patrick Henry Cronin* (Chicago: Rhodes and McClure, 1890), 425; *Chicago Tribune*, "Sale of Dr. Cronin's Books," March 8, 1898. In 1901 Margaret Cronin (widow of Cronin's brother John) received Dr. Cronin's life insurance benefit, $3,420, from the Royal League. *South Side Sun* (Chicago), "Must Pay Cronin Insurance," Dec. 23, 1901. I am grateful to John Corrigan and Ellen Skerrett for alerting me to this information.

212n1 **As press attention turned:** *America: A Journal for Americans*, "Secret, Criminal and Treasonable," July 4, 1889; See for example *Chicago Tribune*, Nov. 18, 1904; Sept. 27, 1911; July 13, 1912. The Carbonari were a loosely organized secret radical nationalist group that began in Italy in the early nineteenth century and spread into France, Spain, and Greece.

212n2 **The parallels were easy to draw:** *Chicago Tribune*, "Eight Held for Selafani Death—Recalls Cronin Case," Nov. 18, 1904; "Sewer Has Murder Mystery—Recalls Cronin Case," Sept. 7, 1911; "Remember Cronin," July 13, 1912.

212n3 **In Chicago folklore:** *Chicago Tribune*, "A Line O'Type or Two," Oct. 23, 1939.

212n4 **In 1900 the Tribune:** *Chicago Tribune,* July 15, 1900; Nov. 6, 1904. The murder may have been the most talked about, though the paper did acknowledge that "even the greatest single tragedy of a great city dwindles with the years until thousands and tens of thousands of Chicago citizens could not tell if that hideous murder was done in 1880 or 1870."

213n1 **A letter from "CST":** *Chicago Tribune,* "In the Wake of the News," Jan. 15, 1927.

213n2 **Writing in the late 1940s:** Casey, *Chicago Medium Rare,* 62.

213n3 **Newspapers published articles:** *Chicago Tribune,* "Famous Mystery Cases in Review: No 4—the Slaying of Dr. Patrick H. Cronin," May 5, 1929. Other cases used in this murder mystery series included "The Murder of Big Jim Colosimo," "The Slaying of the Millionaire Amos J. Snell," and The Knabe Murder Case"; *Chicago Tribune,* "Fight to Return Recalls Famous Flights," Oct. 13, 1932; "His Nimble Mind and Tongue Tell of Old Chicago," Aug. 24, 1941; Delos Avery, "One Way Ride of the 80s," Nov. 17, 1946; Charles Collins, "The Slaying of Dr. Cronin," March 2, 1952. June Sawyers, "A Bloody Step on the Road to Irish Freedom," *Chicago Tribune,* March 13, 1988.

214n1 **In Sherwood Anderson's:** Sherwood Anderson, *Winesburg, Ohio* (1919), new ed. (New York: Viking Press, 1960), 32.

214n2 **In 1992, the journalist:** Mary Maher, *The Devil's Card* (New York: St. Martin's Press, 1992).

214n3 **John Devoy maintained:** John Devoy, "The Story of Clan na Gael," *Gaelic American* (New York), Jan. 31, 1925.

NOTE ON SOURCES

221 **Two lightly fictionalized dime novels:** *Chicago Tribune,* Nov. 16, 1889.

222n1 **Theodore Dreiser, who worked with McEnnis:** Theodore Dreiser, *A Book about Myself* (New York: Boni and Liveright, 1922), 73.

222n2 **McEnnis was convinced:** John Devoy, "The Story of Clan na Gael," *Gaelic American* (New York), Jan. 31, 1925.

ORGANIZATIONS AND TERMS

Clan na Gael Secret, oath-bound Irish republican revolutionary society founded in New York in 1867 following a split in the **Fenian Brotherhood**.

Dynamite War A bombing campaign pursued by Irish American republicans between 1881 and 1885. Men were trained in the United States, then dispatched to Britain to bomb targets including the Tower of London, the Houses of Westminster, Scotland Yard, and London Bridge.

Fenian Brotherhood A revolutionary Irish republican movement founded by John O'Mahony in New York in April 1859. It was the sister organization to the **Irish Republican Brotherhood**.

Invincibles Irish republican society with links to the **Fenians**. It carried out the Phoenix Park murders of Lord Frederick Cavendish and Thomas H. Burke in Dublin in May 1882.

Irish National Land League An agrarian association founded by Michael Davitt in 1879; Charles Stewart Parnell became its president. It organized the Land War of 1879–81 as part of its efforts to improve tenants' rights.

Irish National Land League of America Founded in 1880 as an open, visible organization pledged to support the **Irish National Land League** and later the Irish Parliamentary Party. It was renamed the Irish National League of America in 1883.

Irish Republican Brotherhood (IRB) Founded in Dublin in March 1858 by James Stephens; a secret society dedicated to achieving Irish freedom through force of arms. It was the sister organization of the **Fenian Brotherhood**.

New Departure Organized in 1879 by John Devoy, Michael Davitt, and Charles Stewart Parnell. It linked Irish land reformers, constitutional nationalists, and determined republicans in a campaign to improve tenants' rights in Ireland, restore an Irish Parliament with the granting of Home Rule, and finally achieve the ultimate goal of an Irish republic.

Parnell Commission: A judicial inquiry that sat in London between September 1888 and November 1889 to investigate the claims made by the London *Times*, which linked Parnell with physical force republicanism. Ultimately, Parnell was exonerated.

Skirmishing Fund Established in 1875 by Irish republicans, most notably Jeremiah O'Donovan Rossa and Patrick Ford (*Irish World*). The money raised for the fund was intended to be spent on training young men to use dynamite and to finance bombing raids in Britain. In 1877 John Devoy wrested control of the fund and renamed it the "National Fund."

Society of United Irishmen Founded in October 1791. Inspired by the ideals of the French Revolution, the United Irishmen began as a radical but not a revolutionary society. However, by 1794 it had become a secret, oath-bound revolutionary society dedicated to establishing an Irish republic. Despite the failure of the 1798 Rebellion, the United Irishmen were the inspiration for later generations of Irish republicans.

Triangle Used to describe the leadership of **Clan na Gael** in the mid-1880s. The Triangle referred to Alexander Sullivan, Michael Boland, and Denis Feely.

Young Ireland Cultural nationalists, later revolutionaries. The organization's newspaper the *Nation* was very influential, and its members were behind the failed 1848 Rebellion. Young Ireland and its adherents inspired later generations of Irish nationalists and republicans, particularly through the poetry of Thomas Davis, "A Nation Once Again" (1845), and John Mitchel's book *The Last Conquest of Ireland (Perhaps?)* (1860).

BIBLIOGRAPHY

PRIMARY SOURCES: *Archives*

CHICAGO

Archives of the Clerk of the Circuit Court of Cook County
  Probate records for Father Maurice Dorney, Alexander Sullivan, Margaret Sullivan

Chicago History Museum
  Catalog for Eden Musée, 1890 and 1891—F38QR E4 1890/1891
  Catalog for Epstean's Museum—F38RN N381
  Cronin case scrapbook—F38K.C88 folio
  Cronin and Coughlin case—Prints People
  Old Cap Collier, *Who Murdered Dr Cronin? or, Shadowing the Criminal*, 1889—F38UD.011
    no. 349
  Old Cap Lee, *Who Killed Dr Cronin? or, At Work on the Great Cronin Mystery*, 1889—
    F38UD.B345-Y86

Newberry Library, Midwest Manuscript Collection
  George Ade Papers
    Box 4, folder 169—Whitechapel Club History
    Box 9, folder 359—Whitechapel Club History
  Edward Price Bell Papers
  Robert J Casey Papers
    Box 5, folders 97, 98, and 99
    Box 22, folder 238
  Charles H. Dennis Papers
    Box 12, folder 574—letters and articles from Wallace Rice and regarding the Whitechapel
      Club
  Field Enterprises Records
    Box 30, folders 366–76
    Box 33, folders 413–17
    Series 1—*Chicago Daily News*
    Subseries 5—historical
  Carter H. Harrison IV Papers
    Box 12, folder 657
    Box 20, folders 993 and 1023
  Victor Lawson Papers
    Box 2, folder 4—Outgoing Correspondence, Associated Press, 1892–93
    Box 5, folder 2—Outgoing Correspondence, January 1880–May 1892
    Box 27, folder 60, series 1—Outgoing Correspondence, General Business, March–August
      1889
    Box 28, folder 61—Outgoing Correspondence, December 1888–March 1889
    Box 28, folder 62—Outgoing Correspondence, March–July 1889

Box 29, folder 63—Outgoing Correspondence, August–December 1889
Box 29, folder 64—Outgoing Correspondence, December 1889–May 1890
Box 30, folder 63—Outgoing Correspondence, August 1889–January 1890
Box 95, folder 267—*Chicago Daily News* calendars with Lawson's notes and appointments, 1888–89
Box 125, folders 823–26—Personal General—manuscript by Ozara Davis (1926–27), chapters 1–8

John T. McCutcheon Papers
Reynolds-McBride Family Papers
Memorabilia, 1865–2001, not catalogued, box 1

Northeastern Illinois University, Illinois Regional Archives Depository (IRAD)
Cook County Coroner's Inquest Record Index, 1872–1911, vol. 20, file 6/11/1889

SPRINGFIELD, ILLINOIS
Abraham Lincoln Presidential Library and Museum
Unpublished Federal Writers Project [1936?]—"The Case of Dr. Cronin"

Illinois State Archives
Joliet Prison Records, 243.200, 1857–1916, files 41c–60c
Penitentiary Mittimus files, 1857–1916
Registers of Prisoners, 1847–1975
Supreme Court of Illinois, *People of the State of Illinois v. Daniel Coughlin, Patrick O'Sullivan, Martin Bourk et al.*, 1889, RS # 901.001, 35/13B/65V#, 25939

DUBLIN
National Library of Ireland
Devoy Papers
MS 18001
MS 18012
MS 18015
MS 18016
MS 18018
MS 18041
MS 18048
MS 18054
MS 18058
MS 18142 (1)
Sullivan, Alexander, Henry L. Hoguet, James Lynch, James Reynolds, and Patrick Smith, *Emigration versus Enforced Emigration: Addresses to Chester A. Arthur, President of the United States*, pamphlet (n.p.) of speeches delivered at the White House, Washington, DC, June 23, 1883.

Trinity College Dublin
Davitt Papers
MS 9432/2586
MS 9432/2588
MS 9432/2589
MS 932/2590
MS 932/2591

MS 9432/2599
MS 9432/2600
MS 9432/2601
MS 9432/2956
MS 9532/2583–606

University College Dublin
Desmond Ryan Papers

LONDON
The National Archives of the UK, Foreign Office Papers
FO 5/1707—Fenian Brotherhood in America, May 1878–December 1879
FO 5/1816—Fenian Brotherhood in America, January–March 1882
FO 5/1818—Fenian Brotherhood in America, May–June 1882
FO 5/1861—Fenian Brotherhood in America, April–May 1883
FO 5/1862—Fenian Brotherhood in America, June–December 1883
FO 5/1863—Fenian Brotherhood in America, January 1881–December 1883
FO 5/1928—Fenian Brotherhood in America, January–March 1884
FO 5/1930—Fenian Brotherhood in America, July 1884–January 1885
FO 5/1931—Fenian Brotherhood in America, February–April 1885
FO 5/1975—Fenian Brotherhood in America, January–December 1886
FO 5/2044—Fenian Brotherhood in America, January 1887–December 1888
FO 5/2359—Fenian Brotherhood in America, 1889–97

The National Archives of the UK, Home Office Papers
HO 144/84/a7266—Ireland: Fenians, 1881
HO/144/133/a34707c—Ireland: Fenians, 1884–86
HO 144/145/a38008—Ireland: Fenians, 1884–91
HO 144/196/a46866—Ireland: Fenians, 1887
HO 144/471—Ireland: Fenians, 1887
HO 144/471/x14187—Ireland: Fenians, 1887
HO 144/1536/5—Nationality and Naturalisation: Papers of Sir Robert Anderson
HO 144/1537/1–3—Nationality and Naturalisation: Papers of Sir Robert Anderson
HO 144/1538/5–8—Nationality and Naturalisation: Papers of Sir Robert Anderson
HO 144/588—Police Metropolitan, 1888–1902
HO 144/926/a49962—Parnell Commission, 1889–1912

The National Archives of the UK, Metropolitan Police Papers
MEPO/3/3070—Fenians, 1867–86

PRIMARY SOURCES: **Books**
Adams, Isaac E. *Life of Emery A. Storrs.* Chicago: G. L. Howe, 1886.
Anderson, Sherwood. *Winesburg, Ohio.* Originally published 1919. New ed., New York: Viking Press, 1960.
Anderson, Sir Robert. *The Lighter Side of My Official Life.* London: Hodder and Stoughton, 1910.
———. *Sidelights on the Home Rule Movement.* New York: E. P. Dutton, 1906.
Andreas, A. T. *History of Chicago: From the Earliest Period to the Present Time.* Vol. 3, *From the Fire of 1871 until 1885.* Chicago: A. T. Andreas, 1886.

Anonymous. *The Great Cronin Mystery; or, The Irish Patriot's Fate: By One of America's Most Famous Detectives.* Chicago: Laird and Lee, 1889.

———. *Souvenir of Most Rev. P. A. Feehan's Silver Jubilee in the Episcopacy: 1865–1890.* n.d. [1890?].

——— [Ex-member of Clan na Gael]. *The Cronin Mystery.* Chicago, 1889.

Bailie, Duke. *The Cronin Case: The Assassination of Dr. Patrick Henry Cronin.* Chicago: Rhodes and McClure, 1890.

Bartlett, Thomas, ed. *Life of Theobald Wolfe Tone.* Dublin: Lilliput Press, 1998.

[Beach, Thomas Miller]. *Twenty-Five Years in the Secret Service: The Recollections of a Spy by Major Henri Le Caron.* London: William Heinemann, 1892.

Bennett, Fremont O. *Politics and Politicians of Chicago, Cook County and Illinois.* Chicago: Blakely Printing, 1886.

Cashman, D. B. *The Life of Michael Davitt with a History of the Rise and Development of the Irish National Land League.* Boston: Murphy and McCarthy, 1881.

Dana, Charles A. *The Art of Newspaper Making: Three Lectures.* New York: D. Appleton, 1895.

Davitt, Michael. *The Fall of Feudalism in Ireland; or, The Story of the Land League Revolution.* London: Harper and Brothers, 1904.

De Rousiers, Paul. *American Life.* Translated from the French by A. J. Herbertson. Paris: Frimin-Didot, 1892.

Devoy, John. *Recollections of an Irish Rebel.* New York: Charles D. Young, 1929.

Doyle, Arthur Conan. *The Valley of Fear.* London: Smith, Elder, 1915.

Dreiser, Theodore. *Sister Carrie.* New York: Doubleday, Page, 1900. Reprint of unexpurgated edition, London: Penguin, 1986.

Dunne, Finley Peter. *Mr. Dooley and the Chicago Irish: The Autobiography of a Nineteenth-Century Ethnic Group.* Edited with a new introduction by Charles Fanning. Washington, DC: Catholic University of America Press, 1987.

Dunne, Peter, ed. *Mr. Dooley Remembers: The Informal Memoirs of Finley Peter Dunne.* Boston: Little, Brown, 1936.

Ffrench, Charles. *Biographical History of the American Irish in Chicago.* Chicago: American Biographical Publishing, 1897.

Finerty, John F. *War-Path and Bivouac; or, Conquest of the Sioux.* Chicago: Donohue and Henneberry, 1890.

Flinn, John J. *Chicago, the Marvelous City of the West: A History, an Encyclopaedia, and a Guide.* Chicago: Flinn and Sheppard, 1891.

———. *History of the Chicago Police.* Chicago: Chiago Police Books Fund, 1887. With new introduction by Mark H. Haller, Montclair, NJ: Patterson Smith, 1973.

Freeman, William H. *The Press Club of Chicago: A History.* Chicago: Press Club of Chicago, 1894.

Healy, T. M. *Letters and Leaders of My Day.* 2 vols. London: Thornton Butterworth, 1928.

Hunt, Henry M. *The Crime of the Century; or, The Assassination of Dr. Patrick Henry Cronin.* Chicago: H. L. and D. H. Kockersperger, 1889.

James, Henry. *Letters.* Edited by Leon Edel. Vol. 3. Cambridge, MA: Harvard University Press, 1890.

Kipling, Rudyard. *American Notes.* New York: M. J. Ivers, 1891.

McDonald, John. *Diary of the Parnell Commission: Revised from* The Daily News. London: T. Fisher Unwin, 1890.

McEnnis, John T. *The Clan-na-Gael and the Murder of Dr. Cronin.* Chicago: F. J. Schulte and J. W. Iliff, 1890.

Mitchel, John. *The Last Conquest of Ireland (Perhaps).* London: R. and T. Washbourne, 1860.

Morris, F. M. *The Stranger's Guide: Morris' Dictionary of Chicago with Map.* Chicago: F. M. Morris, 1891.

O'Brien, William, and Desmond Ryan, eds. *Devoy's Post-Bag.* Vols. 1 and 2. Dublin: C. J. Fallon, 1948 and 1953.

O'Connor, T. P. *The Parnell Movement.* New and rev. ed. London: Ward and Downey, 1887.

O'Connor, Thomas Power, and Robert M. MacWade. *Gladstone-Parnell and the Great Irish Struggle.* Philadelphia: Hubbard Bros., 1886.

O'Donovan Rossa, Jeremiah. *O'Donovan Rossa's Prison Life: Six Years in English Prisons.* New York: P. J. Kennedy, 1874.

O'Rell, Max. *A Frenchman in America.* New York: Cassell, 1892.

Ryder, Eliot. *The Household Library of Catholic Poets: From Chaucer to the Present Day.* Notre Dame, IN: Joseph A. Lyons, 1881.

Schaack, Michael J. *Anarchy and Anarchists.* Chicago: F. J. Schulte, 1889.

Schuman, Edwin. *Steps into Journalism: Help and Hints for Young Writers.* Evanston, IL: Correspondence School of Journalism, 1894.

Seeger, Eugen. *Chicago: The Wonder City.* Chicago: G. Gregory Printing, 1893.

Simon, John Y., ed. *The Papers of Ulysses S. Grant.* Vol. 21, *November 1, 1870–May 31, 1871.* Carbondale: Southern Illinois University Press, 1998.

Steffens, Lincoln. *The Shame of the Cities.* New York: McClure, Phillips, 1904.

Stone, Melville E. *Fifty Years a Journalist.* London: Doubleday, 1921.

Sullivan, Louis H. *The Autobiography of an Idea.* New York: Press of the American Institute of Architects, 1924.

Sullivan, M. F. *Ireland of To-day: Causes and Aims of Irish Agitation.* Philadelphia: J. M. Stoddart, 1881.

Sullivan, T. D. *Recollections of Troubled Times in Irish Politics.* Dublin: M. H. Gill and Son, 1905.

Thompson, Slason. *Way Back When: Recollections of an Octogenarian, 1849–1929.* Chicago: A. Kroch, 1931.

Twain, Mark. *Life on The Mississippi.* Boston: James R. Osgood, 1883.

Wagner, Howard. *Assassination of P. H. Cronin, a Murderous Conspiracy.* Chicago: Geo. D. Simonds, 1889.

Wooldridge, C. R. *Hands Up! In the World of Crime.* Chicago: C. C. Thompson, 1901.

PRIMARY SOURCES: *Articles*

Abbot, Willis J. "Chicago Newspapers and Their Makers." *Review of Reviews* 11, no. 65 (June 1895): 647–65.

———. "Women in Chicago Journalism." *Review of Reviews* 11, no. 65 (June 1895): 664.

Becker, Rev. Thomas A. "Secret Societies in the United States." *American Catholic Quarterly Review* 10 (April 1878): 193–219.

Bryan, Charles Page. "The Clubs of Chicago." *Cosmopolitan* 7, no. 3 (July 1889): 211–25.

Lilly, W. S. "The Ethics of Journalism." *Forum* (July 1889): 503–12.

Miller, C. R. "A Word to the Critics of Newspapers." *Forum* (August 1893): 712–17.

Rider, George T. "The Pretensions of Journalism." *North American Review* 135 (November 1882): 471–83.

Shinn, Charles Howard. "The Evils of Newspaper Space-Work." *Writer* 4, no. 1 (January 1890): 5–6.

Sullivan, Alexander. "The American Republic and the Irish National League of America." *American Catholic Quarterly Review* 9 (1884): 35–44.

———. "Parnell as a Leader." *North American Review* 144 (June 1887): 609–24.

Sullivan, M. F. "Catholic Poetry of the English Language." *American Catholic Quarterly Review* 3 (July 1878): 455–81.

———. "Catholic Prelates as American Diplomats." *Catholic World* 68 (March 1899): 752–57.

———. "Concerning Sir Walter Raleigh." *Catholic World* 39 (August 1884): 626–36.

———. "The Fact of Home Rule." *Catholic World* 36 (January 1884): 563–70.

———. "Fashions and Principles in Poetry." *American Catholic Quarterly Review* 2 (1877): 102–23.

———. "How Cornwallis Consolidated the British Empire." *Catholic World* 34 (December 1881): 298–313.

———. "Ireland's Great Grievance." *American Catholic Quarterly Review* 6 (January 1881): 51–91.

———. "Irish Land Bill." *American Catholic Quarterly Review* 6 (July 1881): 508–20.

———. "The Labor Question." *American Catholic Quarterly Review* 3 (October 1878): 721–46.

———. "Recreations with Conservatives and Radicals." *Catholic World* 51 (July 1890): 510–24.

———. "Revival of Manufacture in Ireland." *American Catholic Quarterly Review* 6 (October 1881): 668–82.

———. "The Survival of Ireland." *American Catholic Quarterly Review* 3 (January 1878): 104–30.

Trumbull, General M. M. "The Press as It Is." *Open Court* 3, no. 123 (January 2, 1890): 2060–61.

White, Z. L. "Western Journalism." *Harper's Magazine* 77, no. 461 (October 1888): 678–99.

Wood, Charles H. "The Sullivan Trial." *American Law Register* (1852–91) 25, no. 7, n.s., vol. 16 (July 1877): 385–92.

PRIMARY SOURCES: *Reports and Guides*

Altgeld, John P. *Reasons for Pardoning Fielden, Neebe and Schwab*, June 26, 1893. Chicago, 1893.

A. N. Marquis and Co.'s Handbook of Chicago 1887–8. Chicago: A. N. Marquis, 1887.

Annual Report of the Secretary of Police, Showing the Expenses of the Department for the Various Purposes . . . for Year Ended December 31 1889. Chicago: Barnard and Gunthorp, 1890.

Annual Reports of the Various Departments of the City of Chicago for the Fiscal Year Ending 31 December 1889. Chicago: Barnard and Gunthorp, 1890.

Bench and Bar of Chicago: Biographical Sketches. Chicago: American Biographical, 1883.

Burke, Regina V. June 1889. *Reports of Cases Argued and Determined in the Court of Queen's Bench, Manitoba*. Edited by John S. Ewart. Vol. 6. Winnipeg: Carswell, 1890.

The Daily News *Almanac and Political Register for 1890.* Chicago: Chicago Daily News, 1890.

Galignani's New Paris. Paris: Galignani Library, 1883.

Journal of the Proceedings, the Élite Directory and Club List of Chicago, 1887–1888; 1889– 1890. Chicago: Elite Directory Company, 1887, 1889.

The Lakeside Annual Directory of the City of Chicago, 1889. Chicago: Chicago Directory Company, 1889.

The Lake View Directory. Chicago: R. R. Donnelley and Son, 1889.

Rand, McNally & Co's Bird's Eye Views and Guide to Chicago. Chicago: Rand, McNally, 1898.

Report of the Execution of P. O'Donnell for the Murder of Jas Carey with His Confession and Last Words. Dublin: Nugent, [1883/4].

Report of the General Superintendent of Police of the City of Chicago to the City Council for the Fiscal Year Ending December 31 1889. Chicago: Barnard and Gunthorp, 1890.

Report of the Special Commission on Parnellism and Crime. 12 vols. London: Her Majesty's Stationery Office, 1890.

Report of the Trial and Sentence on Tim Kelly for the Phoenix Park Murders: Important Declaration of the Prisoner from the Dock. Dublin: Nugent [1883].

Report of the United States Commissioners to the Paris Universal Exposition 1878. Vol. 1. Washington, DC: Government Printing Office, 1880.

Reports of Cases Determined in the Supreme Court of the State of Washington. Eugene G. Kreider, reporter. Vol. 21. Seattle: Bancroft and Whitney, 1900.

Reports of the Cases at Law and in Chancery Argued and Determined in the Supreme Court of Illinois. Norman L. Freeman, reporter. Vol. 147. Springfield, IL: Journal Company, 1893.

Reports of the Cases at Law and in Chancery Argued and Determined in the Supreme Court of Illinois. Isaac Newton Phillips, reporter. Vol. 218. Bloomington, IL: Pantagraph Printing and Stationery, 1906.

Sanborn Fire Insurance Maps, Chicago, 1894–97.

Senate Report on the Chicago Police System as Made by the Committee of Investigation, Appointed by 40th General Assembly Special Session 1897–98. Springfield, IL: Philip Brothers, 1898.

Skogan, Wesley G. *Chicago since 1840: A Time-Series Data Handbook, Institute of Government and Public Affairs.* Urbana: University of Illinois Press, 1976.

Thirteenth Annual Report of the Board of Public Works to the Common Council of the City of Chicago for the Municipal Fiscal Year Ending March 31 1874. Chicago: J. S. Thompson, 1874.

Verbatim Copy of the Parnell Commission Report. Dublin: Irish Loyal and Patriotic Union, 1890.

PRIMARY SOURCES: *Newspapers and Periodicals*

Advertiser (Adelaide)—Trove, National Library of Australia

America: A Journal for Americans—Newberry Library, Chicago

Broome Republican (Binghamton, NY)—Chronicling America, Library of Congress, http://chroniclingamerica.loc.gov/newspapers/

Chicago Daily Argus—Chronicling America

Chicago Daily News—Newberry Library, Chicago

Chicago Evening News—Newberry Library, Chicago
Chicago Herald—Newberry Library, Chicago
Chicago Daily Inter Ocean—Newberry Library, Chicago
Chicago Pictorial West—Chicago History Museum
Chicago Times—Newberry Library, Chicago
Chicago Tribune—Newberry Library, Chicago
Chicago Weekly Journal—Newberry Library, Chicago
Citizen—Chicago History Museum
Daily Alta California (San Francisco)—California Digital Newspaper Collection
    (CDNC), Center for Bibliographic Studies and Research, University of California,
    Riverside, http://cdnc.ucr.edu
Daily True American (Trenton City, NJ)— Chronicling America
Frank Leslie's Illustrated Newspaper—Chicago History Museum
Freeman's Journal—St. Patrick's College, Drumcondra, DCU
Gaelic American (New York)—National Library of Ireland
Globe (London)—British Library
Graphic (London)—Newberry Library, Chicago
Harper's Weekly (New York)—Newberry Library, Chicago
Irish Nation (New York)—National Library of Ireland
Irish World—National Library of Ireland
Los Angeles Herald—CDNC
Los Angeles Times—CDNC
National Police Gazette—Newberry Library, Chicago
New York Sun—Chronicling America
New York Times—British Library
Pilot (Boston)—National Library of Ireland
Puck—Newberry Library, Chicago
Sacramento Daily Union—CNDC
San Francisco Call—CNDC
South Side Sun (Chicago)
Times (London)—British Library

SECONDARY SOURCES: **Books**
Adler, Jeffrey S. *First in Violence, Deepest in Dirt: Homicide in Chicago.* Cambridge, MA:
    Harvard University Press, 2006.
Anderson, Patricia. *The Printed Image and the Transformation of Popular Culture 1760–
    1860.* Oxford: Clarendon Press, 1991.
Bachin, Robin F. *Building the South Side: Urban Space and Civic Culture in Chicago, 1890–
    1919.* Chicago: University of Chicago Press, 2004.
Baldasty, Gerald J. *The Commercialization of News in the Nineteenth Century.* Madison:
    University of Wisconsin Press, 1992.
Barrett, James R. *The Irish Way: Becoming American in the Multiethnic City.* New York:
    Penguin, 2012.
———. *Work and Community in the Jungle: Chicago's Packinghouse Workers, 1894–1922.*
    Urbana: University of Illinois Press, 1987.
Barth, Gunther. *City People: The Rise of Modern City Culture in Nineteenth-Century Amer-
    ica.* Oxford: Oxford University Press, 1982.

Bogdon, Robert. *Freak Show: Presenting Human Oddities for Amusement and Profit*. Chicago: University of Chicago Press, 1988.

Brown, Joshua. *Beyond the Lines: Pictorial Reporting, Everyday Life, and the Crisis of Gilded Age America*. Berkeley: University of California Press, 2006.

Brown, Thomas N. *Irish-American Nationalism 1870–1890*. New York: J. B. Lippincott, 1966.

Bulla, David W., and David B. Sachsman, eds. *Sensationalism: Murder, Mayhem, Mudslinging, Scandals and Disasters in 19th-Century Reporting*. Piscataway, NJ: Transaction, 2013.

Búrca, Mícheál de. *The Life and Poems of Michael Scanlan, the Fenian Poet*. Killmalock: Abbey Printing, 1969.

Burchell, R. A. *The San Francisco Irish 1848–1880*. Berkeley: University of California Press, 1980.

Callanan, Frank. *T. M. Healy*. Cork: Cork University Press, 1996.

Campbell, Christy. *Fenian Fire: The British Government Plot to Assassinate Queen Victoria*. London: HarperCollins, 2002.

Casey, Robert J. *Chicago Medium Rare—When We Were Both Younger*. Chicago: Bobbs-Merrill, 1949.

Cohen, Patricia Cline. *The Murder of Helen Jewett: The Life and Death of a Prostitute in Nineteenth-Century New York*. New York: Alfred A. Knopf, 1998.

Cole, J. A. *Prince of Spies: Henri le Caron*. London: Faber & Faber, 1984.

Connell, Evan S. *Son of the Morning Star: General Custer and the Battle of the Little Bighorn*. 2nd ed. London: Pimlico, 2005.

Cronon, William. *Nature's Metropolis: Chicago and the Great West*. New York: W. W. Norton, 1991.

Cummings, Kathleen Sprows. *New Women of the Old Faith: Gender and American Catholicism in the Progressive Era*. Chapel Hill: University of North Carolina Press, 2009.

Curtis, L. Perry. *Apes and Angels: The Irishman in Victorian Caricature*. New York: Smithsonian Institution Press, 1971.

Dale, Elizabeth. *The Chicago Trunk Murder: Law and Justice at the Turn of the Century*. DeKalb: Northern Illinois University Press, 2011.

D'Arcy, William. *The Fenian Movement in the United States: 1858–1886*. Washington, DC: Catholic University of America Press, 1947.

Darrow, Clarence. *Story of My Life*. New York: Da Capo, 1932.

Dennett, Andrea Stulman. *Weird and Wonderful: The Dime Museum in America*. New York: New York University Press, 1997.

Dennis, Charles H. *Victor Lawson, His Time and His Work*. Chicago: University Chicago Press, 1935.

Dreiser, Theodore. *A Book about Myself*. New York: Boni and Liveright, 1922.

Duis, Perry R. *Challenging Chicago: Coping with Everyday Life, 1837–1920*. Urbana: University of Illinois Press, 1998.

Duncan, Hugh Daziel. *The Rise of Chicago as a Literary Center from 1885 to 1920*. Totowa, NJ: Bedminster Press, 1964.

Emery, Edwin, Michael Emery, and Nancy J. Roberts. *The Press and America: An Interpretive History of the Mass Media*. 9th ed. Boston: Allyn and Bacon, 2000.

Emmons, David M. *The Butte Irish: Class and Ethnicity in an American Mining Town 1875–1925*. Carbondale: University of Illinois Press, 1990.

Erie, Stephen P. *Rainbow's End: Irish Americans and Urban Machine Politics, 1840–1985.* Berkeley: University of California Press, 1990.

Ettinger, Patrick W. *Imaginary Lines: Border Enforcement and the Origins of Undocumented Immigration, 1882–1930.* Austin: University of Texas Press, 2009.

Facchini, Rocco, and Daniel Facchini. *Muldoon: A True Chicago Ghost Story; Tales of a Forgotten Rectory.* Chicago: Lake Claremont Press, 2003.

Fanning, Charles. *Finley Peter Dunne and Mr. Dooley: The Chicago Years.* Lexington: University Press of Kentucky, 1978.

———, ed. *The Irish Voice in America: 250 Years of Irish-American Fiction.* 2nd ed. Lexington: University Press of Kentucky, 2000.

———, ed. *New Perspectives on the Irish Diaspora.* Carbondale: Southern Illinois University Press, 2000.

Fennell, Philip, and Marie King, eds. *John Devoy's* Catalpa *Expedition.* New York: New York University Press, 2006.

Fisher, John F., and Joe Nickell. *Crime Science: Methods of Forensic Detection.* Lexington: University Press of Kentucky, 1999.

Friedberg, Susanne. *Fresh: A Perishable History.* Cambridge, MA: Harvard University Press, 2009.

Funchion, Michael F. *Chicago's Irish Nationalists 1881–1890.* New York, Arno, 1976.

Gantt, Jonathan. *Irish Terrorism in the Atlantic Community, 1865–1922.* London: Palgrave Macmillan, 2010.

Golway, Terry. *Irish Rebel: John Devoy and America's Fight for Irish Freedom.* New York: St. Martin's Griffin, 1998.

Green, James. *Death in the Haymarket: A Story of Chicago, the First Labor Movement and the Bombing That Divided Gilded Age America.* New York: Pantheon Books, 2006.

Grossman, James, Ann Durkin Keating, and Janice L Reiff, eds. *The Encylopedia of Chicago.* Chicago: University of Chicago Press, 2004.

Halper, Albert, ed. *This Is Chicago: An Anthology.* New York: Henry Holt, 1952.

Halttunen, Karen. *Murder Most Foul: The Killer and the American Gothic Imagination.* Cambridge, MA: Harvard University Press, 1998.

Harrison, Carter H. *Stormy Years: The Autobiography of Carter H. Harrison, Five Times Mayor of Chicago.* New York: Bobbs-Merrill, 1935.

Heinen, Joseph H., and Susan Barton Heinen. *Lost German Chicago.* Chicago: Arcadia, 2009.

Hirsch, Eric L. *Urban Revolt: Ethnic Politics in the Nineteenth-Century Chicago Labor Movement.* Berkeley: University of California Press, 1990.

Jacobson, Matthew Frye. *Whiteness of a Different Color: European Immigrants and the Alchemy of Race.* Cambridge, MA: Harvard University Press, 1998.

Joyce, William Leonard. *Editors and Ethnicity: A History of the Irish-American Press, 1848–1883.* New York: Arno, 1976.

Kaplan, Richard. *Politics and the American Press: The Rise of Objectivity 1865–1900.* Cambridge: Cambridge University Press, 2002.

Keating, Ann Durkin. *Chicagoland: City and Suburbs in the Railroad Age.* Chicago: University of Chicago Press, 2005.

———, ed. *Chicago Neighborhoods and Suburbs: A Historical Guide.* Chicago: University of Chicago Press, 2008.

Kenna, Shane. *War in the Shadows: The Irish-American Fenians Who Bombed Victorian Britain*. Dublin: Merrion Press, 2013.

Kenny, Kevin. *The American Irish*. New York: Longman, 2000.

———. *Making Sense of the Molly Maguires*. New York: Oxford University Press, 1998.

Kinsley, Philip. *The* Chicago Tribune: *Its First Hundred Years*. 3 vols. Chicago: Chicago Tribune, 1943.

Kirkfleet, Cornelius James. *The Life of Patrick Augustine Feehan: Bishop of Nashville, First Archbishop of Chicago, 1829–1902*. Chicago: Martre, 1922.

Labouchere Thorold, Algar. *The Life of Henry Labouchere*. London: G. P. Putnam's Sons, 1913.

Lewis, Lloyd, and Henry Justin Smith. *Chicago—The History of Its Reputation*. New York: Harcourt, Brace, 1929.

Lindberg, Richard C. *Chicago by Gaslight*. Chicago: Chicago Review Press, 1996.

———. *To Serve and Collect: Chicago Politics and Police Corruption from the Lager Beer Riot to the Summerdale Scandal 1855–1960*. New ed. Carbondale: Southern Illinois University Press, 1998.

Loerzel, Robert. *Alchemy of Bones: Chicago's Leuetgert Murder Case of 1897*. Champaign: University of Illinois Press, 2003.

Lyons, F. S. L. *Charles Stewart Parnell*. London: Collins, 1977.

MacDonald, Fergus. *The Catholic Church and Secret Societies in the United States*. New York: Catholic Historical Society, 1946.

Maher, Mary. *The Devil's Card: A Novel of Murder in 19th Century Irish Chicago*. New York: St. Martin's Press, 1992.

Marrow, Raphael W., and Harriet I. Carter. *In Pursuit of Crime: The Police of Chicago; Chronicle of a Hundred Years, 1833–1933*. Sunbury, Ohio: Flats, 1996.

Mayer, Harold M., and Richard C. Wade. *Chicago: Growth of a Metropolis*. Chicago: University of Chicago Press, 1969.

McCaffrey, Lawrence J. *The Irish Catholic Diaspora in America*. Rev. ed. Washington, DC: Catholic University of America Press, 1997.

McCartney, Donal, and Pauric Travers. *The Ivy Leaf: The Parnells Remembered*. Dublin: University College Dublin Press, 2006.

McConville, Seán. *Irish Political Prisoners, 1848–1922*. London: Routledge, 2003.

McGee, Owen. *The IRB: The Irish Republican Brotherhood, from the Land League to Sinn Féin*. Dublin: Four Courts Press, 2007.

McGerr, Michael. *The Decline of Popular Politics: The American North, 1858–1928*. Oxford: Oxford University Press, 1988.

McMahon, Eileen M. *What Parish Are You From?: A Chicago Irish Community and Race Relations*. Lexington: University Press of Kentucky, 1996.

Meagher, Timothy F. *The Columbia Guide to Irish American History*. New York: Columbia University Press, 2005.

Miller, Donald L. *City of the Century: The Epic of Chicago and the Making of America*. New York: Simon and Schuster, 1996.

Miller, Kirby A. *Emigrants and Exiles: Ireland and the Irish Exodus to North America*. New York: Oxford University Press, 1985.

Monkkonen, Eric H. *America Becomes Urban: The Development of US Cities and Towns 1780–1980*. Berkeley: University of California Press, 1980.

————. *Police in Urban America: 1860–1920*. Cambridge: Cambridge University Press, 1981.

Morris, R. K. *John P. Holland: Inventor of the Modern Submarine*. Annapolis: United States Naval Institute, 1966.

Mott, Frank Luther. *American Journalism: A History; 1690–1960*. 3rd ed. New York: Macmillan, 1962.

————. *A History of American Magazines*. Vol. 2, *1856–1865*. Cambridge, MA: Harvard University Press, 1938.

Murrell, William. *A History of American Graphic Humor (1865–1938)*. 2 vols. New York: Macmillan, 1936.

Newton, David E. *DNA Evidence and Forensic Science*. New York: Facts on File, 2008.

Nord, David Paul. *Communities of Journalism: A History of American Newspapers and Their Readers*. Urbana: University of Illinois Press, 2001.

————. *Newspapers and New Politics: Midwestern Municipal Reform 1890–1900*. Ann Arbor: University of Michigan Press, 1979.

O'Brien, R. Barry. *The Life of Charles Stewart Parnell*. Vol. 1. New York: Harper and Brothers, 1898.

O'Brien, William. *Evening Memories*. Dublin: Maunsel, 1920.

Ó Donghaile, Deaglán. *Blasted Literature: Victorian Political Fiction and the Shock of Modernism*. Edinburgh: Edinburgh University Press, 2011.

O'Donnell, F. Hugh. *A History of the Irish Parliamentary Party—Butt and Parnell— Nationhood and Anarchy: The Curse of the American Money*. Vol. 1. London: Longmans, 1910.

O'Grady, Joseph P. *Irish-Americans and Anglo-American Relations, 1880–1888*. New York: Arno Press, 1976.

Pacyga, Dominic A. *Chicago: A Biography*. Chicago: University of Chicago Press, 2009.

Philpott, Thomas Lee. *The Slum and the Ghetto: Neighbourhood Deterioration and Middle-Class Reform, Chicago, 1880–1930*. Oxford: Oxford University Press, 1978.

Pierce, Bessie Louise. *A History of Chicago*. Vol. 3, *The Rise of a Modern City, 1871–1893*. Vol. 3. New York: Alfred A. Knopf, 1957.

Pollard, H. B. C. *The Secret Societies of Ireland: Their Rise and Progress*. London: Philip Allan, 1922.

Porter, Bernard. *The Origins of the Vigilant State: The London Metropolitan Police Special Branch before the First World War*. London: Boydell Press, 1987.

Roggenkamp, Karen. *Narrating the News: New Journalism and Literary Genre in Late Nineteenth-Century American Newspapers and Fiction*. Kent, OH: Kent State University Press, 2005.

Sanders, John. *Far From the Land: A Story of Irish Betrayal*. London: Forum Press, 1997.

Sappol, Michael. *A Traffic of Dead Bodies: Anatomy and Embodied Social Identity in Nineteenth-Century America*. Princeton, NJ: Princeton University Press, 2002.

Schaaf, Barbara C. *Mr. Dooley's Chicago*. New York: Anchor Press, 1977.

Schneirov, Richard. *Labor and Urban Politcs: Class Conflict and the Origin of Modern Liberalism in Chicago 1864–97*. Urbana: University of Illinois Press, 1998.

Schudson, Michael. *Discovering the News: A Social History of American Newspapers*. New York: Basic Books, 1978.

Short, K. R. M. *The Dynamite War: Irish-American Bombers in Victorian Britain*. Dublin: Gill and Macmillan, 1979.

Slotkin, Richard. *Gunfighter Nation: The Myth of the Frontier in Twentieth-Century America*. New York: Atheneum, 1992.

Smith, Carl. *Urban Disorder and the Shape of Belief: The Great Chicago Fire, the Haymarket Bomb, and the Model Town of Pullman*. Chicago: University of Chicago Press, 1995.

Smith, Gene, and Jayne Barry Smith. *The Police Gazette*. New York: Simon and Schuster, 1972.

Smythe, Ted Curtis. *The Gilded Age Press 1865–1900*. Westport, CT: Praeger, 2003.

Sutherland, Daniel E. *The Confederate Carpetbaggers*. Baton Rouge: Louisiana State University Press, 1988.

Trotti, Michael. *The Body in the Reservoir: Murder and Sensationalism in the South*. Chapel Hill: University of North Carolina Press, 2008.

Tynan, Katharine. *Twenty-Five Years: Reminiscences*. London: Smith, Elder and Company, 1913.

Wade, Louise Carroll. *Chicago's Pride: The Stockyards, Packingtown, and Environs in the Nineteenth Century*. Urbana: University of Illinois Press, 1987.

Wells, H. G. *The Future in America: A search after realities*. London: Harper and Brothers, 1906.

Wendt, Lloyd. Chicago Tribune: *The Rise of a Great American Newspaper*. New York: Rand, McNally and Company, 1979.

Whelehan, Niall. *The Dynamiters: Irish Nationalism and Political Violence in the Wider World, 1867–1900*. Cambridge: Cambridge University Press, 2012.

Willrich, Michael. *City of Courts: Socializing Justice in Progressive Era Chicago*. Cambridge: Cambridge University Press, 2002.

Wright, Sewell Peaslee. *Chicago Murders*. New York, 1945.

Yeats, W. B. *W. B. Yeats: Letters to Katharine Tynan*. Edited by Roger McHugh. New York: McMullen, 1953.

Young, Art. *His Life and Times*. New York: Sheridan House, 1939.

SECONDARY SOURCES: *Articles and Chapters*

Adler, Jeffrey S. "Halting the Slaughter of the Innocents": The Civilizing Process and the Surge in Violence in Turn-of-the-Century Chicago." *Social Science History* 25, no. 1 (Spring 2001): 29–52.

———. "'It's His First Offense. We Might As Well Let Him Go': Homicide and Criminal Justice in Chicago 1875–1920." *Journal of Social History* (Fall 2006): 5–24.

———. "'My Mother-in-Law Is to Blame, but I'll Walk on Her Neck Yet': Homicide in Late Nineteenth-Century Chicago." *Journal of Social History* 31, no. 2 (Winter 1997): 253–76.

———. "'On the Border of Snakeland': Evolutionary Psychology and Plebian Violence in Industrial Chicago, 1875–1920." *Journal of Social History* 36, no. 3 (Spring 2003): 541–60.

———. "Shoot to Kill: The Use of Deadly Force by the Chicago Police, 1875–1920." *Journal of Interdisciplinary History* 38, no. 2 (Autumn 2007): 233–54.

———. "'We've Got a Right to Fight; We're Married': Domestic Homicide in Chicago 1875–1920." *Journal of Interdisciplinary History* 34 (Summer 2003): 27–48.

Appel, John J. "From Shanties to Lace Curtains: The Irish Image in *Puck*, 1868–1910." *Comparative Studies in Society and History* 13, no. 4 (October 1971): 365–75.

Asher, Brad. "The Professional Vision: Conflicts over Journalism Education, 1900–1950." *American Journalism* 11, no. 4 (1994): 304–20.

Aucoin, James L. "The Investigative Tradition in American Journalism." *American Journalism* 14, nos. 3–4 (1997): 317–29.

Bienen, Leigh B., and Brandon Rottinghaus. "Criminal Law: Learning from the Past, Living in the Present; Understanding Homicide in Chicago, 1870–1930." *Journal of Criminal Law and Criminology* 92, nos. 3–4 (2003): 437–534.

Borchard, Gregory A., Gregory A. Bates, and Lawrence J. Mullen. "Publishing Violence as Art and News: Sensational Print and Pictures in the 19th Century Press." In *Sensationalism*, edited by David W. Bulla and David B. Sachsmann, 53–74. Piscataway, NJ: Transaction, 2013.

Brazil, John R. "Murder Trials, Murder and Twenties America." *American Quarterly* 33, no. 2 (Summer 1981): 163–84.

Brown, Michael. "Discriminating Photographs from Hand-Drawn Illustrations in Popular Magazines, 1895–1904." *American Journalism* 17, no. 3 (2000): 15–30.

Brown, Thomas N. "The Origins and Character of Irish-American Nationalism." *Review of Politics* 18, no. 3 (July 1956): 327–58.

Burke, Edward M. "Lunatics and Anarchists: Political Homicide in Chicago." *Journal of Criminal Law and Criminology* 92, nos. 3–4 (2003): 791–804.

Burt, Elizabeth V. "A Bid for Legitimacy: The Women's Press Club Movement, 1881–1900." *Journalism History* 23, no. 2 (Summer 1997): 72–84.

Cheatwood, Derrel. "Capital Punishment for the Crime of Homicide in Chicago: 1870–1930." *Journal of Criminal Law and Criminology* 92, nos. 3–4 (2003): 843–66.

Clark, Emily. "Moving Day." In *The Encyclopedia of Chicago*, edited by James Grossman, Ann Durkin Keating, and Janice L. Reiff. Chicago: University of Chicago Press, 2004.

Clymer, Jeffory A. "The 1886 Chicago Haymarket Bombing and the Rhetoric of Terrorism in America." *Yale Journal of Criticism* 15, no. 2 (Fall 2002): 315–44.

Corrigan, John. "United Irish Societies of Chicago." In *Irish-American Voluntary Organizations*, edited by Michael Funchion, 276–82. Westport, CT: Greenwood Press, 1983.

Cowan, Mimi. "Ducking for Cover: Chicago's Irish Nationalists in the Haymarket Era." *Labor: Studies in Working-Class History of the Americas* 9, no. 1 (2012): 53–76.

Culbertson, Tom. "The Golden Age of American Political Cartoons." *Journal of the Gilded Age and Progressive Era* 7, no. 3 (July 2008): 277–95.

Czitrom, Daniel. "Underworlds and Underdogs: Big Tim Sullivan and Metropolitan Politics in New York, 1889–1913." *Journal of American History* 78, no. 2 (September 1991): 536–58.

Dale, Elizabeth. "'Not Simply Black and White: Jury Power and the Law in Later Nineteenth-Century Chicago." *Social Science History* 25, no. 1 (Spring 2001): 7–26.

———. "*People v. Coughlin* and Criticism of the Criminal Jury in Late Nineteenth-Century Chicago." *Northern Illinois University Law Review* 28 (2008): 503–36.

———. "The People versus Zephyr Davis: Law and Popular Justice in Late Nineteenth-Century Chicago." *Law and History Review* 17, no. 1 (Spring 1999): 27–56.

———. "'Social Equality Does Not Exist among Themselves, nor among Us': *Bayliss vs. Curry* and Civil Rights in Chicago, 1888." *American Historical Review* 102, no. 2 (April 1997): 311–39.

De Nie, Michael. "'A Medley Mob of Irish-American Plotters and Irish Dupes': The British Press and Transatlantic Fenianism." *Journal of British Studies* 40 (April 2001): 213–40.

Denning, Michael. "Cheap Stories: Notes on Popular Fiction and Working-Class Culture in Nineteenth-Century America." *History Workshop* 22 (Autumn 1986): 1–17.

Digby-Junger, Richard. "'The Main Rendezvous for Men of the Press': The Life and Death of the Chicago Press Club, 1880–1987." *Journal of Illinois History* 1, no. 2 (Winter 1988): 74–98.

Doyle, David Noel. "The Irish in Chicago." *Irish Historical Studies* 26, no. 103 (May 1989): 293–303.

———. "The Regional Bibliography of Irish America, 1800–1930: A Review and Addendum." *Irish Historical Studies* 23, no. 91 (May 1983): 254–83.

Dudley Edwards, Owen. "Kipling and the Irish." *London Review of Books* 10, no. 3 (February 1988): 22–23.

East, Ernest E. "The Distillers' and Cattle Feeders' Trust, 1887–1985." *Journal of the Illinois State Historical Society* 45, no. 2 (Summer 1952): 101–23.

Ethington, Philip J. "Vigilantes and the Police: The Creation of a Professional Police Bureaucracy in San Francisco." *Journal of Social History* 21, no. 2 (Winter 1987): 197–227.

Fanning, Charles. "Robert Emmet and Nineteenth-Century Irish America." *New Hibernia Review* 8, no. 4 (Winter 2004): 53–83.

Fedler, Fred. "Exploring the Historical Image of Journalists as Heavy Drinkers from 1850–1950." *American Journalism* 14, nos. 3–4 (1997): 391–410.

Fennell, Philip A. "History into Myth: The *Catalpa*'s Long Voyage." *New Hibernia Review* 9, no. 1 (Spring 2005): 77–94.

Foner, Eric. "Class, Ethnicity, and Radicalism in the Gilded Age: The Land League and Irish-America." In *Politics and Ideology in the Age of the Civil War*, 150–200. Oxford: Oxford University Press, 1980.

Funchion, Michael F. "Irish Chicago: Church, Homeland, Politics and Class—The Shaping of an Ethnic Group, 1870–1890." In *Ethnic Chicago*, edited by Melvin G. Holli and Peter d'Alroy Jones, 8–39. Grand Rapids, MI: William B. Eerdmans, 1981.

———. "The Political and Nationalist Dimensions." In *The Irish in Chicago*, edited by Lawrence J. McCaffrey, Ellen Skerrett, Michael F. Funchion, and Charles Fanning, 61–97. (Urbana: University of Illinois Press, 1987).

Gilfoyle, Timothy J. "The Moral Origins of Political Surveillance: The Preventative Society in New York City, 1867–1918." *American Quarterly* 38, no. 4 (Autumn 1986): 637–52.

Green, E. R. R. "The Fenians Abroad." In *Secret Societies in Ireland*, edited by Desmond Moody, 79–89. Dublin: Gill and Macmillan.

Haller, Mark H. "Historical Roots of Police Behavior: Chicago, 1890–1925." *Law and Society Review* 10, no. 2 (Winter 1976): 303–23.

———. "Urban Crime and Criminal Justice: The Chicago Case." *Journal of American History* 57 (1970): 619–35.

Hartigan, Maureen, Maureen O'Day, and Roland Quinault. "Irish Terrorism in Britain: A Comparison between the Acts of the Fenians in the 1860s and Those of

Republican Groups since 1972." In *Ireland's Terrorist Dilemma*, edited by Yonah Alexander and Alan O'Day, 49–60. Dordrecht: Martinus Nijhoff, 1986.

Humphrey, D. C. "Dissection and Discrimination: The Social Origins of Cadavers in America, 1760–1915." *Bulletin of the New York Academy of Medicine* 49, no. 9 (September 1973): 819–27.

Janis, Ely M. "Anointing the 'Uncrowned King of Ireland': Charles Stewart Parnell's 1880 American Tour and the Creation of a Transatlantic Land League Movement." *German Historical Institute Bulletin*, suppl. 5 (2008): 23–39.

Jensen, Richard. "'No Irish Need Apply': A Myth of Victimization." *Journal of Social History* 36, no. 2 (2002): 404–29.

Kantowicz, Edward R. "Polish Chicago: Survival through Solidarity." In *Ethnic Chicago*, edited by Melvin G. Holli and Peter d'Alroy Jones, 173–95. 4th ed., rev. and exp. Grand Rapids, MI: William B. Eerdmans, 1995.

Kaplan, Richard L. "The Economics and Politics of Nineteenth-Century Newspapers: Market Segmentation and Partisanship in the *Detroit Press*, 1865–1900." *American Journalism* 10, nos. 1–2 (1993): 84–101.

Kelly, Matthew. "Dublin Fenianism in the 1880s: 'The Irish Culture of the Future'?" *Historical Journal* 42 (September 2000): 729–50.

Kemnitz, Thomas Milton. "The Cartoon as Historical Source." *Journal of Interdisciplinary History* 4, no. 1 (Summer 1973): 81–93.

Kenney, Padraic. "'I Felt a Kind of Pleasure in Seeing Them Treat Us Brutally': The Emergence of the Political Prisoner, 1865–1910." *Comparative Studies in Society and History* 54, no. 4 (2012): 863–89.

Kenny, Kevin. "The Molly Maguires in Popular Culture." *Journal of American Ethnic History* (Summer 1995): 27–45.

Kielbowicz, Richard B. "Postal Subsidies for the Press and the Business of Mass Culure, 1880–1920." *Business History Review* 64, no. 3 (Autumn 1990): 451–88.

Landesco, John. "The Criminal Underworld of Chicago in the '80's and '90's." *Journal of Criminal Law and Criminology* 25, no. 3 (1934): 341–57.

———. "The Criminal Underworld of Chicago in the '80's and '90's: II." *Journal of Criminal Law and Criminology* 25, no. 6 (1935): 928–40.

Litwicki, Ellen M. "'Our Hearts Burn with Ardent Love for Two Countries': Ethnicity and Assimilation at Chicago Holiday Celebrations, 1876–1918." *Journal of American Ethnic History* 19, no. 3 (Spring 2000): 3–34.

Lorenz, Larry. "The Whitechapel Club: Defining Chicago's Newspapermen in the 1890s." *American Journalism* 15, no. 1 (Winter 1998): 83–102.

Luning, Paul. "Irish Blood." *Chicago History* 22 (November 1993): 20–37.

Lyne, D. C., and Peter M. Toner. "Fenianism in Canada, 1874–84." *Studia Hibernica* 12 (1972): 27–76.

MacPhee, Graham. "Under English Eyes: The Disappearance of Irishness in Conrad's *The Secret Agent*." In *Empire and After: Englishness in Postcolonial Perspective*, edited by Graham MacPhee and Prem Poder, 101–20. New York: Berghahn Books, 2007.

Makemson, Harlen. "One Misdeed Evokes Another: How Political Cartoonists Used 'Scandal Intertextuality' against Presidential Candidate James G. Blaine." *Media History Mongraphs* 7, no. 2 (2004–5): 1–20.

Marohn, Richard C. "The Arming of the Chicago Police in the Nineteenth Century." *Chicago History* 11, no. 1 (Spring 1982): 40–49.

Martin, F. X. "The 1916 Rising: A 'Coup d'État' or a 'Bloody Protest'?" *Studia Hibernica* 8 (1968): 106–37.

Maume, Patrick. "Parnell and the IRB Oath." *Irish Historical Studies* 29, no. 116 (May 1995): 363–70.

McCaffrey, Lawrence J. "Components of Irish Nationalism." In *Perspectives on Irish Nationalism*, edited by Thomas E. Hachey and Lawrence J. McCaffrey, 1–19. Lexington: University Press of Kentucky, 1989.

———. "Forging Forward and Looking Back." In *The New York Irish*, edited by Ronald H. Bayer and Timothy J. Meagher, 213–33. Baltimore: Johns Hopkins University Press, 1997.

McCartney, Donal. "Parnell and the American Connection." In *The Ivy Leaf: The Parnells Remembered*, by Donal McCartney and Pauric Travers, 38–51. Dublin: University College Dublin Press, 2006.

McMahon, Eileen. "The Irish-American Press." In *The Ethnic Press in the United States: A Historical Analysis and Handbook*, edited by Sally M. Miller, 177–89. Westport, CT: Greenwood Press.

McNamara, Brooks. "'A Congress of Wonders': The Rise and Fall of the Dime Museum." *Emerson Society Quarterly* 20 (3rd Quarter 1974): 201–61.

Meagher, Timothy J. "'Irish All the Time': Ethnic Consciousness among the Irish in Worcester, Massachusetts, 1880–1905." *Journal of Social History* 19, no. 2 (Winter 1985): 273–303.

———. "'Why Should We Care for a Little Trouble or a Walk through the Mud': St. Patrick's and Columbus Day Parades in Worcester, Massachusetts, 1845–1915." *New England Quarterly* 58, no. 1 (March 1985): 5–26.

Mitrani, Sam. "Reforming Repression: Labor, Anarchy, and Reform in the Shaping of the Chicago Police Department, 1879–1888." *Labor: Studies in Working Class History of the Americas* 6, no. 2 (2009): 73–96.

Monkkonen, Eric H. "History of Urban Police." *Crime and Justice* 15 (1992): 547–80.

———. "Homicide in New York, Los Angeles and Chicago." *Journal of Criminal Law and Criminology* 92, nos. 3–4 (2003): 809–22.

Moody, T. W. "Irish-American Nationalism." *Irish Historical Studies* 15, no. 60 (September 1967): 438–45.

Morris, Richard Knowles. "John P. Holland and the Fenians." *Journal of the Galway Archaeological and Historical Society* 31, no. 1 (1964): 25–38.

Nelson, Bruce C. "Revival and Upheaval: Religion, Irreligion, and Chicago's Working Class in 1886." *Journal of Social History* 25, no. 2 (Winter 1991): 222–53.

Ní Bhroiméil, Úna. "The Creation of an Irish Culture in the United States: The Gaelic Movement, 1870–1915." *New Hibernia Review* 5, no. 3 (Autumn 2001): 87–100.

Nicholsen, Michael D. "Identity, Nationalism, and Irish Traditional Music in Chicago, 1867–1900." *New Hibernia Review* 13, no. 4 (Winter 2009): 111–26.

Nord, David Paul. "The Urbanization of American Journalism." *OAH Magazine of History* 6 (Spring 1992): 20–25.

O Broin, Leon. "The Fenian Brotherhood." In *America and Ireland, 1776–1976*, edited by David N. Doyle and Owen Dudley Edwards, 117–32. Westport, CT: Greenwood Press, 1980.

O'Day, Alan. "Imagined Irish Communities: Networks of Social Communication of the Irish Diaspora in the United States and Britain in the Late Nineteenth and

Early Twentieth Centuries." In *Irish Migration and Ethnic Identities since 1750*, edited by Enda Delaney and Donald M. MacRaild, 250–75. London: Routledge, 2007.

———. "Media and Power: Charles Stewart Parnell's 1880 Mission to North America." In *Information, Media and Power through the Ages*, edited by Hiram Morgan, 399–424. Historical Studies, 22. Dublin: UCD Press, 2001.

Rees, Jonathan. "The Natural Price of Ice in America." *Business and Economic History On-Line* 6 (2008). http://www.thebhc.org/publications/BEHonline/2008/rees.pdf

Reiff, Janice L. "What's on Trial." *Labor: Studies in Working Class History of the Americas* 9, no. 3 (2012): 43–46.

Rodechko, James P. "An Irish-American Journalist and Catholicism: Patrick Ford of the *Irish World*." *Church History* 39, no. 4 (December 1970): 524–40.

Ruttenbeck, Jeffrey. "The Stagnation and Decline of Partisan Journalism in Late Nineteenth-Century America: Changes in the *New York World*, 1860–76." *American Journalism* 10, nos. 1–2 (1993): 38–60.

Scatliff, H. Kenneth. "Medical Highlights in Chicagoland: Prominent Chicago Doctor Disappears." In two parts. *Chicago Medicine* 68, nos. 1–2 (January 9 and 23, 1967): 11–14; 67–63.

Schneirov, Richard. "Rethinking the Relation of Labor to the Politics of Urban Social Reform in Late Nineteenth-Century America: The Case of Chicago." *International Labor and Working-Class History* 46 (Fall 1994): 93–108.

Shpayer-Makov, Haia. "Anarchism in British Public Opinion 1800–1914." *Victorian Studies* 31, no. 4 (Summer 1988): 487–516.

Smythe, Ted Curtis. "The Advertisers' War to Verify Newspaper Circulation, 1870–1914." *American Journalism* 3 (1986): 167–80.

———. "The Diffusion of the Urban Daily, 1850–1900." *Journalism History* 28, no. 2 (Summer 2002): 73–84.

———. "The Reporter, 1880–1900: Working Conditions and Their Influence on Their News." *Journalism History* 7, no. 1 (Spring 1980): 1–10.

Toibín, Colm. "Outsiders in England and the Art of Being Found Out." In *Ford Madox Ford: Literary Networks and Cultural Transformation*, edited by Andrzeu Gasiorek and Daniel Moore, 61–80. New York: Rodopi, 2008.

Townend, Paul A. "Between Two Worlds: Irish Nationalists and Imperial Crisis, 1878–1880." *Past and Present* 194 (February 2007): 139–94.

Trotti, Michael Ayers. "The Lure of the Sensational Murder." *Journal of Social History* 35, no. 2 (Winter 2001): 429–43.

———. "Murder Made Real: The Visual Revolution of the Halftone." *Virginia Magazine and Biography* 111, no. 4 (2003): 370–410.

Walch, Timothy. "The Catholic Press and the Campaign for Parish Schools: Chicago and Milwaukee 1850–1885." *U.S. Catholic Historian* 3, no. 4 (Spring 1984): 254–72.

———. "Catholic Social Institutions and Urban Development: The View from Nineteenth-Century Chicago and Milwaukee." *Catholic Historical Review* 64, no. 1 (January 1978): 16–32.

Weaver, Greg S. "Firearm Death, Gun Availability and Legal Regulatory Charges: Suggestions from the Data." *Journal of Criminal Law and Criminology* 92, nos. 3–4 (2003): 823–42.

Whelehan, Niall. "'Cheap as Soap and Common as Sugar': The Fenians, Dynamite and Scientific Warfare." In *The Black Hand of Republicanism: Fenianism in Modern Ireland*, edited by Ferghal McGarry and James McConnell, 105–20. Dublin: Irish Academic Press, 2009.

———. "Skirmishing, *The Irish World*, and Empire, 1876–86." *Éire-Ireland* 42 (Spring–Summer 2007): 180–200.

SECONDARY SOURCES: **Unpublished Theses**

Abramoske, Dan. "Chicago Daily News: A Business History, 1875–1901." PhD diss., University of Chicago, 1963.

Clutterbuck, Lindsay. "The Evolution of Counter Terrorism Methodology in the Metropolitan Police from 1829 to 1901, with Particular Reference to the Influence of Extreme Irish Nationalist Activity." PhD thesis, University of Portsmouth, 2002.

Flewelling, Lindsey J. "Ulster Unionism and America, 1880–1920." PhD thesis, University of Edinburgh, 2012.

McGee, Owen. "Irish Republicanism in the Age of Parnell: The Irish Republican Brotherhood 1879–1893." 2 vols. PhD thesis, University College Dublin, 2003.

Sims, Norman Howard. "The Chicago Style of Journalism." PhD diss., University of Illinois at Urbana-Champaign, 1979.

SECONDARY SOURCES: **Websites and Online Publications**

Ancient Order of Hibernians official website: http://www.aoh.com/pages/aoh_history.html

FamilySearch, https://familysearch.org/pal:/MM9.1.1/MSQW-WNT

Gibson, Campbell. *US Census Bureau Population of the 100 Largest Cities and Other Places in the United States: 1790–1990* (June 1998), https://www.census.gov/population/www/documentation/twps0027/twps0027.html

Mayor DeWitt Cregier's inaugural address, April 15, 1889, Chicago City Council. Chicago Public Library, http://www.chipublib.org/mayor-dewitt-clinton-cregier-inaugural-address-1889/

Spectator (London), "United States Census, 1900," index and images, http://archive.spectator.co.uk/

SECONDARY SOURCES: **Digital Collections**

California Digital Newspaper Collection, Center for Bibliographic Studies and Research, University of California, Riverside, http://cdnc.ucr.edu

Catholic University of America, "Fenian Brotherhood and O'Donovan Rossa Collection," http://archives.lib.cua.edu/findingaid/fenian.cfm

Hansard Parliamentary Debates: Hansard, House of Commons Debates, March 9, 1868, vol. 190, cols. 1215–18, http://hansard.millbanksystems.com/sittings/1868/mar/09

Hansard, House of Commons Debates, April 26, 1875, vol. 233, cols. 1644–45, http://hansard.millbanksystems.com/sittings/1875/apr/26

Library of Congress, Chronicling America, Historic American Newspapers, http://chroniclingamerica.loc.gov/

National Library of Australia, Trove, http://trove.nla.gov.au/

Northwestern University, "Homicide in Chicago 1870–1890," homicide.northwest
ern.edu

Villanova University, Falvey Memorial Library, Digital Collection, "Fenian Brotherhood," http://digital.library.villanova.edu/Collection/vudl:247376

Villanova University, Falvey Memorial Library, Digital Collection, Joseph McGarrity
Collection, http://digital.library.villanova.edu/Item/vudl:101870

INDEX

Page numbers in italics refer to figures.

HISTORICAL STUDIES OF URBAN AMERICA

Edited by Timothy J. Gilfoyle, James R. Grossman, and Becky M. Nicolaides